University, Inc.

University, Inc.

THE CORPORATE CORRUPTION OF AMERICAN HIGHER EDUCATION

Jennifer Washburn

BASIC
BOOKS

A Member of the Perseus Books Group
New York

Hardcover first published in 2005 by Basic Books,
a member of the Perseus Books Group.
Paperback first published in 2006 by Basic Books

Basic Books are available at special discounts for bulk purchases in the United States
by corporations, institutions, and other organizations. For more information, please
contact the Special Markets Department at the Perseus Books Group, 11 Cambridge
Center, Cambridge, MA 02142; or call (617) 252-5298 or (800) 255-1514; or e-mail
special.markets@perseusbooks.com.

Library of Congress Cataloging-in-Publication Data

Washburn, Jennifer.
  University, Inc. : the corporate corruption of American higher education / Jennifer
Washburn.
    p. cm.
  Includes bibliographical references and index.
  HC: ISBN-13 0-978-0-465-09051-8; ISBN-10 0-465-09051-6 (hardcover : alk. paper)
  PBK: ISBN-13 0-465-09052-5; ISBN-10 0-465-09052-4
  1. Business and education—United States. 2. Universities and colleges—United
States—Administration. I. Title.

  LC1085.2.W37 2004
  338.4'3378—dc22
                                           2004028060

06 07 08 / 10 9 8 7 6 5 4 3 2 1

To my parents, Barbara and Deric

Contents

Introduction IX

1 A New Kind of Uprising at Berkeley 1

2 The Lessons of History 25

3 The Birth of the Market-Model U. 49

4 The Republic of Science in Turmoil 73

5 Are Conflicts of Interest Hazardous to Our Health? 103

6 The University as Business 137

7 Dreaming of Silicon Valley 171

8 Paying More for Less: The Commercial Squeeze on Teaching & the Humanities 199

9 The Path Forward: Preserving the Public Domain 225

Acknowledgments 243
Notes 247
Index 309

Introduction

We are living in the information age, a time when a college education increasingly marks the dividing line between fulfilling the American Dream and falling short. In the United States today, attending a top-ranked university is often a prerequisite to finding a financially rewarding (and personally fulfilling) job. But a university degree is ultimately worth far more than this. For most students, the college years mark a time of awakening to a larger world: to history, art, science, culture, to unknown capacities in themselves, to new aspirations and dreams. In the face of spiraling tuition costs, millions of Americans put aside money each year so their children can enjoy these educational riches. For many families, getting a child into a good college is their single greatest priority.

Since 1980, however, and especially over the past fifteen years, a foul wind has blown over the campuses of our nation's universities. Its source is not the stifling atmosphere of political correctness or the influence of so-called "leftist radical professors" that have received so much attention from pundits, journalists, politicians, and gadflies, but a phenomenon that has gone comparatively ignored: the growing role that market forces and commercial values have assumed in academic life.

In higher education today, a wholesale culture shift is transforming everything from the way universities educate their students to the language they use to define what they do. Academic administrators refer to students as "consumers" and to education and research as "products." They talk about branding and marketing and now spend more on lobbying in Washington than defense contractors do.[1] Many have eagerly sought to convert "courseware" into intellectual property that can be packaged and sold over the Internet for profit. Others have allowed whole academic departments to forge financial partnerships with private corporations, guaranteeing these firms first dibs on the inventions flowing out of their labs. In the spring of 2006, Johns Hopkins University raised the commercial bar still further when it allowed a cosmetic firm, Cosmedicine, launched by Klinger Advanced Aesthetics, to use its prestigious name for product endorsements. In exchange, Johns Hopkins had planned on taking a profit-sharing stake in the firm. But shortly after an exposé appeared in the *Wall Street Journal* provoking strong public criticism, the president of the university announced he was pulling out of the deal to preserve "the trust we have earned from the public."[2] In the medical world, professors now frequently endorse pharmaceutical products in which they themselves (or their major funders) have a direct financial stake, blurring the line between academia and marketing.

After World War II, Americans clearly perceived that higher education was a public good, bringing economic, strategic and cultural benefits worthy of generous taxpayer subsidies. Now, politicians increasingly view higher education as a private benefit, forcing colleges and universities to draw more of their operating funds from private donors, industry, and students (in the form of higher tuition fees).

Since the hardback publication of this book, the trend toward privatization of higher education has grown more acute, prompting heightened public debate about its true costs and benefits.[3] Some commentators insist the trend is inevitable. A 2005 book, *Remaking the American University: Market-Smart and Mission Centered*, by Robert Zemsky et al., typifies this new strain of economic determinism. The authors insist we "can no longer expect the public or its political leadership to be particularly moved by the fact that higher education's mission is to educate and conduct research."[4] Zemsky and his coauthors suggest the only way for nonprofit universities to survive in the twenty-first century is by emulating the for-profits, like the University of Phoenix, which are focused on job training, credentialing, and serving market demand. The University of Phoenix has no faculty governance and no tenure; it pays "facilitators" $950 to teach a college-level course ($1,050 if the facilitator has a PhD). Its founder, John Sperling, once famously remarked that the University of Phoenix "is a corporation, not a social entity. Coming here is not a rite of passage. We are not trying to develop. . . [students'] value systems or go in for that 'expand their minds' bullshit."[5] The authors insist universities must accept

the fact that Washington now "consider[s] for-profit and traditional institutions as interchangeable."[6]

This book takes the opposite view. It argues that nonprofit universities
are among the United States' most unique and important economic and
cultural assets, and therefore worthy of special public support. It further
argues that these institutions could never have made the extraordinary
contributions they did, both to American society *and* to industry, throughout the post-war period, were it not for their institutional independence
from both market forces and political dictates.

As this book shows, the current movement toward privatization
mainly took root in the late 1970s, when, in response to heightened competition from Japan and other countries, a powerful nexus of political,
economic, and industrial forces began pushing America's universities to
forge closer ties with private industry, convert themselves into engines of
economic growth, and pump out commercially valuable new inventions.
More and more, the job of teaching students was shunted to the side,
even though the universities' most important public function was to nurture intellectual creativity and talent.

The reformers who pushed these changes were, for the most part,
motivated by noble intentions, genuinely believing that universities could
take on these functions without compromising their core educational
mission. And, in one sense, what they advocated was not entirely new.
Both the computer and the biotechnology revolutions were born out of
academic research labs. Moreover, as far back as the mid-nineteenth century, university professors collaborated with private industry and made
vital contributions to U.S. industrial and agricultural development. The
problem is not university-industry relationships, which have existed for
a long time; it is the elimination of any clear boundary line separating
academia from commerce. Today, market forces are dictating what is happening in the world of higher education as never before, causing
universities to engage in commercial activities unheard of in academia a
mere generation ago. Universities now routinely operate complex patenting and licensing operations to market their faculty's inventions (extracting
royalty income and other profits and fees in return). They invest their
endowment money in risky start-up firms founded by their professors.
They run their own industrial parks, venture-capital funds, and for-profit
companies, and they publish newsletters encouraging faculty members to
commercialize their research by going into business. Often, when a professor becomes the CEO of a new start-up, there is considerable overlap

between the research taking place on campus and at the firm, a situation ripe for confusion and conflicts of interest. The question of who owns academic research has grown increasingly contentious, as the openness and sharing that once characterized university life has given way to a new proprietary culture more akin to the business world.

When researchers at the University of Utah discovered an important human gene responsible for hereditary breast cancer, for example, they didn't make it freely available to other scientists, even though we—the U.S. taxpayers—paid $4.6 million to finance the research.[7] They raced to patent it and gave the monopoly rights to Myriad Genetics, Inc., a start-up company founded by a University of Utah professor, which proceeded to hoard the gene and restrict other scientists from using it.[8] On one occasion, the company actually threatened legal action against Haig Kazazian, chair of the genetics department at the University of Pennsylvania, after he had tried to use the gene in his own breast cancer research. "This is just the tip of the iceberg," Kazazian told the *Chicago Tribune*. "We may end up down the road with a large fraction of the genetic disease testing done under these exclusive kinds of arrangements. That's generally not good for patients, and it's not good for the public."[9]

Such stories are hardly rare these days and are especially common in the sciences, where corporations now fund a growing share of academic research—money that increasingly comes with strings attached. Secrecy and delays of publication have become routine since 1980. Professors frequently sign sponsored-research deals that cede control over the research process to the companies underwriting their work. Were the federal government to engage in some of the practices detailed in the chapters to come—preventing students from publishing their theses on time (in order to protect proprietary secrets), deleting information from academic papers prior to publication, suppressing research studies that uncover significant health threats—it would surely provoke public outrage. The commercial sector's routine violation of these academic norms has been met with comparative silence.

Boosters will tell you that whatever the downsides may be, the heightened commercialism on campus has generated phenomenal benefits for the economy, helping to pull the United States out of the doldrums of the 1970s. This argument has become the conventional wisdom in much of the business press and is repeated like a mantra whenever academic administrators gather at technology-licensing conferences to exchange tips of the trade. But such claims are vastly overblown. Indeed, many economists and experts on innovation—and some prominent members of the business community—have argued just the opposite, warning that the commercialization of higher education may actually impede long-term growth by drawing universities away from their traditional roles. The truth is that few universities are capable of generating the sort of high-tech growth that many state governors now dream about. In fact, only a small minority of schools prove successful at licensing research to industry, despite the enormous time, energy, and money that they have devoted to such efforts in recent years. Although every university president eagerly awaits that blockbuster discovery—the next Google or Gatorade—that would generate millions in royalties, in reality less than two dozen universities in the entire country make significant profits from technology licensing. Hundreds of others barely break even—or lose money.[10] The more universities try to sell politicians on the idea that they can drive local and regional economic growth—justifying their existence in market terms—the more they set themselves up for failure and undermine the basis for their public support.

———————

The new commercial ethos in higher education is affecting more than just the sciences and engineering. It is also changing the priorities of universities in ways that raise disturbing questions about what parents and students are getting in return for the increasingly steep tuitions they pay.

On the vast majority of our nation's campuses today, the most valued professors are not the ones who devote their time and energy to teaching; they are the ones who can bring in the most research money, and whose ideas can be turned into lucrative commercial products and licensed to industry. To be sure, universities have long struggled to maintain the appropriate balance between research and teaching. But the new commercial ethos in higher education has tilted the balance further toward the former of these functions. The same universities that invest millions in high-tech research labs and industrial parks have been whittling down the professoriate, replacing tenured and full-time faculty with part-time adjuncts and graduate students. Whereas star professors in fields like computer science and economics are recruited to campus with six-figure salaries (and assurances that they will have to do little teaching), humanities courses, which form the core of the undergraduate curriculum, are taught to several hundred students at a time in large lecture halls, with graduate student teaching assistants (TAs) bearing nearly full responsibility for the one-on-one instruction and grading. Indeed, with the exception of the smaller liberal arts colleges, the job of undergraduate education often seems like a subsidiary activity at many universities today—a task farmed out to the growing army of part-time instructors who receive no benefits and meager pay.

As one disillusioned grad student explained to me: "Your first semester, the administration makes it clear what the real priorities are: 'We've got to fill seats. We need a body in front of the classroom. Go teach.'" If you want to succeed in academia, he said, what matters are publications, prestige, and grant money. "Forget about teaching. Forget about broadening young people's minds. Whatever you do, don't spend a lot of time on that. It's a waste of time."

Are these the educational values we want our nation's top universities to embrace? Over the past decade, average tuition and fees, adjusted for inflation, increased $5,746 (or 37 percent) at private four-year colleges, and $1,927 (or 54 percent) at public four-year colleges.[11] To pay for these increases, more and more students took out substantial loans, causing the average cumulative debt burden for a graduating senior to rise from $9,250 in 1993 to $19,200 in 2004.[12]

Given this level of economic sacrifice, doesn't every student deserve the very best classroom instruction a university can provide? Even on purely utilitarian grounds, the downsizing of teaching makes poor economic sense. As one American executive from Honda recently noted, the United States' future global competitiveness "will not come from its cheap labor or its abundant natural resources. What will keep America economically vibrant," he said, "will be our intellectual advantage" over other nations.[13]

State governors and legislators, prodded along by the federal government, have exacerbated this trend by pushing universities to pour resources into commercially oriented research centers, in fields like medicine and biotechnology, hoping to spawn "the next Silicon Valley" in their backyards. Many of these same politicians have been considerably less generous when it comes to financing the universities' general funds (which actually go toward educating students). During the period 2001 to 2005, state and local funding per college student dropped to a twenty-five year low, falling from $7,121 to $5,833. Federal support also declined, from $7,881 to $5,862 per student during these years, forcing students and their families to shoulder more of the costs in the form of higher tuition.[14] "That such a substitution"—more money for technology-related programs, less for the basic educational mission—"is going on seems inescapable," wrote Irwin Feller, an emeritus economist at Penn State and an expert on education, "especially in states where governors tout their high technology initiatives at the same time that they propose meager increases for public universities even in flush budget years."[15]

Not surprisingly, these trends have put a squeeze on less commercially oriented fields such as the humanities and social sciences, which at many schools are being neglected or downsized. Under the new corporate style of management in higher education, *Business Week* observed, English professors must demonstrate that Chaucer can pay the bills as effectively as engineering or business classes do.[16] A study in the *Harvard Magazine* concluded that while fields that "make money, study money or attract money" are flourishing, those that do not are languishing.[17] It is true that these changes are partly a reflection of student demand, as a more pragmatic generation of undergraduates selects courses and majors guaranteed to enhance their financial prospects. (Saddling students with high levels of debt also discourages them from even considering less lucrative professions.) Traditionally, however, universities strove to balance careerism and credentialing with the ideal of a liberal education. As Lynne Rudder Baker, a philosophy professor at the University of Massachusetts, cautioned, "The point at which we look to nothing but demand to determine what a university should offer is the point at which the market becomes the enemy of excellence."[18]

Indeed, one could argue that in a knowledge-driven economy it is all the more important that undergraduates are provided not with narrow vocational training but with a broad-based foundation in reading, writing, arithmetic, and science—an education that sharpens students' intellectual faculties, their curiosity about the world, and their ability to think critically and creatively. Because technology and the state of knowledge in nearly every discipline are changing so rapidly, the most valuable skill universities could impart is the capacity to grow intellectually throughout one's lifetime.

Disinterested Research: Going, Going. . . Gone

Visit a college campus today, with its red-brick buildings, manicured lawns, and tree-lined walkways bustling with students, and you are likely to come away charmed by the bucolic setting. What you aren't likely to notice is the growing number of buildings, academic chairs, and institutes that are financed by corporate interests, and that sometimes bear their names: the Ken Lay Center for the Study of Markets in Transition at Rice University, for example, which was renamed after Enron's CEO was indicted. Or the Harvard School of Public Health's Center for Risk Analysis (HCRA), which, as David Brown, a reporter at the *Washington Post*, discovered receives the majority of its funding from industry. In 2001, Brown published an article quoting an HCRA spokesperson who downplayed the significance of a government report on the presence of pesticides and heavy metals in U.S. residents' bodies. Later Brown was shocked to learn that this prestigious Harvard center received 60 percent of its funding from industry sources, including many major chemical and pesticide manufacturers. "It never occurred to me to ask," Brown wrote afterward in a letter to a Harvard dean. "Harvard University has a budget larger than that of some countries. I am surprised it is willing to trade its most valuable thing, its reputation, for a handful of silver."[19]

The truth is it never occurs to most of us to ask. When I began reporting on public health issues in the mid-1990s, I assumed the best place to find disinterested, objective information was at a university. Reporters are far more apt to take the findings of a study published by an academic in a peer-reviewed journal at face value than, say, a corporate press release. Similarly, when a consumer wants to check on the safety of a drug that has just been released on the market, he or she is more likely to trust a study conducted by university scientists than an industry-sponsored one. But much of the university research that we assume is independent often is anything but. Today, at prominent medical colleges, it is not unusual for professors to be paid by drug companies to put their names on review articles and academic papers ghostwritten by industry. These articles are then published in leading medical journals, without any disclosure of corporate involvement. Whereas, in the past, clinical studies at universities were conducted at "arm's length" from the industry sponsor, today these sponsors routinely exert control over the study design, the raw data, and even the way results get reported. This loss of academic independence facilitates the suppression of information the drug industry doesn't want the public to know. In 2006, the *New England Journal of Medicine* accused Merck (and several of its academic coauthors) of failing to report three patient deaths in the 2000 trial that led to FDA approval of its painkiller Vioxx. Four years later the drug was pulled from the market because of its association with heart attacks and strokes.[20] Today, it is not uncommon for the lead investigator and the university itself to own equity in the company sponsoring a drug trial, giving them a direct financial interest in a favorable outcome.

It would be hard to overstate the importance of preserving a space in our culture where the ideal of disinterested inquiry is preserved. Many major public-policy questions Americans will grapple with in the decades to come—global warming, the search for alternative fuels, the safety of genetically engineered crops, international economic development, the regulation of human cloning—will require us to turn to trained experts to help us untangle the complex moral, social, and scientific issues involved. Unfortunately, it has already grown difficult to find disinterested authorities in many fields. A government report recently found that when the Environmental Protection Agency puts together advisory panels to weigh the cancer risks associated with certain chemicals, they are frequently filled with experts who have direct financial ties to chemical manufacturers.[21] More than half the experts hired to advise the U.S. government on the safety and effectiveness of drugs now have financial links (stock ownership, consulting fees, research grants) to companies that will be directly impacted by their conclusions.[22] When a prominent scientific journal, *Nature Neuroscience*, asked Charles B. Nemeroff, the chair of the psychiatry department at Emory University, to review roughly two dozen experimental treatments for psychiatric disorders not long ago, the editors assumed they would receive an impartial assessment. In 2003, however, it came to light that three of the treatments Nemeroff praised in his article were ones he also stood to profit from—including a transdermal lithium patch for which he held the patent. Nemeroff did not disclose these or his many other financial ties to the drug industry in his article.[23]

In my own profession, journalism, it is considered inappropriate to receive gifts or funding from any of the companies or individuals one writes about, because doing so can create bias or, at the very least, the appearance of bias. Shouldn't universities and professors be held to the same standard? It's no secret that part of the reason companies fund academic research is to obtain the imprimatur of a prestigious university. During the 1990s, the tobacco industry realized the best way to fight regulation was to manufacture confusion about the dangers of smoking by paying academic scientists up to $20,000 apiece to write letters in prominent journals and newspapers downplaying the risks of cigarettes.[24] In one instance, the University of Texas even agreed to allow a professor to conduct secret research for tobacco company lawyers over an eleven-year period, in return for nearly $1.7 million.[25]

Less well known was the Enron Corporation's campaign, during the same decade, to buy academic influence by financing prominent research centers at Harvard. One of these, the Harvard Electricity Policy Group (HEPG), churned out no less than thirty-one reports promoting the deregulation of energy markets in California—precisely the kind of market Enron would learn to skillfully exploit. William Hogan, HEPG's research director and a professor at Harvard, advised the state of California to adopt the "Enron model" of electricity deregulation and later, after the market collapsed, coauthored two reports discrediting the idea that companies like Enron had attempted to withhold electricity to improve their own profit margins (even as government investigators were on the cusp of uncovering clear evidence of price manipulation).[26] Meanwhile, Enron paid handsome consulting fees to several professors at the Harvard Business School, which produced a series of glowing studies about the company that would soon make headlines for its accounting scandals.[27] "Harvard University should apologize to the people of California for having sold its research institutes and faculty members to corporations," concluded HarvardWatch, the student and alumni group that investigated and uncovered these ties.[28]

As we'll see, Harvard is by no means alone. All too often today, the names of our nation's most prestigious universities, along with the extraordinary public trust they command, are being bought and sold in similar ways.

The Free-Market Bazaar

To question the growing commercialization of our universities is not to denigrate the value of markets themselves. The problem arises when markets are presumed to be so perfect—so superior to any other form of social organization—that they are permitted to penetrate areas formerly governed by other considerations. "Markets do a great deal well, but they fall far short of being perfectly self-regulating," the economist Robert Kuttner noted. "They often lead to deprivations of personal liberty and economic security that are no less painful for representing authority that is private rather than public. They spill over into realms where they don't belong. . . . A society that was a grand auction block would not be a political democracy worth having. And it would be far less attractive economically than its enthusiasts imagine. . . . Everything must not be for sale."[29]

Unfortunately, we are living in an era when everything increasingly does seem to be for sale. From the operation of prisons to the provision of welfare services for the poor to the conduct of military operations in Iraq, an ideology of free-market fundamentalism has led some ideologues to promote the privatization of everything of late. Companies like Edison have taken over public schools and even entire school districts around the country, and publicly traded corporations have been awarded government contracts to provide services to at-risk youth, the developmentally disabled, and other vulnerable populations, boasting to their shareholders that there are abundant profits to be made in such work.[30]

This book is written out of a belief that although the profit motive plays an important role in our society, so do other values that limit and constrain what unregulated markets will do if left to their own devices. In the past, our universities have played a vital role in this regard, not least by focusing on issues the market ignores. Traditionally, for example, universities tackled public health threats that offered little immediate financial return but impacted millions of lives. They protected and defended the information commons, the pool of public knowledge that is freely available for researchers and creators to use and build upon. Academic scientists also excelled in the performance of research that corporations were reluctant to undertake: undirected "blue-sky" research, risk-taking experimentation, and unconventional inquiry that yielded important practical results over time.

Such research has long played a vital role in stimulating innovation: One 1997 study by the National Science Foundation reported that 73 percent of the scientific research cited in American industrial patents was carried out at universities and other labs funded by the U.S. government.[31] Another study by researchers at the Massachusetts Institute of Technology found that publicly funded research was a "critical contributor" to the discovery of nearly all of the twenty-five most important new drugs introduced between 1970 and 1995.[32] It is thus worth asking whether erasing the distinction between the academic and commercial spheres is really in the best interest not only of the public but of the private sector. As my book will show, the corporate stranglehold on academic science has been most pronounced in medicine, pharmacology, and biotechnology, the same cutting-edge fields that are expected to drive the U.S. economy in the years to come. If universities become little more than appendages of industry, will they be able to generate the innovative ideas needed to sustain our competitive position in the global economy? Many experts believe that our science and innovation systems already are lagging behind those of our competitors.[33] Is further commercialization of the academy really where we should be headed?

Universities have served as a check on market values in another way: by providing an environment where young people have been encouraged to think critically and explore ideas, not because of their dollar value but because of how captivating or original they are. Without this independent academic sphere, would the United States be as open, pluralistic, and democratic a society? As Martha Nussbaum, the American philosopher, explained:

> When we ask about the relationship of a liberal education to citizenship, we are asking a question with a long history in the Western philosophical tradition. We are drawing on Socrates' concept of "the examined life," on Aristotle's notions of a reflective citizenship, and above all on Greek and Roman Stoic notions of an education that is "liberal" in that it liberates the mind from the bondage of habit and custom, producing people who can function with sensitivity and alertness as citizens of the whole world.[34]

To invoke this ideal is not hopelessly quixotic. Nor does it mean we must call on universities to beat a hasty retreat to the ivory tower and wall themselves off from private industry. As I argue in my conclusion, universities should be places that are engaged with the outside world, encourage creative problem solving, and support entrepreneurial thinking. They should have mechanisms in place to facilitate the transfer of new knowledge and inventions to industry and should provide students with the tools and training they need to start up new companies and pursue careers. It is imperative, however, that universities accomplish all of this without sacrificing their autonomy or compromising the values and ideals they have long pledged to uphold.

This book is written for parents, students, professors, administrators, and all those who care about such ideals, who take it as a given that the university's primary mission is still the education of well-rounded citizens and the performance of public research, not merely service to industry's short-term bottom line; who expect academic administrators to stand up to corporations when they threaten to sue a professor who has unearthed information that the public deserves to know; and who want to see the line separating business and academia preserved, even as universities continue to play a role in fueling innovation and stimulating economic growth.

U.S. colleges and universities, whether they are public or private, enjoy enormous levels of public support and tax exemptions because of a belief that they are generating goods that no other market actor would produce without a public subsidy: basic science; liberal education; independent, publishable research. Every year, the federal government pays roughly $20 billion in taxpayer money to subsidize the research at our nation's colleges and universities, and another $60 billion more in loans and grants to help financially disadvantaged students attend these schools.[35] At the state and local levels, taxpayer contributions to higher education now run around $68 billion.[36] In addition, hundreds of thousands of Americans carefully put aside their hard-earned income to pay for tuition, room and board, books, and other expenses needed to send their kids to college. It is up to them—up to all of us—to make sure that the world of higher education is not for sale.

1

A New Kind of
Uprising at Berkeley

In the fall of 1964, at the University of California at Berkeley, a twenty-one-year-old undergraduate named Mario Savio climbed the steps of Sproul Hall and famously denounced his university for bending over backward to "serve the needs of American industry." Savio, the leader of the Berkeley Free Speech Movement, accused the university of functioning as "a factory that turns out a certain product needed by industry" rather than serving as the conscience and critic of society. To the modern ear, such fiery 1960s rhetoric may sound outdated. But to a growing number of critics in the academic world, Savio's words ring more true today than ever.

Since the early 1980s, industry collaborations with universities have grown so extensive that Berkeley's own emeritus chancellor Clark Kerr—once the principal target of Savio's wrath—himself spoke out publicly about the commercial threat to academic life just prior to his death in December 2003. "In the 1960s," Kerr wrote, "I was concerned that too much of the 'evaluative' role [of the university] was aimed more at destruction than at reform and made more use of compulsion than of persuasion. Now I think there is more of a threat to 'independent' appraisals aimed at improving public welfare as against adding to private profit."[1]

Back in 1963, when Kerr published the first edition of his highly regarded classic, *The Uses of the University*, he correctly perceived that the university of the postwar period had evolved into a "multiversity," which faced the daunting task of trying to serve a diverse array of interest groups—government, military, industry, professors, students—while continuing to safeguard its own autonomy.[2] Within the context of the Vietnam War, Berkeley's student radicals seized on the book as an endorsement of outside intrusions into academic life, a blueprint for a brave new world in which universities would serve as mere appendages of the military-industrial complex.[3] At the time, however, Kerr believed that universities—which were then enjoying a "golden age" of government funding for higher education—could effectively manage these multiple roles and still preserve their independence. In hindsight, Kerr's assessment was largely correct. From 1960 to 1980, despite the ghost of McCarthyism and the secrecy that surrounded military research on campus, most universities avoided compromising their core mission in the way that critics like Savio feared. Though their interactions with government and industry increased, universities managed to maintain a high level of institutional autonomy even as their responsibilities proliferated and enrollment expanded.

When I visited Kerr, a balding man with bushy white eyebrows and alert blue eyes, at his home in the hills of El Cerrito in the spring of 2001, he explained why the current proliferation of university-industry ties had led him to revise his views. "The problem arises," he said, "not just because we live in a highly competitive information-based economy, which has encouraged companies to want to get inside academia, but because they are, after all, being *invited* in." With public support for higher education diminishing, he explained, "lots of faculty members and administrators see advantages in getting extra money from private industry, and they may be willing to make concessions which from their own point of view are quite all right, but which are bad for the university." He was particularly worried that a "money-seeking group on the inside" and a "for-profit group on the outside" could collude to undermine the university's mission. "The university ought to remain a neutral agency devoted to the public welfare, not to private welfare."[4]

From his wooded hillside property, purchased in 1946, Kerr had a beautiful bird's-eye view of the University of California at Berkeley (U.C. Berkeley), with its campanile tower visible in the distance. The former chancellor told me he continued to keep close watch over the celebrated university he had once led. Just a few years prior, the school had forged an unusual alliance with a large biotech firm, leaving Kerr, the man once vilified by Berkeley's student radicals, deeply troubled.[5]

On the afternoon of April 13, 1999, a radiant spring day, the Berkeley campus hardly looked like the site of a raging controversy. Sproul Plaza was bustling with activity. Students tossed frisbees and basked in the sunshine on lush green lawns. But inside Room 60 of Evans Hall, a concrete building on the northern edge of campus, the lights were dim and the atmosphere was tense and polarized. There, some two dozen faculty members, mostly professors in the College of Natural Resources (CNR), had gathered to hear the disquieting results of a newly released faculty survey.[6]

The focus of the survey was a controversial agreement that Berkeley had signed in November 1998 with Novartis, a Swiss-based pharmaceutical giant and producer of genetically engineered crops. Roughly two years into the agreement, Novartis's agricultural division merged with another company to become Syngenta.[7] (Despite this name change, however, I will continue to refer to the collaboration as the Berkeley-Novartis alliance.) Under the terms of the agreement, Novartis gave Berkeley $25 million over five years to fund basic research in the Department of Plant and Microbial Biology (PMB), one of four departments within the CNR.

In exchange for the $25 million, Berkeley granted Novartis first right to negotiate licenses on roughly one-third of the department's discoveries, including the results of research funded by Novartis, as well as projects funded by state and federal sources. It also granted the company unprecedented representation—two of five seats—on the department's research committee, which determined how the money would be spent.

That the university had secured funding from a private company was hardly unusual. That a single corporation would provide one-third of the research budget for an entire department at a public university had sparked an uproar. Shortly after the agreement was signed, a newly formed graduate-student group, Students for Responsible Research, circulated a petition blasting the agreement for standing "in direct conflict with our mission as a public university." The *Daily Californian*, Berkeley's student newspaper, published a five-part series on the growing privatization of the university, and a coalition of public interest groups sent a letter to Berkeley's chancellor, Robert Berdahl, charging that the alliance "would disqualify a leading intellectual center from the ranks of institutions able to provide the kind of research—free from vested interest"—that is the hallmark of academic life. Meanwhile, Gordon Rausser, the dean of the College of Natural Resources, sent a message to all professors urging them not to speak to the press and to direct any questions about the agreement to the university's public relations office. Many viewed the memo as a hush order.

"We are here to discuss the position of the faculty," Ignacio Chapela, a professor of microbial ecology, announced as the April 13 meeting began. Chapela, who was then serving as the elected chairman of the college's executive committee (a faculty governing body), snapped on an overhead projector to display the results of the survey. "The Novartis agreement has left the CNR deeply divided," he declared. Although 41 percent of the faculty respondents supported the agreement as signed, more than 50 percent believed that it would have a "negative" or "strongly negative" effect on academic freedom. Roughly half believed that the agreement would erode Berkeley's commitment to "public good research," and 60 percent feared that it would impede the free exchange of ideas among scientists within the college—one of Chapela's own chief concerns.

"When I came to Berkeley," Chapela explained to me after the meeting, "the people who brought me here and who were my closest colleagues were largely in PMB. Now I know that anything I say to these people can be turned around and handed over to Novartis. So I just can't talk to them anymore. If I have a good idea, I'm not going to just give it away." Chapela, like many critics of the deal, is hardly a confirmed opponent of university-industry relations. Before coming to Berkeley, he worked for none other than Novartis—then named Sandoz—and afterward continued to have a relationship with the company. "I'm not opposed to individual professors serving as consultants to industry," he emphasized. "If something goes wrong, it's their reputation that's at stake. But this is different. This deal institutionalizes the university's relationship with one company, whose interest is profit. Our role should be to serve the public good."

The Berkeley-Novartis agreement was not the first major research alliance between a prominent university and a private corporation. As early as 1974, Harvard Medical School signed a $23.5-million agreement with

Monsanto to perform research on cancer tumors. In 1983, Columbia University entered into a multi-million-dollar deal with Bristol-Myers—and there were many more such deals that followed. Yet there is a reason the Novartis agreement touched a particularly raw nerve. For to many people in the academic world, the agreement seemed to mark the culmination of a deeper transformation in which far more was at stake than the fate of one academic department. The agreement came at a time of mounting evidence that commercial criteria were defining the terms of academic life as never before. Take, for example, the comments of Professor J. Patrick Kelly, the Kmart Chair of Marketing at Wayne State University, who told the *Chronicle of Higher Education*, "Kmart's attitude always has been: What did we get from you this year? Some professors would say they don't like that position, but for me, it's kept me involved with a major retailer, and it's been a good thing."[8] At Berkeley itself, buildings increasingly bore the names of corporate donors; industry-sponsored research was ubiquitous; and even academic titles were changing, with Laura D'Andrea Tyson, a former top Clinton adviser, known as the BankAmerica Dean of the Haas School of Business. What's more, the Novartis agreement surfaced at a time when whole new areas of public life—from schools to social services to prisons—were being privatized. The public sector appeared to be shrinking, and was possibly even becoming endangered. If one of the nation's preeminent public universities was willing to lease out its reputation and prestige in this way, where would other academic institutions draw the line? Was it right to ask California taxpayers to finance a higher-education system that effectively granted a foreign-based multinational monopoly control over its research?[9] Such concerns spilled well beyond the Berkeley campus, too. "The Novartis-Berkeley deal can all too easily be portrayed as an institution undermining both its motivation and trustworthiness to provide an independent and impartial view of the most contentious technologies of our time—genetically modified crops," wrote the prestigious science journal *Nature* in an editorial titled "Is the University-Industrial Complex Out of Control?"[10]

At Berkeley, such questions had begun to arouse debate among students. Immediately after the faculty meeting, I made my way to La Burrita, a pub just off campus. There, several members of Students for Responsible Research, the student group formed to investigate the Novartis deal, were meeting to discuss the results of the faculty survey—and to let off steam. "This place has some of the cheapest pitchers around!" said Jesse Reynolds, a graduate student with long brown hair and a goatee, as he poured cold, frothy beer into everyone's glasses.

Unlike the student radicals of the 1960s, these students never expected to lock horns with the university establishment. Reynolds, who studied California water resources, told me he was relatively new to student politics—and politics altogether. "I'm generally one of those people who gripes a lot and does nothing," he explained, stroking his goatee between sips of beer. "But when the best state agricultural college in the country makes this kind of leap, the world is bound to follow. I really fear that."

David Quist, a first-year graduate student in microbiology with short-cropped dark hair and blue eyes, said he had joined the group because he felt that a "business culture" was increasingly permeating the university. At a town hall meeting the previous October, where the Novartis deal was first made public, Dean Rausser had invited concerned students to examine the contract for themselves. "So the next day I came to his office," recalled Quist. "I was given some materials and sat down to take notes. But as soon as an administrator saw me, she said, 'Oh no, you can't do that.'" Quist's notes were confiscated and held at the dean's office for several months. (Wilhelm Gruissem, then a senior professor in PMB, later explained to me that the Novartis negotiations had been conducted in as open a manner as possible, given the need to protect the company's proprietary secrets. But even students within the department felt shut out. Less than a month after the Novartis deal was signed, twenty-three PMB graduate students sent a letter to the faculty complaining that their views had never been solicited, and that they had been "forced to rely on rumors and supposition throughout the negotiation process."[11])

What most concerned Students for Responsible Research was that as university ties to industry grew more entwined, less commercially oriented areas of science would languish. "Let's say you're a graduate student interested in sustainable agriculture or biological control or some other area that is not commercial," said Reynolds. "My guess is you're not going to come to Berkeley, or you'll at least think twice about it."

Some deans and faculty members I interviewed shared this concern. Donald Dahlsten, then associate dean of the College of Natural Resources, told me, "Molecular biology and genetic engineering have clearly risen as the preferred approach to solving our problems, and that's where the resources are going. New buildings have gone up and these departments are expanding while the organismic areas of science—which emphasize a more ecological approach—are being downsized."[12] A tall man with unruly gray hair and an avuncular manner, Dahlsten once chaired Berkeley's world-renowned Division of Biological Control. Today, that agricultural division, along with the Department of Plant Pathology and more than half of all the faculty positions in entomology, are gone— in part, many professors believe, because there are no profits in such work. "You can't patent the natural organisms and ecological understanding used in biological control," explained Andy Gutierrez, a Berkeley entomologist. "However, if you look at public benefit, that division provided billions of dollars annually to the state of California and to the world." In one project Gutierrez worked on, the division helped halt the spread of a pest that threatened to destroy the cassava crop, a basic food staple for 200 million people in West Africa.[13]

Gordon Rausser, the chief architect of the Novartis deal, believes that concerns about the agreement reflect ignorance about both the Novartis contract and the changing economic realities of higher education. When we spoke in his spacious office in the ornate neoclassical Giannini Hall, Rausser insisted that the deal, far from violating Berkeley's public mission, would help to perpetuate the university's status as a top-flight research institution. A professor of agricultural economics who served on the President's Council of Economic Advisors in the mid-1980s and later set up a sideline consulting business, Rausser contends that Berkeley's value is "enhanced, not diminished, when we work creatively in collaboration with other institutions, including private companies."[14] Writing in the Berkeley alumni magazine about the Novartis deal, he argued, "Without modern laboratory facilities and access to commercially developed proprietary databases . . . we can neither provide first-rate graduate education nor perform the fundamental research that is part of the University's mission."[15] Far from draining resources from other academic areas, Rausser told me, the Novartis alliance would benefit the college as a whole because one-third of the money was slated to be spent outside PMB. "I'm sitting here with three science buildings that were built in the 1920s, 1930s and 1940s," he asserted. "I can't get those buildings modernized for first-rate research without resources."[16]

Rausser's perspective is more and more the norm these days, as academic administrators throughout the country turn to the private sector for an increasing percentage of their research dollars. Although the federal government still supplies the majority of the funding for academic research (roughly $21 billion in 2003), the government's share of this support has fallen from a high of 73.5 percent in 1966 to below 60 percent today, even as the cost of doing research has risen sharply.[17] Federal support for the life sciences remains strong; it doubled during the twenty-year period from 1978 to 1998 and then doubled again over the next five years from 1998 to 2003, rising to 70 percent of the total federal budget for academic research. However, over the same five-year period, every other science discipline, including the social sciences, saw its share of federal support shrink (the physical sciences and engineering taking the deepest cuts).[18]

State funding has also declined. Chancellor Robert Berdahl told me that Berkeley had become a "state-assisted institution" rather than a public one, since California supplied just 34 percent of its overall budget, compared with 50 percent twelve years earlier. Other public universities have suffered similar cutbacks, as the share of state budgets going to higher education nationally has shrunk by more than one-third since 1980.[19]

As they rush to forge alliances with industry, universities are not just responding to economic necessity, however; they are also capitalizing on a change in federal law, implemented just over two decades ago, that laid the foundation for today's academic-industrial complex. In 1980, mounting concerns about declining U.S. productivity and rising competition from Japan propelled Congress to pass the Bayh-Dole Act, which enabled universities to patent federally funded research on a large scale for the first time. Universities were offered the opportunity to license campus-based inventions to private companies in exchange for royalties and other fees. The goal of the legislation was certainly noble: to bring ideas out of the ivory tower and into the marketplace more quickly. In subsequent years Congress passed numerous additional laws to foster university-industry ties, including generous tax breaks for corporations willing to invest in academic research.

The Bayh-Dole Act remains controversial. Some credit the act with helping to bring to market countless new products—anti-AIDS treatments, cancer drugs, innovative software—while fueling vast growth in America's booming biotech and computer industries. Others, including a growing number of economists and intellectual property experts, contend that Bayh-Dole's emphasis on privatizing academic knowledge is squeezing out public interest research and weakening the nation's capacity for innovation. What's undeniable is that Bayh-Dole revolutionized university-industry relations. Since the act passed, U.S. universities have seen more than a tenfold increase in the patents they generate, and industry funding for academic research has expanded at an annual rate of 8.1 percent, rising to $2 billion in 2001 (the most recent year for which statistics are available)—or five times more than in 1980.[20] Although industry still supplies only roughly 7 percent of overall university research funding, its support has grown faster than from any other single source, and its influence is generally thought to be far greater than this percentage would suggest.[21] As Denis O. Gray, an expert on university-industry relations, has pointed out, because so much federal research support is now tied to corporate matching grants, cost sharing, and other cooperative research arrangements, industry now directly influences an estimated 20 to 25 percent of university research funding overall.[22]

Like many pressing for greater university entrepreneurship, Rausser contends that the Novartis alliance is consistent with Congress's mandate to transfer academic knowledge to the marketplace for the public's benefit. Far from compromising the university's public mission, he says, the Berkeley-Novartis deal was designed to "extract maximum value for the university," because the traditional terms of engagement were reversed. Instead of allowing the company to initiate the sponsored-research agreement and define its terms, Rausser came up with the novel idea of having PMB draw up a request for proposals, shop it around to various corporate bidders, and select the company that best suited its research needs. The bidding process enhanced Berkeley's leverage, he told me, because "only Novartis had been willing to accept the strict ground rules and safeguards we put forth to ensure that the arrangement complies with the university culture and values."[23]

———

But just how strong those safeguards were is open to question. Eighteen months after the Novartis agreement was signed, concerns about the deal began to spill beyond the campus to the state capital. In the spring of 2000, the California State Senate announced it would convene a hearing to investigate the Novartis agreement's impact on the University of California and its public interest mission.

On May 15, a diverse delegation from the university made its way to the state capitol—a magnificent neoclassical structure with a 120-foot gold-domed rotunda—to give testimony. Among the speakers was the chair of the University of California Student Association, which a month earlier had voted unanimously to oppose the Berkeley-Novartis deal, and a host of professors, students, and administrators, including Gordon Rausser.[24] Although there was little chance of any new bills emerging from the hearing, because the legislative session was drawing to a close, most expected the forum to be a highly charged affair.

They were not disappointed. Senator Tom Hayden, a liberal Democrat from Santa Monica, chaired the hearings. An outspoken critic of the biotech industry, he began by voicing concern that the Berkeley-Novartis contract—and future arrangements like it—could undermine the university's autonomy and its ability to perform disinterested research in the public interest. Hayden expressed his fear that this alliance could inhibit research into the possible adverse effects of genetically modified agriculture, already in widespread use throughout the state.

Joining Hayden was Senator Steve Peace, a Democrat from El Cajon known for both his brilliance and his occasional volcanic outbursts. Although more conservative than Hayden, Peace, the chair of the Senate Budget Committee, was no less concerned that the Novartis deal was structured in a way that failed to safeguard taxpayer interests. "I've read the agreement, and it's very creatively written," he told Rausser when the dean went up to testify, "but certainly it is one that had my lawyers brought it to me, I never would have signed." Peace zeroed in on provisions in the Berkeley-Novartis contract relating to the company's proprietary genomics database. By all accounts, faculty inside PMB believed that having access to Novartis's genomics data was one of the deal's most attractive features. Rausser testified that a handful of large companies, including Novartis, had already staked ownership claims to a sizable portion of the agricultural genome. The faculty in PMB believed that gaining access to this database would enable them to remain scientifically competitive with their counterparts in industry.[25]

Yet under the terms of the contract, Senator Peace noted, professors could access Novartis's data only if they agreed to sign a confidentiality provision that required them to keep the information secret. Rather than advancing public research, these proprietary restrictions would further reduce the amount of agricultural knowledge available in the public domain. Peace was not alone in his concerns. Since the mid-1990s, agricultural experts had been warning that the expansion of proprietary claims on germplasm and other basic biological research tools was hampering public-sector plant breeding, enabling a small number of private firms to gain near monopoly control over the global food system.[26] "Can you produce any professors who have gotten access to this data or research . . . without signing a confidentiality agreement?" Senator Peace asked Rausser.

"That is not knowledge that I have," Rausser replied.

Senator Peace followed by asking what might happen if, after having signed a confidentiality agreement, professors were to come upon information "which they believe to be of significant danger to the public [or] to the environment." Did the contract address such a scenario?

"No," Rausser replied. "All contracts by their very nature are incomplete."

The senator did not hide his irritation at this abrogation of the public interest. "I may not understand this highfalutin bio[tech] stuff," he stated icily. "But I do understand contracts."[27]

When Senator Hayden took over the questioning, the subject was oversight. "The governance structure seems very peculiar to me," said Hayden, referring to the two committees that had been formed to oversee implementation of the agreement. The first body, Hayden noted, was a monitoring group composed of six members—three representatives from the university and three from the company. This sounded balanced, except that two of the three university representatives were Dean Rausser and Joseph Cerny, then vice chancellor of research, or as Hayden put it, "two people who had engineered the agreement." The third was an independent faculty member.

"So five of six of the monitoring committee overall are [aligned] with Novartis, or with the University-Novartis deal," Hayden observed. "That wouldn't pass muster in either house of the Legislature as effective oversight. It just wouldn't make any sense."[28]

Hayden then turned to the second oversight body, a five-person research committee charged with determining *how* the Novartis money would be allocated. Two of the five members were representatives from Novartis; the other three were university appointees. Hayden inquired whether it was true that each of the university representatives, who had a hand in selecting proposals for funding, was "prohibited from having a conflict of interest."

"Yes. That's a University policy," replied Rausser.

"By being on this five-member committee, your testimony is that [the faculty] would be excluding themselves from any research funding?" Hayden repeated.

"No. I am not testifying to that," said Rausser.

"So members can allocate funds to themselves?" Hayden continued.

"Yes, they can."[29]

Adopting a prosecutorial style, Hayden then ticked off the specific dollar amount of research funding that each committee member had received from Novartis. "Dr. Gruissem got, himself, $200,000. Dr. Kutsu, $125,000. Dr. Staskawicz, $200,000. That's among a list of maybe twenty-five total research awards in 1999."[30]

Incredulous, Senator Peace interjected, "So all three? Am I hearing—?" Hayden repeated the amounts.

"Does that disturb you at all?" Peace demanded.

"No," Rausser replied. "Because the faculty elected, on the Research Committee, those faculty members who were doing, in their minds, the most meritorious research."

After these testy exchanges continued some time longer, Rausser seemed eager to change the tenor of the discussion. He emphasized that the Novartis alliance had always been "designed as an experiment," with important checks and balances in place. In particular, he noted, an external research group was due to conduct "a two-and-a-half-year review" to evaluate the effectiveness of the deal and its wider ramifications for the university. "There's overwhelming support on the part of not only the PMB faculty, [and] the College of Natural Resource faculty, but the Academic Senate faculty on the Berkeley campus that this be conducted as an experiment."[31]

The External Review

Close to a year after the senate hearing, I returned to Berkeley to see how the "experiment" was turning out. Two and a half years had lapsed since the Berkeley-Novartis alliance began. But the "two-and-a-half-year review"—or progress report by external examiners—had still not materialized. In fact, it was not yet under way.

The delay was generating considerable rancor on campus. Prior to signing the Novartis deal, the administration had made a verbal commitment to the Academic Senate, Berkeley's faculty governing body, that an external study would be an integral part of the deal. That pledge dated back to the fall of 1998, when the administration first asked the Academic Senate to offer "advice and comment" on an early draft of the proposed Novartis contract.[32] After reviewing the proposal, the faculty voiced many concerns.[33] Realizing they lacked the time and ability to adequately resolve these issues, however, the Senate began pressing for the alliance to be treated like "an experiment," so that an independent team of researchers could both monitor its progress and study its broader impact on the university. "We regard an *on-going assessment of the institutional impact of the agreement to be essential*," wrote Robert Brentano, a professor of medieval history and then chair of the Senate, in a November 1998 letter to the administration. "A proper assessment will require early selection of an independent research team, acquisition of adequate resources, and appointment of an advisory group of national stature which will assess implementation of the agreement over the next five years."[34] Soon afterward, the administration and the faculty struck a deal: The Novartis alliance would go forward with only minor modifications, and an external team of researchers would be selected to monitor and study its progress.

But ever since that time, Senate members told me, the administration had been dragging its feet. "We had expected to have this going by now so midway through the process we could learn if we were beginning to go off track," said Todd LaPorte, chair of the ad hoc Senate committee charged with examining the deal. Unfortunately, added Robert Spear, another leading Senate member, "finding the money [to finance an external study] wasn't really high on the administration's agenda."[35]

Finally, in early 2002, more than three years into the agreement, a ten-member research team from Michigan State University was selected to evaluate the collaboration.[36] Initially, the faculty felt some measure of relief. But this diminished somewhat when, in October, the administration decided to release its own *internal* mid-term study of the Novartis deal, which optimistically concluded that the alliance had "brought considerable benefit . . . with few, if any, countervailing costs." *Science* magazine, summing up the study, hailed the Novartis deal as a "smashing success."[37] When asked to comment, Spear tactfully responded, "While I find no reason to doubt the facts presented in the [internal] report, it is important to keep in mind that it emanates from the administrative office that was centrally involved in negotiating the agreement in the first place."[38]

When the external reviewers at Michigan State issued their final report in July 2004, they reached a starkly different conclusion. The

Berkeley-Novartis alliance "was outside the mainstream for research contracts with industry," they wrote. "While an intriguing experiment, there appears to be little rationale for repeating the approach."[39] Lawrence Busch, the sociologist who led the study, told the *Chronicle of Higher Education* that "universities as institutions can only be objective observers on the scientific and regulatory scene to the extent that some distance remains between them and industry funding sources." This deal created the impression that the department was "on the dole," he said, and "biased toward the funding source."[40]

The external reviewers also objected to the university's "stewardship of public funds," noting that Berkeley's decision to award up-front proprietary rights to Novartis "fell short of at least the spirit of the NIH's [National Institutes of Health's] guidelines" by effectively allowing one company to exert a monopoly over the department's best research, irregardless of whether it was funded by Novartis or by U.S. taxpayers."[41] Interestingly, although Berkeley did seek patents on twenty discoveries made during the contract period, Novartis-Syngenta never licensed any of them, an outcome suggesting that it got relatively little commercial value out of the collaboration.[42]

The report did take pains to stress that the critics' worst fears had not occurred: There was no evidence that Novartis-Syngenta had strong-armed any of the university's scientists into pursuing more commercially oriented research. The department of PMB had always been primarily focused on basic research, and it remained so. However, the report suggested this wasn't all that surprising: "The very distinction between basic and applied has of late disintegrated. Especially with respect to molecular biology, what is considered breakthrough in basic research one day may well be a tool or product the next."[43] In other words, Novartis had allied itself with PMB not to make its research more applied, but to access basic science that might have commercial potential.[44]

The Maize Controversy

One of the most troubling fallouts from the collaboration, noted the Michigan State reviewers, was the intense polarization it had created on campus between pro-genetic-engineering researchers (who had ready access to industry support) and those more skeptical (who were increasingly starved for resources).[45] As it happened, Ignacio Chapela, the microbial biology professor who had organized the faculty survey and had become a vocal critic of the Novartis deal, stumbled into the middle of this contentious battleground when his bid for tenure came up for review and was denied in November 2003. Instantly, large numbers of faculty protested the decision, questioning whether it was driven by an objective assessment of Chapela's scholarship—or by politics.

The external review team did not deliver an opinion on whether Chapela should have gotten tenure, but it did discuss the case, noting that "there is little doubt" that the Berkeley-Novartis deal had played a role in the decision.[46]

The controversy surrounding Chapela's bid for tenure really began in the fall of 2001, when he and his graduate student, David Quist, published a study in the journal *Nature*, reporting that foreign DNA material from genetically modified (GM) plants was showing up in native varieties of corn in southern Mexico, even though Mexico had banned the planting of modified corn since 1998.[47] Corn was first cultivated in Mexico ten thousand years ago, and it remains the center of that plant's genetic diversity around the world, which helps to explain why both the Mexican government and the environmental community reacted nervously to the study's findings.[48] Like all of *Nature*'s papers, Chapela's study was rigorously peer-reviewed by expert scientists prior to being accepted for publication. Yet the moment it was released, it became the subject of heated debate perhaps—not surprisingly, given the financial stakes involves.[49]

In the biotech world in recent years, a number of respected scientists who have published research critical of GM agriculture have found both their scholarship and their personal integrity challenged, often by large agricultural interests with profits riding on the research. (For example, when Cornell professor John E. Losey published a study showing that monarch butterfly caterpillars exposed to pollen from GM cotton became sick and died in lab studies, his research was roundly attacked by industry-funded scientists, and an aggressive public relations campaign was launched against him.[50]) What was striking about the Chapela and Quist study was that many of the authors' harshest critics had direct ties to PMB, the department that had signed the deal with Novartis. Both of the letters *Nature* published challenging the validity of Chapela's research, for example, were written by current and former researchers in PMB.[51] Michael Freeling, a PMB professor, and others in his department went so far as to sign a petition calling for a full retraction of Chapela's paper.[52]

With both sides accusing the other of having impure motives, it became increasingly difficult to judge the study on purely scientific grounds.[53]

In fact, virtually nobody disputed Chapela and Quist's finding that genetically modified plants had contaminated native maize in Mexico. The disagreement was over the significance of that finding. Biotech supporters maintained that such contamination posed no danger, whereas critics worried that this kind of genetic migration could erode the corn plant's genetic diversity and create other long-term ecological problems. A second conclusion in the Chapela paper, concerning the movement of foreign DNA around the corn plant, was more controversial, as the testing method was judged to be too unreliable. In the end, *Nature* did not retract the peer-reviewed study, but it did do something unparalleled in its 133-year history: The journal printed an editorial note stating that the "evidence available is not sufficient to justify" the original publication and calling upon readers to judge the science for themselves.[54]

Not surprisingly, the study and the surrounding controversy became a central issue in Chapela's tenure decision. At first, the College of Natural Resources voted 32 to 1 in favor of tenure (with three abstentions). Then, an ad hoc tenure committee composed of five experts chosen for their ability to evaluate Chapela's research voted unanimously in his favor. But when the case reached the final arbiter, the budget committee—with members from across the college—tenure was denied. Immediately, controversy erupted. Wayne Getz, a professor of insect biology who had sat on the five-person ad hoc committee, charged that the process had "gone awry." The chair of that same committee, who had originally voted in favor of tenure, rescinded his recommendation. It then came to light that a member of the budget committee, Jasper Rine, a professor of genetics, had ties to the biotech industry that may have colored his judgment, provoking further dissension. When this book went to press, the case was still being appealed and Chapela was filing a lawsuit.

Ultimately, the most damaging legacy of the Berkeley-Novartis agreement was its effect on the university's perceived independence and its public trust. What the Chapela case revealed was that a sizable segment of the Berkeley faculty had simply lost faith in the administration's capacity to oversee a fair assessment of Chapela's scholarship, free of political or commercial bias. In the past, universities had been largely responsible for monitoring only their professors' potential conflicts of interest, wrote the Michigan State reviewers. But "the [Berkeley-Novartis agreement] raised issues of a different sort. In this case, it is the *institution's* potential for conflict of interest relative to the funds it receives that is at issue."[55]

Berkeley's belated attempt to evaluate the Novartis experiment serves as an apt parable for what has happened nationwide as university-industry collaborations have proliferated since the early 1980s. Although the Bayh-Dole Act ushered in a new era of commercial engagement—one unprecedented in both its scope and its scale—these collaborations have been subject to precious little independent scrutiny. At most schools, in fact, such partnerships do not even fall under the purview of faculty governing bodies, because they are not considered directly relevant to curricular or academic affairs. Thus, there has been little opportunity for the broader campus community to weigh in on the costs and benefits of these agreements, or to evaluate how they fit into the university's broader educational and research mission. The oft-cited need to protect corporate proprietary interests has also tended to keep information about these deals tightly controlled; the contracts themselves are frequently not made public. At Berkeley, the only reason the Academic Senate had input was because Robert Berdahl (who took over as chancellor just as the Novartis negotiations were coming to a close) insisted that the faculty be consulted.

Given all the controversy it stirred, you might think the Berkeley-Novartis deal would have diminished California's thirst for large-scale alliances of this kind. It did nothing of the sort. Across the U.C. system, university-industry partnerships accelerated. In December 2000, for example, Governor Gray Davis announced an ambitious plan to finance three new California Institutes for Science and Innovation (CISI) to boost the state's economy and generate high-tech jobs through targeted research in biotechnology, telecommunications, and nanosystems. The plan was sharply criticized in a front-page story in the *San Francisco Bay Guardian* titled "The Selling of the UC System."[56] In announcing the winners of the governor's statewide competition for public funds, Richard Atkinson, then president of the U.C. system, proudly noted that the new research centers have "inspired an unprecedented level of collaboration . . . with private industry," a fact that was hardly surprising given the way the state had structured its competition. Davis had pledged he would provide approximately $100 million annually in public funds for each of four new science institutes over the next three years, but receipt of this money was contingent on each institute's being able to raise at least twice that amount on its own. The winning proposals generated an astonishing $1.4 billion in matching funds, including pledges from federal sources and more than two hundred private companies. Among the corporations that had pledged support, Governor Davis boasted, was "almost every blue chip company in America."[57]

One of the largest of these CISI projects is the Institute for Bioengineering, Biotechnology, and Quantitative Biomedicine (otherwise known as "QB3"), which is housed jointly at U.C. campuses in San Francisco, Berkeley, and Santa Cruz. QB3 takes a multidisciplinary approach to the diagnosis and treatment of disease, combining chemistry, engineering, mathematics, and medicine, and seeks to radically enhance the academic-industrial interface. At its main San Francisco headquarters at Mission Bay, a three-hundred-acre site that was still under construction when I visited, an estimated nine thousand University of California at San Francisco scientists will be housed at research facilities located at the core, surrounded by an industrial park that is slated to be filled with biomedical companies—many of them start-up firms founded by U.C. professors. "Academic scientists form only a part of the continuum of activities that comprise the long road toward commercialization," explained Christopher Scott, then the assistant vice chancellor at UCSF, who gave me a guided tour of the campus. At Mission Bay, Scott said, all the activities necessary to foster commercialization would be fully integrated into the academic experience, including: venture-capital management services, business incubator facilities, entrepreneurship classes for Ph.D. students in traditional science programs, frequent exchanges between the medical school and surrounding business schools, and much more.

Scott viewed the QB3 project, much like the Berkeley-Novartis agreement, as a "grand experiment." In an essay, he wrote that "if Silicon Valley has informally created a geographical locus for innovation and economic diversity, then perhaps [Mission Bay] will do the same for the next surge of the biomedical industry."[58]

The vision is certainly bold, but is the public university system the appropriate locus for such a commercial experiment? How far do such ventures risk pulling universities from their primary educational missions? Are universities even capable of effectively administering venture-capital funds, industrial parks, and other such commercial operations? *Should* they be asked to perform these functions at a time when state support for higher education is declining? (During the period 2000–2003, when these expensive commercial-research centers were being launched, state spending on the U.C. system declined by 14 percent, even as enrollment climbed 18 percent.[59]) Most champions of academic-industry partnerships rarely pause to consider such questions.

Dean Rausser, for example, frequently expressed surprise at the level of opposition the Novartis agreement provoked, noting that the alliance was only one of many similar initiatives across the state. Under a program known as Industry-University Cooperative Research, started in 1996, the U.C. system has actively encouraged faculty collaborations with industry. One program, known as MICRO for microelectronics research, has generated more than $100 million in private investments for U.C. investigators. Another, BioSTAR, solicits industry matching grants for collaborative research in the area of biotechnology. Its marketing slogan: "*When it comes to biotechnology, UC means business.*" From 1993 to 2003, as a result of such initiatives, industry-sponsored research at the U.C. system grew 97 percent in real terms (from $65 million to $155 million).[60]

But if commercial collaboration extends beyond the Berkeley-Novartis agreement, so do the accompanying problems. In the U.C. system alone, several incidents have occurred in which companies have sought to quash academic freedom—with serious implications for the American public. Consider the case of Betty Dong. In December 1990, Dong, a clinical researcher at UCSF, discovered that a widely prescribed thyroid medication—Synthroid (levothyroxine)—was no more effective than three cheaper competing drugs, including several generics. At the time, Synthroid was the third-most-dispensed drug in the country, taken by 8 million Americans each day. Dong's findings stood to influence the health choices of vast numbers of U.S. consumers.

They also stood to have a major impact on the bottom line of Boots Pharmaceutical (later Knoll Pharmaceutical Co.), her corporate sponsor, which upon learning of Dong's conclusions immediately sought to bury the results. Over the next four years, Boots/Knoll waged a vigorous campaign to discredit the study and prevent publication, claiming that the research was flawed. Two university investigations found nothing but the most minor and easily correctable problems in Dong's research and concluded that the company's attacks were "harassment" designed to prevent publication of results that the company simply didn't want the public to know.[61]

At first, UCSF's legal counsel supported Dong's decision to submit her study for publication in the prestigious *Journal of the American Medical Association (JAMA)*, despite a restrictive clause in her university-approved contract that required company approval. The study passed through *JAMA*'s peer-review process and was scheduled to be published in its January 25, 1995, issue. Several weeks before the issue went out, however, Boots/Knoll threatened to sue. UCSF, fearing an expensive court battle, urged Dong to withdraw her manuscript from publication, which she did. Hoping to add a final nail to the coffin, the company then published a portion of Dong's data in a competing medical journal, giving it a far more favorable spin.

By this point, it seemed unlikely that Dong's research would ever see the light of day. That changed only after a reporter from the *Wall Street Journal* learned of the study's existence and published an article exposing what had happened.[62] Soon, pressure from the Food and Drug Administration compelled Boots/Knoll to back down, and the study finally appeared in *JAMA*—nine years after it was originally completed.

The lengthy delay in the study's release was a huge victory for Boots/Knoll, enabling the company to sustain Synthroid's dominant position in a $600-million market for drugs to control hypothyroidism.[63] For the general public, it was another story. If an equally effective generic or brand-name preparation were substituted for Synthroid, Dong and her colleagues estimated that people suffering from hypothyroidism and other conditions would have saved $365 million annually.[64] The publication of these findings prompted numerous lawsuits, including two massive class-action lawsuits, filed on behalf of all Synthroid users and thirty-seven states, alleging that Knoll had defrauded them of hundreds of millions of dollars in inflated costs. In 1999 and 2000, the company agreed to pay $179 million to settle these group claims.[65]

More recently, conflicts within the U.C. system morphed into a public scandal involving a potentially serious threat to the environment and public health. Tyrone B. Hayes, a biologist at U.C. Berkeley, often finds himself referred to as the "frog man" for his extensive knowledge of the beloved four-legged amphibians found in ponds and backyards across the country. In 1998, the same year that Berkeley signed its $25-million deal with Novartis-Syngenta, Hayes accepted a smaller $100,000 individual grant from Ecorisk, Inc., a consulting firm hired by Novartis-Syngenta, to study the effects of its most popular weed killer, atrazine, on frogs. Although few Americans know the chemical atrazine by name, it happens to be the most heavily applied herbicide in the United States, used on two-thirds of the nation's corn and sorghum acreage, on 90 percent of its sugar cane acreage, and on golf courses and residential lawns. Some 60–70 million pounds of the herbicide are applied annually to U.S. crops, and traces of it can be found in streams, waterways, and even rainwater throughout the United States, especially after the planting season.

Hayes's research quickly turned up disturbing results: Exposure to atrazine appeared to disrupt the sexual development of male frogs, causing their voice boxes to shrink. Worse, these males started to develop ovaries and become demasculinized. Atrazine appeared to be one of a family of chemicals known as endocrine disruptors that, even in minute traces, can significantly interfere with the hormones that regulate key biological activities, both in wildlife and in humans. Hayes wondered whether this effect explained why fifty-eight amphibian species had disappeared or become extinct in the past twenty years, and another ninety-one endangered.[66]

Hayes was sure other scientists would take interest in his findings. What he didn't know is that the contract he had signed gave Ecorisk *and* Syngenta ultimate control over publication.[67] (Again, just as in the Betty Dong case, the U.C. grants office had somehow allowed this glaring breach of academic freedom to slip into the contract.) Ecorisk promptly brought in its Atrazine Endocrine Risk Assessment Panel, a consulting group chaired by Ronald J. Kendall, a professor at Texas Tech University, to evaluate and analyze Hayes's results. As time passed, Hayes grew convinced that the panel's true purpose was to forestall publication of his research. If he continued to participate in this process, Hayes wrote in a November 2000 resignation letter to the company, "It will appear to my colleagues that I have been part of a plan to bury important data."[68]

After resigning, Hayes managed to pull together new funding (from W. Alton Jones, the World Wildlife Fund, and the National Science Foundation) to continue his research, the first part of which he published in the *Proceedings of the National Academy of Science* in April 2002. The study had an immediate impact because the Environmental Protection Agency (EPA) was, at that precise juncture, reviewing the safety of atrazine to determine whether it should be reauthorized for use as an herbicide in the United States.

The EPA's scientific panel had been leaning in favor of reapproval until it saw Hayes's findings, which showed that extremely low levels of exposure to atrazine—as low as 1 part per 10 billion in water—could cause tadpoles to develop into frogs with both male and female sexual organs. If Hayes's results were accurate, then serious hormone disruption was occurring at concentrations thirty times lower than the EPA's then-approved levels.[69] At the time of the EPA hearing, much of Europe had already banned atrazine because of safety concerns. (In October 2003, the European Union extended the ban to all of Europe.)

Aware of the consequences, Syngenta and Ecorisk quickly moved to discredit Hayes's study. On June 20, 2002, they issued a press release announcing that "three separate studies by university scientists have failed to replicate" his findings. None of the studies had been published in peer-reviewed journals; all had been underwritten by Syngenta. One study, coauthored by Texas Tech's James A. Carr, Ronald Kendall (head of the Ecorisk consulting group), and others, did eventually find its way into print, in the journal *Environmental Toxicology and Chemistry*—where Kendall happened to be an editor.[70] Prior to publication, a quote from Kendall appeared in a company press release. "As research on this issue continues," he said, "one thing is certain. No conclusions can be drawn at this time on atrazine and its purported effect on frogs."[71]

How independent were these studies? Syngenta told the EPA that the Texas Tech study "was conducted under the direction and auspices of an independent scientific panel." But as Goldie Blumenstyk, an investigative reporter at the *Chronicle of Higher Education*, discovered, this statement was highly misleading. The $600,000 contract Texas Tech signed with Ecorisk stated that all research data and analyses belonged to Ecorisk "and/or its client." Furthermore, any publication of the research required "appropriate review and written permission by Ecorisk."[72]

In October 2002, Hayes published a second study in *Environmental Health Perspectives* (and a shorter piece in *Nature*), based on field research in the Midwest examining native populations of frogs at eight different sites, seven of which had detectable traces of atrazine. At one of these sites, in Wyoming, 92 percent of the male frogs had immature eggs growing inside of them. At six of the other sites, the researchers found levels of hermaphrodite frogs ranging from 10 to 40 percent. The only site where they found no abnormal males was the one where no traces of atrazine had been detected.[73]

Once again, Hayes's research came under attack. This time, in addition to the Ecorisk panel, his critics included a Fox News commentator; the Kansas Corn Growers Association; and the Triazine Network, an association of a thousand growers and herbicide manufacturers. These industry groups challenged the validity of Hayes's research and, under an arcane law known as the Data Safety Quality Act of 2001, petitioned the EPA to disregard all his findings. Despite these efforts, in June 2003 the EPA's scientific advisory panel ruled that there was "sufficient evidence" to hypothesize that the country's most widely used herbicide, atrazine, does cause sexual abnormality in frogs. The panel found six of the studies it reviewed, showing a variety of alarming defects including the development of multiple testes and multiple ovaries, both persuasive and significant.[74]

Four months later, however, when the EPA issued its final ruling, it reversed course and reapproved atrazine for use as a weed killer in the United States. Critics suspect that Syngenta's $6.5 billion in annual revenues and heavy funding of atrazine research may have distorted the scientific debate. Fueling such suspicion was the fact that Kendall, who oversaw $600,000 worth of Syngenta-funded research at Texas Tech, sat on the board of the EPA's scientific advisory panel on atrazine, as well as its endocrine disruptor screening committee, which also would have been involved in any final decision on the herbicide's approval.[75]

As these stories clearly reveal, were it not for the existence of fiercely independent academic scholars like Dong and Hayes, the American people would have virtually no way of accessing important information that, despite having a direct bearing on their lives, powerful interest groups often would prefer to keep buried.

The commercial threat to the academy is not confined to the University of California. Nor are the consequences relevant merely to professors in the sciences, a point made eloquently in recent years by Berkeley's own chancellor, Robert Berdahl. Although he has remained steadfast in supporting the Berkeley-Novartis agreement, in a speech at the University of Erfurt in Germany, Berdahl warned that market forces are encroaching on the academic sphere in unforeseen and potentially dangerous ways. "With the new capacity of some faculty—biologists, engineers, computer scientists, and business school faculty—to earn substantial amounts outside the university, there can be a corresponding devaluation of the work of humanists and social scientists," Berdahl cautioned. "It is worrisome that the great challenges posed by the advent of the new technologies . . . are fundamentally issues of ethics and public policy. Who will guide us through the moral and policy thicket of this new age if the humanists and social scientists are weakened by the overwhelming drive of market forces in a university-industrial complex?"

Berdahl further asserted that "the perception of the objectivity of our faculty may be compromised and with it the confidence that their research is dedicated to the public good." He went on to cite a theoretical example—"an extreme example," he said—of a scientist studying lung cancer whose research was funded by tobacco companies.[76] The example is not, alas, so extreme. In 2000, Karl Keen, the chair of U.C. Davis's nutrition department, presented research at a major scientific conference showing that consuming chocolate was good for your heart. "The findings are very promising," reported Keen, "and suggest that, with balance and moderation, chocolate can contribute to a healthy diet."[77] The study was financed by Mars, the maker of M&Ms, Milky Way, and Snickers.

2

The Lessons of History

While the college student has been learning a little about the bar-
barous and petty squabbles of a far-distant past, or trying to master
languages which are dead . . . the future captain of industry is hotly
engaged in the school of experience, obtaining the very knowledge
required for his future triumphs.

—Andrew Carnegie[1]

History has figured prominently in recent debates about the commercialization of higher education. At the height of the Novartis
controversy, Gordon Rausser, Berkeley's dean, defended the alliance by in-
voking the past. Writing in the school's alumni magazine after Robert
Berring, a professor at the law school, had penned a scathing critique of
the agreement, Rausser fired back:

Professor Berring assumes that Berkeley's commercial collaborations are new and necessarily dangerous, but ignores the very
heritage that has allowed the University to thrive. We are, after all,

one of the original land grant universities whose stated purpose was to marry scientific insight with practical knowledge to improve agricultural productivity. This might not sound like commerce, but it was and still is.[2]

Rausser had a point. Certainly in comparison with their European counterparts, universities in the United States have always displayed a strong utilitarian bent. In founding the University of Virginia in 1825, Thomas Jefferson sought to provide "an useful American education." He recommended the study of agriculture because "it is the first in utility," and expressed appreciation of the natural sciences, civil history, and law because of their direct application to nation building.[3]

This utilitarian conception of education reflects deeply ingrained American values. As a nation of pioneers, pragmatists, entrepreneurs, and businesspeople, Americans have long taken to viewing knowledge as a means to *other* ends, rather than a value in and of itself. For the typical nineteenth-century American, noted the historian Henry Steele Commager, "education was his religion"—provided that it "be practical and pay dividends."[4] Richard Hofstadter shrewdly observed that although Americans professed universal admiration for the "man of intelligence," they didn't necessarily feel the same way about *intellectuals*. The intellectual heroes of the United States have tended to be inventors such as Thomas Edison and Benjamin Franklin, practical men whose contributions arose largely through direct interaction with the "real world." Common sense over abstract learning, hands-on experience over erudition: this has long been an unspoken national creed. Within such a culture, it's no surprise that universities have often sought to legitimize their existence by emphasizing their utility: training students for practical careers in engineering, medicine, and law; providing expert advice to various sectors of society, including private industry; generating scientific and technological breakthroughs to spur economic growth.

But although all of this is true, it hardly follows that the level of commercial engagement in higher education today is unexceptional—or that universities have been guided *solely* by utilitarian aims. Throughout American history, there have been prominent voices—academic leaders, scientists, educators, public intellectuals—who forcefully called on universities to preserve their autonomy, and honor their commitments to teaching and pure intellectual inquiry. At times, those voices have seemed in the minority. Yet their influence has been lasting and profound.

Indeed, much of what we value most about higher education today—academic freedom, the commitment to open inquiry and disinterested research, the ideal of a well-rounded education—exists because such voices warned against allowing external forces (religious authorities, the government, the private sector) to threaten these distinctive values. Rausser may be right that universities in the United States have never been as removed from the marketplace as many contemporary critics now imagine. Yet it is precisely because they have stubbornly resisted forsaking their independence and refused to adopt narrow market values (even as their responsibilities have grown) that universities have played a unique and vital role in American life.

The first American colleges were training grounds of a sort—not for industry but for the clergy. The colonial-era colleges (with the exception of the College of Philadelphia, which was nonsectarian) operated under the direct influence and control of the various religious denominations that had taken root in America. The first of these institutions, Harvard College, was founded in 1636 by Puritans less than two decades after their arrival on the shores of New England.[5] As one contemporary observer wrote in *New England's First Fruits* (1643), after erecting shelter, a house of worship, and the framework of government, "one of the next things we longed for, and looked after, was to advance Learning and perpetuate it to Posterity."[6] By the middle of the next century, many of the great private institutions that remain with us today had been founded: Princeton (1746) by Presbyterians; Columbia (as King's College, 1754) by Episcopalians; Brown (1764) by Baptists; and Rutgers (as Queen's College, 1766) by members of the Reformed Church.[7]

These early American colleges were never merely theological seminaries, however, and their admissions policies did not prescribe religious tests.[8] Although they graduated large numbers of ministers, the curriculum was modeled after the English college's version of a medieval course of study.[9] It consisted chiefly of cultivating "mental discipline" and sharpening young men's faculties through the prescribed study of Latin, Greek, mathematics, logic, and moral philosophy.[10] By modern standards, the early colleges had many weaknesses: Teaching was carried out largely by recitation, and scholarly inquiry was arid, uninspired, and bound by tradition. But many of the principles these early schools championed carried over to the modern university, including the belief that education should instill moral principles, build character, and provide a common core of cultural knowledge, as well as emphasize linguistic and literary attainment and critical thinking.[11]

Religious leadership limited the autonomy of the early colleges, but the need to protect academic freedom was already a clearly articulated goal, one whose origins could be traced back to the first medieval European universities of the twelfth century. Despite the power of the European church, these universities enjoyed an exceptional degree of intellectual freedom. Faculty managed to secure a high level of autonomy, including the right to govern their own internal affairs. (When external powers tried to intervene, scholars often threatened to strike or, in extreme cases, relocate to another town.[12]) Though inherited patterns of deference to philosophic authority—as well as the desire to attain salvation—limited the scope of that freedom, the early universities in Bologna, Paris, and Oxford engaged in rigorous intellectual inquiry and disputation of a kind quite exceptional for the period. Within medieval society, these academies were looked upon as centers of power and prestige because of the great importance attached to learning, and because of the growing need for educated clerics and civil servants. As Hofstadter noted, the early medieval universities were "autonomous corporations, conceived in the spirit of the guilds; their members elected their own officials and set the rules for the teaching craft." Licenses to teach were granted by the emperors, popes, or kings, but "internal matters of institutional governance were in the hands of those immediately connected with learning."[13]

No such latitude existed in America, where academic scholars failed to win these powers of self-governance. The founders of the first two colonial colleges, Harvard, and William and Mary, initially sought to emulate the European tradition of faculty control but after a brief period of dual governance opted to transfer authority to an external board of laymen trustees, known as overseers or visitors.[14] "In this respect," explained Hofstadter,

> American higher education is a deviant among the educational systems of the Western world [and] also without parallel among the other learned professions within the United States. Doctors and lawyers would be appalled . . . at the thought that their professional standards and practices should be exposed to control by laymen. But few Americans find it at all surprising that the govern-

ing decisions of American learning are formally in the hands of laymen whose substantive knowledge of education as such, or of the
various disciplines they preside over, is about as limited as the ordinary layman's knowledge of medicine or law.[15]

This academic governance structure arose in part because the nation
was young, lacked an established tradition of scholarship, and had no organized teaching profession.[16] Be that as it may, placing power in the
hands of an external board, as Abraham Flexner and other educators have
noted, wound up posing a persistent challenge to academic freedom.[17] In
time, the faculty would win broad powers over hiring and curricular decisions (and even some measure of participation in university governance),
but the legacy of external control inevitably had the effect of making
American universities more susceptible to outside influence.

After 1787 the early colonial college system started to wither. Sectarian
controversies gradually loosened religious control over higher education,
and the states, which until then had subsidized religious colleges, stopped
providing tax assistance to sectarian organizations. Along with this growing secularism came the settling of the frontier and the imperatives of
nation building, which forced universities to alter their mission or risk
growing obsolete. In 1804, the federal government, seeking to foster public education, began to grant federal lands to states west of the
Appalachians to endow new universities.[18] It was the first of many steps
that would lead to the gradual displacement of the old-time college, which
was too insular and elitist to suit the needs of an emerging democratic nation filled with aspiring artisans, farmers, and professionals.

A new emphasis on the pragmatic uses of higher education, unthink-
able in classical Europe, gathered steam. In 1862, Congress passed the
Morrill Act, which expanded land-grant assistance to the states for educational purposes. The act specifically instructed the land-grant colleges
to teach "agriculture and the mechanical arts . . . in order to promote liberal and practical education of the industrial classes."[19] This act laid the
foundation for the public university system that Gordon Rausser described, with its strong commitment to technical training and public
service. Meanwhile, a group of prominent academic reformers—Charles
W. Eliot of Harvard, Andrew D. White of Cornell, and Francis Wayland

of Brown—emerged to advance a more utilitarian model of higher education. Seeking to make education more relevant to the nation's growing scientific and professional needs, the utilitarians advocated expanding the curriculum to include new programs in business, law, engineering, and medicine. "There has existed for the last twenty years a great demand for civil engineers," noted Wayland in 1850. "Has this demand been supplied from our colleges? We assume the single academy at West Point . . . has done more towards the construction of railroads than all our one hundred and twenty colleges combined."[20] From 1824 to 1861 an array of new technical schools were built—Rensselaer Polytechnic Institute (1824), Harvard's Lawrence Scientific School (1847), Yale's Sheffield Scientific School (1847), and the Massachusetts Institute of Technology (MIT) (1861)—precisely in order to meet the needs of a modernizing society.[21] Their formation coincided with the birth of a public high school system, without which the expansion of higher education would have been impossible, and the emergence of great personal fortunes capable of financing institution building on an unprecedented scale. After the Civil War, university expansion depended heavily on wealthy patrons like Ezra Cornell, Cornelius Vanderbilt, Johns Hopkins, and John D. Rockefeller.[22] As David A. Hollinger observed, a signal accomplishment of the generation of Eliot, White, Daniel Coit Gilman (of Johns Hopkins), William Rainey Harper (of Chicago), and others was the enormous amount of relatively unrestricted money they obtained from these private sources to build their institutions.[23]

The utilitarians fervently believed that higher education should shed its elitist past. As Benjamin I. Wheeler, president of the University of California, expressed it, "A university is a place that rightfully knows no aristocracy as between studies, no aristocracy as between scientific truths, and no aristocracy as between persons."[24] It was a quintessentially American sentiment, and with the rapid settlement of the new continent and the birth of new industries, it naturally won out over the earlier focus on rigid classical training for a gentlemanly elite. As education came to be viewed increasingly as the key to social advancement, more and more universities adopted the elective system, freeing students to select their own course of study instead of adhering to a prescribed curriculum. At public universities, tuition was lowered to broaden access. The land-grant colleges meanwhile embraced a new ideal of public service, offering instruction to farmers in breeding, soil science, and other technical fields.[25]

The commitment to public service was perhaps best exemplified by the University of Wisconsin at Madison. Founded in 1848 to give "the *whole* people of the State an educational institution suited to their wants," the university gradually extended its educational programs to serve the needs of local agriculture, industry, and government.[26] Wisconsin dairy farmers saved hundreds of millions of dollars when scientists at the university developed the agricultural "short course" and the Babcock fat test and dedicated their discoveries to the public.[27] Later, during the Progressive era, when "Fighting Bob" La Follette was state governor, the university mobilized around the "Wisconsin Idea," a two-part plan that involved bringing university advisers into local government (in the form of a "brain trust"), and developing extension programs to educate citizens throughout the state.[28]

Unfortunately, though it unquestionably brought benefits and helped to modernize the university, this new emphasis on utility also fostered an unmistakable strain of anti-intellectualism.[29] In 1892, Chancellor James H. Canfield of the University of Nebraska scorned "the institutions that seem to love scholarship and erudition for their own sake; who make these ends and not means; who hug themselves with joy because they are not as other men, and especially are not as this practical fellow, who always wishes to know what may be done with what he is to receive."[30] All too many universities embraced a crude vocationalism, allowing academic standards to erode, equating education with mere training, and forgetting that the quest for knowledge had intrinsic worth.

It was in reaction to these trends that, beginning in 1900, a small but influential group of educators, among them Woodrow Wilson, the president of Princeton, and Abbott Lawrence Lowell, who succeeded Eliot at Harvard, arose to defend the classical liberal arts education. For these "advocates of liberal culture," to borrow the historian Lawrence Veysey's term, the growing focus on utility and narrow specialization needed to be counterbalanced by a renewed commitment to cultural understanding, breadth of knowledge, and critical thinking. Most of these reformers embraced Matthew Arnold's definition of culture: "a wide vision of the best things which man has done or aspired after." Although critics dismissed this movement as elitist, most of its adherents actually shared Arnold's belief that liberal culture and democracy went hand in hand. As the critic Russell Jacoby pointed out, Arnold believed all citizens within a democratic polity, not just the elites, should have access to culture and the arts.[31]

By the turn of the century, even many advocates of utility, such as Andrew D. White, the former president of Cornell, had begun to voice misgivings. From his retirement in 1908, White wrote, "There is certainly a widespread fear among many thinking men that in our eagerness for these new things we have too much lost sight of certain valuable old things, the things in university education which used to be summed up under the word 'culture.'"[32] In the decades to follow, prominent educators such as Robert M. Hutchins of the University of Chicago and Norman Foerster of the University of Iowa would criticize the excessive focus on vocationalism and help launch a movement to reinstate a prescribed liberal arts curriculum during the early undergraduate years. Their efforts bore fruit, as universities across the country added or reintroduced general humanities courses to their curriculums during the 1920s and 1930s.[33]

Just as the advocates of liberal culture reacted against an excessive emphasis on "utility" in higher education, so, too, did a group of educators and scientists influenced by the German university and its commitment to "pure research." These reformers hoped to emulate the German conception of *Wissenschaft*, or "science," which connoted a dignified, sanctified pursuit of knowledge for its own sake. In contrast to the American focus on practical applications, the German research method was motivated by the desire to uncover truth and expand the frontiers of knowledge. Accordingly, research was judged not by its utility but by a small community of peers who could verify its accuracy (for example, through replication of an experiment) and assess its value in relation to the existing knowledge within a particular scholarly field.[34] The German model placed strong emphasis on academic freedom. "To the German mind," wrote the historian James Morgan Hart, "if either freedom of teaching or freedom of learning is wanting, that institution no matter how richly endowed, no matter how numerous its students, no matter how imposing its buildings, is not . . . a *University*."[35]

The founding of Johns Hopkins University, in Baltimore in 1876, served as the catalyst for the adoption of the pure research model. It also marked the birth of graduate education in the United States. Hopkins adopted the German format of teaching through lectures, seminars, and laboratory work, bringing faculty and graduate students together—in the role of mentor and trainee—to pursue their investigations in close collaboration. By the turn of the century, numerous other colleges and universities had adopted this emphasis on pure research and graduate-level instruction.[36]

In the academic sciences, two radically different models of research thus vied for influence. In the pure research model, wrote the historian Walter Metzger, "the searcher was to be independent, not only with respect to his conclusions, but to his choice of an area of work. To fill the gaps in knowledge that continuing inquiry revealed, to conduct investigations as the logic of a discipline directed—these were to be the functions of academic inquiry. Practical results might be forthcoming, but inquiry should be allowed to push against any of the frontiers of knowledge, and *not merely along that border where material benefits were promised"* (emphasis added).[37] The utilitarian model, by contrast, was aimed at generating discoveries and perfecting skills of practical benefit to industry, agriculture, and other professional endeavors. A tug of war arose between researchers who sought to make the university responsive to practical needs and those eager to preserve their scholarly independence and freedom from outside control.

American Industry and the Academy

Many of the fundamental tensions that continue to pervade higher education today—pure versus applied research; the place of the humanities in a business-oriented, pragmatic culture; the struggle between preserving autonomy and serving outside interests—first surfaced in the nineteenth century. Fueling many of these debates was the growing influence of private industry. For by the turn of the century, the United States was no longer a nation of farmers and small businesspeople. It had become an industrial power, and a wave of mergers, acquisitions, and scientific breakthroughs had spurred the rise of large corporations eager to maximize their technical and managerial expertise.

The emergence of the chemical and electrical industries quickly gave rise to specialized fields of engineering. Realizing that university research and training could have a direct bearing on their industrial interests, companies such as General Electric, Westinghouse, Dow, du Pont, and AT&T swooped in to recruit graduate students, to finance research, and to establish consulting relationships. During the interwar years, the aerospace industry forged close ties with the California Institute of Technology (Caltech), Stanford, and MIT.[38] The University of Pennsylvania's Wharton School created a special division of industrial research that would perform contract investigations on problems of labor and management. The Harvard Economic Service conducted business forecasts for private subscribers. Michigan, Minnesota, Illinois, and MIT all performed extensive contract work for industry in their programs of engineering.[39] Beginning in 1912, some universities even established third-party mechanisms for patenting and licensing professors' research discoveries.[40]

State universities were often particularly subject to the needs of local industry and the priorities set by state legislatures. The University of Akron developed close ties with the local rubber industry. Kentucky and North Carolina worked extensively on developing technologies for processing tobacco.[41] The University of Minnesota, which ran a Mines Experiment Station with its own blast furnace, helped the local mining industry develop new methods for extracting low-yield iron ore from the Mesabi Range.[42]

But not all universities followed this path. Some charters, like MIT's, written in 1861, specified that the school should aid "by suitable means the advancement, development, and practical application of science in connection with arts, agriculture, manufactures, and commerce." (As MIT president Paul Gray boldly asserted in 1981, "Our academic roots are in American industry."[43]) But other schools, such as Princeton and Yale, leaned more heavily toward the liberal arts and pure research. Cornell and Chicago were "academic crossbreeds," seeking to strike a balance between pure science, applied research, and liberal instruction.[44]

Still, corporate influence over academic affairs grew nearly everywhere, in part because the development of new fields of specialization was costly. In the past, universities had drawn the bulk of their support from religiously motivated donors, philanthropists, alumni, and tuition fees.[45] Public universities received additional support from the states and the federal government (in the form of land grants). The federal government did not yet play a role in funding research, because educators and politicians had a deep-seated fear that government support would compromise academic autonomy.[46] No comparable skepticism existed toward industry and private donors—even though their support increasingly came with strings attached. The endowments of chairs of philosophy at both Cornell and Berkeley had explicit ideological limitations based on the wishes of benefactors. At Cornell, Veysey wrote, the influence of lumber magnate Henry W. Sage was so great that "he could make or break presidents as well as faculty."[47] Increasingly, universities succumbed to the political dictates of their wealthy patrons, as when Professor Henry Carter Adams was dismissed from Cornell for delivering a prolabor speech that annoyed a powerful donor.[48]

As the influence of the business class grew, so did its representation on the boards of trustees governing the universities. Charles and Mary Beard observed that by the turn of the century, "the roster of American trustees of higher learning read like a corporation directory."[49] One study of board membership at twenty private and state universities found that by 1900, 64 percent of the trustees were businessmen, bankers, and lawyers.[50] Often the trustees' conception of their authority differed sharply from that of the faculty. "As to what should be taught in political science and social science," wrote one business trustee at Northwestern University, "they [the professors] should promptly and gracefully submit to the determination of the trustees. . . . If the trustees err it is for the patrons and proprietors, not for the employees, to change either the policy or the personnel of the board."[51] A poll taken in 1900 of the boards of trustees at seven major universities confirmed the prevalence of this view.[52]

In time, the limits of this corporate largesse grew more apparent. In 1925, George Ellery Hale, an influential scientist at Caltech, and U.S. secretary of commerce Herbert Hoover spearheaded a national campaign to raise $20 million from private industry to finance basic research. Hale was convinced that businesses would support a National Research Fund, since industry stood to benefit enormously over the long term. To his disappointment, he soon discovered that most companies would contribute only if they could gain monopoly control over the results, and the campaign thus collapsed.[53] The Stanford University physics department also turned to industry in the 1930s, but many of its physicists grew disillusioned after clashing with their corporate sponsor over secrecy, corporate control of the research agenda, and the appropriate balance between research and development work.[54]

Even at MIT, an institution long committed to industrial partnerships, controversy arose as industry funding began to crowd out the space for academic research. Beginning in 1903, MIT, inspired by schools like Johns Hopkins, sought to broaden its mission beyond engineering to include basic science and graduate-level studies. As part of this reorientation, it established the Research Laboratory of Physical Chemistry, headed by Arthur A. Noyes, which was dedicated to pure research along the German model. The Noyes laboratory was housed somewhat incongruously in the same department as William Walker's Research Laboratory of Applied

Chemistry, which focused on industrial problems and was funded almost entirely by corporations. Noyes and Walker immediately clashed over the training and education of chemists and engineers. Whereas Noyes was committed to giving students a solid foundation in basic science, Walker preferred to impart more practical on-site training at selected industrial firms.

Tension between the two men came to a head in the spring of 1919, when Walker wrote to MIT president Richard C. Maclaurin threatening to resign if Noyes was not demoted from his position. Maclaurin succumbed and asked Noyes to withdraw from the chemistry department, prompting Noyes to resign and relocate to Caltech, where he helped launch that institution's rise to academic prominence.[55] Shortly after, Walker was appointed to oversee a new office of industrial relations, and the school embarked on a major campaign—known as the Technology Plan—to raise money from businesses for the school's general endowment.

The campaign helped MIT build up the nation's fifth-largest endowment, but it also revealed the perils of relying too heavily on industry support. According to Roger L. Geiger, the Technology Plan "turned out to be a one-time windfall rather than a model for sustained cooperation." When MIT approached industrial sponsors after the initial five-year period, most companies refused to renew their subscriptions, seeing little direct payoff to their own bottom line.[56] The administration also drew criticism from the faculty, which charged that too many of the school's contracts involved trivial industrial development projects of little academic value. One contract with the Vacuum Oil Company, for example, enlisted professors to develop oil containers that wouldn't leak during shipment. Meanwhile, the Humble Oil Company and other firms refused to permit publication of academic research.[57]

By the end of the decade, even MIT's trustees began to grow uneasy, fearing that the institute was losing its ability to remain competitive in academic science. Following the departure of Noyes and other renowned scientists, MIT's standing in chemistry and physics dropped in national comparisons.[58] In 1930, Princeton physicist Karl T. Compton took over as president of MIT with a clear mandate from the trustees to strengthen the school's academic reputation and its commitment to basic science. Compton immediately implemented a series of tough new restrictions on industry consulting and in several instances refused lucrative contracts from companies. When General Electric, one of MIT's largest funders, sought a consulting relationship with a faculty member in 1939, Compton refused. "We want our staff members to be as useful to industry as possible, but we cannot 'sell out' our laboratories or staff to any one company," he declared. The Great Depression of the 1930s and the volatility of industry funding confirmed the wisdom of his approach. As the historian John Servos observed:

> What had appeared initially as a natural and beneficial alliance of businessmen and applied scientists revealed itself in the 1930s to be a temporary and unstable partnership. . . . Contributions to the support of applied research at MIT and other American educational institutions were marginal expenses to most businesses; when the need to economize became urgent, they were among the first costs to be cut.[59]

But it was faculty, not administrators, who most acutely perceived the toxic effect that a business mind-set could have on academic life. As industrial influence over academia grew, a growing chorus of critics emerged. John Jay Chapman, a writer and educational reformer, complained in 1909, "The men who control Harvard to-day are very little else than business men, running a large department store which dispenses education to the million." The renowned educator and philosopher John Dewey—a pragmatist who hardly believed universities should wall themselves off from the real world—wrote in 1902, "Institutions [of learning] are ranked by their obvious material prosperity, until the atmosphere of money-getting and money-spending hides from view the interests for the sake of which money alone has a place."[60]

The most acerbic critique came from Thorstein Veblen, the radical economist whose famous book *The Higher Learning in America* (published in 1918 but written the preceding decade) excoriated academic administrators for subordinating scholarly ideals to commercial imperatives. "The ideals of scholarship are yielding ground, in an uncertain and varying degree, before the pressure of businesslike exigencies," Veblen warned, accusing administrators and trustees of seeking to transform higher education into "a merchantable commodity, to be produced on a piece-rate plan, rated, bought and sold by standard units."[61]

Of mounting concern in the scholarly community was the growing number of professors being arbitrarily dismissed because of their political views rather than any objective evaluation of their academic performance. When Thomas Elmer Will, the president of Kansas State Agricultural College, conducted a survey in 1901, he found that a large number of the faculty targeted for dismissal over the previous decade had expressed views challenging the prevailing economic and social order. Richard T. Ely, a professor of economics at the University of Wisconsin, was put on trial in 1894 for "heretical" social and economic writings. A year later, the University of Chicago dismissed Edward W. Bemis from the economics department for endorsing antimonopoly views.[62] Cases such as these led Will and others to conclude that industrial powers—which were threatened by such viewpoints—had gained excessive influence over academic affairs.[63]

The Edward Ross case at Stanford was particularly important in mobilizing the faculty. Ross was a highly regarded economist and the secretary of the American Economics Association. After Leland Stanford, the university's founder, died in 1893, his widow, Jane Stanford, assumed control of the school's affairs and immediately took a strong disliking to Ross. In a university founded by a Republican railroad magnate—who had built his empire on the backs of cheap immigrant labor—Ross dared to call for municipal ownership of utilities and a ban on Asian immigration. He also spoke out in defense of the socialist Eugene V. Debs and was a proponent of free silver at a time when most economists were gold Republicans. For several years Jane Stanford pressed David Starr Jordan, the university's president, to silence Ross. "When I take up a newspaper . . . and read of the utterances of Professor Ross," she wrote in one missive, "and realize that a professor of the Leland Stanford Junior University . . . thus steps aside, and out of his sphere, to associate with the political demagogues of this city . . . it brings tears to my eyes. I must confess I am weary of Professor Ross, and I think he ought not to be retained at Stanford University."[64] In 1900 Jordan caved in to his benefactor's intolerance and dismissed Ross. Ross's firing marked the nadir of academic freedom, but it also helped spark its revival. One year later, seven Stanford professors resigned in protest. Among them was Arthur O. Lovejoy, a professor of philosophy who later played a pivotal role in founding the American Association of University Professors (AAUP), the organization that launched the academic freedom movement.[65]

The creation of the AAUP in 1915, by Lovejoy, John Dewey, and other prominent educators, marked a crucial turning point in the history of American higher education. Until then, professors in the United

States had virtually no legal rights protecting their intellectual freedom or job security. Numerous court cases had affirmed that universities were "private corporations" whose trustees and regents had the right, unless a school statute specified otherwise, to dismiss professors at will.[66] The AAUP's principal aim when it released its first report on academic freedom was to establish a new set of legal rights to protect professors from arbitrary firings. But its founders also had a more ambitious goal: to tie the interests of the faculty more broadly to those of the university. The AAUP realized that granting professors greater control over academic affairs would naturally curtail the power of the trustees and other external interest groups, thereby carving out a unique space in American society where intellectuals could express views that challenged the status quo without fear of retribution. Instances where academic freedom had been curtailed, the AAUP noted, often centered on "the expression of opinions which point toward extensive social innovations, or call in question the moral legitimacy or social expediency of economic conditions or commercial practices in which large vested interests are involved."[67]

After the AAUP released its new guidelines, egregious violations of academic freedom continued. In 1924, the organization reported that the Phelps-Dodge Corporation had pressured the University of Arizona to dismiss a professor of agricultural chemistry after he had testified before the state legislature that copper-smelting fumes were harming local crops.[68] But over the course of the next few decades, the principles of academic freedom (including the validation of the peer-review process in assessing the quality of scholarship, and faculty authority in defining standards of achievement, promotion, and tenure) became woven into the fabric of American higher education.

These principles would be tested anew as World War II thrust upon universities a new set of responsibilities, and vastly enhanced the federal government's role in financing higher education. But university leaders and professors had learned a great deal from their previous interactions with industry, and in time, they managed to preserve and strengthen their hard-won academic freedoms.

The Federal Government and the University

The year was 1944. Allied victory in Europe was virtually assured, and President Franklin Roosevelt, weary of the war, was already beginning to think about peace. He called an adviser into his office to discuss postwar science policy.

"What's going to happen to science after the war?" the president asked.

"It's going to fall flat on its face," the adviser quipped.

"What are we going to do about it?" said Roosevelt.

"We better do something damn quick."

The adviser whom Roosevelt consulted was Vannevar Bush, a brilliant engineer known for his wit and charm who was then serving as head of the Office of Scientific Research and Development, the agency responsible for overseeing wartime science. A former MIT professor and dean, Bush was the son of a working-class Universalist preacher from Provincetown whose seafaring ancestors, stretching back over six generations, were among the earliest settlers of Massachusetts. A scientist and inventor of considerable renown, Bush had cofounded the electronics firm Raytheon in the mid-1920s and won worldwide recognition for developing the electromechanical analog computer. But it was World War II that transformed Bush—a bespectacled scientist famously pictured in his white lab coat, peering at a test tube and smoking a pipe—into an American icon and forever altered the relationship between the federal government and U.S. universities.[69]

During World War I, interactions between university scientists and government agencies had occurred off campus: Researchers contributing to the war effort were inducted into service and assigned to federal laboratories. But in the spring of 1940, after the Roosevelt administration tapped him to mobilize the nation's scientists and engineers for World War II, Vannevar Bush decided to organize things differently. He put the nation's scientists to work by issuing federal research contracts and grants directly to the universities, institutes, and industrial laboratories that employed them. Thus, ironically, it was Bush, a conservative critic of the New Deal and an opponent of government expansion, who opened the way for millions of dollars in federal funding to pour into universities, thereby breaking down the government's historic aversion to any direct federal role in financing higher education.

Ever true to his academic roots, however, Bush designed a federal grant system that afforded university scientists a remarkable degree of autonomy and flexibility. Hoping to minimize political intrusions into the scientific sphere, he appointed civilian scientists, not government bureaucrats, to head up a new National Defense Research Committee charged with overseeing the disbursement of federal funds. What's more, federal contracts during the war were careful to specify that the government was purchasing the research itself, not any anticipated outcome or finding.

Bush's new approach proved a masterstroke. Two of the largest research and development efforts of the war were the Manhattan Project, which began largely at university campuses before moving to Los Alamos, New Mexico, and the Radiation Laboratory at MIT, a crash program to advance the Allies' radar capabilities.[70] The extraordinary wartime accomplishments of university scientists—the building of the atomic bomb; the development of penicillin; path-breaking research on radar, fuses, and rocket propulsion; new medical breakthroughs with blood plasma—proved that academic science was an important national resource.[71]

After his meeting with Roosevelt, Bush realized that American taxpayers might lose interest in funding science after the war—especially basic science that had no obvious or immediate practical utility. Fearing that a unique opportunity might be lost to capitalize on the public's newfound appreciation of the university, Bush convened a panel of leading academics to formulate a vision for postwar science policy. In July 1945, the panel produced a 192-page document dramatically titled *Science: The Endless Frontier*.[72] Heralding basic science as the "seed corn" for all future technological advancement, the report laid out a blueprint for an unprecedented union between government and academia—a national policy aimed at fostering open-ended, blue-sky research on a massive scale. Though he was a conservative, Bush thus laid the groundwork for what Linda Marsa aptly termed "a New Deal for science," seeking to preserve a realm where university research was performed free of market dictates.[73] "It is chiefly in these [academic] institutions that scientists may work in an atmosphere which is relatively free from adverse pressure of convention, prejudice, or commercial necessity," wrote Bush in *The Endless Frontier*. "Industry is generally inhibited by preconceived goals, by its own clearly defined standards, and by the constant pressure of commercial necessity." Of course there are exceptions, he acknowledged, "but even in such cases it is rarely possible to match the universities in respect to the freedom which is so important to scientific discovery."

Just as he had done during the war, Bush took pains to grant academic scientists the maximum degree of autonomy so that they could pursue their research "free from the influence of pressure groups, free from the necessity of producing immediate results, free from dictation by any central board." To achieve these objectives, Bush proposed the creation of a new national science foundation, headed by civilian scientists, which would be dedicated to supporting truly basic research.[74]

The report was an instant success, landing on the best-seller list and serialized in *Fortune*. Unfortunately, however, Bush's central objective—the creation of the National Science Foundation (NSF)—did not come to pass until 1950 because of strong disagreements in Washington about whom, exactly, the agency should be accountable to.[75] This delay proved extremely costly. As Roger Geiger noted in his superb history, *Research and Relevant Knowledge*, the failure to establish the NSF immediately after the war meant that the task of funding academic science quickly fell to an array of mission agencies—the Atomic Energy Commission and the U.S. Army, Navy, and Air Force—which were heavily weighted toward military objectives. Nevertheless, the original goal of fostering basic science was not entirely lost: Improbable though it may seem, the Office of Naval Research managed to disburse millions of dollars annually to academic scientists under terms that largely accorded with Bush's original vision. So did the National Institutes of Health (NIH), which assumed responsibility for funding medical research. The NIH budget soared from $3.4 million in 1946 to $50.5 million in 1951.[76] At both agencies, academic scientists were granted a high degree of autonomy, research was unclassified and publishable, and truly fundamental research was supported.

Still, by the time the NSF was born, the military had already established a firm grip on postwar federal science policy, and the universities' much-celebrated autonomy was dangerously slipping away. That year, in 1950, 87 percent of *all* federal funding for academic research came from the Pentagon and the Atomic Energy Commission.[77] (By contrast, initial appropriations for the NSF were miniscule—a mere $3.5 million in 1952.) For many universities, this flood of defense money meant, in the words of Cold War scholar Stuart W. Leslie, "bigger budgets, better facilities, more political clout in Washington, ever more sophisticated military hardware, and even a few Nobel prizes."[78] But it also meant new infringements on academic freedom. Laboratories that signed on to multi-million-dollar weapons projects quickly found themselves thrust into a world of secrecy that was anathema to academic life. Faculty and students who worked on classified projects were forbidden to publish their research, or to share it with academic peers. Many top universities permitted graduate students to work on classified theses.[79] Prominent institutes, such as MIT's Center for International Studies and the Harvard-based Russian Research Center, also maintained close ties to the Central Intelligence Agency (CIA), the Federal Bureau of Investigation (FBI), and other intelligence and military agencies, which deeply compromised their objectivity. An official government study from 1952 found that "fully 96 percent of all reported [government] funding for social sciences at that time was drawn from the U.S. military."[80] In essence, the university had become an indispensable partner in what Senator J. William Fulbright would later term the "military-industrial-academic complex."[81]

Much of this military R&D took place at the large federal-contract laboratories, which were based at universities, such as Caltech's Jet Propulsion Laboratory (aeronautical and space sciences); MIT's Lincoln Laboratory (air defense); Berkeley's Lawrence Livermore Laboratory (nuclear weapons); and Stanford's Applied Electronics Laboratory (electronic communications and countermeasures).[82] In hindsight, noted Geiger, "one might legitimately ask why [federal contract labs] operated under university contracts at all."[83] Indeed, one wonders whether universities would have been better served by declining this management role altogether and permitting individual professors to take extended leave from campus to work at the federal labs, thereby keeping the distinction between academic research and federal weapons development clear.

The heavy skewing of federal money toward military ends unquestionably shaped the overall direction of academic research. In 1959, Louis Smullin, one of the founding fathers of MIT's Research Laboratory of Electronics, proposed redirecting a portion of MIT's research toward the "major non-military engineering problems of the modern world," including alternative energy sources, air traffic control, soil conservation, and desalinization of sea water. Because of the dominance of military funding, however, the proposal went nowhere. Twenty years later, Smullin reflected that because of military distortion, "we don't really know what to do with our fancy, sophisticated engineers and scientists, in terms of the ordinary daily needs of people."[84]

Government funding distortions may also have prevented universities from taking a stronger stand against the ideological excesses of the Cold War. During the political witch-hunts of the late 1940s to the mid-1950s, which peaked under Senator Joseph R. McCarthy in 1950–1954, the United States was consumed by a near-hysterical fear of communism. With the notable exceptions of the University of Chicago and the University of Wisconsin, many of the nation's colleges chose to cooperate with congressional and state committees seeking to expose and purge individuals with leftist sympathies or suspected ties to the Communist Party.[85] Universities required faculty to sign loyalty oaths and disavow communism as a condition of their employment; some even launched their own internal investigations. The result was an extraordinary abridgement of both constitutional rights and academic freedom. At the height of the purges, in 1953, more than one hundred faculty were subpoenaed, the result being at least thirty dismissals.[86]

Yet although much that is profoundly regrettable can be traced to the Cold War, it was the Cold War that ultimately served as the catalyst for an era of unprecedented public support for higher education—one in which academic values became ascendant once again.

When the United States learned on October 4, 1957, that the Soviet Union had successfully launched Sputnik I into orbit around the earth, the federal government's commitment to higher education dramatically changed. A nation that had invested heavily in its scientific and technological capabilities suddenly felt its supremacy threatened. In the space race against the Soviets, the United States appeared to be losing. Panicked officials in Washington immediately pledged to increase the capacity and effectiveness of the nation's educational system, and to reinvigorate academic science by renewing the commitment to basic research.[87]

At long last, Vannevar Bush's vision for the public financing of civilian academic research came to fruition. The NSF budget rose from $16 million in 1956 to $130 million in 1959, and by 1966 it had reached a whopping $480 million.[88] Overall federal spending on university research increased from $456 million in 1958 to roughly $1.3 billion in 1964, a doubling of the national effort relative to the gross national product. The character of federal funding also changed: In 1958, 62 percent of academic research was considered basic; six years later the figure rose to 79 percent.[89] Federal support for medical research skyrocketed—so much that by the early 1960s the NIH had surpassed the Department of Defense (DOD) as the largest single funder of academic research.[90]

The impact of Sputnik went well beyond science. In 1958, building on the earlier success of the GI Bill, Congress passed the National Defense Education Act (NDEA), which offered loans to college students (partially forgiven for those who became teachers), fellowships to graduate students, and funding for languages and international studies. Previously,

Congress had shunned any direct federal funding for higher education (as distinct from research), but passage of the NDEA, in response to a perceived "educational emergency," turned the tide.[91] In subsequent years, Congress expanded the NDEA, provided money for building construction (to meet a projected enrollment boom), and assumed a much larger role in funding academic disciplines, such as foreign languages, that could not otherwise find support. Eventually, the desire to nurture and sustain a broad range of disciplines, as well as the arts, led to the establishment of the National Endowment for the Humanities and the National Endowment for the Arts in 1965.[92]

These developments coincided with a dramatic increase in the proportion of young people attending college. During the Kennedy and Johnson administrations, the federal government sought to ensure that all Americans regardless of economic background or race would have the opportunity to attend college. Tuition assistance, affirmative action programs, and the establishment of a state-level community college system helped to bring large numbers of previously excluded groups into higher education. In 1950, only 6.2 percent of Americans over twenty-five had completed four years of college. Three decades later that number rose to 16.3 percent.[93] By 1972, the nation had a comprehensive system of need-based student financial aid, as well as a college student population far more reflective of American society than ever before.[94]

As dramatic as these changes were, there was one sector—military research—that remained virtually untouched by these post-Sputnik reforms. The elevation of basic research had been achieved primarily through increases to the budgets of NSF and NIH, leaving Pentagon funding of academic science largely unchanged.[95] After 1966, however, the university's participation in the military-industrial complex drew heightened criticism from both faculty and students. Military research that had gone unquestioned for decades now became a focal point of controversy amid the mounting protests against the Vietnam War, which had prompted students to uncover explicit ties between weapons manufacturers and their own universities. In January 1969, a group of MIT faculty stunned the academic world when they announced a research stoppage and called on academic scientists to reevaluate their cozy relationship with the military. A protest manifesto signed by some forty-eight faculty members—most of them scientists and engineers—challenged MIT scholars "to devise means for turning research applications away from the present emphasis on military technology toward the solution of pressing environmental and social problems."[96] At Stanford, faculty and students protested the school's extensive covert contracts with the CIA and other classified campus research.[97] Students at Columbia fought pitched battles with the police over the university's affiliation with the Institute for Defense Analysis, and students at American University and George Washington University forced their administrations to divest from off-campus research institutes in the social and behavioral sciences sponsored by the U.S. Army.[98]

The rise of the antiwar movement and the student left forced a long-overdue debate about the compatibility of Pentagon research with the university's broader educational mission. Many schools grudgingly acknowledged the price they had paid for allowing military funding to distort their research priorities and, under pressure from the faculty and students, terminated some of their most explicit defense-oriented institutes and weapons laboratories. Other schools responded by banning all classified research from campus.[99] In Congress, Senators J. William Fulbright and Mike Mansfield introduced a rider to the Military Authorization Act of 1970 that sought to redirect more federal money to the NSF for basic science. But Congress was in no mood to expand NSF funding at this time. The antimilitarization movement reached its climax *not* when the post-Sputnik expansion was at its height, but when it was already waning and rapidly giving way to the economic stagnation of the 1970s. Instead, both the Pentagon and the NSF saw their budgets decline.[100]

By the mid-1970s, the "golden age" of federal support for higher education was effectively over, and the academic community was thrust into a period of growing financial insecurity and reflection. Where had the university arrived, and where was it headed? The emergence of the federal grant system had brought unquestionable gains. America's research universities were now considered among the best in the world because of their extraordinary achievements in science and technology and the high caliber of their education. They were more accessible and democratic than in the past; their areas of specialization and expertise more expansive; their academic achievements more universally recognized. Universities, both public and private, had evolved into "public trusts" that were deserving of extensive government support and tax exemptions because of the indispensable civic functions they performed. Although national security objectives had profoundly distorted federal science policy after World

War II, there was by the 1960s an extraordinary commitment on the part of the government to provide research grants that were fully consistent with the university's core academic principles. The government accepted that academic research was an essential part of the national scientific infrastructure, and that American universities were the best qualified to educate and train the next generation of citizens, scientists, and public leaders.

The difficulty was whether and how these gains could be maintained. For the same federal grant process that had brought so many tangible benefits also presented significant challenges. As the university grew in size and stature (becoming a "multiversity," to use Clark Kerr's term), it also had to respond to a variety of disparate interest groups—federal agencies, state legislatures, the military, private industry, scientists, faculty, student advocates—all of whom had different conceptions of the "uses" of the university. The more functions the university took on, the more bloated, bureaucratic, and costly it was to operate. Larger enrollments also resulted in the adoption of a mass-lecture system, in which the professor of an introductory course was asked to teach anywhere from one hundred to five hundred students at a time. In this mass-education system, critics noted, many of the most valuable personal and emotional dimensions of teaching disappeared.

Perhaps the biggest problem was that the university—formerly a close-knit community of scholars and students—had become highly decentralized by the mid-1970s. Scientists and humanists lived in two separate spheres with little contact; the professional schools for business, law, and medicine operated as semiautonomous institutions; scientists involved in defense-oriented research worked in isolated facilities; and faculty across all disciplines, including the humanities, increasingly sought to be relieved from their undergraduate teaching duties to devote more time to their own research, publication, and consulting. To a greater extent than ever before, professors pursued their own personal agendas, with little regard for the university as a whole. Critics on the left, who had begun by defending the university's need for autonomy against the demands of the national security state, themselves began to politicize the academy to advance their own ideological and social agendas. Many reformers of the 1970s sought to turn the university into an agent of social change to alleviate poverty in local communities, end racism, and accomplish other political and social objectives. In this regard, their mission was not unlike that of other external constituencies that were pulling the institution away from its core research and teaching functions to perform a public service.

In short, there were fewer internal constituencies dedicated to preserving the university's autonomy—and even fewer that were prepared to defend the old-fashioned concept of pursuing knowledge for knowledge's sake. None of this boded well for the academic world's ability to weather the next great challenge to its autonomy: the effort to realign universities with the needs of industry in the service of economic growth.

3

The Birth of the
Market-Model U.

In 1973, when Stanley Cohen, a professor of genetics at Stanford University, and Herbert Boyer, a biochemist at the University of California at San Francisco (UCSF), successfully transferred genetic material from an African clawed toad into bacterium—getting it to replicate or clone—they had little idea just how far-reaching the impact of their research would be. Genes are segments of DNA that carry the instructions for creating the individual proteins that make up a living organism. Cohen and Boyer's technique opened up the revolutionary prospect of creating bacteria that could serve as living factories for human protein.[1] Both researchers perceived that their breakthrough would open whole new vistas in genetic engineering. They did not imagine that it would soon give rise to a new multi-billion-dollar industry—biotechnology—that would, in turn, help to transform the relationship between academia and the commercial world.

One person who took an early interest in the Cohen-Boyer discovery was Niels Reimers, a former engineer who had migrated from industry to academia and now served as Stanford's patent administrator. In the spring of 1974, Reimers came across an article in the *New York Times* in which Stanley Cohen speculated that, one day, it might be possible to create recombinant bacteria capable of manufacturing antibiotics or human insulin. Though Cohen still believed such practical applications were a long way off, Reimers' eyes lit up as he envisioned the enormous power—and potential commercial impact—of recombinant DNA technology. Having just set up a new office at Stanford to patent and license academic inventions internally, he quickly perceived that the gene-splicing invention might be a valuable jewel capable of generating significant royalty income both for Cohen and Boyer (as inventors)—and for their respective universities.

Reimers was a pioneer in the mid-1970s, one of a handful of academic administrators ambitiously trying to expand the university's role in patenting academic research. In his view, commercially useful inventions had been laying fallow in the laboratory for too long, in large part because universities had shirked any direct involvement in commercial affairs. Reimers sought to change this by giving universities a direct financial stake in the commercialization of faculty research. Shortly after reading the *Times* article, he approached Cohen and Boyer about allowing Stanford to patent their gene-splicing technique. Although both scientists were initially reluctant, they eventually agreed—a decision that instantly sparked controversy within the academic world.[2]

Patenting was by no means new to academia, but it had a complex history. In 1925, the University of Wisconsin set up an affiliated foundation—the Wisconsin Alumni Research Foundation (WARF)—to manage the school's licensing activity, making it an early leader in patenting academic research. A year earlier, Henry Steenbock, a professor at the School of Agriculture, had filed patents on a process for irradiating foodstuffs with ultraviolet rays to enhance vitamin D formation, which proved helpful in eliminating rickets as a childhood disease. WARF licensed the Steenbock patents to Quaker Oats on an exclusive basis, a deal that proved extremely lucrative for the University of Wisconsin. Several other public universities followed in Wisconsin's footsteps. But by and large, most universities remained ambivalent about patents, believing that, with few exceptions, academic knowledge should be placed in the public domain without proprietary restrictions. The prevailing view, as the historian Daniel J. Kevles wrote, was that "knowledge wrested from nature in universities ought to be bestowed upon the world free of charge, not exploited for profits by the universities."[3]

Concerned that commercial interests might compromise the university's autonomy, many schools permitted their faculty to patent and license research only through an independent third party. One of the earliest of these, which grew to service large numbers of universities, was the Research Corporation, founded in 1912 to commercialize pollution control technology developed by Frederick Cottrell, a professor in the chemistry department at Berkeley. Cottrell realized that in the case of some embryonic inventions, companies might not be willing to invest in commercial development without some form of patent protection, so he established the Research Corporation as an independent nonprofit to provide professors with a vehicle for filing patents when doing so was commercially necessary. Early in this process, Cottrell rejected the possibility of having the University of California manage this commercial activity directly. "A danger was involved," he wrote, "particularly should the experiment prove highly profitable to the university and lead to a general emulation of the plan. . . . The danger this suggested was the possibility of growing commercialism and competition between institutions and an accompanying tendency for secrecy in scientific work."[4]

The commercial dangers Cottrell anticipated proved real. The University of Wisconsin, through its direct affiliation with WARF, soon found itself embroiled in a number of unsavory controversies. Starting in the 1930s, public health professionals and the press began to question whether WARF's monopoly control over irradiation technology and its licensing practices were inflating the price of vitamin D milk and other enriched food products. In 1943, the federal government brought an antitrust suit against the foundation for its alleged refusal to license irradiation technology to manufacturers of oleomargarine. Because its patent was about to expire anyway, WARF agreed to surrender the vitamin D patent to the public. However, the foundation's troubles did not subside. In 1965 and again in 1970, the government filed lawsuits against WARF, accusing it of impeding scientific advances through its restrictive licensing practices.[5] As a result of this negative publicity, even MIT—a school with a long history of industrial collaboration—avoided following the WARF model. Vannevar Bush, then a professor with several patents to his name, warned MIT president Karl Compton that any direct involvement in patenting might bring criticism from politicians and industrial firms and thereby tarnish the university's reputation. In 1937, when Compton expanded the school's patenting and licensing activity, he signed a contract with the Research Corporation to avoid embroiling the university in commercial decisions.[6]

When Stanford announced its plans to patent the Cohen-Boyer invention, many professors in the biomedical community voiced misgivings.[7] One reviewer, asked to comment on the patent application, wrote, "I am concerned that given the fundamental nature of the work and the number of scientists involved, either directly or indirectly, that this patent will not reflect favorably on the public service ideals of the University."[8] Within academic medicine, it was still widely believed that commercial interests stood in direct conflict with the university's commitment to public health and the broad dissemination of knowledge. Because patents could be used to restrict access to health-related inventions, many professors deemed them fundamentally antithetical to the academic mission.[9] In 1955, when newscaster Edward R. Murrow asked Jonas Salk who owned the patent to his polio vaccine, he famously replied, "Well, the people, I would say. There is no patent. Could you patent the sun?"[10] Harvard, Chicago, Yale, Johns Hopkins, and Columbia all had policies on the books that explicitly forbade patenting of biomedical research.[11]

What made patenting particularly controversial in the case of the Cohen-Boyer invention was the extremely basic nature of the discovery and the fact that during the previous thirty years large numbers of scientists, financed by the U.S. taxpayer, had laid the intellectual foundation for this breakthrough discovery. Science had always been a cumulative process. Why should Cohen and Boyer (or their respective universities) be permitted to claim sole ownership of this collective academic scholarship and reap all the financial dividends? Many professors, upholding the tradition of open academic science, insisted that fundamental research of this kind should not be owned by anyone but should be made freely available to all members of the scientific community without proprietary controls. Otherwise, they cautioned, scientific exploration could be dangerously impeded.

Cohen himself shared many of these qualms. "My initial reaction to Reimers's proposal," he recalled in 1982, "was to question whether basic research of this type could or should be patented and to point out that our work had been dependent on a number of earlier discoveries by others."[12] Reimers countered that without patent protection, commercial development of the gene-splicing technology might be thwarted. "Through a patent we might be able to get an exclusive license to a company to develop recombinant insulin . . . ," he would later recall telling Cohen. "You can't get drugs developed today without some proprietary protection because they require an investment of a couple of hundred million dollars for R&D."[13]

Reimers's argument to Cohen was deeply flawed. The gene-splicing technique was a broad platform technology—a fundamental tool needed for all research in the field of genetic engineering—so there was never any danger that it would not be utilized, both in academia and industry, without a patent. Although Reimers was correct that patent protection *can* be critical in the development of many early-stage drug discoveries, in the case of the Cohen-Boyer invention it most certainly was not. As Reimers himself admitted in 1997, "whether we licensed [the gene-splicing technique] or not, commercialization of recombinant DNA was going forward."[14]

If commercial development wasn't Reimers's true goal, why was he so intent on patenting the Cohen-Boyer invention? The main reason was money. Reimers wanted to demonstrate that patents could be a lucrative new source of revenue for the university. Initially, Reimers had considered licensing the technology exclusively to a handful of companies for restricted fields of use, but he soon realized this wasn't advisable because it would prevent large numbers of researchers from gaining access to the technology. (Had Stanford actually pursued an exclusive license, there is little doubt it would have been catastrophic to the emerging field of biotechnology.) Instead, Reimers chose to license the gene-splicing technique nonexclusively.[15] Under a nonexclusive license, anyone can access the technology; in this case, the only catch was they had to pay Stanford a modest fee to use it. Because large numbers of researchers were eager to utilize the technique, Reimers figured that a modest licensing fee would add up to a handsome sum—and he was right. In total, the Cohen-Boyer discovery would generate some $300 million for Stanford and UCSF—which received half the proceeds because of Boyer's role as a coinventor—making it one of the most lucrative licensing deals in academic history.[16]

Within the academic world, pursuit of a nonexclusive license was highly unusual. Because a nonexclusive license didn't provide the licensee with any monopoly protection over the technology, it also didn't serve any function in fostering commercial development or "technology transfer." The only real purpose, Reimers candidly observed in 1997, was to generate revenue: "A nonexclusive licensing program, at its heart, is really a tax. . . . But it's always nice to say 'technology transfer.'"[17]

Taxing researchers who use an academic invention in order to skim profits was an idea inherently difficult to square with the university's status as a nonprofit institution ostensibly driven by noncommercial goals.

In the past, most universities had carefully weighed the possible benefits of patenting with its potential costs to the public domain, open communication, and other central features of the academic culture. Now, Reimers was advancing a very different rationale for academic patenting: It was legitimate for the university to stake proprietary claims on faculty inventions not only as a mechanism to facilitate commercial development, but purely as a source of income for the university itself.

———————

At the same time that Stanford was experimenting with new ways to extract profits from biotech research, Herbert Boyer was busy exploring commercial opportunities of his own at UCSF. A burly former high school football player who preferred blue jeans to tweed jackets and regularly took part in demonstrations against the Vietnam War, Boyer was something of a maverick in the academic world, a brilliant scientist who nevertheless felt cloistered in the ivory tower. In the spring of 1975, Boyer became excited about the possibility of using recombinant DNA technology for the development of new medicines and therapies.[18] The idea came to him, he would later recall, after he took his eldest son to the doctor to have his growth hormone levels tested. The boy turned out to be fine, but in talking with the doctor Boyer learned that children whose growth has been stunted because of a pituitary gland deficiency required treatment with human growth hormone. Unfortunately, the doctor said, the hormone was available only from human cadavers and therefore difficult to obtain. By the time Boyer returned home, his mind was racing with what genetic engineering might one day accomplish. "You know, we could make human growth hormone" in the laboratory, he told his wife. "All we have to do is isolate the gene."[19]

As luck would have it, in January 1976 Boyer received a call from Robert Swanson, a venture capitalist with a background in chemical engineering who shared Boyer's passion for commercializing recombinant DNA technology. The two men immediately hit it off. At their first meeting, they went out for drinks at a local watering hole near the medical school that was frequented by scientists and lab rats. After several rounds of beer, each agreed to put up $500 to form a partnership. They even came up with a name for the company that night. Playing with the words "genetic engineering technology," Boyer settled on it: Genentech.[20]

In April 1976, Genentech was officially incorporated. Unlike earlier academic spin-offs, which had emerged from within the electronics and computer-engineering departments of many universities but then quickly moved off campus, Genentech maintained exceptionally close ties to the university. Indeed, the company soon began operating its main research hub from inside Boyer's lab on the USCSF campus.[21] Boyer himself retained his faculty appointment, even as he grew increasingly involved in running the company. To save money on overhead, Swanson and Boyer also negotiated sponsored-research deals with UCSF and other academic institutions and brought together a team of talented academic investigators to work with the company.

Boyer was motivated by noble intentions. Like many professors who had toiled for years in the insular world of academe, he thrilled to the idea of being able to apply his academic knowledge to the real world. "The money was not a driving factor," he would later explain. What excited him was the opportunity "to take the technology and the science to some pragmatic level, which a lot of people never had the opportunity to do."[22] Much like Reimers, Boyer regarded the merger of academia and industry as an unqualified good—What could be wrong with using the power of the market to push academic research in new directions?—while failing to consider the potentially deleterious long-term consequences.

Among his peers, Boyer's efforts to build his company's proprietary-research portfolio from inside his academic lab—a model that would soon be widely emulated—raised eyebrows. Many professors within the Department of Biochemistry and Biophysics considered Boyer's financial stake in Genentech—and his simultaneous receipt of research funding from the company—a blatant conflict of interest.[23] Faculty in the Academic Senate and the medical school expressed concern that proprietary secrets could hinder open communication in the lab.[24] A UCSF committee charged with examining Genentech's sponsored-research agreement found that with one exception, those interviewed believed the company's presence had led to serious disruptions within the department. "A recurrent theme," the committee wrote, "was that people were loath to ask questions and give suggestions in seminars or across the bench, for there was a feeling that someone might make money from someone else."[25]

Boyer was too distracted by the pressures of launching a new company to pay much attention to the criticism. The race was on for Genentech to prove to its investors the practical utility of recombinant DNA technology—

and the stakes were high. Other prominent academic scientists at Harvard and UCSF were hotly pursuing similar lines of inquiry. On December 1, 1977, the company held a press conference at the Biltmore Hotel in Los Angeles to announce that it had succeeded in cloning and expressing the human brain hormone somatostatin. Boyer proudly told reporters, "The man on the street can now finally get a return on his investment in science." The comment was telling. Previously, the public had been willing to fund higher education primarily to advance the frontiers of science and train the next generation. If economic dividends were forthcoming, that was an added bonus. Now, Boyer seemed to be saying that the public should expect a tangible commercial return on its academic investment.

Genentech's next goal was to synthesize human insulin using the techniques of genetic engineering. The process was slow and arduous, but in early September 1978 the team held a press conference to announce their success. The firm's compelling story instantly made front-page news throughout the country: A tiny biotech start-up had succeeded in opening the world's eyes to the shimmering promise of biotechnology.[26] On October 14, 1980, the company went public in a frenzied stock offering. Genentech's asking price was $35 per share. A mere twenty minutes after trading began, the price shot up to $89 per share. By lunchtime, Swanson and Boyer were each worth approximately $82 million on paper. By day's end, the company was valued at $529 million. Genentech had no products to market yet, noted the *Washington Post*, "but investors loved it."[27]

Both the Cohen-Boyer discovery and the rise of Genentech generated immediate ripple effects throughout the academic world. Venture capitalists began scouting academic labs for promising new research. Pharmaceutical firms signed large-scale sponsored-research agreements with academic biology departments. New biotech start-ups—including Biogen, Genetic Systems, Hybritech, and hundreds of others—began to sprout up across the country, mainly on the basis of discoveries made by gray-bearded professors.[28] Soon, nearly every molecular biology professor had a consulting arrangement with a company, served on its scientific advisory board, or held equity in a small start-up venture of his or her own.[29] "They actually told me I could name any amount, literally write my own check," one Harvard researcher told the *Washington Post* after he had received a steady stream of industry offers.[30] Never before had university professors been able to command such a high commercial price tag.

The birth of biotechnology played a central role in laying the groundwork for future changes in academic-industry relations. However, it was only one of several factors that converged in the late 1970s to drive commercialization forward. Significant shifts were now also occurring in the global economy—as well as within American society—that prompted universities to reexamine their mission.

For one thing, the extraordinary expansion of federal government support for academic science and engineering began trickling to a halt. Between 1960 and 1968, this funding had grown at a 14 percent annual rate. From 1968 to 1974, as money was poured into the Vietnam War and the United States experienced its first oil shock, the rate of growth slowed to zero.[31] The great postwar economic boom that had fueled two decades of unprecedented national expansion was, in fact, coming to an end, and a new era of stagnation and intense foreign competition was getting under way. In 1971, a trade deficit registered in U.S. manufactured goods for the first time in the postwar era.[32] Suddenly, politicians began to fear that the United States was losing its competitive edge, as rising industrial powers like Germany and Japan leapfrogged ahead in fields such as auto manufacturing and electronics.

Economic uncertainty prompted the federal government to reevaluate its role in funding higher education. The old Cold War view that U.S. scientific and technological supremacy depended on a strong federal commitment to basic science and advanced education gradually lost its vitality. By the mid-1970s, a new preoccupation with economic competitiveness began to catch hold. On March 16, 1972, President Richard M. Nixon delivered a speech to Congress calling on the National Science Foundation and other federal agencies to foster industrial innovation by "stimulating non-Federal investment in research and development" and "improving the *application* of research and development results" (emphasis added). A year later, the NSF set up a series of experimental programs designed to foster university-industry research partnerships.[33] In 1978, under the leadership of Richard Atkinson, the NSF added the more substantial University-Industry Cooperative Research Projects Program. A principal requirement of all these new grants was that academic investigators obtain joint funding from industry and work collaboratively with corporate sponsors to increase the likelihood that their federally funded research would be "relevant to industrial goals."[34] In many respects, these new programs signaled the emergence of a U.S. industrial policy, but because direct government handouts to industry were politically unpalatable, NSF's programs masqueraded under the traditional rubric of academic grants. No one bothered to consider how routing industrial support through the university would affect academic culture—or scientific innovation over the long-term. The fact that such programs first emerged at NSF—historically a bastion of basic science—sent a clear message to the academic community that federal funding priorities were changing.

Also changing were the needs and expectations of U.S. industry. By the latter half of the 1970s, it was apparent that knowledge, wrested from basic science, would play an increasingly important role across many industrial sectors. According to Henry Etzkowitz and Andrew Webster, experts on science policy, the world economy had entered "a new stage of economic growth, with knowledge and therefore intellectual property as the engine of industrial development." Traditional economic drivers such as monetary capital, natural resources, and mechanical innovations were losing their salience.[35] What mattered more was the ability to harness cutting-edge ideas.

Many U.S. companies found themselves woefully unprepared for this new knowledge-driven economy. Over the course of the 1960s and 1970s, according to NSF statistics, industry had significantly cut back on long-term, basic-oriented research performed at industrial laboratories. Many large companies shut down their most acclaimed research facilities, making it more difficult to keep up with developments on the frontiers of science.[36] In the pharmaceutical sector, the emergence of biotechnology literally caught the industry unawares. Most drug firms had entirely ignored the field of molecular biology and thus had no internal expertise to draw on when the Cohen-Boyer invention was announced.[37] Other industries, too, discovered that basic research emerging inside the university was increasingly relevant to their operations. According to Louis Branscomb, then vice president and chief scientist at IBM, even traditional manufacturing was becoming more "process-oriented rather than assembly-oriented," so it required "much greater involvement with fundamental properties of the materials being worked."[38] The historic division that had separated basic and applied science—though never perfectly delineated—appeared to be eroding.

Previously, industry had been content to wait for basic research results to emerge from laboratories at a more leisurely pace. "Now," the historian David Dickson wrote, "it needed to know what was going on in the laboratory as it happened—and, if possible, before it happened."[39] The problem, noted the sociologists Walter Powell and Jason Owen-Smith, was that in many of the most rapidly developing fields—such as advanced television systems, biotechnology, computers, optics, and semiconductors—"research breakthroughs were distributed so broadly across both disciplines and institutions that no single firm had the necessary capabilities to keep pace."[40] The logical solution, industry thought, was to establish closer ties to federally financed researchers at the universities, who could provide access to cutting-edge science at deeply discounted prices. As Edward E. David, president of the Exxon Research and Engineering Company and Nixon's former science adviser, explained in 1979, "The time has come for a closer and more intimate relation between industry and academia."[41]

University administrators were quick to seize on this realignment of political and economic interests to advance their own goals. They had been searching for a new rationale to sustain the federal government's commitment to higher education. Now they believed they had found it. If the university could repackage itself as a source of technological innovation capable of enhancing U.S. economic competitiveness, it could not only satisfy the government's demand for "relevance" but appeal directly to industry for further support. In the late 1970s, advocates of this new strategy began pushing on various fronts to encourage greater interaction between universities and business. High-profile academic-industry conferences were organized. New associations, including the Business-Higher Education Forum, founded in 1978 by the American Council on Education, emerged. Universities and industry even joined hands to lobby against federal regulations that both believed were hampering productivity.[42] Most administrators realized industry support would never approach the magnitude of government spending, but they saw it as a way to make up for federal declines while potentially changing the academic culture for the better.

Thus, by the late 1970s, several concurrent developments—the leveling off of federal science and technology spending, the birth of biotechnology, the emergence of a new knowledge-driven economy—had converged to align the interests of universities and industry as never before. To consummate this marriage, however, more than overlapping interests were needed. A legal and political mandate from Washington was also required. It came, in 1980, in the form of an obscure yet profoundly influential piece of legislation called the University Small Business Patent Procedures Act, later known as the Bayh-Dole Act.[43] This landmark legislation tore away any remaining taboos against the patenting of academic knowledge; it also permitted *all* universities to begin patenting and licensing federally sponsored research on a large scale for the first time.

———————

The Bayh-Dole Act represented perhaps the most sweeping change in federal science-and-technology policy since Vannevar Bush had laid out his blueprint for postwar science. It instantly altered the mechanisms by which billions of dollars in taxpayer-financed research would be delivered to the public and ushered in an era of unprecedented university-industry collaborations. Strangely, however, though its impact was profound, the story of Bayh-Dole's passage into law is not well known and has received little scrutiny. It is an important and intriguing story, which exposes both the political machinations that led to the act's passage and the surprising weakness of the economic evidence on which it was based. A look back at this history also raises enduring questions regarding the act's long-term impact on the nation's economy and its innovation system—questions that were largely ignored during legislative debates at the time.

Congress's original intent in passing the Bayh-Dole Act was to reverse the United States' precipitous economic decline during the 1970s. Senators Birch Bayh (Democrat of Indiana) and Bob Dole (Republican of Kansas), the bill's primary sponsors, argued that federal patent reform was necessary to jump-start U.S. industrial competitiveness during a time when the nation was facing a growing trade deficit with Japan. "The damaging impact of federal patent policy on the economy is dramatic," proclaimed Senator Dole on the opening day of Senate hearings. "That we have lost our leadership role to Japan in the fields of electronics and shipbuilding is no accident."[44] A steady drumbeat of news stories published during the lead-up to the hearings captured the nation's mood. "Something's Happened to Yankee Ingenuity," blared a headline in the September 3, 1978, *Washington Post*. A month later, *Time* magazine ran a story forebodingly titled "The Innovation Recession." On June 4, 1979, the cover of *Newsweek* screamed out, "Has America Lost Its Edge?" Each article played up the same theme: The United States, once a leader in technological innovation, was in danger of becoming a second-rate power. Bayh-Dole's supporters—an alliance of university patent administrators, small-business groups, and influential legislators—persuasively argued that liberalization of federal patent policy could reverse this ominous trend. They pointed to the $26 billion that the federal government spent annually on research and development and asserted (incorrectly, it turned out) that most of this research was simply gathering dust on government shelves rather than being commercialized by private industry.[45]

The problem, they said, was that federal patent law was preventing effective university-industry collaborations. First, there were more than twenty policies governing the ownership and licensing of taxpayer-financed research across all the various federal agencies. Second, in most cases, the government retained ownership rights—or title—to these sponsored inventions, and often it was reluctant to license them exclusively, preferring to make them broadly available to everyone. According to Bayh-Dole's supporters, the government's aversion to exclusive licensing was the single greatest impediment to commercialization. "In all but exceptional cases," said Frederick Andrews, the vice president of research at Purdue University, in testimony before Congress, "exclusive licenses are required by industrial sponsors before they will undertake the huge expenditures needed to move federally funded work . . . from the drawing board into the commercial marketplace."[46]

The Bayh-Dole Act proposed creating a uniform federal patent policy that would grant small businesses, universities, and nonprofits automatic ownership rights to taxpayer-funded research. Under the act, small firms that contracted with the federal government would receive automatic exclusive rights to their research, and universities and other noncommercial entities would be free to patent and license their discoveries in exchange for royalties and other fees.

The effort to overhaul federal patent policy generated considerable unease in Congress, especially among liberal members of the legislature, who tended to look askance at granting private industry monopoly control over taxpayer-financed inventions. In February 1980, for example, Russell Long (Democrat of Louisiana), the powerful chairman of the Senate Finance Committee, charged that one version of the House reform bill was among "the most radical and far-reaching giveaways I have ever seen."[47] Admiral Hyman Rickover, the "father" of the nation's nuclear fleet and a leading spokesperson for the opposition, testified that giving private firms exclusive rights to inventions generated at public expense essentially required the public to pay twice for the same invention—once through taxes to support the research that yielded the invention, and then again through higher monopoly prices and restricted supply when the invention reached the market.[48]

The Bayh-Dole bill also conflicted with an important strand of economic thought, which held that patents could have the effect of impeding—rather than enhancing—widespread use of *basic* scientific and technological information. In the late 1950s and early 1960s, Richard Nelson and Kenneth Arrow, then both economists at RAND, published pioneering work on the social returns to scientific research, arguing that scientific knowledge tended to be "nonrival" in use and therefore less suitable for patent protection. Unlike a standard economic good (a candy bar, for example), which is sold and quickly consumed, a nonrival good (such as the gene-splicing technique) may be used simultaneously by many different parties in diverse applications, without diminishing any one person's ability to benefit from the use of that good. Thus, Nelson and Arrow reasoned, the public interest would be best served if most of this nonrival, basic science remained in the public domain, because any policies restricting access to that knowledge (such as exclusive licenses or secrecy provisions) would only impose substantial costs on the excluded parties, and on the economy as a whole, by stifling open competition and inventive activity.[49]

Nelson and Arrow's work was developed at a time when the federal government's role in complementing the market was widely recognized, but they were hardly the first to adopt a cautionary approach to patenting fundamental knowledge. Dating back to the early days of the Republic, the granting of "monopoly rights" to ideas was viewed with considerable wariness. The nation's very first patent administrator, Thomas Jefferson, affirmed the desirability of keeping nonrival ideas free of proprietary restraints. "If nature has made any one thing less susceptible than all others of exclusive property," wrote Jefferson in 1813, "it is the action of the thinking power called an idea. . . . He who receives an idea from me, receives instruction himself without lessening mine; as he who lites his taper at mine, receives light without darkening me."[50] Jefferson recognized that patents and copyright protection provided an important incentive to encourage private investment in the creation of new products; that is why Article 1, Section 8, of the U.S. Constitution grants creators the power to obtain, for a limited period of time, "exclusive right to their respective writings and discoveries." Yet he was also keenly aware of the need to balance property rights with the preservation of a public domain for basic ideas, stressing that the central task of American patent law was to "[draw] a line between the things which are worth to the public the *embarrassment of an exclusive patent,* and those which are not" (emphasis added).[51] Patents were potentially "embarrassing," in Jefferson's view, because the United States was an open society whose strength rested on the free exchange of ideas, and also because they were known to exclude would-be competitors and raise prices, and thereby generate economic inefficiencies.

Federal patent policy prior to Bayh-Dole was based on this Jeffersonian desire to maintain an appropriate balance between property rights and the public domain. After World War II, when the federal government assumed a central role in funding science and technology, each federal agency was permitted to develop its own patent policy based on its mission and research needs. Some agencies, like the Department of Defense, adopted a "license policy" that gave industry contractors the option of taking title to federally sponsored inventions, so long as the government received a royalty-free license to use the technology at any time. Others, such as the Atomic Energy Commission and the Department of Agriculture, preferred to follow a "title policy," whereby the agency retained the title to all sponsored inventions and made them broadly available through the public domain or nonexclusive licenses. Until the mid-1970s, the "titlists" and "licensees" remained locked in a political stalemate, effectively ensuring that the federal government would retain its commitment to keeping much of its sponsored research free of proprietary controls, where it could be used as the wellspring for future innovation and discovery.[52]

One of the most striking features of the Bayh-Dole Act was that it all but ignored this long-standing federal commitment to preserving the public domain. It made no distinction between nonrival scientific knowledge, which had the potential to be widely utilized if broadly disseminated, and other kinds of knowledge, which might require exclusive licensing to encourage commercial investment and development. In the view of Bayh-Dole's proponents, explained Rebecca Eisenberg, a law professor at the University of Michigan, "the public domain was a treacherous quicksand pit in which discoveries sink beyond reach of the private sector. If the results of federal-sponsored research were to be rescued from oblivion and successfully developed into commercial products, they would have to be patented and offered up for private appropriation."[53]

Considering what a radical departure Bayh-Dole represented, it is surprising how little opposition and debate it generated at the time. Only a few years earlier, a similar bill had met with considerable resistance and died

before even coming to a vote.[54] The Bayh-Dole legislation and its compan-
ion bill in the House, by contrast, passed by large majorities, and
President Jimmy Carter signed the act into law during a lame-duck session
in December 1980.[55] During these hearings, the act's economic logic went
largely unchallenged. There was no mention of Nelson and Arrow's work
on the public funding of science, and little attention was paid to the government's historic role in preserving the scientific commons.[56] Admiral
Rickover, the opposition's main spokesperson, resorted to inflated rhetoric that alienated even more sympathetic liberal allies.[57]

Opponents also failed to challenge the economic data that Bayh-Dole's
supporters presented during the hearings—even though the data were inaccurate and highly misleading. Over and over again, legislators and
witnesses recited the same alarming statistic drawn from the Federal
Counsel on Science and Technology (FCST): Of the more than twenty-
eight thousand patents lying in the government's portfolio in 1976, fewer
than 5 percent were licensed to industry for commercial development.[58]
The message couldn't have been more clear: The federal government had
an abysmal track record of bringing its inventions into commercial use.
Another frequently cited statistic, pulled from a 1968 Harbridge House
study, asserted that rates of utilization of government-funded patents were
much higher when industry contractors (23.8 percent), as opposed to the
federal grant-making agencies (13.3 percent), retained the title to sponsored inventions.[59] Statistical evidence such as this went a long way
toward convincing legislators that transferring patent rights, and licensing
authority, to universities and small businesses was essential if Congress
hoped to promote commercial exploitation of taxpayer-financed research.

Yet, as Rebecca Eisenberg's research has demonstrated, the data underlying these claims did not support this conclusion at all, primarily because
of a "selection bias" in the pool of patents selected for study. The vast majority of the patents examined in both the FCST sample (63 percent) and
the Harbridge House sample (83 percent) had been funded by the
Department of Defense, a "license" agency that permitted industry contractors, in nearly all cases, to retain the title to sponsored inventions. As
a result, noted Eisenberg, the overwhelming majority of the patents held
by the federal government in both study samples were not simply "lying
fallow," as Bayh-Dole's supporters had argued; they represented technologies that had been offered to industry and *turned down*, presumably
because they lacked short-term commercial potential. The data, therefore,

failed to support the Bayh-Dole argument that a title-in-contractor policy would result in higher rates of commercialization.

Because these statistics measured only "numbers of patents licensed," they also provided an incomplete picture of the "utilization" of government-sponsored research. As the authors of the Harbridge House study noted, "It was common knowledge that government-owned inventions may be used without a formal license" and therefore "probable that more inventions are being used than are noted in the government records." Finally, these data considered only research performed by *industry contractors* and were therefore of questionable relevance concerning the utilization of *university*-based research (which was frequently transferred to industry without a license through the public domain).[60]

In part, the weakness and disorganization of the opposition reflected the overriding fear about declining U.S. competitiveness. Many liberals were reluctant to oppose legislation widely seen as a way to spur U.S. competition. As *Science* magazine reported in 1979, "The critics of such legislation, who in the past have railed about the 'giveaway of public funds,' have grown unusually quiet. The reason seems clear. Industrial innovation has become a buzzword in bureaucratic circles." Even Long and Gaylord Nelson (Democrat of Wisconsin), two of the legislation's most prominent critics, elected not to "actively oppose" the bill, and played only a limited role in the debates.[61]

But deeper probing shows that the weakness of the Bayh-Dole opposition had to do with another factor: the political savvy of a little-known government bureaucrat named Norman Latker. Latker was a veteran public servant who served as legal counsel at the Department of Health, Education, and Welfare (HEW) from 1965 to 1980. Though largely ignored in previous histories, Latker played a crucial role behind the scenes in bringing the legislation forward and carefully steering it past the liberal opposition.[62]

A civil engineer and patent lawyer by training, Latker emphatically believed that patents were the best way to stimulate commercial use of taxpayer-financed research. Shortly after his arrival at HEW, he embarked on a personal crusade to reform the federal patent system. In 1968, he pushed through a new Institutional Patent Agreement (IPA) program at HEW—often described as the precursor to Bayh-Dole—which granted universities "with approved technology transfer capability" automatic title to agency-sponsored inventions, including the right to license those inventions exclusively to private industry.[63] Latker's IPA program was enormously popular, and had the immediate effect of encouraging universities to set up their own internal patenting and licensing programs. It was through an IPA that Niels Reimers set up the technology-transfer office at Stanford and filed his controversial patent on the Cohen-Boyer technique, six years before Bayh-Dole. In 1973, the National Science Foundation set up an IPA program of its own, modeled on the one at HEW, giving a further nudge to academic patenting.[64]

As luck would have it, Latker's administration of the IPA program put him in constant contact with an emerging group of university patent officers, who shared his interest in federal patent reform. The more vested the universities became in negotiating lucrative licensing deals with private industry, the more they resented federal policies that restricted their ability to privatize publicly funded research. Linked through a professional association—the Society of University Patent Administrators—and through a newsletter Latker regularly published on the arcana of federal patent law, this small but influential group (including Niels Reimers, Howard Bremer of the University of Wisconsin, Ralph Davis of Purdue, and others), soon joined Latker in his quest to overhaul federal patent law.[65]

Robert Weissman, the author of an important early dissertation on Bayh-Dole, noted that because universities represented a constituency to which most liberals felt sympathetic, they were highly successful in convincing Democratic legislators to drop their historic opposition to the privatization of public research. When I interviewed Latker in 2003 at his law firm, Browdy and Neimark—where he assists universities filing patent claims—he confirmed this for me: "We figured out, early on, that the universities had a direct phone line to their senators and representatives, whoever they wanted. Because they appeared on the surface to be moving in the best interest of the country, as opposed to their own self-interest, they were always listened to."[66]

It was this powerful new constituency of university patent officers that convinced Senators Birch Bayh and Bob Dole to sponsor patent reform legislation. In August 1977, HEW ordered an internal review of its patent policies and slowed down processing of individual patent applications, providing Latker and his allies with a timely political opening.[67] The agency had concerns that exclusive licensing of taxpayer-financed research might contribute to higher health care costs and stifle competition "in those cases where competition could bring the fruits of research to the public faster and more economically." But HEW's decision to stall patent applications gave the opposition just the ammunition it needed. When Latker and the university lobbyists brought their concerns to Congress, they had little trouble convincing Senators Dole and Bayh that bureaucratic red tape was hampering commercial development.[68] At a press conference, held in September 1978, Dole accused HEW of "stonewalling" twenty-nine requests for patent rights to valuable medical discoveries developed with NIH support. These included potential advances in diagnosing and treating cancer, arthritis, hepatitis, and muscular dystrophy. "HEW's decision to effectively suppress these medical breakthroughs is without precedent," Dole charged. "Rarely have we witnessed a more hideous example of overmanagement by the bureaucracy."[69] Later that month, Dole and Bayh introduced the University Small Business Patent Procedures Act, which Latker both conceived and drafted.

Latker's main objective when he crafted the Bayh-Dole bill was to win liberal support and thereby break the political stalemate between the titlists and the licensees that had blocked earlier attempts to liberalize federal patent law. His decision to grant automatic patent rights to universities and small businesses—while excluding large companies—was carefully calibrated to achieve this goal. As Bhaven Sampat, an economist at Georgia Tech and the coauthor of a trenchant study of Bayh-Dole, noted, the exclusion of large corporations effectively undermined the traditional liberal argument that such a policy would favor big business and lead to a concentration of economic power.[70]

Hoping to diminish liberal fears about private profiteering at public expense, Latker also packed the legislation with various safeguards, most of which he drew from his earlier IPA program. These included a "march-in" provision that enabled the federal government to terminate an exclusive license if the licensee failed to take effective steps to bring the invention into practical application within three years; a royalty-free license for the federal government to use the technology at any time; and explicit limits on the duration of exclusive licenses (five years from commercial sale or eight years from the date of the license). He also added a "recoupment fee," requiring institutions to pay back a share of any licensing income or sales to the federal government to recoup for U.S. taxpayers.[71]

It was an impressive list. The only trouble was that not *all* of the IPA's safeguards actually made it into the legislation—and, in cases where they did, they didn't survive for long. HEW's IPA contracts contained strong language requiring university grantees to make good-faith

efforts to license technology nonexclusively (on a "royalty free or reasonable royalty basis") to all qualified parties, *before seeking an exclusive
license*.[72] Yet Latker left this language out of the Bayh-Dole Act entirely.
The recoupment fees were eliminated when the House and Senate met in
conference to reconcile their respective patent reform bills. When I asked
Latker, in 2003, about their swift disappearance, he quickly interjected
and said, "We all hated [the recoupment fee provision], but we felt this
was a way of buying off the opposition. . . . It was a political ploy."
Several years later, the time limits on exclusive licenses were also removed
as part of a 1984 amendment to Bayh-Dole, written and pushed by
Latker. It's hard to escape the conclusion that these safeguards were mere
window dressing designed mainly to broaden political support.

Even the exclusion of big business, which had proved so important in
winning liberal support, turned out to be little more than a political
sleight of hand. Latker correctly judged that allowing small businesses
and universities to license research exclusively simply wouldn't arouse
the same level of opposition as granting those same monopolistic rights
to large corporations. Small businesses were credited with generating 50
percent of the nation's innovation, so giving them a leg up—particularly
during an economic crisis—could hardly be a bad thing. As for the universities, most liberals continued to see them as disinterested institutions
that could pose no real economic threat. Nevertheless, Bayh-Dole's supporters faced a tricky problem: What if large corporations lobbied to
defeat Bayh-Dole because it gave their small-business rivals a competitive
advantage? As was confirmed to me by Howard Bremer, one of the legislation's key backers, Latker and the university lobby quietly resolved
this problem by striking a backroom deal with big business prior to the
act's passage. (Weissman also confirmed this in an 1989 interview with
Niels Reimers.) The deal was this: The corporations agreed not to vigorously oppose the legislation; in exchange, Bayh-Dole's supporters
pledged to lobby for an extension of the act to large firms after congressional passage was assured. "What you have to realize is that the large
companies adopted a hands-off policy on the legislation," Bremer told
me in 2003. "There was kind of a tacit agreement with them that they
would not come in and raise questions and testify; [They] would just
have a hands-off approach."[73]

Latker sought to honor his agreement with big business as expedi-
tiously as possible. Shortly after Bayh-Dole passed, he attempted to bring
in legislation that would extend the title-in-contractor policy to large cor-

porations. The university lobby also testified in favor of a blanket transfer of government title to large firms. After these efforts failed, Latker
went to the White House, where he found the incoming president,
Ronald Reagan, and his advisers highly receptive to his concerns. "They
had some kind of an affinity for what I was doing," Latker told me, still
sounding thrilled by his good fortune. "They gave me every latitude that
I needed to get things done."[74] On February 8, 1983, Reagan issued a
Presidential Memorandum, drafted by Latker, which instructed all executive agencies to extend the Bayh-Dole Act's title-in-contractor
provisions to large corporations. A subsequent 1987 Executive Order
made the policy permanent.[75]

The Bayh-Dole Act was truly the brainchild of Norman Latker. His
success in amending and fine-tuning the legislation meant that in the end,
the act was a strikingly different piece of legislation from the one that
Congress originally approved in 1980. Latker's tenacious efforts opened
the way for full-scale privatization of public research, and for a raft of
other new laws that would further cement the bond between higher education and big business. These included generous tax breaks for
corporations willing to invest in academic research; a revision of the antitrust laws that permitted universities, industry, and the federal
government to pool their research capabilities; and myriad new federal-
grant programs designed to stimulate university-industry research
collaborations.[76] In 1986 Congress also passed the Federal Technology
Transfer Act, a federal parallel to Bayh-Dole, drafted by Norman Latker,
which encouraged government labs to become more active in patenting
and licensing, and to forge cooperative research-and-development agreements (known as CRADAs) with private industry.[77] Three years later, the
National Competitiveness Technology Transfer Act extended these licensing provisions to all contractor-operated national laboratories. The
collective effect was a dramatic increase in the overall amount of publicly
financed research now subject to proprietary commercial control—and
the birth of a new paradigm in American higher education variously described as the "second academic revolution," the "entrepreneurial
university," or simply "academic capitalism."[78]

———

Just as the economic logic that lay behind this new paradigm wasn't questioned, neither was its broader effect on higher education. Virtually no

one who testified during the Bayh-Dole hearings bothered to ask any questions about the legislation's potential impact on the academic culture, academic freedom, conflicts of interest, or the tradition of open science.

Yet the impact was bound to be profound. In the past, most universities had assiduously avoided any direct commercial involvement, both because it was considered beyond their realm of expertise and because it was seen as conflicting with their core academic mission. Now Congress had removed the stigma long associated with such activity.[79] By giving universities the opportunity to generate royalties and other revenues—indeed, positively encouraging them to do so—Bayh-Dole introduced a profit motive directly into the heart of academic life.

This new profit orientation was vividly expressed in the spring of 1981 when William F. Massy, Stanford's vice president for business and finance, voiced concern, during a faculty meeting, that the "natural income of the fruits of research" accruing to the university from patent and licensing fees was not commensurate with the true value of the research, and that "windfall profits" might be going to others. "It's important that we find means by which the university can participate in the entrepreneurial returns that come from those things that we create here," he concluded.[80]

Never before had university leaders expressed such an explicit desire to maximize their own "entrepreneurial returns" from academic knowledge. Eager to capitalize on their professors' research, universities began pursuing lucrative licensing deals with private industry, setting up venture-capital funds, and investing in their own professors' start-ups. The number of schools operating their own technology-transfer offices jumped from 25 in 1980 to 200 a decade later. By 2000, virtually every research university in the country would be running its own patenting and licensing operation.[81] The number of patents granted annually to academic institutions also skyrocketed, from a mere 264 in 1979 to more than 3,200 in 2001.[82] Whereas in the past universities had transferred knowledge to industry largely through open channels—the education and training of students, faculty consulting for companies, sabbaticals, publications, and conferences—from here on in the emphasis would be on staking proprietary claims to research, and then licensing it to industry.

As we've seen, these developments were not solely attributable to the Bayh-Dole Act. The emergence of biotechnology, shifts in federal science policy, and the rise of a knowledge-based economy had already propelled administrators like Niels Reimers to see dollar signs in their professors' discoveries.[83] But now every university in the country would begin to dream of patenting its very own Cohen-Boyer invention—a multi-million-dollar cash cow that would generate a continuous flow of revenue—and they didn't have to apply for an Institutional Patent Agreement or a special waiver to do it. Back in 1955, when Jonas Salk invented the polio vaccine, he shunned patenting, viewing his research as a "public good." By the mid-1980s, such an attitude would seem touchingly quaint.

The ability to stake a proprietary claim to federally funded research, as part of a sponsored-research deal, immediately encouraged private industry to forge closer ties with the academy. Because the universities' labor force, labs, and research were already heavily subsidized by the federal government, industry was virtually guaranteed a relatively good return on its investment.

During the first half of the 1980s, dozens of multiyear, multi-million-dollar contracts were announced, most of them far larger in scope than corporate-sponsored agreements of the past. Du Pont gave $6 million to the Harvard Medical School for genetics research; Hoechst, the West German chemical giant, dolled out $50 million to the Massachusetts General Hospital for medical research; ten companies contributed $7.5 million for a new computer center at Stanford; Monsanto gave $2.3 million to Washington University for biomedical research; and Sohio gave $2 million to the University of Illinois for plant-molecular-genetics research.[84] In each of these sponsored-research deals, industry targeted its money on specific areas of research and expected tangible returns: exclusive rights to any valuable inventions, the ability to review manuscripts prior to publication, and other benefits.

That all of this would happen without raising deeper questions about the potential impact on academic culture is both telling and troubling. In the decades to come, while pundits debated how political correctness and identity politics were transforming higher education and corrupting the formerly pristine search for truth, few would bother to contemplate how another factor—private money—was doing so. Although conservatives accused universities of bending over backwards to mollify minority groups and women, they were curiously silent about the corrupting influence of another interest group: big business.

For their part, academic leaders almost universally embraced the new "economic competitiveness" mandate, much as their predecessors had embraced a "national defense" mandate for higher education after World War II. Most welcomed the opportunity to boost their access to both federal and industrial funding, expand their research capabilities, and bring power and prestige to their institutions. By and large, academic leaders took it for granted that the university would learn to balance its commitment to teaching and research with its new commercial mission. "Almost uniformly," observed the historian Roger Geiger, "universities in the 1980s made the judgment that the inducements to commercial activities outweighed the possible risks to their core academic roles."[85] Conflicts between the worlds of academia and private industry could always be managed, these administrators reasoned.

But just as the military ties spawned during the Cold War had proven more difficult to manage than most anticipated—leading to blatant violations of academic freedom and a skewing of the research agenda—the new market orientation would come with innumerable costs.

4

The Republic of
Science in Turmoil

In a classic paper published in 1942, the sociologist Robert K. Merton likened the culture of science to the ideals of communism. Intellectual property was commonly shared; discoveries were freely exchanged. "The scientist's claim to 'his' intellectual 'property,'" Merton wrote, was "limited to that of recognition and esteem," and scientific knowledge was assumed to be a public good.[1]

This tradition of openness within the sciences, stemming from the German model of research, is intimately connected to academic culture itself, which has long been dedicated to open inquiry and the sharing of ideas. Judging professors on their research, teaching, and publications fostered a collegial environment where information was broadly disseminated. Furthermore, by rewarding professors for their "priority of discovery"—for being the *first* to uncover a new mathematical formula, a scientific theorem, a philosophical theory—the culture of academia encouraged the rapid creation of new knowledge, hastened public disclosure, and enabled peers to evaluate and replicate new research findings to ensure their accuracy, thus serving to broaden the stock of reliable knowledge available in the public domain for future exploration.[2]

Today, one of the greatest threats posed by the growing financial ties between universities and private industry is the erosion of this open scientific culture, which Michael Polanyi would famously dub the "Republic of Science" in 1969.[3]

Scientists who perform industry-sponsored research routinely sign legal contracts requiring them to keep both the methods and the results of their work secret for a period of time. From a corporate sponsor's point of view, secrecy makes perfect sense: It prevents potential competitors from pilfering ideas before the company can secure proprietary rights to a professor's inventions. Although companies sometimes gift universities unrestricted money, more often than not they want assurances that they will *own* any inventions stemming from their support.

In many respects, this proprietary corporate culture is fundamentally at odds with the university's culture of openness and sharing. Finding an appropriate balance between the two has proven difficult. The National Institutes of Health, for example, recommend that universities allow corporate sponsors to prohibit publication for no more than one or two months (the time normally required to apply for a patent), but lengthier delays have become standard. In 1994, researchers at Massachusetts General Hospital surveyed 210 life science companies and found that 58 percent of those sponsoring academic research required delays of more than six months before publication.[4]

"One of the most basic tenets of science is that we share information in an open way," said Steven A. Rosenberg of the National Cancer Institute, one of the country's leading cancer researchers. "As biotech and pharmaceutical companies have become more involved in funding research, there's been a shift toward confidentiality that is severely inhibiting the interchange of information." Rosenberg reported that he has frequently been asked to sign confidentiality agreements to obtain access to basic scientific reagents and research tools—some agreements lasting up to ten years. Once, when he refused to sign such an agreement, he was denied access to information he needed for a clinical trial involving an experimental cancer treatment.

"The ethics of business and the ethics of science do not mix well," explained Rosenberg. "When I began doing research twenty years ago, sharing of research materials was much more common. Today, the whole issue is in the closet. People don't like to talk about it because to do their research a lot of people are signing these confidentiality agreements. This is the real dark side of science."[5]

Such concerns are not merely anecdotal. Research conducted by David Blumenthal and Eric Campbell, health policy researchers at Harvard University, suggests that data withholding and publication delays have become far more common, particularly in the life sciences, where commercial relationships have grown dramatically in recent years. In a survey of 2,167 life science faculty, Blumenthal found that nearly one in five of them had delayed publication for more than six months to protect proprietary information. The same survey also found that academic scientists now frequently withhold information from one another. Thirty-four percent of those surveyed reported they had requested and been denied access to research results or products developed by other university scientists,[6] despite Albert Einstein's famous aphorism: "The right to search for truth implies also a duty: One must not conceal any part of what one has recognized to be true."

Of course, information withholding within academia is not always driven by commercial imperatives; academic competition and a scientist's desire to advance his or her own career can be sufficient motivation. Nevertheless, Blumenthal found that professors involved in "commercializing research" (defined as research that has resulted in patent applications, patents, licenses, trade secrets, products under regulatory review, or start-up companies) were *three times more likely* to have delayed publication of their research for six months or more, and *nearly two and half times more likely* to have refused to share information with other university scientists.[7]

———

Worse than the problems of enforced secrecy and publication delays is the possibility that corporate sponsors may be manipulating manuscripts or suppressing unwelcome research to serve their commercial interests. The presumption of investigator objectivity is one of the most cherished principles in the academic sciences. Without it, universities would cease to be places dedicated to impartial inquiry and truth seeking. Yet this is a realm where, once again, the interests of business and those of academia can, and frequently do, collide.

How prevalent is such corporate meddling? The question has received surprisingly little scholarly attention, but what research does exist is not encouraging. One survey of major university-industry research centers in the field of engineering found that 35 percent would allow corporate sponsors to delete information from papers prior to publication.[8] This does not, of course, mean that censorship of this kind occurs at such a rate across the university. Even so, one has to wonder how often corporations meddle in the research process without anybody's raising objections or taking notice. A professor who steps forward to challenge a corporate sponsor is, after all, risking a lot: time-consuming and contentious battles, future industry funding, sometimes even his academic career.

Danger on the Job

In November 1994, a thirty-six-year-old worker at a textile factory visited the occupational medicine clinic of David Kern, a professor of medicine at Brown University. Kern's clinic was located at Memorial Hospital, a sprawling thirteen-acre teaching institution in Pawtucket, Rhode Island, that is affiliated with Brown's medical school. When Kern examined the patient, he discovered a rare interstitial lung disease (ILD) that inflames the fragile walls of the lung's air sacs and impairs breathing. Because the disease is typically found in just 1 in 40,000 people, most of whom are elderly, Kern immediately wondered whether perhaps the patient's ailment was work-related. He decided to turn the case into an occupational-health investigation for his medical students. On December 2, after obtaining permission from the worker's employer, Microfibres, Inc., a Pawtucket company that manufactures nylon-flocked fabrics, Kern and his students visited the plant to take air samples. Before embarking on this one-hour educational visit, Kern signed a standard corporate confidentiality agreement forbidding the disclosure of trade secrets. As he had signed such documents during factory visits many times before, it never occurred to him that doing so this time would come back to haunt him.[9]

The tests failed to identify any cause for the worker's ailment, and the project ended.

More than a year later, however, another worker visited Kern from the same Microfibres factory with virtually identical symptoms. Believing that this second case (again involving a young worker) might signal a pattern, Kern convinced the company to hire him as a consultant to conduct an investigation.

Memorial Hospital's Rick Dietz, assistant vice president of marketing and development, drew up the payment arrangements for Kern's consulting activities in February 1996. As is common at many academic teaching hospitals, the fees Microfibres paid Kern went directly to Memorial. But there was one glaring oversight: The hospital did not require Microfibres to sign a written contract. In an interview, Kern said he pressed Microfibres to sign an agreement that his own occupational-health clinic had prepared, which would have underscored his academic right to publish. But when his efforts were rebuffed, Kern pressed ahead with his investigation, anxious to discover the cause of his patients' illness. In a matter of months, he turned up 6 additional cases of ILD—a total of 8 cases in a workforce of 150. He also unearthed an earlier medical journal article describing a similar outbreak in a nylon flocking factory in Canada. Soon, armed with what he believed was sufficient evidence to prove the existence of a new lung disease, Kern informed the company of his plans to publish his findings in a paper that he would present at the annual meeting of the American Thoracic Society in May 1997.

In response, Microfibres threatened to sue, citing the confidentiality agreement Kern had signed during his educational visit, dated fifteen months before his paid consulting activities began.

Kern's first instinct was to contact Brown University's grants office. The office referred him to Peter Shank, associate dean of medicine and research. After reviewing Kern's documentation, Shank wrote, "I see no way in which you can publish results of your studies at the company without their written approval. . . . You should immediately withdraw your abstract to the national meeting."[10]

Kern was stunned. He, his assistant, and Charles Kuhn, the chief of pathology, immediately requested a meeting with Shank to lay out why, in their view, the university should not back down. A significant public health issue was at stake, they pointed out. Kern's research had uncovered a cluster of potentially fatal illnesses in a sector of the labor force not previously thought to be vulnerable. One Canadian who worked in a flocking factory had already died, and two others were seriously ill. In addition, the researchers noted, Kern's paper would not divulge any "trade secrets." The information he required had been obtained through a combination of state and federal right-to-know laws, knowledge of processes and materials generic to the flocking industry, previously published medical articles, and physical exams of volunteer workers. In other words, even if one accepted the company's claim that the earlier confidentiality agreement should apply, Kern wasn't violating it. In light of all this, the researchers argued, both Kern and Brown Medical School had a professional and moral obligation to make these findings public.[11]

But Shank was not persuaded, insisting that the agreement prevented Kern from publishing.

And the situation soon went from bad to worse. On December 23, 1996, Kern received a memorandum from Francis Dietz, the president of Memorial Hospital and the father of Rick Dietz, who had negotiated Kern's consulting arrangement with Microfibres. Dietz Sr. instructed Kern to "withdraw [his] abstract from publication or presentation before the deadline date of January 15, 1997." The hospital, he added, was shutting down his occupational-health program "effective immediately."[12] (Memorial has insisted that the decision to close Kern's program was made well before the Microfibres controversy and was not retaliatory, but Dietz's memo addressing both issues in subsequent paragraphs makes this statement implausible.)

That spring, word began to circulate within the scholarly community about the suppression of Kern's research. Donald J. Marsh, dean of Brown Medical School, and other top administrators soon found themselves deluged with letters from prominent academics supporting Kern.[13] "Dear Dr. Marsh," began one April 11, 1997, letter from Howard Frumkin, then-chair of public health at Emory University:

> I am a graduate of Brown. Since I left there 20 years ago, I have considered it an institution that embodies core values of scholarship, honesty, and integrity. I am confident that Brown does not wish to be identified with the suppression of scientific findings, the compromise of professional ethics, the concealment of important public health information, the active collusion between a truculent local company and a university-affiliated hospital, and the closure of vigorous, essential educational programs. I appeal to you to work to reverse the University's and the hospital's position in this matter.[14]

Dean Marsh sought to distance Brown University from what was rapidly turning into a public embarrassment, going so far as to portray the university as an outside party to the dispute. In a letter and subsequent interviews with the *Providence Journal* and the *Boston Globe*, Marsh first asserted that Memorial Hospital had acted on its own without consulting Brown (a position he was quickly forced to admit was untrue).[15] Later, Marsh stated that Kern's Occupational and Environmental Health Program was never a formal "program" at the medical school, and therefore that the administration lacked any authority to intervene.[16] Kern strongly disputed this, noting that he had taught at the university for eleven years and was a full professor of general internal medicine and occupational health. Many of the courses he taught satisfied degree requirements for students enrolled at Brown Medical School.[17] The deeper problem, according to an internal Brown investigation, was that the university's affiliation agreement with its teaching hospital failed to spell out the faculty's academic rights and responsibilities, or to establish clear lines of authority.[18]

Despite considerable pressure to back down, David Kern went forward with the publication of his paper.[19] On May 21, 1997, bucking the threats from Microfibres and the warnings of his own university, Kern attended the American Thoracic Society conference. There, before some ten thousand pulmonary physicians who had gathered from around the world, he presented evidence documenting what appeared to be a new lung disease. He was roundly praised for his work and left the conference feeling at least partially vindicated. Still, there was one aspect of the event that needled him. While he was answering questions beside his poster presentation in a large conference hall, Kern recalled, Brown representatives roamed the room distributing flyers that read, "Brown University supports the Academic Freedom of Dr. David Kern."[20]

Kern was incredulous, but the message was entirely consistent with Dean Marsh's new public relations stance. Realizing that Kern was not going to back down, the university now portrayed itself as the embattled professor's champion. "Dr. Kern has published his abstract and will present his work to the American Thoracic Society," Dean Marsh wrote in a letter to Brown faculty just prior to the event. "I believe his rights to publish have been preserved."[21]

The letter didn't mention the price Kern was forced to pay to have his rights so "preserved." Less than a week after returning from San Francisco, David Kern opened his mailbox and found two letters from Vartan Gregorian, Brown's president at the time, and Francis Dietz. The letters informed him that his teaching and research positions were being eliminated. Later that same fall, the Centers for Disease Control officially recognized the new disease Kern identified, flock worker's lung.

So why *did* Brown abandon Kern in the midst of this affair? Searching for an answer, I tracked Kern down where he was living near the coast of Maine, and working as a doctor of internal medicine at the Penobscot Bay hospital. A soft-spoken man with wavy brown hair and a gentle manner,

Kern does not come across as a man spoiling for a fight, nor does he seem embittered.

At first, Kern was reluctant to revisit his past at Brown. Over time, however, he sent me reams of documents about the case. As I pored over these, it was hard not to conclude that Brown's actions were at least partially shaped by the institution's own financial interests. In July 1996, a mere five months after Kern's consulting activities began, Brown Medical School and Memorial Hospital announced a major new partnership, centered on the construction of a $4.3-million Center for Primary Care. In an interview with the *Providence Journal*, Rick Dietz admitted that Microfibres had been approached about making a donation just weeks after Kern's consulting relationship fell apart.[22] This was also right around the time when the university and the hospital were negotiating with Microfibres over Kern's right to publish.

Microfibres, like many local businesses, already had close connections with the hospital. James McCulloch, the company's owner, and two other family members sat on Memorial's board, and Microfibres was one of eight companies that had helped fund the construction of the hospital's histology lab.[23]

That wasn't all. During the summer and fall of 1996, the Brown Medical School was soliciting a major grant from the state of Rhode Island to launch a new Center for Cellular Medicine dedicated to nurturing biotech companies in the state.[24] Kern told me that a light went off for him when he saw the Spring 1998 issue of *Brown Medicine*, the medical school's in-house publication.[25] The issue was devoted to entrepreneurial faculty who had launched their own start-up companies and highlighted the role that the Center for Cellular Medicine (now the Slater Center for Biomedical Technology) would play in building up a new biotech corridor in the state of Rhode Island. "It's possible that the university hoped Microfibres' owner would donate a million dollars to Brown, as he did to the Dartmouth medical school," Kern told me in an interview. "But I don't think that was the real issue. The thinking was: We can't allow faculty to jeopardize this close working relationship with industry in the state."

Shading the Truth

Proponents of university-industry ties do not deny that such stories are troubling but insist they are rare. There are thousands of industry-sponsored studies completed every year, after all, with no conflicts reported. As universities have grown more sophisticated in collaborating with industry, proponents maintain, they have become more adept at negotiating contracts that prevent such abuses from occurring.

There is a measure of truth to this. Certainly cases like David Kern's— where professors are willing to risk their careers in the face of pressure from their corporate sponsor—*are* rare, although, as we'll see in subsequent chapters, by no means unheard of. Far more common are instances where corporations exert influence over academic research that is more subtle—and hence more difficult to detect. As Mildred Cho, a senior research scholar and associate director of Stanford's Center for Biomedical Ethics, explained, "When you have so many scientists on boards of companies or doing sponsored research, you start to wonder: How are these studies being designed? What kinds of research questions are being raised? What kinds aren't being raised?" For every David Kern who steps forward in such cases, an unknown number of researchers voluntarily toe the company line or succumb to more discrete forms of influence.

At the University of Florida, for example, controversy erupted following disclosure that Charles Thomas, a criminologist at the school who advised the state on prison policy, had pocketed $3 million in consulting fees from the private-prison industry (in which he also owned stock). Thomas's views on private prisons have been quoted frequently in the pages of the *New York Times* and the *Wall Street Journal*, and he has trumpeted the virtues of "full-scale privatization" in testimony before Congress.[26] "I'm really kind of astounded that the state university system would tolerate something like this," said a member of the state ethics commission, which slapped Thomas with a $20,000 fine.[27]

As Marcia Angell, a lecturer at Harvard Medical School and the former editor in chief of the *New England Journal of Medicine*, explained, a close and remunerative relationship to a company "naturally creates goodwill on the part of researchers and the hope that the largesse will continue. This attitude can subtly influence scientific judgment in ways that may be difficult to discern."[28] Consider Enron's influence on research at Harvard, where, as already mentioned, the Harvard Electricity Policy Group churned out a whopping thirty-one reports promoting the deregulation of energy markets in California—this while receiving funding from Enron and other energy firms that stood to benefit from precisely such a policy. Or the influence that major chemical, oil, gas, and pharmaceutical companies wield over the Harvard Center for Risk Analysis (HCRA), which receives 60 percent of its funding from private sources, most of it stemming from large corporations—Exxon, Monsanto, Eli Lilly & Co., AstraZeneca—that have a direct stake in the outcome of its research on regulatory matters.[29]

Harvard's extensive financial conflicts first came to light after the HCRA's longtime director, John D. Graham, was nominated by President George W. Bush to become the government's "regulatory czar" at the Office of Information and Regulatory Affairs (part of the Office of Management and Budget). Graham's nomination was controversial and prompted Congress to launch a series of hearings exploring HCRA's research record and its sources of funding. The hearings revealed that Graham's center, which offers courses and degree programs to some 500 Harvard students every year, solicited tobacco money and worked with the tobacco industry to disparage the risks of secondhand smoke. (Harvey Fineberg, a dean at the Harvard School of Public Health, demanded that one check from Philip Morris be returned. In response, Graham wrote to the company asking if it might send the $25,000 back to HCRA via its subsidiary, Kraft Foods, instead.[30]) Graham's HCRA also argued that cell phone use by drivers should not be restricted, even though its own research, which was funded by AT&T Wireless Communications, showed that such use could lead to a thousand additional highway deaths a year.[31] As a member of the EPA's scientific advisory board subcommittee on dioxin, a known human carcinogen, Graham argued that reducing dioxin levels might "do more harm . . . than good"; he even went so far as to argue that dioxin might prevent rather than cause cancer in some cases. His Harvard center, meanwhile, was heavily funded by dioxin producers.[32]

Sometimes the sheer volume of industry money pouring into a particular research field can significantly distort the scientific debate. In his book *The Heat Is On: The High Stakes Battle over Earth's Threatened Climate*, the reporter Ross Gelbspan documented how fossil fuel companies have bankrolled numerous academic studies that downplay the threat of global warming, thereby sustaining the perception that global warming is still unproven, and distorting the public policy debate.[33]

One of the government's top scientists studying the Exxon *Valdez* oil spill in Alaska, meanwhile, has publicly voiced concern that it has become all but impossible to find academic scholars who don't have financial ties to the oil industry.[34] The chief sponsor of Stanford University's new Global Climate and Energy Project, for example, kicking in $100 million over ten years, is Exxon Mobil. In return for such largesse, Exxon Mobil and the other corporate sponsors get to decide which academic projects are selected for funding.[35]

Corporate interference with academic freedom can also take the form of intimidation and harassment, as scientists studying agricultural pollution have recently learned. James Zahn, a former researcher at Iowa State University's USDA (U.S. Department of Agriculture) Agricultural Research Service lab, was told by his supervisors he could not publish or speak publicly about finding antibiotic-resistant bacteria in air emissions from hog farms. Pork producers, who paid for up to a third of Zahn's research, claimed that his work did not fit the lab's mission, and his bosses silenced him.[36] Similarly, a local pork growers group attempted to intimidate Steven Wing, a professor of epidemiology at the University of North Carolina, Chapel Hill, shortly after he released a paper on the poor health of residents living near hog farms. The group issued press releases discrediting Wing's research and tried to force the university (under the state's open records law) to compel him to disclose his study volunteers' names, even though these rural, low-income residents had been promised full confidentiality in order to secure their participation. Afterward, Wing said he felt his position at the university was far less secure.[37]

Many scholars balk at the notion that merely accepting industry grants or holding a financial stake in a company sponsoring academic research will bias a professor's work. They note, rightly, that government financing of university research is far larger in quantity and can result in biases of its own. The current NIH budget, for example, is heavily skewed toward AIDS research, which dwarfs spending on illnesses like cardiovascular disease and Alzheimer's that kill far more Americans each year.[38] As many thoughtful observers have pointed out, however, important distinctions must be drawn between the kind of influence government and corporations tend to wield. For one thing, federal research funding is determined through a democratic decisionmaking process; corporate funding, by contrast, is dictated by what is best for each company's bottom line. Furthermore, although abuses certainly have occurred in the past, the American public has been remarkably vigilant in rejecting government interference with academic freedom. Vannevar Bush assiduously tried to insulate the federal grant-making process from politics by having all grants decided through a meritocratic, competitive peer-review system.[39]

Obviously there is no similar system in place for corporate-sponsored research, even though a vast body of work suggests such research is far from impartial. Mildred Cho, for example, coauthored a study in the *Annals of Internal Medicine* that found that 98 percent of papers based on industry-sponsored research reflected favorably on the drugs being examined, compared with 79 percent of papers based on research not funded by industry.[40] An analysis published in the *Journal of the American Medical Association* found that studies of cancer drugs funded by the pharmaceutical industry were nearly *eight times less likely* to reach unfavorable conclusions than similar studies funded by nonprofit organizations.[41] Another study in the same journal found that 94 percent of review articles by tobacco-industry-affiliated authors concluded that passive exposure to tobacco smoke is not harmful, compared with just 13 percent of authors with no industry ties.[42] Of course, it is possible that this sharp skewing of research outcomes results less from any overt manipulation of the research and more from companies' preselecting scholars whom they judge to be more sympathetic to their viewpoint. Regardless, the results are unambiguous. As a systematic review of 1,140 clinical trial studies published by Yale researchers in 2003 concluded, from cancer to arthritis to cholesterol, the evidence is overwhelming that when research is industry-sponsored, it is "significantly more likely to reach conclusions that [are] favorable to the sponsor" compared with non-industry-funded research.[43]

Given all of this, might the public begin to see academics less as stewards of truth and more like hired hands? Or, worse than hired hands, as interested parties? More and more, professors not only accept industry grants to support their research but also hold stock in or have other financial ties to the companies funding them. Professors of engineering and business have long done consulting for outside companies, but now they are actually going into business themselves and becoming part owners of the firms commercializing their research.[44]

Financial entanglements between researchers and corporations have grown so common that the Securities and Exchange Commission (SEC) has detected the trend and investigated numerous academic researchers suspected of engaging in insider trading. In a case filed in Pennsylvania, the SEC charged Dale J. Lange, a Columbia University neurologist, with pocketing $26,000 in profits after Lange bought stock in a company that was about to release promising new findings concerning a drug to treat Lou Gehrig's disease. Lange had good reason to expect the stock to soar because he had conducted the confidential clinical trials himself.[45]

Students Speak

The fabric of academic science has become so riddled with commercial entanglements that they have even started to take a noticeable toll on graduate students. Early in their academic careers, most young scientists are asked to choose one professor, or mentor, who will instruct them in both the technical and ethical aspects of good scholarship and scientific practice—a relationship that usually lasts for the duration of their apprenticeship training and beyond. As one professor wrote, the "research group is like an extended family or a small tribe, dependent on one another, but led by a mentor, who acts as their consultant, critic, judge, advisor, and scientific father."[46] Lately, though, research groups at many schools have come to behave less like an extended family than like a cut-throat business enterprise.

According to Drummond Rennie, an editor at the *Journal of the American Medical Association*, the intellectual property battles now surfacing inside university labs have grown both more numerous and more difficult to adjudicate. "I've talked to scores and scores of people who allege misconduct, and most of them are entirely right," he told the *Chronicle of Higher Education* in 2002. "In some labs it's routine to steal other people's work." Too often the junior scientists are willing to be abused, Rennie said: "They know their advisor is stealing their work, but they think they need to stay and get a good recommendation."[47]

Nelson Kiang, an emeritus professor at MIT who organized a conference on "Secrecy and Science" in March 1999, worries that instead of learning proper academic protocol, many young scientists—particularly those working extensively under corporate contracts—are being taught to accept the inhibiting power of money over science. "One hears of many students at MIT who complain about not being able to publish their theses in a timely fashion," Kiang said, "but when we tried to involve them in the conference, not a single one would participate, and they actually asked us specifically not to be named. Of course, it's not surprising. They fear that if they come forward, they might get into trouble with their supervisors."[48] At Brigham Young University, the dean of graduate studies even has a readily accessible form posted online titled "Request to Secure Theses and Dissertations," which enables professors and students to restrain publication of student research for a specified amount of time in order to protect commercial or proprietary research.[49]

Remarkably little analytical attention has been paid to how commercial restraints on publication and the free flow of knowledge may be affecting the education and training of students. Many administrators and faculty are quick to point out that these interactions with industry benefit their students educationally and provide employment opportunities after the students graduate. Both of which may certainly be true. One survey of more than two thousand life sciences faculty found that 60 percent believed that industry-sponsored research enhanced career opportunities for students.[50] But the widespread assumption that these relationships are wholly beneficial may also be leading many institutions to overlook problems.

In one Harvard study, David Blumenthal and Eric Campbell found that roughly 57 percent of the life science companies they surveyed reported that "confidential, proprietary information sometimes or often emerges from their sponsorship of graduate students and postdoctoral fellows; *88 percent reported that their university contracts often require students and fellows to keep such information confidential*" (emphasis added). The authors cautioned that "graduate students and postdoctoral fellows may be particularly affected by industry policies on secrecy," because they frequently rely "on the prompt publication of research findings in order to secure their first jobs."[51]

In 2002, Campbell told me that all the anecdotal evidence he had gathered through confidential interviews (in preparation for a possible upcoming survey) suggested that intellectual property and secrecy were critical issues in the lives of students. "We had students tell us all the time that they used to lock up their lab notes at night because they didn't want anyone else to steal their ideas," he explained. "That world is full of stories of students who make up duplicate lab books with false data in them, students who work from midnight to nine in the morning, when the lab is mostly empty, so they don't have to tell anyone what they're working on—industry-funded research or research with high commercial potential."[52]

During the Cold War, the federal government's demand that students' theses and dissertations be kept confidential to protect national security generated vocal opposition in the academy. Today, by contrast, the growing commercial restraints on students are barely discussed, partly, no doubt, because these students are frequently afraid to speak out and it can be difficult to substantiate their stories. Personal testimonials like the one below from two students at Stanford are rare indeed.

A View from Inside

I first became acquainted with David Zapol, a young man in his mid-twenties, with dark eyes, olive skin, and a thin athletic build, while he was working at Pharsight Corporation, a small firm that did modeling and simulation of drug development for pharmaceutical companies. When I contacted Zapol in 2002, I had one simple question: Why had he abandoned his Ph.D. studies at Stanford? His father, Warren Zapol, is an eminent scientist at Harvard Medical School, and I'd heard through the grapevine that he was deeply troubled by the circumstances surrounding his son's departure from Stanford. David told me he finally felt ready to talk; speaking out, he said, might prevent other young scientists from falling into the same predicament he had.

David Zapol began his story by vividly recalling the excitement he felt when he first met Garry Nolan, the dynamic young assistant professor who recruited him to Stanford and later became his mentor. At the time, Zapol was an ambitious student from MIT, intent on finding a cure for HIV. "Garry convinced me that Stanford was the place for me," Zapol said. "We got along wonderfully." Shortly afterward, Zapol was awarded a highly prestigious National Science Foundation fellowship that would pay for his graduate studies at Stanford.[53]

When Zapol joined Nolan's lab in June 1996, he found the atmosphere every bit as exciting as he had imagined it would be. The lab was filled with bright young people doing cutting-edge research. Nolan, who had a joint appointment in the Departments of Molecular Pharmacology and of Microbiology and Immunology at Stanford Medical School, was widely regarded as a rising academic star—not to mention a budding entrepreneur. On June 14, 1996, he officially cofounded and incorporated Rigel Pharmaceuticals, Inc., a start-up company based on a genomic screening technology that he had invented and later patented together with another graduate student, Michael Rothenberg. Stanford subsequently licensed this technology exclusively to Nolan's firm.[54]

Richard Popp, Stanford's then senior associate dean for academic affairs, told me in an interview that the school was careful to draw a clear boundary between Nolan's academic lab and Rigel. "The lab was not to be a research or development arm for the company," he said, "and the students understood this."[55] However, according to Zapol, these boundary lines quickly grew blurry.

Shortly afer his arrival at Stanford, Zapol remembers sitting down with Nolan to map out the HIV-related research he was going to pursue as part of his Ph.D. thesis.[56] At first, Zapol was extremely excited about the project and relished the idea of collaborating with Nolan. But there was one problem: His thesis was built around the same genomic screening technology (the intracellular peptide libraries) that now lay at the core of Rigel's business portfolio. What's more, prior to delving into his own research, Nolan had asked Zapol to partner with Michael Rothenberg on the "proof of concept" for Rigel's new technology, drawing him directly into the company's commercial orbit.

Around the lab, Zapol started to hear rumors about graduate students and postdocs being given consultancy positions and possibly even future stock options in Nolan's new firm. "I remember debating with my mother about how much [of this commercial activity] was appropriate and feeling conflicted about it," he told me. "You know, clearly, if it's my adviser who's starting a company, it's exciting to see it get off the ground. But at the same time, if I can't get time with my adviser and he's completely preoccupied, then as a student I start to wonder if my education isn't being compromised."[57] David's mother, Nikki Zapol, was no stranger to the tensions her son was now confronting, having worked for many years at the interface between academia and industry, including serving as director of corporate-sponsored research at Massachusetts General Hospital, Harvard's teaching hospital, and later as legal counsel for the hospital's parent company. At the time, she mostly trusted that Stanford would be carefully managing the situation, but that proved not to be the case.

According to Zapol, one day in late July 1997, Michael Rothenberg came into the lab, evidently quite distraught. He told Zapol he had just been over at Rigel's offices and had seen their proof-of-concept results featured in a company presentation for investors, without any acknowledgment of their authorship. Both students were totally perplexed as to how their preliminary, unpublished results, which only Nolan and they were privy to, had migrated over to the company. Zapol told me both he and Rothenberg believed their research would first be published in a peer-reviewed academic journal. Because publication is the coin of the realm in academia, this was extremely important to both of them.

When I asked Nolan to respond to Zapol's allegations concerning Rigel's misuse of his students' data, he replied in writing, "I do not have a memory of this event." He emphasized that his decision to found Rigel stemmed from a genuine desire to advance public health, not to get rich.

"My story is far from unique—there are many investigators (MDs, PhDs) who are driven by these motivations. . . . I am pleasantly surprised every time I see the ideas coming from my lab helping the public. . . . It gives me great pleasure to teach the students how to effectively walk the academic-industrial divide." Nolan also sharply disputed Zapol's contention that the boundary between his academic and commercial research was ill-defined. "It was very clear that students could not work on company-directed projects in the laboratory at Stanford," he asserted. "The truth is there was a clear delineation of my roles. Stanford demanded it and I was fully accountable for separating my dual responsibilities as an academic mentor and the founder of a start-up company."[58]

But Zapol didn't see it that way. And, as it turns out, neither did Michael Rothenberg.

When I managed to track down Rothenberg in September 2004, he initially expressed strong reservations about speaking out publicly on an issue that was, for him, very personal. He also said he was concerned that his struggle might be misinterpreted by others in the academic community. After I explained that I only wanted to establish whether there was any truth to Zapol's allegations, he agreed to corroborate to the extent that he could. It turned out that Rothenberg had corresponded with Nolan, and his e-mail records fully substantiated Zapol's account. In one August 3, 1997, e-mail, for example, Rothenberg made explicit reference to "Rigel's inappropriate use of my data without referencing me" and thanked Nolan for meeting with him the previous day to discuss his concerns.[59] In his reply later that same day, Nolan wrote that he had already spoken with the company's executive vice president, Donald Payan, who "reiterated once again that he HAS been referencing you verbally as the person who did the hands-on experiments in my lab." Nolan reported that Payan also "had no problems" with adding Rothenberg's name to the company's presentation and citing him as the data's author.[60]

On the one hand, Nolan seemed to acknowledge the legitimacy of Rothenberg's concerns, but later on in the same e-mail, he also scolded his pupil for speaking so forthrightly. "Please, do not be referring to this situation as 'Rigel's inappropriate use of my data without referencing me,'" he warned. "Be careful what you say." Nolan then recounted for Rothenberg a cautionary tale about when he was still pursuing his Ph.D. and he publicly accused a well-known Stanford professor of using "false data" in a scientific presentation. His outspokenness generated a "firestorm" on campus that nearly resulted in his dismissal from school.

But Rothenberg had done nothing even remotely similar to what Nolan was describing; he had merely written a personal e-mail to his mentor about what he felt was an inappropriate use of students' data. Rothenberg interpreted Nolan's story as a warning not to speak out.

———————

David Zapol said his faith in his mentor was badly broken after this incident. As a young scientist, he knew his academic career hinged on having an adviser who could provide strong personal and intellectual guidance. Nolan seemed unable to provide either. According to Zapol, Nolan was often absent from the lab, tending to his own business, and had started to miss scheduled meetings to discuss Zapol's research. What's more, whenever Zapol tried to voice his discomfort concerning the ever-blurring boundaries between Nolan's academic and commercial pursuits, he found his adviser's responses both evasive and disapproving.

Less than a month earlier, in June 1997, Nolan and his students had met with Richard Popp and Craig Heller, two of Stanford's top medical school deans, to discuss the Rigel partnership. Zapol came away from that meeting convinced that neither Nolan nor Stanford was truly committed to preserving an independent academic research sphere. The deans explained that they had already signed off on an intellectual property agreement that allowed "know-how," related to the licensed technology, to flow freely from the lab to Rigel for a limited period of time (a fact that both Nolan and Dean Popp confirmed for me).[61] Zapol also understood that the school had equity and other direct financial interests in Nolan's company, making it far from a neutral player. At first, Zapol told me, he tried to speak up and ask questions of the deans concerning the lab's relationship to the firm, but his voice soon fell silent when he realized that virtually no one else from Nolan's lab was talking. "It suddenly dawned on me," he said, "that certain lab members had been offered positions as consultants in the company, so they had no incentive to blow the whistle." According to Zapol, after the meeting, Nolan yelled at him for being so outspoken and said that if he wasn't able to look on the bright side and only saw the negative in things, he should consider leaving the lab. Rothenberg, who was present during this encounter, told me he was upset by Nolan's reaction and his evident anger. The expressed purpose of that meeting was to permit the students to air their concerns about what the deans themselves acknowledged was a unique situation. Now, one of those students seemed to be in trouble for doing just that.

Later that summer, after the data incident, Zapol gave notice to Nolan that he was leaving the lab, and he embarked on a year-long leave of absence from school.

——————

Rothenberg, for his part, chose to remain in Nolan's lab a while longer. However, in April 1998, roughly nine months after Zapol's departure, he, too, picked up and left the lab prior to completing his Ph.D. He transferred to the lab of another well-known Stanford professor, defended his thesis on an entirely new subject, and graduated with an M.D.-Ph.D. in cancer biology in 2002. Given how unusual it is for two highly talented graduate students to leave their mentor's lab midstream, I pressed Rothenberg to tell me more about why he had left.

The root of the conflict, once again, stemmed from the failure to draw any clear distinctions between Nolan's academic research and his business pursuits. Initially, Rothenberg had trusted Nolan when he suggested that licensing their research to Rigel would be a win-win situation for everyone. Rigel managed to raise an initial $6 million on the basis of the technology—a portion of which went to help finance Nolan's academic lab.[62] Rothenberg believed that transferring academic knowledge to industry was extremely important, enabling scientific discoveries to have a direct bearing on public health. But he soon came to believe that in this case, the transfer was premature. "Our research was still unproven. We hadn't published anything on it yet," he told me. "If the technology had already been shown to work, perhaps it could have been used by Rigel and by our lab for different purposes. But it was not fully developed. . . . Once Rigel's scientists possessed my methods and reagents, we were starting at the same point and working independently toward the exact same goal. Except that they had the advantages of significantly more manpower and funding."[63]

In other words, Rothenberg suddenly discovered, much to his dismay, that he was in direct competition with his mentor's company. What would happen if Rigel's scientists completed the proof of concept before he did, and he was beaten out of an academic publication despite his years of hard work on the original research? How would he complete his Ph.D.? After much effort, Rothenberg succeeded in getting a provision added to the consulting agreement Rigel asked him to sign that guaranteed he would be named as an author on the first major publication to stem from Stanford's technology, regardless of where it originated. (Unfortunately, even this guarantee didn't prove very helpful: The only publication Michael Rothenberg's name would appear on was a summary chapter he authored based on a scientific presentation, not the first peer-reviewed article stemming from Stanford's licensed technology.)

But the tensions between Nolan's firm and his lab continued to simmer just beneath the surface. In April 1997, shortly after this contract issue was resolved, Rothenberg received an e-mail from Rigel's Donald Payan warning him to be careful about making contact with Professor Kit S. Lam, an expert on peptides. "Garry forwarded to me communication between yourself and Kitt [sic] at University of Arizona. You should know that he is one of the founders of Selectide a major competitor of ours . . . !" wrote Payan. "The guys here will be less than pleased if ideas that they give you re. structures etc . . . end up in the hands of Selectide. Get my drift?"[64]

Rothenberg's correspondence with Lam had begun before Rigel's inception, and he was shocked by this apparent effort to restrict his collaboration with another university scientist. Once again, however, Nolan's response to the incident was decidedly ambiguous. "I will talk to Don," he wrote in a May 4, 1997, e-mail to Rothenberg. "He is treating you as a member of the team but forgets the boundaries I think about what he can ask for." However, in the same e-mail, Nolan urged Rothenberg to discontinue any further communication with Lam until he (Nolan) could look into the matter further.[65] Not wanting to cause problems, Rothenberg said he cut off the collaboration.

Summing up his reasons for leaving Nolan's lab, Rothenberg explained, "All of this was new to me. I had no previous experience navigating academic-industrial relationships, and I needed help. When I had a concern, I went to Garry. I thought he would agree that the actions and behavior of the people at the company were inappropriate. However, he seemed more worried about how my concerns would be perceived by others than about dealing effectively with their cause. As far as I could tell, nobody but Garry was actually monitoring the lab's interaction with the company."[66]

In June 1998, David Zapol returned to Stanford in the hopes of finding a new academic lab to join where he could complete his Ph.D. He met with David Botstein, a renowned biochemist at Stanford. As soon as Botstein heard Zapol's reasons for leaving Nolan's lab, he immediately called Phyllis Gardner, then Stanford's senior associate dean of education. Unfortunately, as luck would have it, this move proved disastrous.

Zapol had been told the meeting with Gardner would be confidential, but when he walked into her office, he was shocked to find that Nolan had been invited to attend. Because the power relationships were so clearly unbalanced, Zapol tried to speak as little as possible, petrified that he might damage his academic prospects forever. In an e-mail to Botstein, sent the next day, he briefly recounted the outcome of the meeting. After Nolan left the room, he wrote, Gardner "told me that unless I have 'hard data' she cannot pursue Garry. But I was under the impression that I only was being asked to provide information for someone else's investigation, not to initiate the demise of my former advisor."[67] (Botstein, now at Princeton, declined to speak on the record about the Zapol case.)

In response to my written questions, Gardner said she had invited Nolan to attend this meeting because she happened to run into him in the hallway. With hindsight, she admitted it was probably a "mistake." Gardner also suggested that Stanford had thoroughly investigated Zapol's allegations and found them without merit. "I was told by Dean Popp," she wrote, "that appropriate COI [conflict-of-interest] review had taken place, with input from multiple students, on two separate occasions without a finding of impropriety." However, in a separate interview, Dean Popp told me that to his knowledge there had been no independent investigation of the Zapol case. Dean Gardner also posited that the real reason Zapol was disgruntled was because he hadn't acquired any intellectual property rights to Nolan's research (a view also echoed by Nolan).[68] But this explanation seems implausible, given that all the research Zapol worked on had already been patented and licensed to Rigel well before Zapol ever joined the lab. Rothenberg also told me he had no recollection of Zapol's expressing any interest in acquiring intellectual property rights.[69]

Soon after the Gardner meeting, David Zapol decided to abandon his Ph.D. and give up his dream of becoming a scientist. His father and mother were crushed.

Though the Zapols felt powerless to change the situation at Stanford, the moment they learned in early 1999 that a group of powerful faculty at the Harvard Medical School were pushing to loosen restrictions on stock ownership and other forms of corporate compensation, they were determined to speak out. Firmly opposed to such a move, Warren Zapol wrote an impassioned letter to Harvard's conflict-of-interest committee: "I feel compelled to relay to you that I have had a recent personal experience which I believe illustrates the inevitable temptations and resulting complications that result from having graduate students working under a mentor with an equity stake in a start-up company."

After briefly laying out the details of his son's case, he confessed that he found Stanford's refusal to properly investigate David's allegations suspicious: "I could only believe that the potential of another Cohen-Boyer windfall [a reference to Stanford's lucrative genetics patent] had so completely poisoned the atmosphere at Stanford that the institution itself was incapable of objectivity in this situation." As a parent, he said, "I am extremely disappointed to see a budding young scientist crushed by the greed of his mentor and institution."[70]

Warren Zapol couldn't prove that Stanford's negligence had been financially motivated, but he certainly wasn't wrong to suspect that financial conflicts might have played a role. When Rigel was founded, both Stanford and Nolan took substantial equity in the company. In 2000–2001, the university sold its shares for over $900,000.[71] Patent records from 2004 also reveal that Stanford owns at least six of Nolan's patents. One of these is listed among twenty-one Stanford inventions that have generated a cumulative royalty income for the school of *"between one and five million dollars each."*[72] If any of Rigel's inventions become successful drugs, Stanford also stands to earn substantial royalty income. In early 2004, Rigel had two potential drugs in clinical trials—one for asthma and allergies, another designed to attack the hepatitis C virus.

In the end, Harvard's committee decided *not* to weaken the school's conflict-of-interest standards, mostly because, in the middle of its deliberations, news broke out that a young boy had died in a gene therapy experiment at the University of Pennsylvania (where, as we'll soon see, both the university and the lead investigator had a direct financial interest in the product being tested). But Warren Zapol's letter did have an impact. After the committee disbanded, Harvard adopted new guidelines designed to better protect students whenever they are assigned to work on research in which their mentor has a financial interest.[73] The Zapols hope that similar guidelines will be adopted by other universities, where student protections remain weak—or nonexistent.

Friction between students and faculty over intellectual property and the ownership of ideas is not a new problem, though it continues to be largely overlooked. In 1981, shortly after Bayh-Dole passed, controversy arose at the University of California at Davis (U.C. Davis) after evidence surfaced that Ray Valentine, a professor in the College of Agricultural and Environmental Sciences, had interlocking ties to various agricultural firms.[74] Just days after U.C. Davis signed a $2.3-million contract with Allied Chemical to provide research support to Valentine and four other professors—in exchange for exclusive rights to any resulting inventions—it emerged that Allied had also paid $2.1 million for a 20 percent stake in Calgene, Inc., a small biotech firm cofounded by Valentine. Eventually, Valentine was forced to sever his ties to Allied. But in the spring of 1982, new details surfaced regarding Valentine's treatment of his students. A memo from JaRue Manning, a graduate adviser, revealed that four of five graduate students working under Valentine had elected to transfer out of his lab after he told them they would have to clear their research projects with Calgene. As one postdoc put it, "Calgene gets first crack at all our ideas." Students were even told to switch their thesis topics or their funding would be cut off, even though some had already spent more than two years on their thesis work.[75]

More recently, the computer science field has become wracked with commercial conflicts. In June 1999, John Guttag, the head of the electrical engineering and computer science department at MIT, became so concerned about the growing migration of students into professors' start-up companies that he wrote the faculty a letter: "My perception is that an increasing number of our students are being hired to work at companies in which MIT faculty members play a significant role." He noted that bringing students into these ventures in the middle of their training raised "some serious issues with respect to potential conflicts of interest, and has already put some of our students in difficult situations." Difficult, indeed: In one case, reported in the *Wall Street Journal*, William Koffel, a junior at MIT, refused to hand in a homework assignment to M. Frans Kaashoek, his professor, because he feared doing so might violate his employment agreement with an outside company, Akamai Technologies, Inc., cofounded by another MIT professor. Koffel explained that because his work for Akamai overlapped with his homework assignment, he was bound by a nondisclosure agreement (NDA). Three other students in

Kaashoek's class subsequently announced they were in the same predicament. "I felt the students were getting a bad deal," said Kaashoek. "The students should be able to do any assignment at MIT. I'm not going to let it happen again. It's ridiculous that an NDA is going to set the content of my course." The dispute didn't end there. F. Thomas Leighton, the professor who had founded Akamai, told the *Journal* that he suspected the reason Kaashoek—who operates his own company—had assigned that particular homework was to learn more about Akamai's progress, as the two companies were potential competitors.[76] A little more than a year later, similar problems surfaced at MIT's famous Media Laboratory, a center for innovative research that receives 90 percent of its funding from industry.[77]

As a rule, students are reluctant to speak out publicly when they are having problems with their mentors. However, the growing number of lawsuits that students now file against their mentors suggests that this may be changing. Joany Chou, a molecular geneticist at the University of Chicago, for example, fought a pitched legal battle against her former mentor, Bernard Roizman, alleging that he had gone behind her back and filed a patent on a new gene she had discovered related to the herpes virus, without listing her as a coinventor. The university's patent office then licensed the discovery to Roizman's own start-up company.

Chou first tried to appeal to the university, insisting that the discovery was the culmination of her fourteen years of research as a graduate student and postdoc in Roizman's lab. But she was rebuffed. Later, when she took her case to court, a federal judge in northern Illinois ruled that Chou had no "legal standing" to bring a lawsuit because as an employee of the university, her work was university property. In July 2001, however, the U.S. Appeals Court for the Federal Circuit in Washington, D.C., unanimously reversed the lower court's decision, permitting Chou's case to go forward.[78] In its ruling, the court stated that professor Roizman had a fiduciary duty to care for his pupil—a duty that prevented him from "seeking any selfish benefit for himself at the expense of [Chou]."[79]

Some professor CEOs readily acknowledge that juggling business and education is not easy. At the 2001 annual meeting of the Midwestern Association of Graduate Schools, both the entrepreneurial professors who were featured speakers admitted to experiencing difficulties on this score. "Now here's the punch line," said Garland Marshall, a professor of molecular biology and pharmacology at Washington University and the founder of two companies. "There's no way to avoid conflict; there is no way to serve two masters. You can be the best-intentioned person in the world, but there is going to be a conflict." The previous year, Marshall explained, he suddenly realized that a problem he had assigned to a postdoc was one his own company had already solved. Because of confidentiality restrictions, however, he was obligated to remain silent. "I knew the solution. I knew exactly how to solve that problem but I couldn't tell him," he told the audience. "It's not a good situation to be in."

Marshall said he had been on partial leave from the university for the past five years because of his demanding business activities. "It is not a question of where your body is—it is a question of where your mind is," he said. "If you are worried about where you are going to get that next billion dollars, that's not worrying about how your graduate student is doing."

William Wold, the chair of the molecular microbiology and immunology department at St. Louis University Medical School, echoed this sentiment. Wold introduced himself as the president and CEO of a small start-up, Virex, which is trying to develop new genetic treatments for cancer. The company, he noted, was being run out of his own academic lab on campus. "When I started this whole business, I was an academic scientist and I was really motivated by the idea of bringing biotech industry money into the department," he explained. "I thought that I could handle both being a scientist and the president of a small company, that there really wouldn't be a conflict of interest. But, of course, that was wishful thinking. It turns out that my activities with Virex *do* interfere with my duties as chair [of the department] and as a scientist mentoring students."

He continued, "I'm sure that every one of you is thinking 'Is this really a proper thing to do?' I don't know. . . . I rationalize this by thinking that in the long run this is going to be good for everybody because our goal is to develop an anticancer drug. So I try not to worry about the conflicts of interest."

During the question period, I asked Wold how he planned to handle intellectual property in cases where graduate students and postdocs were assigned to work on company-related research. "We really don't have any rules at our university to deal with that," he admitted.[80]

The Fox Guarding the Hen House

Breaches of academic freedom and conflicts of interest as disturbing as the ones I've described occurring recently at U.C. Berkeley, Brown, Stanford, and numerous other schools are not new—and neither are these universities' inadequate and often badly compromised attempts to address them. The truth is, concerns about the corrupting influence of money in academe—and failed efforts to deal with the problem—are nearly as old as the Bayh-Dole Act itself.

The most obvious way for universities to rein in their burgeoning commercial conflicts would be for them to adopt stringent conflict-of-interest regulations and disclosure rules designed to curb the potential for abuse. However, since the early 1980s, when Congress began pressing for improved regulation, these universities have vigorously opposed efforts to impose tighter conflict-of-interest restrictions on professors who receive federal research grants. The university leadership has always maintained that any effort to impose regulation from the outside would violate academic autonomy. However, its own efforts at self-regulation have been distinctly unimpressive.

In the spring of 1982, for example, five prominent university presidents, from MIT, Harvard, Caltech, Stanford, and the U.C. system, along with six heads of industry, met in seclusion at the Pajaro Dunes resort on the California coast to see if they could hash out a new set of common principles to guide their growing research collaborations.[81] Two years had lapsed since the passage of Bayh-Dole, and serious conflict-of-interest scandals were already surfacing and attracting unwanted publicity. The whole imbroglio at U.C. Irvine with Ray Valentine and his students was just one of many such cases then coming to light. In Washington, Al Gore, then a junior congressional member from Tennessee, chaired hearings to investigate a $50-million contract between Harvard's Massachusetts General Hospital and Hoechst, the German chemical company, the details of which Harvard had been trying to keep confidential. Gore noted that the ostensible purpose of Bayh-Dole was to stimulate U.S. economic competitiveness. "Now, isn't it a little unfair to the American taxpayers," said Gore, after a twenty-year-long investment in federal research support, ". . . to give the cream of the results to a foreign company that gets exclusive rights?"[82] Those participating in the Pajaro Dunes conference feared that unless they quickly adopted their own conflict-of-interest guidelines, regulations would be imposed from outside. Yet, in the end, they achieved remarkably little. The conference's final statement on managing conflicts of interest was widely criticized for its vagueness. "Although we see no single 'right' policy," the statement read, "we do believe that each university should address the problem vigorously."[83]

After this failed attempt at reform, serious commercial conflicts continued to surface at Harvard and at several other prominent research institutions.[84] In 1988 and 1989, Representative Ted Weiss (Democrat of New York) held two explosive hearings to investigate scientific misconduct in the nonprofit research sector.[85] Afterward, Congress began pressing the National Institutes of Health (NIH) to adopt more stringent conflict-of-interest rules to better safeguard the integrity of taxpayer-financed research. In the fall of 1989, responding to this request, the Department of Health and Human Services (HHS), of which the NIH is a part, proposed new conflict-of-interest guidelines and opened them up for public comment. The guidelines called on the nation's universities to better manage their conflicts of interest by requiring professors who receive federal funding to disclose *all* of their financial interests, and to divest themselves of any stock they might own in companies that would stand to profit from the outcome of their work.[86] Less than four months later, however, the guidelines had been quashed.

HHS secretary Louis W. Sullivan capitulated to intense pressure from universities and the biomedical industry, noting that it is "important that we not impose on our scientific community regulatory burdens which may be unnecessary or counterproductive."[87] HHS was inundated with more than seven hundred letters, most of them highly critical, like this one from Karl J. Hittelman, associate vice chancellor at the University of California at San Francisco: "Not the least of our objections is the insidious assumption that . . . the university biomedical community is motivated primarily by venality and is incapable of effective self-regulation. This arrogation of guilt has generated a policy that is unnecessarily intrusive, restrictive, and administratively burdensome." Nearly all of the nation's top universities wrote letters rejecting the government's proposed rules, saying that universities should be left to address the conflict-of-interest problem themselves.[88]

After HHS backed down, nothing happened for another six years. Then in 1995, the federal government finally succeeded in pushing through new conflict-of-interest rules, which would apply to all academic researchers funded by HHS or the National Science Foundation. But the rules, which remain in place today, were far weaker.[89]

Essentially, the current rules require professors who receive grants from HHS or NSF to disclose their financial holdings to their university employers. These holdings include any salary, consulting fees, honoraria, stock holdings, or intellectual property rights valued at $10,000 or more per year from a for-profit entity, as well as any ownership interests of more than 5 percent in such entities. The institution, in turn, is required to notify the federal funding agency of any financial conflicts it deems relevant to the project.

But the HHS/NSF policy has glaring holes. Although it mandates that serious conflicts of interest must be managed and/or eliminated, it leaves the determination of what action is to be taken, if any, entirely up to the university. The policy also doesn't provide any guidance on which conflicts warrant serious attention, nor does it impose any prohibitions, such as banning financial conflicts outright in the area of human subject research. Significantly, the policy also says nothing about *institutional conflicts of interest*.

The result, not surprisingly, is that university conflict-of-interest rules vary widely. One comprehensive survey of the written policies at one hundred academic institutions found that only 55 percent of schools required disclosure of conflicts of interest from *all* faculty, and only 19 percent specified *any limits* on researchers' financial ties (such as equity) to corporate sponsors.[90] Worse yet, under this fragmented system, there is enormous pressure on universities to keep their policies lax. Schools with tighter restrictions run the risk of losing talented faculty to competing schools with more permissive policies, where the financial rewards and commercial prospects are likely to be greater. Those who doubt that the current system encourages weak conflict-of-interest regulations need only look at Harvard. When Harvard considered relaxing its conflict-of-interest rules in 1999–2000, one of the principal reasons it cited was the need to recruit and retain talented faculty.[91] Obviously, if Harvard, an Ivy League institution, expressed this concern, one can only imagine the pressures felt by the University of Nebraska and Ohio State University to keep their policies more lenient.

Another conspicuous problem with the HHS/NSF policy is that it does not require universities to make any of the information they compile on their faculty's financial conflicts available to the public. Many academic journals now require their authors to disclose corporate financial ties. But in practice, reporting is astonishingly poor. In a 2001 study, Sheldon Krimsky, a professor of public policy at Tufts University and an expert on conflicts of interest, found that a mere *0.5 percent* of the 61,134 papers appearing in 181 peer-reviewed journals contained statements about the authors' financial ties. More recent studies have found similarly low levels of reporting.[92]

Some argue that this is as it should be. Kenneth Rothman, an epidemiologist at the Harvard School of Public Health and a former editor of the journal *Epidemiology*, likened mandatory reporting of financial ties to a form of academic "McCarthyism," as any such link has an inherently "pejorative connotation." According to Rothman, "policies of mandatory disclosure thwart the principle that a work should be judged solely on its merits. Although intended to raise scientific discourse to a higher standard of ethics, these new disclosure policies themselves contribute to new ethics problems, by abridging the right of honest scientists to an impartial hearing of their work."[93]

However, many ethicists challenge Rothman's logic. Dennis F. Thompson, the founding director of Harvard's Center for Ethics and Professions, wrote that financial disclosure rules, far from being prejudicial, function to ensure that the public will not lose trust in the scholarly enterprise as a whole. Thompson noted:

> The rules do not assume that most physicians or researchers let financial gain influence their judgment. They assume only that it is often difficult if not impossible to distinguish cases in which financial gain does have an improper influence from those in which it does not. . . . Given this general difficulty of discovering real motives, it is safer and therefore ethically more responsible to decide in advance to remove insofar as possible factors that tend to distract us from concentrating on medical and scholarly goals.[94]

In some respects, the whole debate reflects how far the academic world remains from dealing seriously with the issue: *Disclosure* of potential conflicts of interest is, after all, a far cry from eliminating them outright, as many professions not only recommend but require. In the legal profession, for example, attorneys are prohibited from taking on cases in which they have a financial interest or other explicit conflicts that might be seen to compromise their professional integrity. The same is true of judges.

Perhaps none of this hand-wringing should surprise us, however. Efforts at reform have proceeded under the assumption that universities can be trusted to manage these commercial interactions themselves. It's a nice idea. But are academic institutions really capable of performing this function? There is good reason to be skeptical, for the Bayh-Dole Act not only encouraged private investment in academic research but also profoundly changed the motivations and the culture of the university itself. Far from being independent watchdogs capable of dispassionate inquiry, universities are increasingly joined at the hip to the very market forces the public has entrusted them to check, creating problems that extend far beyond the research lab.

5

Are Conflicts of Interest
Hazardous to Our Health?

James Kahn is, in many respects, an unlikely symbol of the growing clashes between academia and industry. A professor of medicine at the University of California at San Francisco (UCSF), Kahn always valued collaborations with the private sector. Like other clinical investigators, he viewed the interests of academia and industry as complementary, not adversarial. After all, new medical breakthroughs are beneficial to patients only if they can be developed into safe and marketable drugs or devices; this kind of development makes effective collaboration a necessity. Like most of his colleagues, Kahn depended on a combination of government and industry grants to fund his research. But in 1999, Kahn's long-cherished academic values collided with a corporate sponsor committed to little more than its own bottom line.

Kahn was the lead investigator on a massive clinical-drug trial funded by the Immune Response Corporation (IRC) of Carlsbad, California, which involved 2,527 patients at seventy-seven medical centers. The purpose of the trial, launched in 1996, was to test the company's AIDS drug, Remune, to see if it enhanced survival rates or slowed down progression of the disease. The drug was an experimental vaccine—an inactivated form of the HIV virus—developed by the late Jonas Salk, inventor of the polio vaccine. (Although Salk had famously declined to patent his polio vaccine, later on, in the new, more commercial atmosphere that followed Bayh-Dole, he became a co-founder of IRC.) Remune was designed to boost the patient's immune system and assist other drugs in combating the virus. Agouron, a unit of Pfizer, Inc., had already licensed the U.S. rights and was eagerly awaiting the study's results. But when the trial was terminated, Kahn and his colleagues found that the drug was, in fact, no more effective than a placebo, or sugar pill. It simply didn't work.

Kahn and another doctor, Steven Lagakos, a prominent biostatistician at Harvard, were eager to make their findings public. But IRC, which had sizable profits riding on the study, immediately contested their interpretation of the data. And on September 1, 2000, IRC slapped both Kahn and the university with a legal suit, demanding $7 million to $10 million in compensatory damages for harming its business.[1]

Five months after the IRC suit was filed, I traveled to San Francisco General Hospital to interview James Kahn. Arriving at his office in the early morning, I learned that Kahn had unexpectedly been called to duty at the hospital. Like many professors of medicine, Kahn not only performs research and teaches but is also a practicing physician in a busy urban hospital. His secretary apologized for any inconvenience, but the change actually afforded a rare glimpse into Kahn's life, far removed from the litigation and media attention that now surrounded him.

The secretary escorted me to the AIDS clinic, known as the Positive Health Program, where Dr. Kahn had been called in early that morning. San Francisco General, one of UCSF's principal teaching hospitals, is a sprawling medical facility located in the heart of the city. Like most public hospitals, San Francisco General will admit any patient who needs to be seen. Some have insurance, many do not. Evidence of disrepair and financial strain are visible everywhere, yet the facility continues to employ some of the best academics in their fields, who, like Kahn, are on the cutting edge of medical research. The AIDS clinic serves an estimated thirty-five hundred patients annually, and is housed in an older building set apart from the main hospital complex. To get there, we traveled up a dingy, claustrophobic elevator to the sixth floor, where the halls were painted bright saffron yellow. Near the elevator bank a bald man with a crimson face rocked back and forth uncontrollably as if mentally agitated, or in extreme pain. Farther down the hall, a woman, rail thin, wandered aimlessly in a circular pattern, while nurses hurried by.

"This is life in a city hospital!" said Dr. Kahn in a spirited voice as he greeted us by the entrance of a small room reserved for the hospital staff. "I'm afraid we're stretched so thin that when someone is out, we have to pull resources from wherever we can."[2]

An amiable man in his late thirties with dark hair and soft brown eyes, Kahn projects both personal warmth and authority. His fleshy round face was tanned and he wore a white lab coat, as well as a pressed shirt, tie, dark slacks, and loafers. Kahn was juggling a variety of urgent health needs on the hospital floor that morning, but he seemed exceptionally calm.

The room we met in was white, clean, and cramped. A large box of doughnuts lay open on the counter, sugary fuel to keep the staff going through their long hours. Before beginning the interview, Kahn conferred with a third-year medical student he was supervising. Together, they reviewed the medical care of each patient on the floor. Some patients were clearly dying, as the virus had not been caught soon enough for them to benefit from the latest drug cocktails. Others were suffering the side effects associated with those drugs, compounded by years of poor health. Periodically, an inquiring nurse or another resident on the floor came in to ask something. Kahn responded to each interruption with the same good-natured calm. "Do you feel OK with everything?" he asked his student when they had finished. "You don't feel overwhelmed? Come to me if you have any questions." Rolling a chair over to where I was seated, Kahn jumped right into discussing his recent confrontation with IRC.

Initially, he explained, the company had been enthusiastic about having independent academics associated with the study. "It gave everybody confidence that people with nothing to gain financially would be involved with the study and accurately evaluate it," he said. While Kahn served as the study's primary investigator, IRC paid 35 percent of his academic salary, but he and his colleagues were careful not to accept any other outside compensation, such as honoraria, consulting fees, or equity: "We didn't want even the faintest hint of impropriety to cast doubt on our decisions and our actions."

In the beginning, Kahn noted, the research team had had "complete autonomy." He and Lagakos designed the study themselves, without any corporate interference. As is increasingly common in a trial of this magnitude, they also persuaded the company to hire an independent data safety monitoring board (DSMB)—a group of experts who can monitor each of the experimental treatment groups during the study. If it should become clear that one set of patients was disadvantaged or suffering serious adverse effects, the DSMB could step in and stop the trial—which is precisely what happened in the case of Kahn's study.

Three years into the Remune trial, the DSMB determined that IRC's drug was ineffective, and that patients would be better off taking other treatments. As a publicly traded company, IRC was obligated to report this decision to the SEC and to its own investors. According to Kahn, this was when trouble began. "The company wrote in its press release that although the trial was being canceled, a subset of the data showed positive results," he explained, choosing his words with evident care. "We didn't see that and felt that it shouldn't be stated in that way." In reality, Kahn said, the company was "data dredging," because the subset of data they now wanted to include was not part of the original, approved trial protocol. Kahn and his colleagues insisted on removing their names and any references to themselves from the document.

A patient with a gaunt face and bright blue hair wandered into the staff-only area where we were talking. Kahn briskly stood up and took a few moments to speak to him, then resumed our conversation.

"We had anticipated receiving the final data set for analysis in December of 1999," Kahn recalled. "But our attempts to get this set were met with considerable resistance from the sponsor." Kahn and his fellow researchers already had what he estimated was approximately 95 percent of the complete trial data—data that were virtually identical to what the DSMB had used as the basis for shutting down the trial. But as the primary investigator, Kahn knew he had a right—indeed, an obligation—to see the *complete* trial data. "We tried not to make our requests for data over the telephone," Kahn told me. "We documented everything with e-mails, sending the correspondence around to everyone so everyone could see the effort that we were going through."

The correspondence speaks volumes. On January 17, 2000, IRC informed Kahn that it had "'locked' the final database." "Our plan for the final analysis is to perform the analysis at IRC," the letter stated. Firing back an e-mail the following day, Kahn wrote, "This is completely unacceptable . . . To suggest that analysis and manuscript preparation should be removed from the study team and empowered to IRC is a break in the agreement and faith we shared. . . . I would not have enrolled a single patient with the understanding that the data would not be analyzed with care by an independent group." Lagakos was even more succinct: "It is critical that we receive the complete database, with no modifications to any of the data."

Still the company refused to back down: "We will provide the final database to you provided that . . . no publication or public disclosure . . . may be made without the prior express written consent of the sponsor's medical director (which may be withheld at the sole discretion of the sponsor)."[3]

Unwilling to sign away his academic freedom, Kahn faced a dilemma. Plenty of physicians might have reasoned that it would be better to drop the fight for publication at this stage. After all, the trial had already been safely terminated. Why stir up the waters? Once word got out that Kahn was not a "team player," how many companies would sponsor his research in the future? Where would he obtain the funding he needed for other important research he hoped to pursue?

But Kahn reasoned differently. "Independent university investigators play a very important role in drug and device development," he told me. "Their participation is a key factor in you having confidence that the medicine you put in your body is good for you. It's not a 100 percent guarantee, but the expansion of knowledge—independently performed and scrupulously honest—is the bedrock of why I do what I do."

Kahn was concerned that patients who had enrolled in the trial might not be given accurate information about the results. He knew that other studies had been proposed involving the same drug, and he wanted to be certain his colleagues—as well as future patients—were aware of his findings. "There was a certain amount of feistiness in me," Kahn admitted. "I just felt wronged. I felt that these people were setting a bad example and precedent."

In September 2000, Kahn and his coinvestigators submitted their manuscript along with a complete copy of their e-mail correspondence with IRC to the *Journal of the American Medical Association (JAMA)*. A mere three weeks after the journal announced it would publish the study, IRC filed suit for damages.[4] "I was very worried," Kahn recalled. "You know, I've got a family and kids, and the letter stated I would be held personally liable."

Kahn's employer, UCSF, never wavered in its defense of Kahn. A close look at the contract, however, suggests that UCSF had learned remarkably little about negotiating with industry since its earlier debacle involving Betty Dong (discussed in Chapter 1). On the one hand, the agreement asserted that the "University shall own all Data collected by the Principal Investigator." A little farther down in the same paragraph, however, it stated that the "raw data from the clinical studies" will be treated differently: "The parties acknowledge and agree that [the] *University shall not acquire any ownership interest or use or publication rights in such raw data"* (emphasis added). Apparently, in its eagerness not to alienate a potential corporate funder, the university had accepted language that was extremely unclear concerning publication.[5]

Fortunately, in spite of this weak language, the university proved victorious. On November 1, 2000, Kahn and his coauthors successfully published their findings in *JAMA*, and ten months later an arbitration panel ruled in the university's favor.[6] Catherine DeAngelis, *JAMA*'s editor, commented on the highly unusual circumstances that surrounded their decision to publish: "The data set is incomplete, but the investigators, peer reviewers and editors believe it to be of sufficient merit to warrant the conclusions. Our decision to publish this study is based on the belief that the integrity of the research process must be protected and preserved."[7]

———

Kahn was reluctant to make generalizations about his own experience: He considered his case "quite extreme" and believed it unrepresentative of what most academics who collaborate with industry encounter. Certainly many industry-sponsored trials are well designed, well executed, and correctly analyzed. But was Kahn's experience really such an anomaly?

With the possible exception of business schools, industry's penetration into the nation's medical schools has been more sweeping than in any other sector of the university. Pharmaceutical companies sponsor daily lunches for medical students, during which they market their latest drugs; they ply professors with fancy dinners, gifts, luxurious trips, and free prescriptions designed to influence their medical decisions and prescribing habits. These academic "opinion leaders" consult for, or hold equity in, the same firms that manufacture the drugs they are studying, while also often accepting generous fees to join their corporate advisory boards and speakers' bureaus. Sometimes they even hold the patent to the drug or device being tested. In a study of eight hundred scientific papers published in leading journals of medicine and molecular biology, Sheldon Krimsky, a professor of public policy at Tufts University, found that slightly more than *a third* of the lead authors based at research institutions in Massachusetts had a significant financial interest in their own reports. These included owning related patents, or holding an executive, advisory, or major equity position in a company with a stake in the research.[8] So pervasive are such ties that journal editors now frequently complain they can no longer find academic experts who do not have a financial interest in a drug or therapy they would like to review.[9]

This may be good news for corporations, but it is anything but good news for ordinary citizens. Indeed, the growing nexus between universities and the pharmaceutical industry could not come at a worse time. The cost of pharmaceutical drugs—and health care in general—in America continues to skyrocket. Expensive new drugs are aggressively marketed on TV and in doctors' offices the moment they hit the market. Yet physicians warn that many of these hyped prescriptions are simply "me-too drugs" that vary only slightly from medications already on the market, despite being far more expensive.[10] As mentioned earlier, research suggests that publicly funded science, most of it performed at universities, was a "critical contributor" to the discovery of *nearly all* of the twenty-five most important breakthrough drugs introduced between 1970 and 1995.[11] If university scientists lose their independence, who will perform this pathbreaking research and objectively evaluate the safety and effectiveness of drugs already on the market?

Unfortunately, it is this scholarly independence that is now in jeopardy. "The boundaries between the academic medical colleges and the drug companies are becoming ever more porous," said Marcia Angell, a senior lecturer at Harvard's School of Public Health and former editor in chief of the *New England Journal of Medicine (NEJM)*. "It used to be that academic medical colleges said, 'OK, we will take this industry grant and do the study, but our researchers are going to retain the data; they are going to analyze the data.' Now this arm's-length relationship has broken down."[12]

Take the issue of who controls the data from a large clinical trial. Although the Kahn case was unusual in reaching litigation, corporate control over trial data is far from uncommon. In the fall of 2001, the editors of twelve prominent medical journals collectively announced that they would refuse to publish research on new prescription drugs unless the authors provided assurances that they had had unimpeded access to the data and were fully responsible for the paper's conclusions. The announcement was an extraordinary admission of just how extensive industry control over medical research had become. The editors noted that more and more, the authors of scientific papers—even authors based at prestigious universities—did not have access to the complete trial data. In some cases, the editors observed, authors were unable to publish without prior authorization from the corporate sponsor.

The journal editors pointed out that publication of clinical studies in respected peer-reviewed journals is the "ultimate basis for most treatment decisions," so it is essential that the data be gathered and presented in "an objective and dispassionate manner." Medicine is only as good as the science on which it is based, and if that science is not objective and honest, then patients can be seriously harmed. The editors noted "that the current intellectual environment . . . may threaten this precious objectivity." Until recently, university medical centers contributed to the "quality, intellectual rigor, and impact of such clinical trials," they explained, "but as economic pressures mount, this may be a thing of the past."[13]

Indeed, there are strong indications that university-based medicine is losing its hallowed objectivity. After conducting an extensive review of the medical literature for an article in the *NEJM*, Thomas Bodenheimer, an internist at UCSF, found that academic investigators were rapidly ceding to industry the control over nearly every stage of the clinical research process.[14]

In the past, for example, it was common for university scientists to initiate the research protocol. Now, however, studies are frequently conceived and designed in the company's own pharmacological and marketing departments, thus removing this formative stage of the research from academic hands almost entirely. The company then shops the study around to various academic institutions (and a growing number of competing for-profit entities as well), in search of investigators to conduct the research. Although most companies would still prefer to sign up a prominent academic who can lend the study credibility and prestige, these scientists have far less influence than they used to. As university medical schools have grown more dependent on industry grants to sustain their operations (and more commercial themselves), their professors have become increasingly more willing to accept an industry-initiated protocol as is, without modification, even though the study may be largely designed to secure a company's market position. Should a professor choose to reject the study or insist on changes not agreeable to the sponsor, another university scientist will very likely be more solicitous. In this way, industry is slowly changing the direction of academic research, causing it to be far more market-driven and less directed toward truly important science.[15]

Not surprisingly, wrote Bodenheimer, exercising control over trial design makes it far easier for companies to build biases into their research—some easier and some harder to detect. One analysis by Paula Rochon, published in the *Archives of Internal Medicine*, found that in 54 percent of corporate-sponsored arthritis drug trials, the dose of the funding company's drug was higher than that of the comparison drug, so that the results were clearly skewed in the sponsor's favor.[16]

Another disturbing trend in university medicine today is the growing use of ghostwriters and "guest writers." Readers may see a prominent academic's name at the top of a research article or review, but that scholar may or may not be the person who actually wrote the paper. Frequently, a big-name professor or department chair is invited to appear as a "guest author," even though she or he had no involvement in the research. Or in the case of company-initiated studies and reviews, the manuscript may have been ghostwritten by a medical communications company working for the drug maker, and its author may have been paid an honorarium to attach his or her name to it. The average reader thus *thinks* the study bears the stamp of approval of an independent academic scholar, when in fact this is nothing more than an illusion. *The Lancet* commented on this alarming phenomenon in an editorial, noting with some bitterness that "the pinnacle of success, presumably, is to sign up a prominent academic" to lend an aura of objectivity and prestige to the company's research.[17]

One dramatic case of pseudoauthorship came to light when Wyeth-Ayerst sought to boost market demand for Redux, one part of the then highly popular "fen-phen" diet drug combination. Wyeth's marketing plan centered on the placement of nine articles in medical journals touting the benefits of Redux for its use as a diet drug. It hired a company called Excerpta Medica to help draft the manuscripts and pay doctors to review and sign the articles. If this company successfully placed an article in a journal, there would be no mention of Wyeth whatsoever. But Excerpta maintains that all its authors were told of the company's association with the manufacturer. One of the many doctors who signed Excerpta's papers was Richard Atkinson, a renowned obesity expert at the University of Wisconsin at Madison.[18] Atkinson denied having any knowledge of Excerpta's connection to Wyeth, but as an independent academic he nonetheless agreed to lend his name to a company he apparently knew little about. In a deposition on January 15, 1999, Wyeth-Ayerst executive Jo Alene Dolan admitted that her company had written the article for Atkinson, stressing that all drug companies ghostwrite articles. Shortly before the article could be published, Redux was pulled from the market because of its association with serious heart and lung problems.[19]

Troyen Brennan, a professor at Harvard's School of Public Health, is another physician who was contacted by a ghostwriting firm, Edelman Medical Communications. The company's pitch shocked him. "The caller said that I would not really have to do much work on this project," recalled Troyen. "I would discuss the matter with them, and they would then have a professional writer compose the editorial, which I could modify as I saw fit. I would earn $2,500 for what was estimated to be several hours of work."[20] The practice of ghostwriting has become extremely prevalent, raising troubling questions about the trustworthiness of the science appearing in even the most prestigious medical journals.[21] As Richard Horton, the editor of *The Lancet*, caustically observed in 2004, "Journals have devolved into information-laundering operations for the pharmaceutical industry."[22]

Regulating access to the raw data from a large, multisite trial, as occurred in the Kahn case, is yet another tactic the drug industry commonly deploys to skew medical research in its favor. Sometimes the principal investigators are given unimpeded access, but increasingly companies prefer to control the data themselves. Frequently, explained Bodenheimer, studies are designed with multiple end points (or measurable outcomes), so that it is relatively easy for the company to "publish those end points favorable to their product and bury data on less favorable end points."[23]

Recently, M. Michael Wolfe, a gastroenterologist at Boston University, publicly disclosed that Pharmacia Corporation, the manufacturer of the blockbuster arthritis drug Celebrex, had duped him in precisely this manner. In the summer of 2000, the *Journal of the American Medical Association (JAMA)* asked Wolfe to write a review of a Celebrex study showing that the drug was associated with lower rates of stomach and intestinal ulcers and other complications than two older arthritis medications (diclofenac and ibuprofen). Wolfe found the study, tracking eight thousand patients over a six-month period, persuasive and penned a favorable review, which helped to drive up Celebrex sales. But early the next year, when he had occasion to review the same study again—this time while serving on the Food and Drug Administration's arthritis advisory committee—Wolfe was flabbergasted by what he saw. Pharmacia's study had run for one year, not six months, as both Wolfe and *JAMA* had been led to believe. When the complete data set was considered, most of Celebrex's advantages disappeared because the ulcer complications that occurred during the second half of the study were disproportionately found in patients taking Celebrex. "I am furious . . . I wrote the editorial," Wolfe told the *Washington Post*. "I looked like a fool. But . . . all I had available to me was the data presented in the article." None of the original study's sixteen authors, *including eight university professors*, had spoken out publicly about the suppression of data. All the authors were either employees of Pharmacia or paid consultants of the company.[24]

Industry also manipulates academic research by suppressing negative studies altogether. Consider the recent medical scandal surrounding the class of antidepressants known as selective serotonin reuptake inhibitors (SSRIs), which have been linked to an increased risk of suicidal thinking and behavior in young people.[25] Throughout the latter half of the 1990s, the number of young Americans being given Prozac, Paxil, Zoloft, and other antidepressants skyrocketed. By 2002, roughly 11 million prescriptions had been handed out. Boys under the age of twelve diagnosed with "conduct disorders" were the fastest-growing group.[26] The bulk of the published academic literature strongly supported treating depressed children and adolescents with SSRIs. As it turns out, however, this recommendation was at odds with what the complete research record showed.[27] In early 2004, an FDA scientist reviewed all fifteen pediatric SSRI studies in the agency's files, including many that had never been published. In all but three of those studies, young patients suffering from depression experienced no greater improvement taking an SSRI than they did with a placebo, or sugar pill.[28] Given that university scientists were involved in a large portion of this research and duty-bound to publish, how did so much of this negative evidence drop from public view?

In June 2004, this question made its way into the headlines when New York attorney general Eliot Spitzer filed suit against GlaxoSmithKline (GSK), the manufacturer of Paxil, charging that the company had "engaged in repeated and persistent fraud by misrepresenting, concealing and otherwise failing to disclose" information showing that its drug was not only ineffective in treating child and adolescent depression but also linked to an increased risk of suicidal thoughts and self-injurious behavior. GSK had funded five studies on Paxil and childhood depression, only one of which ever got published. Taken together, however, the data clearly showed that those children who took Paxil were approximately *two times more at risk* of becoming suicidal than those taking a placebo.[29] Parents of children who had committed suicide, along with a small minority of psychiatrists, had been suggesting for some time that there appeared to be a link between SSRIs and suicide, but until these revelations, their concerns had been largely discredited.

Unfortunately, GSK wasn't the only company burying research in this way. When Andrew Mosholder, a senior FDA epidemiologist, examined twenty-two pediatric studies, he found that children taking a wide range of antidepressants were also nearly twice as likely as those given a placebo to show signs of becoming suicidal—a finding which his FDA supervisors initially sought to suppress but which was later corroborated by an independent research team at Columbia University.[30] What was perplexing was that *nearly all* of the published literature, authored by many of the leading lights of academic psychiatry, had arrived at the opposite conclusion: SSRIs were safe and effective in treating depression in youngsters.

Or was this *really* what their academic studies showed?

When the FDA and other independent scientists took a closer look, they found a striking discrepancy between what these esteemed academic psychiatrists had written in their papers—and what the data actually revealed. In a surprising number of cases, the benefits of these drugs were overstated, and the problems were downplayed or buried.[31] The only GSK study of Paxil that ever got published, for example, concluded that the data "provides evidence of the safety and efficacy of [Paxil] in the treatment of adolescent depression."[32] (On the basis of this one study, GSK launched a massive promotional campaign telling its sales representatives going out to doctors' offices that Paxil had "REMARKABLE Efficacy and Safety in the treatment of adolescent depression."[33]) But when an FDA examiner studied the data more closely, he found the authors' claims highly exaggerated, as the drug actually failed on the protocol's two primary measured outcomes.[34] The study also concluded that "most adverse events were not serious," when, in fact, seven of the children who took Paxil had to be hospitalized after suffering severe adverse effects from the drug.[35]

Eighteen of the Paxil study's twenty-two authors were university scholars. Its lead author, Martin B. Keller, is a highly acclaimed psychiatrist and chair of the psychiatry department at Brown University, who has extensive ties to the drug industry. In 1998, when the Rhode Island attorney-general's office forced Keller to forfeit hundreds of thousands of dollars in state grant money to settle a financial fraud inquiry, it came to light that Keller had received more than half a million dollars from drug companies that year, most of it from the same firms whose drugs he had touted in journals and at medical conferences. According to the *Boston Globe*, Keller's financial ties were so numerous that they prompted the National Institute of Mental Health to review its conflict-of-interest rules.[36] The most recent publicly available data shows that as of June 2003, Keller had been consulting for at least seventeen major drug firms, including Wyeth-Ayerst, Merck, Bristol-Myers, Eli Lilly, and Pfizer, while also working under a $25-million research grant from Wyeth-Ayerst.[37]

It is impossible to prove a direct causal relationship between Keller's funding sources and the distortions found in his research. But at least three other studies authored by prominent academic psychiatrists on the pediatric use of SSRIs evidenced similar distortions—and all the authors had financial ties to the manufacturers. One of these was a 2003 study published in the *Journal of the American Medical Association* led by Karen Wagner, a renowned psychiatrist and director of the Division of Child and Adolescent Psychiatry at the University of Texas Medical Branch. The study claimed that the antidepressant Zoloft was "effective and well tolerated for children and adolescents." But when the FDA and other outside experts examined the data from the two pooled studies more closely, they again found that the drug had failed to demonstrate positive outcomes.[38] In fact, according to one analysis, when data left out of the published study were included, Zoloft had "an unfavorable risk-benefit balance."[39] In other words, the risks associated with taking the drug were greater than the anticipated benefits. At the time of this study, Wagner reported receiving research money from numerous pharmaceutical companies, consulting for ten drug firms, and participating in speakers' bureaus for Abbott Laboratories, Eli Lilly, GlaxoSmithKline, Forest Laboratories, Pfizer, and Novartis. The study itself had been funded by Pfizer, the maker of Zoloft, and the "study supervisor" held stock options in the company.[40] Finally, the FDA criticized two Prozac studies (1997, 2002) for overstating the drug's efficacy in treating childhood depression.[41] Both studies had been led by Graham Emslie, a professor at the University of Texas Southwestern Medical Center, and financed by Eli Lilly, the maker of Prozac. Emslie receives research support from industry; he also consults and serves on speakers' bureaus of numerous drug companies, including Bristol-Myers, Eli Lilly, and Wyeth-Ayerst.[42]

In December 2003, when this research finally came to light, it prompted a quick response from the British drug authority, which recommended that doctors not prescribe SSRI antidepressant drugs to children under 18, citing a two- to threefold increase in the risk of suicidal behavior, and insufficient evidence of benefit. Nearly one year later, in October 2004, the FDA announced that all such antidepressants must carry a "black box" warning label linking the drugs to an increased risk of suicidal thoughts and behavior in children and teenagers.[43]

———————

If the pharmaceutical industry's ability to influence and distort academic medicine were confined to the field of psychiatry, the implications might be less frightening. But running down the list of drugs recently pulled from the market because of adverse events and deaths or falsely promoted for conditions they didn't actually treat—Rezulin, the diabetes drug; Redux (or fen-phen), the diet drug; Retin-A, the antiwrinkle cream; Neurontin, the epilepsy drug—one finds that a remarkable number of prominent university professors (with close financial ties to the manufacturers) played a central role in lobbying for these drugs to be approved, recommending them to other doctors, and, in many cases, urging that they remain on the market long after problems or lack of effectiveness were known.[44] Not infrequently, the university scientists who shill for the drug companies most aggressively are also the biggest-name professors in their fields, a fact suggesting that academic medicine is becoming tainted to its core.[45]

When Wyeth-Ayerst, for example, was trying to get its diet drug, Redux, approved for sale in the United States, it faced a serious hurdle: Patients in Europe who had taken a drug identical to Redux had an increased chance of getting a rare life-threatening lung ailment known as pulmonary hypertension. To combat this negative health profile, the company packed an FDA hearing room with a who's who list of the nation's top academic obesity experts, including JoAnn Manson of Harvard and Gerald Faich of the University of Pennsylvania—all of whom were paid consultants to Wyeth-Ayerst or other companies involved in the sale of Redux. The company also recruited expert "opinion leaders," such as George Blackburn, a renowned obesity expert at Harvard, to testify before the Medical Society of Massachusetts for approval of the drug. Blackburn and other academic luminaries also joined the company's "Visiting Important Professors Program" and were paid thousands of dollars in honoraria to fly to fancy resorts and promote Redux at medical conferences. Not surprisingly, the drug handily won market approval, and prescriptions in the United States began to soar.[46]

Soon, however, evidence of the drug's association with lung damage surfaced once again, and the company turned to leading university scientists to do damage control. When an international group of scientists published a study in the *New England Journal of Medicine* warning that patients who took Redux (as part of the fen-phen diet drug combination) for longer than three months had a significantly higher risk of developing pulmonary hypertension, an accompanying commentary in the same issue of the journal significantly downplayed the gravity of their findings, suggesting that obesity was a far greater health danger than the risk of lung failure. The authors of this commentary were none other than Manson and Faich, whose financial ties to Wyeth were never disclosed.[47] "I was outraged when I saw that," Stuart Rich, a professor at Rush Medical College, told the *Chronicle of Higher Education* when the ties were exposed. "The study was the only scientific study that said these diet pills kill people."[48] One day after this study came out, Wyeth-Ayerst drafted a $5.8-million budget to pay for new research studies. An internal company memo said the money was needed to "establish and maintain relationships with opinion leaders at the local and national level to communicate to their colleagues the benefits of Redux and to encourage its use."[49] Among the many doctors willing to heed the company's call was Richard Atkinson, the obesity expert at the University of Wisconsin, whose name appeared on a company-authored article. "Let me congratulate you and your writer," wrote Atkinson in a thank-you letter to the ghostwriting firm. "Perhaps I can get you to write all my papers for me!"[50]

A virtually identical story could be told about Rezulin, Warner-Lambert's controversial diabetes drug. When the NIH launched a national study to investigate Rezulin's effectiveness, twelve of the twenty-two scientists selected to oversee the research (many of them based at universities) had significant financial ties to the manufacturer. Some years later, the FDA convened a scientific advisory panel to examine new data showing that patients on Rezulin had a perilously high risk of liver failure (an estimated twenty-eight patients had already died). Nine prominent university scientists from Harvard, UCLA, and other schools delivered testimony downplaying the drug's health risks. Although *all* of these professors had financial ties to Warner-Lambert, the FDA was persuaded to keep the drug on the market. The British government banned Rezulin in December 1997. But the FDA waited until March 2000 to take similar action, by which time the drug had been associated with 391 deaths, including 63 that involved liver failure.[51]

Universities, Medicine, and the Market: A Short History

What all of these examples reveal is that commercial forces are rapidly undermining the delicate foundation of trust that underlies academic medicine. It wasn't always this way.

In fact, historically, the nation's medical colleges served as the standard-bearers of the medical profession, helping to advance medical science and build up its reputation in large measure through a firm insistence on drawing clear boundaries between academia and business.[52]

In the nineteenth century, medicine was not the respectable profession we know today; it attracted some able men along with a large number of "irregular physicians," opportunists, and charlatans. In his authoritative account, *The Social Transformation of American Medicine*, Paul Starr showed how, well into the twentieth century, the practice of medicine suffered from internal dissension, an insecure social standing, and a lack of public trust. Medical knowledge itself was still primitive, and many of those who purported to be doctors were either quacks selling nostrums or folk healers selling herbs or other local remedies. Within the profession itself, there were sharp disagreements among various sects—Mormons, Eclectics, Christian Scientists, homeopaths—each of which held competing medical theories.[53]

To advance the goals of the profession, the nation's physicians had to "assure the public of the reliability of their 'product'" and build trust in their medical expertise, explained Starr. They also had to grapple with a more difficult question: "What sort of a commodity is medical care?"[54] Like many professional groups, physicians decided the most effective way to build up their public credibility was to make it clear that their medical decisions were guided by science and expertise, not by narrow commercial interests. "In the physicians' view," wrote Starr, "the competitive market represented a threat not only to their incomes, but also to their status and autonomy because it drew no sharp boundary between the educated and the uneducated, blurred the lines between commerce and professionalism, and threatened to turn them into mere employees."[55] Doctors knew that if they failed to gain their own professional autonomy, they risked becoming mere hired hands or "contract physicians" to private industry; as a result, a third party would not only dictate their fees but, potentially far worse, exert control over their medical decisions and intervene in the sacred physician-patient relationship. The key to securing their autonomy lay in establishing codes of conduct in medicine that were higher than the minimal rules governing the marketplace. What better way to do this than to call on the nation's nonprofit medical colleges to uphold the highest standards of scientific rigor, quality, and ethical judgment?[56]

Most of America's first medical schools arose in tandem with its colleges and universities. The University of Pennsylvania established a medical faculty in 1765. Kings College (now Columbia University), Harvard, and Dartmouth followed suit shortly thereafter.[57] Yet it took considerably longer for American medicine itself to advance. The true revolution began with the founding of the Johns Hopkins School of Medicine in 1893, which helped to give pure scientific research, along the German model, a permanent and privileged place in American higher education.[58] Soon after its founding, the United States began making significant scientific and medical advances. Surgery was transformed by Joseph Lister's concept of germ-free environments and the use of carbolic acid spray. The first radical mastectomy was performed at Johns Hopkins in 1891, and X-rays were discovered by Wilhelm Roentgen in 1895.[59]

Yet, until the early part of the twentieth century, medical education as a whole remained quite backward; U.S. medical colleges still couldn't hold a candle to their European counterparts. "The ignorance and general incompetency of the average graduate of American Medical Schools, at the time when he receives the degree which turns him loose upon the community, is something horrible to contemplate," wrote Harvard president Charles Eliot in the early 1870s. "The whole system of medical education in this country needs thorough reformation."[60] Among the greatest impediments to reform was the large number of commercial schools of dubious educational merit, which functioned as degree mills and fostered unrestrained competition.[61]

In 1904, concerned about the profession's lagging reputation, the American Medical Association (AMA) embarked on a campaign to raise educational standards so that these proprietary enterprises might be put out of business. Aiding this effort was a 1910 survey of the nation's medical schools, commissioned by the Carnegie Foundation and conducted by the noted educator Abraham Flexner. The survey decried the "wave of commercial exploitation" that had swept through university medical schools and proprietary institutions alike.[62] In graphic detail,

Flexner exposed evidence of fraudulent marketing, meager instruction, laboratories with no equipment, and reeking corpses that had not been properly disinfected. Armed with Flexner's report, the AMA succeeded in winning widespread state support for the implementation of stricter accreditation standards.[63] By 1922, the number of medical schools had been whittled down from 160 in 1906 to 81. Many commercial schools were forced to shut down.[64]

Seeking to gain "sovereignty over medical care" and raise its stature, noted Starr, the fledgling medical profession also advanced another goal: the banishment of profit-making business from medical practice itself. Awareness of the potentially corrupting influence of money on medicine had already been well established. Moses Maimonides, a physician of the twelfth century, famously appealed to God not to let "thirst for profit" or "ambition for renown" interfere with the doctors' commitment to his patients.[65] But given that most doctors were paid on a fee-for-service basis, it was never possible to completely wall off business from medicine. And some physicians argued vociferously that their business activities should not be regulated at all. The professional societies, however, realized that excessive profiteering threatened to erode the profession's standards and credibility. The AMA adopted its first code of ethics at its national conventions in 1846 and 1847. This code affirmed that physicians should not own patents on surgical instruments or medicines and should avoid unnecessary patient visits to prevent the appearance of interested motives.[66] Later the AMA sought to curb fee splitting, kickbacks, and other common practices by which doctors reaped financial rewards for making patient referrals. The AMA also looked unfavorably on doctors' owning pharmacies, dispensing medical products, and running advertisements. The American College of Surgeons required its members to sign an oath pledging to shun "unwarranted publicity, dishonest money-seeking and commercialism."[67]

To be sure, as Marc A. Rodwin argued persuasively in his book *Medicine, Money, and Morals*, the doctors' record of self-policing was spotty. By and large, the profession avoided enforcing any of its new codes through disbarment or other penalties, leaving it entirely to the discretion of individual physicians whether to abide by them or not. Most important, unlike lawyers, public servants, and other professionals who serve as fiduciaries for their clients, the medical establishment never implemented any normative conflict-of-interest standards—an omission that has haunted the profession ever since.

Despite these ethical gaps, by mid-century the profession rested on a more solid base, and university medical colleges stood poised to make extraordinary advances. Public recognition of the importance of scientific research during World War II resulted in a massive infusion of public dollars: Between 1941 and 1951, the federal budget for medical research grew from $3 million to $76 million.[68] By 1966 the creation of the federal Medicare and Medicaid insurance programs for the elderly, disabled, and indigent had opened up a new stream of generous reimbursements, which the universities' hospitals used to further subsidize the high cost of medical research, teaching, and training.[69] By the mid-1950s, vaccines had been developed to protect children against a series of traditional childhood killers: whooping cough, tetanus, diphtheria, measles, and rubella. When epidemiologists at the University of Michigan announced in 1955 that the polio vaccine had been proven safe and effective, the nation erupted in celebration.[70] The wonders of medicine appeared virtually unlimited, and the esteem of the nation's medical colleges grew.[71]

After thirty years of steady public support, however, politicians and employers grew anxious about the nation's soaring medical costs. Between 1950 and 1970, national health care expenditures rose from $12.7 billion to $71.6 billion, reaching 7.3 percent of GNP.[72] Efforts at cost containment soon ushered in the rise of for-profit health maintenance organizations and other managed-care plans. The university hospitals were the first to feel the financial hit because, unlike their competitors, they relied on health care reimbursements to subsidize a variety of other public goods: teaching, research, and indigent care.[73] Then, from 1974 to 1984, the universities experienced a sharp slowdown in the growth of NIH spending.[74] Having grown accustomed to an extraordinary degree of autonomy, physicians now found themselves operating in a far more commercial environment, with diminished control over both their professional lives and their medical decisions.[75]

Many physicians responded to this new competitive landscape by becoming more entrepreneurial themselves, investing in an array of health care businesses, including diagnostic laboratories, dialysis units, freestanding surgical centers, nursing homes, and hospital chains. In 1980, Arnold Relman, the editor in chief of the *New England Journal of Medicine*, became the first prominent physician to sound the alarm about the rise of a dangerous new "medical-industrial complex." In this and subsequent articles, Relman warned that physicians' direct financial stake in health care businesses would destroy the public's trust in the medical profession and the doctor's ability to serve patients as an "honest, disinterested trustee." Health care services were not like other market commodities, Relman cautioned, because "informational inequalities" make the patient highly dependent on the doctor for unbiased medical advice. [76]

Despite these early warnings, neither the universities nor the professional associations imposed any significant constraints on the growing entrepreneurial activities of their professors and physicians, leaving them ill prepared for the sudden emergence of commercial biotechnology and the passage of the Bayh-Dole Act. University medical schools were among the first to negotiate large-scale institutional agreements with industry; they were also leaders in taking equity in professors' start-up companies, running venture-capital funds, setting up incubators, and extracting royalty revenue from an increasingly entrepreneurial faculty. The same medical school faculty who had once dedicated themselves to raising the scientific and ethical standards of their profession by clearly separating medicine from the marketplace were now pushing to tear down the walls dividing academia and business.

The Loss of Autonomy

These days it is not only individual professors who have allowed themselves to become "captured" by the drug industry but the medical colleges as well. Consider what happened recently at the University of Toronto, a school that has been aggressively pursuing academic-industry alliances along the U.S. model.

In 2000, David Healy, a well-known psychiatrist based at the University of Wales, accepted an offer to become the director of the Mood Disorders Program at the University of Toronto's Centre for Addiction and Mental Health. Healy, a noted expert on the history of psychiatry, was one of the few academics who tried to sound the alarm early on about the SSRIs, and their capacity to trigger suicidal behavior. That November, Healy was invited to deliver a lecture at the center on the history of psychopharmacology, in which he mentioned his concerns about a possible link between Prozac and suicidal behavior in some patient populations. Soon afterward, Healy received an e-mail from David Goldbloom, the center's chief physician, informing him that his university appointment had been rescinded: "It is with regret that I am advising you that the Centre has decided to withdraw its offer of a position as Clinical Director of the Mood and Anxiety Disorders program. . . . Essentially, we believe that it is not a good fit. . . . This view was solidified by your recent appearance at the Centre in the context of an academic lecture."[77] Neither Goldbloom nor the university ever spelled out their reasoning, but it wasn't very hard to figure out. At the time, the center was the recipient of a $1.5-million gift from Eli Lilly, the manufacturer of Prozac, and 52 percent of its funding came from corporate sources.[78] In May 2002, Healy settled a $9.4-million lawsuit against the University of Toronto, in which he accused the institution of muzzling his free speech and violating his academic freedom.[79]

Healy's experience would come as no surprise to Nancy Olivieri, a medical professor at the University of Toronto who, a few years earlier, had also found herself hung out to dry when her research challenged the interests of a powerful financial donor. John Le Carré's novel *The Constant Gardener*, though fictional, is thought to be drawn at least in part from this dramatic case.

In 1995, Olivieri published a largely favorable study on the benefits of an iron chelation agent, called *deferiprone*, in the treatment of thalassemia, a genetic blood disease that afflicts millions of people throughout the world.[80] As Olivieri's clinical trials progressed, however, she found disturbing evidence that the agent was frequently ineffective and possibly even harmful. Olivieri felt it was important to notify her patients who had volunteered for the trial. But when she voiced her concerns to her sponsor, Apotex, a large generic-drug maker based in Canada, the company insisted that her interpretation of the data was incorrect. Olivieri then approached the Research Ethics Board, a hospital committee charged with monitoring clinical trials. The board agreed with Olivieri's assessment and mandated that the consent form be revised to inform patients of the new safety concerns. When Apotex learned of this move, it promptly shut down Olivieri's trial and terminated her research contract. Not long afterward, when Olivieri notified the company of her intent to publish in the *New England Journal of Medicine*, Apotex threatened legal action.[81] (Shortly after the trial was terminated, Olivieri's coinvestigator, Gideon Koren, received substantial additional research funding from Apotex and published favorable findings on the company's drug, without disclosing the source of his funding.[82])

Throughout the controversy, both the University of Toronto and the Hospital for Sick Children (HSC), where Olivieri worked, refused to provide her with legal assistance, citing a contract she had signed barring disclosure of her findings without "the prior written consent of Apotex." Neither institution appeared bothered by its own role in Olivieri's predicament. "The truly remarkable thing about [the secrecy provision in the Olivieri contract] is that it came to be written at all," wrote Robert A. Phillips, executive director of the National Cancer Institute of Canada, and John Hoey, editor in chief of the *Canadian Medical Association Journal,* in a 1998 article discussing the case. "That an internationally renowned children's hospital would have no formal mechanism to scrutinize contracts . . . is astounding."[83] Olivieri admitted that signing such a restrictive disclosure policy was naïve, but she did not act alone when she breached its confidentiality provisions: The decision to notify patients of the new safety concerns had been endorsed by the university hospital's own Research Ethics Board.[84]

Word quickly spread about the Olivieri case, and the University of Toronto was flooded with letters from prominent academic scholars asking the administration to intervene. The story soon leaked to the press, and in October 1998 the *Canadian Medical Association Journal* uncovered a possible explanation for the university's behavior: Both the university and the hospital had been courting Apotex for large donations, including one grant of more than $20 million for the university and another of $10 million to finance its affiliated hospitals. Later, the CEO of Apotex said these gifts were "part of an even more ambitious and generous philanthropic discussion" that could total "$55 million."[85] Despite the growing negative publicity, on January 6, 1999, HSC dismissed Olivieri from her position as director of the Program in Haemoglobinopathy (with the university's consent) and issued a "gag order" prohibiting her and other hospital staff from discussing the case.[86]

These actions prompted various Canadian faculty associations and leading health experts to intercede. Finally, after several weeks of sustained pressure, University of Toronto president Robert Prichard reversed course, reinstating Olivieri at the Toronto Hospital. But the controversy wasn't over yet. Nine months after Olivieri was reinstated, information surfaced that Prichard had lobbied top Canadian officials—including the prime minister—on behalf of Apotex, pressing the government to change its drug patent regulations. As the *Toronto Star* bluntly put it, the university's president had become "a drug lobbyist."[87] Soon after the story broke, Prichard admitted that the reason he had lobbied for Apotex was that he feared the proposed regulations would make it impossible for the company to make its promised $20-million donation to the university's new molecular biology center. Prichard's negotiations with Apotex dated back to when the company had been actively trying to keep Olivieri from publishing her research.

Human Guinea Pigs

Nowhere has the impact of commercialism been so clear and so damaging to the reputation of universities as in the area of clinical research involving human subjects. If the medical profession didn't have large numbers of patient volunteers who were willing to enroll in experimental drug trials—many of them conducted at universities—medical progress would grind to a halt. These human "guinea pigs" literally put their lives on the line for the advancement of medicine, trusting that their doctors will treat them with dignity and respect. But the commercialization of academic medicine has not served these patients well, gravely compromising the public trust on which all medical science depends.[88]

Starting in 1999, a series of deaths and scandals turned the public spotlight on the nation's universities, exposing the elaborate financial and commercial conflicts that now pervade clinical medicine. The first case to capture national media attention was that of Jesse Gelsinger, an eighteen-year-old boy from Tucson, Arizona, who died in a gene therapy experiment at the University of Pennsylvania.

Jesse had volunteered to be a subject in the Penn study for purely altruistic reasons. The study sought to find a cure for a rare liver disease known as ornithine transcarbamylase (OTC) deficiency syndrome. Although Jesse had a mild form of this disease, he did not stand to benefit from the study, because his own liver condition was already being effectively controlled through a combination of medication and a strict diet. According to his father, Paul Gelsinger, Jesse thought that by participating he could help researchers find a cure for infants who suffer a more deadly form of the disease. Based on their conversations with the doctors at Penn, the family believed the risks were minimal.[89]

On the afternoon of September 14, 1999, however, Paul received an urgent call from Penn's investigators informing him that the large dose of genetically engineered viruses they had infused into Jesse's liver had caused a massive reaction. Paul stayed in regular contact with the doctors and eventually flew to Pennsylvania to be with his son, but by the time he got there his son was already dying. Jesse's liver failed, his blood thickened into jelly, and his kidneys, brain, and other vital organs shut down. Four days after the initial infusion he was brain-dead.

Though he suffered terrible grief, Paul initially defended the scientists at Penn, trusting that they had done what they could to save his son's life. Over time, however, he came to accept a far more disturbing and painful portrait of what had happened. When the FDA and other auditors launched an investigation, they discovered that Penn's highly esteemed researchers had flagrantly violated federal rules designed to protect human subjects. Their findings shut down the OTC trial and other studies as well.

The FDA found that in earlier experiments, monkeys given gene transfer injections similar to the one Jesse received had died or suffered serious adverse events. Penn's investigators had neglected to tell the agency about this outcome until after Jesse died, and they failed to mention this critical information on patient consent forms.[90] Federal auditors also found that Penn's researchers did not halt the study and alert the FDA, as required, when volunteers suffered serious toxic reactions prior to Jesse's participation.[91] And even though Jesse's blood ammonia levels rose too high to meet the criteria for enrollment, investigators admitted him into the study anyway.[92]

After his son's death, Paul was equally shocked to learn that the study was riddled with financial conflicts. Both James Wilson, the lead investigator, and a former dean at the medical school held patents on some aspects of the experimental procedure.[93] Wilson and the University of Pennsylvania also held stock in Genovo, Inc., a biotechnology company that Wilson himself had founded, and that provided approximately 20 percent of the research budget for the lab. In exchange for this funding, Genovo had exclusive rights to develop Wilson's research into commercial products. In short, both Wilson and the university stood to profit if the study was successful.[94]

Despite the public outcry surrounding Gelsinger's death, Genovo was eventually sold to a larger company; Wilson's stock options, as a result, were reportedly worth $13.5 million, and the university's equity stake was valued at $1.4 million.[95]

The Gelsinger case forced the federal government to confront what was happening to academic medicine. What it discovered was startling. In the fall of 1999, the National Institutes of Health sent out a notice to all gene therapy investigators reminding them that adverse events and deaths must be reported. To their amazement, officials were suddenly flooded with 652 new adverse-event reports from eighty institutions, none of which had been previously reported (as federal guidelines require).[96] Although they had thought that Jesse Gelsinger was the first person to die as the result of a gene therapy experiment, it turned out that at least seven earlier deaths had not been reported to the NIH. Wilson was by no means the only renowned university scientist with a direct financial stake in his research. Jeffrey Isner, a cardiologist at Tufts University who oversaw experiments in which two patients died, was a major shareholder in the company funding his trial.[97] Further inquiry revealed that many investigators and their corporate sponsors now treated adverse events as "confidential commercial information" and were reluctant to make them public.[98]

From 1999 to 2001, federal regulators restricted or shut down research at twenty institutions—many of them prominent universities—for violations of the human research protection rules. The crackdown came at a time when funding for biomedical research was skyrocketing. Many more clinical trials were being conducted, and an already-weak oversight system was staggering from the strain of too much work. "Too many researchers are not adhering to standards of good clinical practice," wrote Donna Shalala, then secretary of Health and Human Services, in an editorial published in September 2000. "These were not isolated incidents on the fringes of science. Instead, these troubling problems occurred at some of our most prestigious research centers and involved leaders in their fields of study."[99]

Experts estimate that nearly 3 million Americans volunteer annually to participate in fifty to sixty thousand ongoing clinical trials. These experiments are critical in determining whether the vast array of new drugs and therapies developed in the nation's laboratories will prove effective in curing diseases and saving lives. Medical research usually begins with extensive laboratory testing on animals. If the results are promising, investigators generally file a new-drug application with the FDA and navigate through three phases of testing on humans. The first phase, usually performed on twenty to a hundred subjects, tests toxicity, the way the drug is absorbed into the body, and what dosage levels are safe. The second phase, conducted on up to several hundred people, tests whether the drug is effective. Only about one-third of experimental drugs successfully complete both phases. Drugs that make it to the third phase are tested on several hundred to thousands of subjects to establish a more thorough understanding of their effectiveness, benefits, and side effects. The system is intentionally rigorous to ensure that only drugs that are safe and have proven health benefits are released to the public.[100] However, since the late 1990s, a series of federal investigations have identified serious deficiencies in the oversight system designed to uphold these standards.

The main mechanism for protecting human subjects is the local institutional review board (IRB). Typically, each university has its own IRB, composed of faculty members, administrators, and at least one independent representative from outside the institution. The IRB is charged with reviewing and approving each study that is undertaken to ensure that the human subjects will be protected, and ethical parameters will be followed throughout the course of the trial. But according to George Annas, chair of the health law department at Boston University's School of Public Health, the IRBs are increasingly compromised. "Money is the most corruptive force driving the research system right now," said Annas. "IRBs are under tremendous pressure to approve research, because research brings in money to medical schools and hospitals which are desperate for it."[101] According to the Office of the Inspector General at Health and Human Services, "the expansion of managed care, the increased commercialization of research [and] the increased number of research proposals" have "presented major disruptions and challenges" for IRBs. "IRBs are inundated with protocols and adverse event reports," HHS noted. "With limited personnel and few resources, many IRBs are hard-pressed to give each review sufficient attention."[102]

Federal oversight is not much better.[103] Both of the agencies that oversee human subject research—the FDA and the Office of Human Research Protections—have the power to suspend research. But according to federal audit reports, they rarely conduct on-site inspections while clinical trials are in progress; therefore, violations are often identified too late for the human subjects involved.[104] To make matters worse, privately funded research is subject to federal oversight only if it is submitted to the FDA as part of a new-drug application. Large areas of commercial research are totally unregulated.[105]

The current oversight system was designed to give universities a high degree of flexibility and autonomy. But with universities and medical schools under increasing financial pressure—and with many directly involved in commercial activities themselves—the system is badly broken. Cutbacks in Medicaid support for teaching hospitals (as a result of the 1997 Balanced Budget Act) and the rise of managed care have resulted in significant budget shortfalls at the nation's medical schools. Although spending on basic research by the National Institutes of Health remains robust, universities have suffered losses on the clinical research side that have made them far more reliant on drug companies for support. Today, 80 percent of all clinical research is funded by the pharmaceutical industry, not by the government.[106]

To make matters worse, precisely when medical colleges began feeling the financial squeeze, the pharmaceutical industry started shifting a large portion of its drug research away from academic medical colleges to an array of new, for-profit outfits known as contract research organizations (CROs) and site management organizations (SROs). (The CROs provide drug companies with central oversight and management of their clinical trials, at both academic and private research sites, and SROs organize private physicians' offices into trial networks and oversee the rapid recruitment of patients.[107]) Universities and their affiliated hospitals used to perform the vast majority of the nation's clinical drug research, but now much of it has moved to the private sector. In 2000, academic medical centers received just thirty-four cents of every dollar that industry devoted to clinical research, down from seventy-five cents per dollar in the early 1990s.[108]

Studies indicate that these commercial entities do complete clinical trials faster and more cheaply than their academic counterparts—an obvious virtue for an industry that says it loses an estimated $1.3 million every day it is delayed in winning FDA drug approval. But private-sector competition also appears to be fostering a precipitous decline in research standards. In 1999, the *New York Times* reported that private doctors' offices were being bombarded with enticements from industry: "Improve Your Cash Flow," "Discover the Secret for Obtaining More Funded Studies." These have contributed to a nearly threefold increase in the number of private physicians, outside the university setting, experimenting on human subjects since 1990. According to the *Times*, 70 percent of the doctors involved in these trials had taken part in three or fewer previous drug studies, indicating their general lack of research experience. During its ten-month investigation, the *Times* uncovered numerous cases in which doctors relaxed eligibility criteria for patient enrollment in trials, fabricated data, and handed off their professional responsibilities to untrained nurses and staff. In one case, bodily fluids that met certain lab values were stored in an office refrigerator, ready to be substituted for the urine or blood of patients who did not qualify for studies.[109]

Heightened competition has also intensified the search for human subjects. The faster patients are enrolled in a clinical trial, the sooner it can start. The drug industry has resorted to paying doctors financial incentives ranging from $1,000 to $6,000 for each new patient recruited. Top recruiters can earn anywhere from $500,000 to $1 million a year. At the 2001 annual meeting of the American Academy of Allergy, Asthma and

Immunology, an industry representative told a group of investigators, "No longer will you get $2,500 per patient, you will get X dollars if you recruit 5 patients before week four, and if you don't, that's it and we are going to close the site."[110] The danger, as HHS has warned, is that physicians, motivated by financial rewards, will recruit patients into clinical trials who do not meet the enrollment criteria or have been given insufficient information about their other medical options.[111]

Hoping to better compete in this new research landscape, some thirty academic medical colleges have set up centralized clinical trial offices modeled on those in the private sector. Their purpose is to streamline academic research, adjust to the market's faster time horizons, and win back industry grants. Michael Leahey, director of the central Office of Clinical Trials at Columbia University and New York Presbyterian Hospital, believes that by making operations more efficient and industry-friendly, universities can bring research back into the academy and prevent standards from further deteriorating.[112] But can universities really uphold those standards when they've grown so dependent on commercial revenue themselves? Marcia Markowitz, director of the Office of Clinical Trials at the University of Pennsylvania, told a research trade publication that "one goal [of her office] is to increase the number of trials, and thereby increase the revenue."[113] During its 2000 inauguration, Harvard's Clinical Research Institute boasted it would "raise its share of industry-sponsored clinical research to at least $140 million over the next five years," up from $40 million.[114]

Universities have gone out of their way to assure the public that their clinical trials meet the highest standards of "scientific excellence" and "academic rigor." But not everyone is buying it.

One person deeply skeptical is Alan Milstein, an attorney based in New Jersey who represented the Gelsinger family, and subsequently took on similar cases against several other major academic research centers, including one affiliated with the University of Oklahoma and the University of Washington. An insurance specialist with black-and-silver-streaked hair, Milstein acquired the Gelsinger case by accident (through a prior family connection to his firm). He had never filed a medical malpractice suit before. But after reading up on the history and ethics of human experimentation—and learning that clinical research abuses like those at Penn were far from isolated—what began as an intriguing but straightforward legal case soon turned into a personal crusade. The potential to win a lucrative claim or settlement didn't hurt either: Although the amount is confidential, observers estimate that the Penn settlement was between $5 million and $10 million.

Milstein believes that universities have come to think they are immune from legal action in clinical research—and he's determined to change that. Other attorneys have shied away from taking on experimental research cases, as the legal obstacles to proving malfeasance are significant. Universities have consistently argued that research violations are the aberrant behavior of individual investigators. However, Milstein says responsibility can often be traced to the universities' top administrators, who frequently ignore evidence of problems—or try to sweep them under the rug.[115]

At Penn, for example, an internal Conflict of Interest Standing Committee (CISC) was set up to review James Wilson's financial connection to Genovo, Inc. well before Jesse Gelsinger's death. In 1995, Neal Nathanson, Penn's vice dean for research and training, told the committee that "the Genovo case might be the most important case which the CISC will ever deal with." The professors who sat on this committee voiced serious concerns: "Since Dr. Wilson's research efforts will be directed towards the solution of a problem in which he has a financial interest in the outcome, how can Dr. Wilson assure the University that he will not be conflicted when making decisions that could have an impact on . . . his intellectual property?" Buried in the committee's minutes was another prescient question: "How can Dr. Wilson and the University avoid liability for any damages if a patient died from any of the products produced or studied at the University?" Despite hours of internal deliberation, the committee failed to mandate that these conflicts be eliminated, allowing both the university and Wilson to retain their equity interests in Genovo.[116]

Some observers believe that taking universities to court, as Alan Milstein has done, will create more problems than it solves, dissuading the public from enrolling in clinical trials and slowing the advance of medical research. "Malpractice suits have done little to raise the quality of medical care, so why would they fix clinical research?" asked Robert M. Nelson, chairman of the institutional review boards at Children's Hospital of Philadelphia, when I interviewed him. "Getting a monetary award eight years later," he argued, "doesn't do any good for changing practices at the time of the trial."[117]

But others say these lawsuits are a by-product of the glaring weaknesses in the current oversight system—a system that depends almost entirely on university self-policing. Consider the case of Protocol 126, a failed blood cancer experiment conducted at the world-renowned Fred Hutchinson Cancer Research Center, affiliated with the University of Washington—otherwise known as "the Hutch." The purpose of the experiment, which ran from 1981 to 1993, was to reduce the incidence of side effects stemming from bone marrow transplants in leukemia patients. But in March of 2001 an exhaustive investigation by *Seattle Times* reporters Duff Wilson and David Heath revealed that the twelve-year experiment was plagued with problems: Patients were not properly informed about the risks of the experimental treatment, their alternative medical options, or the extensive financial interests that both the center and its doctors had in the drugs being tested. Equally worrisome, the Hutch repeatedly disregarded both the deteriorating health of the patients and the numerous objections raised by members of its own internal oversight body—the IRB.[118]

As early as 1981, when Protocol 126 first came up for review, the IRB questioned the lack of sufficient animal research; inadequate informed consent; and misleading patient information suggesting that if the experimental transplant failed, patients could obtain a second, standard transplant without difficulty. According to documents obtained by the *Seattle Times*, it was known at the time that second transplants were fatal about 95 percent of the time. Such concerns prompted the IRB to reject the protocol and insist on revisions, but later, after changes had been made in the board's membership, a second IRB granted approval with only minor modifications. Because so many underlying problems remained, however, subsequent IRBs continued to detect problems and raise objections.

Early in 1983, for example, the Hutch adopted a new conflict-of-interest policy stating that scientists "shall not participate in any (research) involving the Center in which the member has an economic interest." Yet, when the IRB inquired about the financial conflicts rumored to exist in Protocol 126, E. Donnall Thomas, one of the trial's lead investigators and a prominent Hutch scientist, denied there were any. In truth, all three principal investigators—Thomas, John Hansen, and Paul Martin—as well as a Hutch-affiliated foundation had substantial stock holdings in Genetic Systems, the company that owned the exclusive rights to three of the drugs being tested. All three also had employment or consulting positions with the company, while retaining their joint appointments at the University of Washington and the Hutch. (Although Protocol 126 would ultimately fail to show any treatment benefits, the value of these professors' stock soared after Genetic Systems was successfully sold to Bristol-Myers in 1985 on the basis of the company's promising research portfolio.)

When the IRB directly questioned Thomas about his conflicts, he fired back a furious reply: "I think Committee members have not only an obligation to review the ethical aspects of this work, but also an obligation to assist us and not impede our research." Under federal law, however, the IRB has only one mission: to protect the rights of human subjects. Six weeks later, IRB chairman Henry Kaplan wrote to Robert Day, the Hutch's president, requesting an independent investigation of Protocol 126. Day promptly turned down the request, saying it would be too costly and would reveal secrets to the Hutch's competitors.

In 1984, Hutch investigators admitted in an article published in the medical journal *Blood* that the rate of transplant-graft failure using their experimental method—40 percent at the time—was "an highly unusual outcome."[119] But the trial proceeded, even as patients continued to die at an alarming rate. Over this period, the IRB continued to press for revisions in the study protocol, some of which were gradually implemented. But the Hutch refused two additional IRB requests for independent reviews. In response to the last of these requests, Frederick Appelbaum, the head of the Hutch's clinical research division, told the IRB chair to stop complaining about conflicts of interest and "accept the fact that those of us in cancer research are intrinsically honest individuals who are trying our best."

When the Hutch finally terminated the experiment, the rate of graft failure was at least 24 percent, versus the expected 1 percent. The rate of cancer relapse for patients in the trial was 100 percent, versus the expected 25 percent. Eighty out of eighty-two patients who enrolled in Protocol 126 died. The *Times* estimated that at least twenty of those deaths were directly attributable to the experimental treatment.

Public dismay over the extensive financial entanglements in clinical research triggered congressional hearings and a two-day NIH symposium in August 2000. E. Greg Koski, director of the newly upgraded Office of Human Research Protections (housed under the secretary of Health and Human Services), told a packed audience, "Conflicts of interest are very real, very serious and a threat to our entire endeavor. During the last five years, they may have gotten out of control."[120]

After the hearings, momentum for reform continued to build. Two of the nation's top medical journals, the *Journal of the American Medical Association* and the *New England Journal of Medicine*, devoted special issues to the subject of human clinical research and conflicts of interest.[121]

David Korn, then head of governmental affairs at the Association of American Medical Colleges, wrote an editorial acknowledging the need for reform: "Some forms of alleged financial conflicts of interest, both individual and institutional, that recently have come to public attention would seem to be unacceptable and should be prohibited."[122]

Finally, in January 2001, HHS secretary Shalala rolled out "new draft interim guidelines on financial conflicts in human subject research" and submitted them for public comment.[123] Financial conflicts had become a growing problem throughout the academic world, but the proposed guidelines were intentionally narrow, focusing only on the area of human subject research. The mildly worded draft proposal suggested that IRBs, when assessing the ethical merits of a particular study, should be informed about the investigators' potential financial conflicts as well as any institutional conflicts and how they are managed. When such ties cannot be eliminated, HHS stated, this information should be included in the patient consent form. The draft was an attempt to harmonize federal rules and give greater guidance to university administrators, without imposing any specific prohibitions. But as one observer noted, "Even this gentle prodding was too much for academic leaders."[124]

In March, virtually all the major university consortiums—including the Association of American Medical Colleges (AAMC), the Association of American Universities (AAU), the Council on Government Relations, and the National Association of State Universities and Land Grant Colleges—demanded that the HHS guidelines be withdrawn. Rather than cooperate with the government, the organizations were adamant that universities should be left to develop conflict-of-interest policies of their own.[125] In a striking reversal, the AAMC's Korn asserted in a letter to *Science*, "Despite a seeming rush to judgment by political leaders and the media based on a few anecdotal reports, convincing empirical evidence that investigators' (or institutions') related financial interests in their research pose a significant threat to the integrity of that research is lacking."[126] Hoping to forestall federal regulation, both the AAMC and the AAU pledged to convene high-level panels to formulate a new consensus on university conflict-of-interest policies.

"Universities are bastions of free inquiry," said Arthur Caplan, a bioethicist at Penn, when I asked him about the universities' defensive response. "Regulation is not in the culture. They just see it as obtrusive. . . . Universities stand for those values of self-regulation and community oversight. I'm not saying they always work, but that culture is very deep."[127] Caplan is certainly correct about higher education's deep-seated aversion to any outside meddling, an instinct that stems from a long and noble tradition of academic freedom. But in the current commercial climate, this plea for self-regulation has a profoundly disingenuous ring.

Despite overwhelming evidence of problems and enormous political pressure to act, the federal government quietly abandoned its proposed conflict-of-interest guidelines. Although some reforms were enacted—including new education and training requirements for clinical investigators and their staff—the most serious recommendations proposed by Shalala and a presidential National Bioethics Advisory Committee (fines of up to $1 million for research violations, and the creation of one unified federal office to monitor all research) were never implemented.[128]

The government's back-pedaling provoked consternation within the public health community but was barely noted in the press. Nobody seemed to recall that the scenario was eerily reminiscent of what had taken place in 1989, when Congress had uncovered numerous research abuses involving conflicts of interest and had tried to impose tougher conflict-of-interest guidelines once before. In 2001, as in 1989, the higher-education world's response was the same: "Don't interfere. We will address the conflict-of-interest issue ourselves."

By the end of 2001, after many months of deliberation, both the AAU and the AAMC released their long-awaited reports outlining how the academic community proposed to do this. Remarkably, *all* of their recommendations were voluntary. The AAU's report emphasized that these were "suggested operating guidelines intended to help reduce the variation among institutions"; the AAMC stressed that its recommendations were intended to serve as "a model for baseline standards and practices without limiting the prerogative of institutions to implement conflict of interest policies in a manner best suited to local needs." Although both reports offered candid discussions of how universities might better manage or eliminate conflicts of interest, they failed to offer any consensus position on what policies *all* institutions should be *required* to follow. Financial interests related to human subject research should be avoided, both reports noted, except in "compelling circumstances."[129]

Once again the academic establishment had successfully fended off federal conflict-of-interest rules.* But most independent observers were far

---

*On May 12, 2004, the Department of Health and Human Services did release a new "Guidance for Human Subject Protection," but this version was systematically watered down. It was offered only as a series of "points to consider," and the agency was careful to emphasize that "this document is nonbinding, and does not change any existing regulations [or] impose any new requirements"(*Federal Register*, 69(92), May 12, 2004: 26393–26397).

from sanguine about the universities' capacity to regulate themselves—
and they had good reason to be. A 2003 study, for example, revealed that
nearly half the faculty who serve on university IRBs, charged with protecting human subjects, also serve as consultants to the drug industry.[130] In
2002, another survey of 108 university medical schools found that universities were routinely signing corporate-sponsored research agreements
that failed to protect their professors' basic academic freedoms: Just 1 percent of researchers were guaranteed unimpeded access to the complete
trial data; only 5 percent of research contracts required that the results be
published.[131] Thus, by continuing to insist on "self-regulation," universities and their medical schools would seem to be further undermining the
delicate foundation of public trust that the medical profession had once
fought so hard to build.

6

The University as Business

*The field of technology transfer offers all manner of intriguing possibil-
ities to help stimulate technological innovation. . . . With this bright
promise, why does the prospect of technology transfer arouse anxiety
on the campus of almost every distinguished research university? . . .
[The causes for concern flow from a sense that these programs] are
likely to confuse the university's central commitment to the pursuit of
knowledge and learning by introducing into the heart of the academic enterprise a new powerful motive—the search for commercial
utility and financial gain.*

—Derek Bok, former president of Harvard University[1]

The commercial hub of nearly every American research university is
its technology-transfer office. When I visited Stanford's Office of
Technology Licensing (OTL) not long ago, it occupied the third floor of
a drab concrete building just off the main loop that circles the palm-
studded Palo Alto campus. This otherwise unprepossessing spot is the
envy of universities across the country. Inside the main lobby, encased in

handsome wooden frames along the walls, I was greeted by impressive displays, highlighting the various patents and products the office had helped to bring to market. One described a valve that creates high-resolution images on the surface of a silicon chip; another depicted a new case-management system for heart failure that the nation's hospitals might want to license.

The OTL's mission is to commercialize professors' discoveries, manage Stanford's growing patent portfolio, and carry out the provisions of the Bayh-Dole Act. On the day of my visit, the office was churning with activity: Dozens of licensing staff were poring over faculty inventions, investigating their commercial prospects, and searching about for potential industry partners. "We're producing about 250 inventions per year, roughly one in three of which gets patented," Jon Sandelin, then a senior OTL associate, told me. Stanford regularly ranks among the nation's top ten universities in licensing revenue (more than $50 million in 2002)[2]—a success Sandelin credited to creating the right entrepreneurial environment. "You have to understand—initially the department chairmen and school deans weren't thrilled by having this new activity that was diverting the attention of their faculty away from teaching and research," he said. "So how do you offset that? You make them stakeholders—you make them beneficiaries."[3]

Once professors and their departments learned that they could earn a cut from inventions, said Sandelin, they became distinctly more enthusiastic about bringing their ideas to the OTL. To reinforce the message, the OTL conducts aggressive outreach, organizing lunches with department heads; publishing a newsletter, *Brainstorm*, that touts the latest faculty discoveries; and dangling financial rewards in front of would-be inventors. One such enticement is the Research Incentive Fund, launched in the 1990s to help professors convert academic concepts into "prototype products." "Got an idea for the next great whatchmacallit but don't have the funds to move from hypothesis to thesis?" an issue of *Brainstorm* asked. "This fund might just be your answer."[4]

The OTL also conducts regular training sessions with Stanford faculty on the ins and outs of starting their own companies. For instructional purposes, the school even created its own mock-up of a Monopoly board depicting the exciting, if risky, road that would-be professor-entrepreneurs must traverse—from coming up with that original "gee whiz!" idea and drafting a business plan to attracting venture capital and launching a start-up—before passing "Go" and earning a payout.[5]

Not surprisingly, this overtly probusiness message—now being promulgated aggressively at nearly every research university in the country—has encouraged academic-industry collaborations to flourish. In addition to the large-scale institutional contracts such as the U.C. Berkeley-Novartis alliance, there are smaller corporate-sponsored research agreements and consulting deals brokered between individual faculty members and firms; industrial affiliate programs; and a burgeoning number of university-industry research centers (UIRCs). The UIRCs may involve everything from close research collaborations between industry scientists and faculty on applied projects to more fundamental investigations with broader potential industrial applications. A comprehensive survey published in 1994 counted more than 1,050 UIRCs in the United States, over half of them launched in the 1980s.[6] Affiliate programs, also known as liaison programs, usually operate on a membership basis, with corporations agreeing to pay an up-front annual fee in exchange for privileged access to university expertise and resources. At Carnegie Mellon's Magnetic Technology Center, for example, firms such as IBM and Kodak pay an annual fee of $750,000, which permits them to designate three topics each for the center's academic investigators to pursue.[7] At the University of Utah's College of Pharmacy, meanwhile, companies pay a basic membership fee in exchange for "early announcements on research progress, first options for licensing technologies, a set number of consulting hours from faculty, and a seat on the board of directors for the affiliates program."[8]

Being more business-friendly and catering to industry's needs has had a number of direct payoffs for the university sector. First and foremost, it has helped to boost the inflow of cash. Industry funding for academic research has grown faster than from any other source since the 1980s, rising from $264 million in 1980 to $2 billion in 2001 (the most recent year for which statistics are available).[9] Although industry supplies roughly 7 percent of academic research funding nationally, at individual schools the percentages are far higher. Duke University now draws 31 percent of its research and development budget from industry. At Georgia Institute of Technology, MIT, Ohio State, Penn State, and Carnegie Mellon, these percentages have now jumped to 21, 20, 16, 15, and 15, respectively. Surprisingly, even many of the smaller, less prestigious research universities are highly dependent on industry funding, including Alfred University (48 percent); the University of Tulsa (32 percent); and Lehigh University (22 percent).[10]

Ultimately, though, the most striking feature of this burgeoning academic-industrial complex is not the large amounts of private capital flowing into university coffers. As we've already seen, throughout the modern era, professors have received funding from private corporations and have performed research that helped spur industrial development. What's truly new—and dangerous—is the degree to which market forces have penetrated into the heart of academia itself, causing American universities to look and behave more and more like for-profit commercial enterprises.

North Carolina State, Johns Hopkins, Harvard, and numerous other universities, for example, now operate their own venture-capital funds to bankroll, promote, and profit from commercially promising academic research.[11] Some 174 universities have affiliated business incubators ready to house and seed new companies.[12] The University of Chicago, renowned for its classical tradition, has created a nonprofit, the ARCH Development Corporation, whose mission, in part, is to launch new start-up companies based on faculty inventions.[13] At Chicago as at other schools, the focus on profit has grown increasingly raw and undisguised. After Glenn D. Steele, Jr., the dean of Chicago's medical school, removed 50 percent of his faculty department heads, for example, he bluntly told *Business Week* that he planned to begin "insinuating the place . . . with entrepreneurial people"—a clear statement that commercial acumen would be an important new qualification for academic promotion.[14]

The new breed of academic-industry partnerships is increasingly structured less like traditional sponsored-research deals than like commercial joint ventures. Johns Hopkins, for example, has teamed up with Genetics Institute, Inc., to launch a separate company—MetaMorphix, Inc.—to research diseases of the nervous system. Genetics Institute has invested $3.8 million, for a 58 percent share of the company, and Johns Hopkins has contributed nineteen genes in exchange for a 42 percent share and future royalties.[15]

Back in 1980, when Harvard first flirted with the idea of investing in a professor's start-up company, it generated an outpouring of negative publicity: An editorial in the *New York Times* cautioned that the nation's universities "must be careful not to lose their academic souls."[16] Today, however, it is common for universities to take equity in their professors' start-up ventures (in lieu of royalties), thus giving these schools a direct financial stake in the commercial (rather than purely academic) success of their professors' research. In 2001, the Association of University Technology Managers estimated that some 180 universities owned stakes in 886 start-up ventures. Princeton, the quintessential ivory tower, held equity in seven firms—one of which returned an impressive $4 million in licensing revenue.[17] More recently, Stanford University announced it would sock away an estimated $190 million from its equity stake in Google, an online search-engine company founded by two Stanford graduates, which went public in 2004.[18]

Not all such investments prove so lucrative, however—and they can be financially risky. During the 1980s and early 1990s, for example, Boston University (BU) poured $85 million (nearly a fifth of its endowment) into Seragen, a biotech firm specializing in cancer research, which several BU professors had founded. Convinced that the company would generate windfall profits, BU president John Silber also personally invested heavily in Seragen and persuaded numerous other professors and trustees to do likewise. Unfortunately, from 1991 to 1997 Seragen lost almost $150 million. The university, which at one point owned 91 percent of the company's stock, was accused of egregiously mismanaging the school's endowment to prop up the company and protect the trustees' investments.[19]

One might think such a debacle would serve as a cautionary tale for other schools. Far from restraining universities, however, the difficulty of turning a profit seems only to have made them more ambitious. Several universities, such as the University of Louisville in Kentucky, have launched their own for-profit firms to commercialize and market faculty research. The University of Pittsburgh, meanwhile, recently acquired a foundering biotech firm.[20] Stanford has already pushed beyond mere patenting to invest more than $1 million in developing its own brand-name product, Sondius-XG, a sound-synthesis technology that the university now markets in conjunction with Yamaha. Why? Because unlike patents, which expire after twenty years, brands have the potential to generate revenue forever.[21]

A Win-Win Proposition?

There is something appealing, even elegant, about the new market ideology that animates many current academic administrators, including Stanford's Jon Sandelin, who perceive all this heightened commercialism as a win-win proposition for everyone involved. By helping faculty bring their inventions into commercial use, these modern-day utilitarians seek to generate new revenue for their academic institutions—revenue that can be used to provide monetary rewards to the faculty inventors, fund the technology-transfer operation, and, if substantial profits are forthcoming, help pay for future academic research. In 2002, universities generated an impressive sum—nearly $1 billion in licensing and royalty income—from their efforts to commercialize academic inventions.[22]

To Sandelin and his colleagues, the passage of Bayh-Dole was a stroke of genius, and perfectly in keeping with America's long tradition of free enterprise and entrepreneurship. By giving universities and their professors a direct financial stake in their research, the act provided an important incentive for universities and their faculty to devote more time and resources to commercializing their discoveries. When Marie and Jerry Thursby, economists at Georgia Tech and Emory University, respectively, asked industry representatives to rate their reasons for increasing links with academia, 31 percent noted that *greater university receptivity to licensing* was extremely important. What's more, Thursby and Thursby found, in the case of 40 percent of licensed academic inventions, the faculty member remained involved in subsequent commercial development.[23] To administrators like Sandelin, the benefits of this commercial activity are obvious: Not only does it speed up the transfer of knowledge to industry, enhancing national economic growth, but it also steers much-needed capital into cash-starved academic institutions.

The most important cheerleader for the Bayh-Dole Act is the Association of University Technology Managers (AUTM)—a membership organization comprising roughly three thousand tech-transfer managers from more than three hundred universities, research institutions, and teaching hospitals—which routinely publishes a variety of statistical surveys and reports that tout the virtues of academic commercialism.[24] Among the eighty-four universities that have responded consistently to AUTM's surveys over the period 1991–2000, disclosures of new inventions by academic investigators shot up an impressive 84 percent, new patent applications rose 238 percent, license agreements 161 percent, and royalties more than 520 percent.[25] In 2000, AUTM reported that business activity associated with sales of products stemming from academic research during the previous year totaled more than $40 billion; this, in turn, supported more than 270,000 jobs and contributed $5 billion to the nation's tax revenues at the federal, state, and local levels.[26]

These AUTM data, frequently referenced in the press, certainly sound impressive—and have helped to convince members of Congress and state legislators that it *pays* to make universities more entrepreneurial and commercially savvy. *The Economist*, citing AUTM's data, recently went so far as to declare the Bayh-Dole Act "possibly the most inspired piece of legislation to be enacted in America over the past half century."[27] However, these figures don't tell the whole story.

One fundamental problem with the AUTM surveys is that they fail to address a crucial analytic question: What share of the university-based inventions generated since 1980 were commercialized *because* of the institutions created under Bayh-Dole, and what share *would have been commercialized anyway*? As Bhaven Sampat, an economist at the Georgia Institute of Technology, explained to me in an interview, until this basic question can be answered, it really isn't possible to measure Bayh-Dole's true economic impact at all.

Sampat pointed, by way of example, to software technology that Vanu Bose invented and developed in the late 1990s while he was a graduate student at MIT. (Bose's father, Amar Gopal Bose, is the well-known MIT professor-entrepreneur of Bose Corporation fame.) If a statistician at AUTM were to tally up the total economic activity that the younger Bose's software company, Vanu, Inc., is generating five years from now, the figures would probably look impressive, explained Sampat. "But they wouldn't tell us anything about Bayh-Dole." Why? "Because it is quite clear from publicly available records," he said, "that Bose's technology was moving forward and going to get commercialized, with or without any patenting or licensing activity on the part of MIT's tech-transfer office."[28] Ironically, in a 1999 *Wall Street Journal* article, Bose accused his alma mater of trying to extract such exorbitant licensing fees and royalties at the outset that he feared the university's involvement would cause his company to tank, rather than aid it in getting off the ground.[29] "Therefore," continued Sampat, "to attribute all this entrepreneurial and economic activity to the influence of Bayh-Dole and the intellectual property regimes it put in place simply wouldn't be accurate." Other economists share Sampat's skepticism. Richard Nelson, an emeritus professor at Columbia University, wrote, "My strong suspicion is that a good share of the technology transfer that has occurred [since Bayh-Dole] would have proceeded as widely and as rapidly as in fact it did, *even if there had been no claiming of intellectual property rights by the university*" (emphasis added).[30]

It is extremely difficult for researchers to obtain the kind of license-specific information that became public in the Bose case. Therefore, many economists remain unconvinced by AUTM's numbers. Unfortunately, there are currently no other independent efforts under way to measure Bayh-Dole's long-term economic impact. Although the U.S. government funds an estimated 58 percent of university-based research, it does not collect any comprehensive data on academic licensing, relying instead on AUTM's data. As the General Accounting Office (GAO) wrote in 1998, "Despite the perception that Bayh-Dole is working well, none of the federal agencies or universities we contacted evaluated the effects of Bayh-Dole," thus the act's true impact on technology transfer and the economy remains unknown.[31]

The Bayh-Dole Act does require universities to inform federal agencies about any taxpayer-financed inventions they produce, but in 1999 the GAO reported that the government's own records were "inaccurate, incomplete, and inconsistent." Two years later, the NIH acknowledged that information concerning the development of new drugs and technologies by academic institutions was "neither systematically nor consistently" reported, even when substantial taxpayer funding was involved.[32] Because AUTM remains the only entity that routinely collects university technology-transfer data, its statistics are routinely cited in the press without any mention of the data's limitations. More rarely still do news outlets address AUTM's potential bias as a source: In addition to being a membership association for academic tech-transfer professionals, the group, formerly known as the Society of University Patent Administrators, was once also a key lobbyist for the passage of Bayh-Dole.

Defenders of Bayh-Dole dismiss such criticism. Prior to the act's passage, they contend, most university inventions simply languished inside the ivory tower, unexploited by private firms. Thus, any successful technology transfer after 1980 must be attributable largely to Bayh-Dole. As AUTM's then president Pat Harsche told a reporter in 2003, "A lot of technology sat on the shelf before universities really began to apply for patents. . . .There was no incentive to take it off the shelf."[33]

This oft-repeated argument is enormously popular—but also wrong.

As the work of such noted economists as Nathan Rosenberg and Richard Nelson demonstrates, U.S. research universities made vital contributions to the nation's economic and industrial growth long before Bayh-Dole.[34] Throughout the modern era, in fields ranging from agriculture to engineering to computer science, wrote Nelson, universities have had a "well-known record of strong performance in doing research that contributed to technological progress and industrial development, and strong efforts in technology transfer,"—even though, in the past, these were "almost always accomplished without the university claiming any intellectual property rights."[35]

The latter point underscores a third problem with AUTM's patenting and licensing data. The figures tell us nothing about *non*proprietary methods of transferring academic knowledge and skills to industry, such as publishing, consulting, one-on-one relationships, and the training of students. These "open" methods of transferring technology and knowledge are admittedly more difficult to quantify and track. Yet studies suggest that their significance to industrial progress is anything but trivial—even today, when so much of the current focus in academia is on proprietary methods of technology transfer. In a large-scale survey of industrial R&D managers published in 2002, Nelson and two other researchers, Wesley Cohen and Jonathan Walsh, asked respondents to rank the different channels by which they had benefited from university-based research. These authors found that in a majority of industries, the most important channels were publications, conferences, consulting, and other informal methods of information exchange—the very same *open pathways* that Bayh-Dole's champions so frequently try to discredit. Interestingly, patents and licenses ranked near the bottom of this list—the lone exception being the pharmaceutical sector. A survey of the faculty in MIT's Departments of Mechanical and Electrical Engineering, published the same year, reached a similar conclusion, finding that patents actually constitute a very small fraction of the knowledge transfer from these applied-research laboratories.[36]

What troubles Nelson and other scholars is the possibility that in placing such a premium on patenting and licensing, Bayh-Dole may actually disrupt many of these older, nonproprietary methods of bringing academic knowledge into practical use, with unknown consequences for the health and vitality of the broader innovation system.[37] Because of the new commercial mind-set in the academic world and recent changes in intellectual property law, there is good reason to be concerned.

The Disappearing Knowledge Commons

In the summer of 1998, a National Institutes of Health working group issued a report warning that changes in the way universities now guard their intellectual property could endanger the free exchange of gene sequences, reagents, and other basic research tools that are the building blocks for future scientific discovery. The NIH said it was dismayed to learn that universities now routinely impose onerous legal conditions—known as material transfer agreements (MTAs)—on these research tools that are every bit as restrictive as those applied by private industry, even when these tools have been generated through public funding. The restrictions include requirements that the university be allowed to review manuscripts prior to publication; legal provisions extending the university's ownership rights to all future discoveries deriving from use of its materials; and prohibitions on the materials being used in any research that is already subject to licensing obligations with another institution.[38] In addition to restricting access, noted the working group, these burdensome proprietary conditions can introduce disturbing inefficiencies into the scientific process, causing even the simplest exchange of data between two scientists to become mired in costly red tape and time-consuming legal reviews.

The NIH's report strongly rebuked the university community for turning its back on the "gift economy" that traditionally prevailed in academia and replacing it with a new, more profit-oriented conception of knowledge and ideas as private property. "[Universities] have no duty to return value to shareholders, and their principal obligation under the Bayh-Dole Act is to promote utilization, not to maximize financial returns," the working group noted. "It hardly seems consistent with the purposes of Bayh-Dole to impose proprietary restrictions on research tools that would be widely utilized if freely disseminated. Technology transfer need not be a revenue source to be successful."[39]

Historically, of course, one of the central missions of the university was to nurture and protect the information commons, the pool of knowledge and ideas unencumbered by ownership claims that is freely available to researchers and the public at large. Like our national parks, timber, and water resources, this pool of knowledge—much of it funded by U.S. taxpayers—is a crucial part of the public domain. Unfortunately, in recent years, despite the revolution in information technology, the size of the knowledge commons has diminished, as more and more ideas, subject to restrictive patents and licenses, get cordoned off behind high proprietary fences.

One reason for this shrinking commons is the more expansive conception of intellectual property law that the U.S. courts embraced around the same time that lawmakers began calling on universities to become more entrepreneurial. In 1980, the year Congress passed Bayh-Dole, the U.S. Supreme Court issued a landmark ruling, *Diamond v. Chakrabarty*, that affirmed that a genetically altered, living organism—in this case, an oil-eating bacterium—was a product of human invention and therefore eligible for patenting. Prior to this time, living organisms tended to be viewed as acts of nature and, save for a few narrowly defined exceptions, were excluded from patenting. As Sheldon Krimsky explained in his book *Science in the Private Interest*, the *Diamond v. Chakrabarty* ruling instantly "opened up the floodgates for the patenting of cell lines, DNA, genes, animals and any other living organism that has been sufficiently modified by humans to qualify as 'products of manufacture.'"[40] Indeed, in defending this vast expansion of intellectual property law, Chief Justice Warren Burger wrote in his majority opinion that "anything under the sun that is made by man is eligible for patenting."[41]

The same year *Chakrabarty* was decided, the Supreme Court issued another ruling, *Diamond v. Diehr*, that extended patent protection to applications of laws of nature and mathematical formulas.[42] Shortly after, Congress pressed to further extend the reach of U.S. patent law through the creation of a new, specialized court of appeals for the Federal Circuit dedicated to handling intellectual property claims. As the legal scholars Arti Rai and Rebecca Eisenberg observed, the new appeals court significantly "relaxed the standards normally required for patent protection, such as proof of the practical utility of an invention and its lack of obviousness," making it far easier to patent early-stage research in the biomedical arena and other fields.[43] Other reforms pushed through during the same period also extended the term limits on copyright protection, thus further slowing the pace at which knowledge reenters the public domain.

The collective effect of these changes was dramatic, as Seth Shulman observed in his trenchant 1999 book *Owning the Future*. Virtually overnight, vast new realms of knowledge fell into private hands. In the late 1980s, for example, Agracetus, a Wisconsin-based biotechnology firm, successfully inserted foreign genes into cotton and managed to obtain a surprisingly broad patent on *all genetically engineered* cotton. When researchers at the NIH treated two girls with a rare genetic disorder, they parlayed their discovery into a patent on *all ex vivo human gene therapy*.[44] What made many of these new patents so unusual, noted Shulman, is that they granted their owners monopolistic control over whole new conceptual realms, whose boundaries were still being actively explored. Rather than issuing a patent on one particular improved version of a mousetrap (which would appropriately reward the inventor's creativity), it was as if the U.S. Patent Office had suddenly decided to award a broad patent on the *very concept of trapping mice itself*—thus, in effect, discouraging others from trying to invent new, and possibly even better, mousetraps in the future. Historically, the U.S. courts have been wary about allowing patents on inventions, where their "utility" is not narrowly defined. As the U.S. Supreme Court concluded in *Brenner v. Manson*, a 1966 case involving an allegedly novel process for making steroids, awarding too broad a patent "may confer power to block off whole areas of scientific development, without compensating benefit to the public."[45]

A recent example of this trend toward the issuance of overly broad patents surfaced in 2000 when the U.S. Patent Office awarded Human Genome Sciences a controversial patent on the CCR5 receptor. At the time of its filing, the company had no idea that this receptor was actually the route by which HIV/AIDS enters a human cell—a discovery made only six months later by an independent team of researchers. Now, however, despite not having known about this crucial medical function, HGS has a monopoly on the receptor and can insist that any scientist wishing to use it must obtain a license and pay fees and royalties.[46]

The breadth and scope of this shift in the ownership of knowledge has been truly startling. Today, companies exert monopoly control over the basic building blocks of computer code (formerly an open, government-financed system that gave rise to the public commons we now call the Internet); doctors hold patents on medical procedures they once shared openly with their peers; and drug companies hold title to many of the world's most valuable medicinal plants and microorganisms, which indigenous peoples and local healers have used freely for generations. As James Boyle, a prominent intellectual property expert, has observed, the current effort to privatize the knowledge commons "makes the monopolies of the nineteenth-century robber barons look like penny-ante operations."[47] Under this radical reinterpretation of U.S. patent law, even our own genetic makeup as humans has effectively been placed on the auction block as fierce competitions have sprung up between private firms and government scientists to see who will be the first to fully map the human genome. Companies like Human Genome Sciences, Incyte, and Celera have all spent millions in the hope of patenting the human genome for commercial gain, and public-sector scientists have raced to keep as much of the genetic code as possible freely available in the public domain.[48]

Within such a context, it would certainly seem more vital than ever for our nation's universities to rededicate themselves to protecting the knowledge commons, so that the basic building blocks of science continue to be freely available for future invention and discovery. Unfortunately, however, the intrusion of a market ideology has caused these institutions to move in precisely the opposite direction. Inspired by Bayh-Dole, academic tech-transfer officers across the country now race to file proprietary claims on everything from DNA sequences and protein structures to disease pathways and algorithms—discoveries whose greatest value is as a platform for future invention. In fact, as of the late 1990s, U.S. universities actually held more patents on DNA sequences than private industry. While the total number of new gene patents issued between 1990 and 1999 rose from 400 to 2,800, academia's share increased from 55 percent to a whopping 73 percent.[49] Even U.S. government labs, operating under the federal equivalent of Bayh-Dole, have largely embraced this gold-rush mentality and joined the patenting frenzy. In 1991, for example, forsaking its commitment to the public domain, the NIH filed the first-ever patents on anonymous gene fragments, known as expressed sequence tags (ESTs). Ironically, it was a private firm—Merck & Co.—that first rose up to oppose the NIH and its ill-conceived decision to patent such early-stage genetics information.[50]

The Innovation Pipeline in Jeopardy

It is not merely the quantity of university-held patents that is troubling but, even more important, the *way* these institutions are choosing to license those patented inventions to private firms. Before Bayh-Dole, you may recall, the federal government required universities operating under an Institutional Patent Agreement—the precursor to Bayh-Dole—to make good-faith efforts to license their taxpayer-financed research *nonexclusively* on a "royalty-free or reasonable royalty basis," precisely in an effort to protect open competition and discourage monopolistic control and pricing. When he drafted the Bayh-Dole legislation, however, Norman Latker removed this cautionary language almost entirely, granting universities free rein to license their research however they saw fit, with only minimal government oversight. Latker and his colleagues argued that because a large percentage of academic research is embryonic—or far from commercial application—*exclusive licensing* was the only way to induce a private firm to invest in commercial development.

In some respects this logic was perfectly sound. Few would deny that exclusive licensing can be very important in certain cases; however, a growing body of scholarship suggests it simply isn't true that *all, or even most,* embryonic research needs to be patented and licensed in order to be successfully brought into practical use. Indeed, an examination of the patent portfolios at Stanford and Columbia, published in 2002 by Jeannette Colyvas, Michael Crow, and other scholars, reveals that the academic technology-transfer process is far more heterogeneous than the Bayh-Dole Act assumed. The authors did identify some inventions, such as the glaucoma treatment Xalatan, that would very likely never have been commercialized without an exclusive license. Yet the same study turned up numerous other inventions that did *not* require proprietary licenses in order to promote commercial development. Of eleven inventions examined in detail, Colyvas and her colleagues identified seven that the universities' assertion of property rights did *not* induce corporate interest in, because "strategically located people in industry were well aware of the university research projects even before the universities began to market the inventions."[51] In many cases, companies were quite willing to exploit an embryonic academic invention without any license at all, because they had sufficient confidence that their research would lead to a profitable line of inquiry and, ultimately, to a final product that they could then patent.[52]

The truth is that the walling off of basic, embryonic research behind an exclusive license that isn't absolutely necessary imposes serious, long-term costs on the research community—and the broader economy. This is particularly true when the research in question is so-called nonrival research. As mentioned before, a candy bar is the quintessential rival good: It is quickly consumed and cannot be broadly shared without being diminished in usefulness. By contrast, when you are dealing with an economic good that is nonrival, as a large portion of academic research is—a mathematical theorem or a genetics technique, for example—then use of that good by additional parties, or in additional applications, poses *no real economic costs.* As Richard Nelson noted in his classic 1959 essay, "The Simple Economics of Basic Scientific Research," "The types of advances that are likely to result from basic research projects often take a long time to uncover, and very often have practical value in many fields. Consider the range of advances resulting from Boyles' gas law or Maxwell's equations." Because few firms operate in so wide a field of economic activity, he reasoned, it is highly unlikely that any one patent holder can capture the full economic value of this early-stage research. Therefore, it is far preferable to place a sizable portion of this nonrival knowledge in the public domain, where it can spur creative competition among scientists and diverse paths of inquiry.[53]

Increasingly, this simply isn't happening, thanks to the growing tendency for universities and their scholars to treat knowledge like a commodity. Consider the University of Wisconsin's recent handling of a breakthrough discovery in the field of stem cell research. In the 1990s, Professor James Thomson, working under a grant from the National Institutes of Health, succeeded in deriving stem cells from rhesus monkeys and macaques. The discovery generated enormous excitement within the scientific community, as these primitive cells can turn into virtually any type of tissue or organ and thus may have enormous potential value in the treatment of degenerative diseases such as multiple sclerosis, Alzheimer's, and Parkinson's.[54] By 1998, however, the university's technology-licensing arm—the Wisconsin Alumni Research Foundation (WARF)—had succeeded in obtaining an exceptionally broad patent on Thomson's discovery, covering *all lines of embryonic stem cells for primates (including humans), along with the actual method for isolating them*. The patent effectively gave WARF the power to determine which U.S.-based scientists could work with primate embryonic stem cells, under what conditions, and for what purpose.[55] Rather than making its stem cells available to everyone on a non-exclusive basis, WARF elected to grant an *exclusive* commercial license to the Geron Corporation, based in Menlo Park, California. This license encompassed many of the most important stem cell types—heart, bone, nerve, pancreatic, blood and cartilage—and their therapeutic uses. (Later, WARF scaled back the license in response to pressure from the National Institutes of Health, but Geron retained control over three of the most medically significant stem cell types, the crown jewels of regenerative medicine.)[56]

Many in the scientific community were outraged. In 2001, during a congressional hearing chaired by Senator Arlen Specter (Republican of Pennsylvania), one witness estimated that because of this monopoly, nearly half of all money the federal government provides for stem cell research would very likely be diverted to the University of Wisconsin and Geron in the form of royalty payments.[57] There was also widespread concern at the time about restrictions on access due to WARF's onerous license provisions, which included a $5,000 licensing fee, royalty payments, and a "reach-through" provision that gave WARF (and by extension Geron) first dibs on commercializing research stemming from the use of its cell lines. One outraged scientist, Douglas Melton of Harvard, told the *New York Times*, "Those conditions would mean that I am the ideal employee of Geron. They don't pay my salary, they don't pay my benefits, but anything I discover they own."[58]

As is so often the case with intellectual property disputes, the general public and mainstream media had no knowledge of this controversy—until August 9, 2001, the day President George W. Bush announced in a widely publicized televised address that the federal government was scaling back funding for human-embryonic stem cell research because of opposition from pro-life and religious groups. Under the new policy, the federal government would restrict public funding exclusively to scientists working with stem cell lines that had *already been developed prior to Bush's announcement*. The administration's sudden policy change greatly inflated the value of the University of Wisconsin's cell lines—and made it all the more imperative that scientists be able to access this valuable taxpayer-financed research. Yet the Bush administration and the NIH found they were highly constrained in their ability to intercede, because of provisions in Bayh-Dole that allow the government to intervene only in "exceptional circumstances."[59] Instead, the NIH worked to convince WARF and Geron in a series of backdoor meetings that, in addition to harming the University of Wisconsin's reputation, maintaining restrictive access to this taxpayer-financed research could drastically slow the pace of scientific development. In the end, WARF caved in and agreed to lift many of the more onerous licensing conditions; it also applied legal pressure to Geron, successfully scaling back its exclusive rights from a total of six cell types to three. This outcome enabled the Bush administration to save face. But it did nothing to address the larger question of whether fundamental, taxpayer-funded research should be subject to such restrictions in the first place.[60]

As with stem cells, so with transgenic mice—genetically engineered mammals that are critical research tools for scientists studying the many diseases that mice and humans share. In 1991, Baylor College of Medicine filed a patent on a new transgenic mouse—known as the p53 or "knockout" mouse—that had a tumor-suppressor gene knocked out or missing. As was the case with the University of Wisconsin's stem cells, all the original research that had gone into developing the p53 mouse had been underwritten by U.S. taxpayers, yet instead of making it broadly available to academic researchers, Baylor decided to license the mouse *exclusively* to a private company called GenPharm (now Taconic). The company, in turn, imposed restrictive conditions on use, including limits on breeding and licensing fees that most academic scientists considered objectionable (as the fees could quickly amount to thousands of dollars per lab).

It was at a prestigious scientific conference held at Cold Spring Harbor Laboratory in 1992 that the p53 mouse controversy really blew up.[61] Baylor was not the first university that had chosen to license a valuable basic research tool so restrictively. Back in 1985, Harvard set off a smoldering debate when it filed for an extremely broad patent on a genetically engineered mouse—known as the oncomouse—and licensed it exclusively to Dupont, creating considerable headaches for scientists wishing to use the mouse.[62] Now three hundred aggrieved scientists, led by Harold Varmus, a Nobel Prize–winning virologist at the University of California at San Francisco, publicly expressed their opposition to Baylor's mouse license, and called for the immediate establishment of a national repository at Jackson Laboratories (or "the Jax") in Bar Harbor, Maine, to distribute transgenic mice inexpensively to all academic scientists without proprietary restrictions. Despite the stature of the scientists involved in this effort, however, neither Baylor nor its corporate licensee would back down—so the p53 mouse controversy dragged on for another seven years.[63] Baylor refused to make its mouse freely available for academic distribution, and some time later, when MIT developed its own version of the p53 mouse and passed it along to the Jax, Baylor charged that both the school and its distributor were infringing on Baylor's original patent. Under the Bayh-Dole Act, Baylor's position was legally defensible, and in December 1999 the school compelled MIT and its distributor to pay royalties. Nonetheless, many scientists considered Baylor's actions reprehensible, as the imposition of royalties only added to the cost of making the p53 mouse available for academic research.[64]

The p53 and oncomouse controversies were partly responsible for leading the NIH, starting in 1996, to start investigating the universities' handling of basic research tools.[65] What it found was so shocking that it eventually led the agency, then under the direction of Varmus, to issue new guidelines in December 1999, calling on universities to refrain from imposing overly restrictive licenses on basic research tools financed by the U.S. taxpayer.[66] Because most university licensing records are kept strictly confidential (to protect corporate proprietary secrets), it's hard to know how closely this new advisory is being adhered to, but the lack of any true enforcement mechanism suggests that compliance is probably limited. When David Mowery and his colleagues obtained rare access to invention disclosures and licenses at two prominent academic institutions over the period 1986–1992, they found that a surprisingly high fraction of *all* academic inventions—as high as 90 percent of licenses in the University of California system and nearly 60 percent of licenses at Stanford—were licensed on a relatively *exclusive* basis.[67] Tom Doetschman, a geneticist at the University of Cincinnati who has created some 120 exotic strains of transgenic mice, recently told *Science* magazine that he felt increasingly "old-fashioned" for continuing to make his research tools freely available through the public domain.[68]

Old-fashioned, perhaps, but Professor Doetschman is by no means alone in believing that openness and sharing are critical to the scientific enterprise. In April 2003, the Royal Society, Britain's leading scientific academy, issued a report calling for freer access to scientific databases and other basic scientific information, and requesting that universities refrain from aggressively pursuing so many patents.[69] Three months after the Royal Society's pronouncement, a group of fifty-nine leading economists and scientists—including Nobel laureates Joseph Stiglitz (2001, economics) and John Sulston (2002, medicine)—wrote a public letter to the World Intellectual Property Organization, asking that it begin promoting more "open" models of innovation that don't rely on patents. There is evidence, the letter asserted, that a high level of innovation can be achieved in some areas of the economy without proprietary protection, and that "excessive, unbalanced, or poorly designed intellectual property protections may be counterproductive."[70] The property rights thicket has grown so dense post–Bayh-Dole that some worry the end result will be to *hamper* rather than foster innovation. As Richard Nelson wrote in 2003, we must not forget that "the market part of this Capitalist engine rests on a publicly supported scientific commons."[71]

In an influential paper, Michael A. Heller and Rebecca Eisenberg, legal scholars at the University of Michigan and Columbia University, respectively, argued that the problem with imposing excessive proprietary restrictions on early-stage, or "upstream," research is that it could result in a dangerous "anticommons" forming around one of our most vital public resources—knowledge—and thus stifle downstream research and innovation. "The tragedy of the anticommons," they explained, "arises when a user needs access to multiple patent inputs to create a single useful product. Each upstream patent allows its owner to set up a tollbooth on the road to product development, adding to the cost and slowing the pace of [innovation]."[72]

Of course, the tragedy is all the more egregious when one recognizes that taxpayers are footing the bill for so much of this upstream research—paying, in effect, for the building and maintenance of a public library of knowledge to which they themselves are subsequently denied access. "The whole issue of university involvement in patenting publicly funded research is sort of weird from a traditional economics perspective," Sampat explained to me in an interview. "Traditionally, the reason governments are involved in supporting science and technology is because markets do a poor job alone. Because it is difficult to prevent the new knowledge generated by one company from spilling over to others, profit-maximizing firms are not going to invest in socially optimal levels of R&D; the market alone will tend to underinvest." There are two ways to correct for this: Either the government can decide to issue patents that give companies limited-time monopolies on their research, or the government can fund the research itself. "What is so unusual about Bayh-Dole," Sampat observed, "is that it applies these two approaches simultaneously, first by choosing to fund the research out of the public purse, and then by opening the way for the universities to license those results exclusively to private firms."[73] In essence, this arrangement creates a double subsidy that flies in the face of traditional economic theory. To the extent that these practices stifle competition and facilitate monopolistic pricing, this could leave U.S. taxpayers shortchanged.

Putting Profits First

Proponents of academic commercialism tend to downplay the idea that heightened patenting and licensing jeopardize the free exchange of ideas—or the traditional mission of the university. In their view, the emergence of a knowledge-driven economy made it inevitable that society's conception of intellectual property law would change—and just as inevitable that our nation's universities would feel compelled to play a more direct role in commercializing new knowledge. As AUTM president James A. Severson reassuringly told Congress in 2000, "Patents to genetic discoveries made during university research can be pursued *without* disrupting the core values of publication and sharing of information, research results, materials, and know-how" (emphasis added).[74] According to Severson, because academic scholars who apply for patents are also obligated to publish their research (with only minimal delays), the public's interest in the open dissemination of new knowledge is protected.

In reality, however, publication does nothing to ensure that outside investigators will be permitted unrestricted access to the underlying technology, reagents, data, or techniques described in an academic paper. It is the university tech-transfer office that often controls that access. And under Bayh-Dole, there is a perverse incentive for these offices to seek the *most restrictive license possible*, as it will almost always be preferable to the corporate licensee, and more financially lucrative for the university. "Exclusive licenses typically command higher royalties," Rai and Eisenberg explained, "and companies holding exclusive licenses are more willing to reimburse for patent costs and to provide additional grant funding to the inventor."[75] The NIH working group was absolutely right to remind universities that "their principal obligation under the Bayh-Dole Act is to promote utilization, *not to maximize financial returns*." But given the explicit financial rewards Bayh-Dole placed in front of these cash-starved universities, is it any surprise that such warnings have mostly fallen on deaf ears? A large-scale survey by Jerry Thursby and other prominent economists found that university tech-transfer officers now list "revenue" as their *number one priority*—not widespread use of their technology, or even effective commercialization.[76]

More and more, our nation's leading universities are behaving in ways that suggest money is what ultimately guides their decisionmaking. Consider some of the creative ways universities have sought to extend the longevity of their patents in recent years to maximize their royalty revenue. In the late 1970s, Barnett Rosenberg, a professor at Michigan State University (MSU), developed two widely prescribed cancer drugs, cisplatin and carboplatin, that have been widely credited with helping to extend or save innumerable patients' lives. For MSU, the discovery was like hitting the jackpot. The university licensed Rosenberg's invention, financed largely with taxpayer grants, to Bristol-Myers Squibb, and by 1999 it had raked in more than $160 million in royalties. Having tasted wealth, however, MSU wasn't eager to give it up. As the patents neared their expiration date, the university and its licensing agent, Research Corporation Technology, tried something unusual: They applied for a second patent on cisplatin, slated to kick in before the original one expired.[77]

From a purely financial standpoint, this was clearly good for MSU's bottom line. But did it benefit the public? In fact, MSU's action prevented four generic manufacturers from marketing a far cheaper version of the anticancer drug, prompting the companies to take the university to court. In 1999, the U.S. District Court in New Jersey rejected MSU's second patent as "obviousness-type double patenting" and ruled in favor of the generic drug makers.[78]

More recently, Columbia University sought to keep Richard Axel's famous cotransformation patent alive by mimicking the tactics of the drug industry. A highly valuable technique for enabling animal cells to be used in manufacturing human proteins, the Axel invention was already one of the most lucrative licenses in academic history. Since 1981, the school had raked in an estimated $300–$400 million.[79] Yet, in early 2000, just months before the Axel patent was set to expire, Columbia launched a lobbying campaign on Capitol Hill designed to reap an even greater windfall. Enlisting the help of a Columbia alumnus, Senator Judd Gregg (Republican of New Hampshire), the university attempted to slip a provision into an unrelated appropriations bill that would have extended the Axel patent for an additional fourteen to eighteen months.[80] Michael Crow, the head of Columbia's tech-transfer office at the time, estimated that had the extension been successful, it would have steered another $100 million into the university's coffers. Outraged industry representatives and legislators blocked it from going through.

But Columbia didn't back down. Borrowing another page from the drug industry's book, the university applied for, and eventually won, a controversial new patent on the Axel invention that extended its ownership claims to 2019. It did so even though, over the previous two decades, more than thirty biotech and pharmaceutical firms had already licensed the Axel invention, using it to develop an array of valuable new medicines: Avonex (for multiple sclerosis); Cerezyme (for Gaucher disease); and Activase (for removal of blood clots). Collectively, these companies had already paid Columbia hundreds of millions of dollars in royalties, including roughly $70 million from the Genentech corporation alone. Because all of Columbia's original patents on the Axel invention were originally slated to expire in August 2000, the companies were naturally startled to wake up one morning and find that they were now expected to continue paying royalties for an *additional* twenty years. Predictably, they fought back. By the end of 2003, Columbia was a defendant in three separate lawsuits, involving a total of five major biotech firms. "Columbia obtained its patent protection, reaped very significant rewards, and now the inventions have passed into the public domain," explained Donald R. Ware, an attorney representing several of the companies. "The industry wants Columbia to play by the rules that everybody else plays by, which is you have an invention, you get a patent, and you get one 17-year term."[81] Needless to say, it seems doubtful that students, parents, and alumni would be very happy to learn that Columbia was now diverting its educational dollars to this sort of exorbitant legal defense.

In their zeal to maximize revenue, many schools are not only engaging in unsavory battles to extend the life of their patents but also getting into embarrassing legal skirmishes with their own students and professors over the rights to potentially lucrative ideas.

In the most extraordinary case to date, Petr Taborsky, a student at the University of South Florida (USF), in Tampa, wound up on the chain gang of a maximum-security state prison after colliding with his university over the rights to a discovery he had made while he was an undergraduate. Taborsky, an émigré from Prague, had been working as a research assistant on an academic project sponsored by the Florida Progress Corporation, a local holding company. At the end of the sponsored research period, Taborsky claimed he had gotten permission from Robert Carnahan, a dean in the College of Engineering, to begin working on his own experiments, following a different approach, which he planned to use as the basis for a master's thesis. But as soon as Taborsky made his research breakthrough, which had obvious commercial utility as a way to remove ammonia from wastewater, USF and Florida Progress immediately asserted proprietary rights to his discovery. The university filed criminal charges against Taborsky, and spent more than *ten times* the amount of the original research grant on legal counsel alone. Taborsky was convicted of stealing university property and trade secrets and sent to a maximum-security prison, where he began serving on a chain gang in 1996. Eventually, the case grew into an embarrassing media spectacle, prompting then governor Lawton Chiles to intervene and offer Taborsky clemency. After the criminal trial was already over, the U.S. Patent Office acknowledged that Taborsky was the *sole inventor* of his discovery, not Carnahan, the university, or Florida Progress.[82]

Prior to Bayh-Dole, such disputes were unheard of. Professors by and large viewed their profession as a calling; they gave much of their research away for free, and they didn't hold executive positions or have other personal financial interests in the companies funding their research. Whatever business dealings they had were largely conducted off campus, on their own time or during consulting hours. Now, the battle to control and own ideas has led to costly litigation that pits universities against their own professors. In 2002, *The Scientist* reported that the University of New Mexico had filed lawsuits against four of its professors over a seven-year period for allegedly absconding with inventions that were the property of the university. With one exception, the university won all of its claims. In 1996, a jury awarded $2.3 million to two professors, Jerome Singer and Lawrence Crooks, who filed suit against the University of California for shortchanging them on royalties resulting from their path-breaking research on magnetic resonance imaging, a widely utilized medical test known as the MRI. An appeals court found that the university had improperly sheltered revenue by dramatically discounting the patents it had licensed to manufacturers in exchange for more than $20 million in research funding. And such cases are merely the tip of the iceberg.[83]

Equally disturbing are the growing numbers of professors who are battling their own universities over the right to keep their research freely accessible in the public domain. Such conflicts have grown particularly divisive in the field of computer science, where the birth of the Internet was predicated on the willingness of university-based programmers to work collaboratively in an open, nonproprietary manner. Chris Johnson, a computer science professor at the University of Utah, haggled with his tech-transfer office for two years before he finally convinced the officers there to allow public release of a software platform he and his research team had developed. "We wanted to open-source it," Johnson told *Salon.com*, referring to the nonproprietary release of computer code, but the tech-transfer office repeatedly asserted that doing so "would undermine its commercial value." Johnson and his research team rejected the university's argument, because they knew their software, known as SCIRun, was a foundational program that would be far more valuable if other programmers were free to access it, and build on it themselves. In another recent case, Steven Brenner, a computational biologist at U.C. Berkeley, reported that it took several months—and hundreds of dollars in legal fees—for him to persuade the U.C. tech-transfer office to grant him an open-source contract with his university. Since then, numerous other professors have contacted Brenner to learn how they, too, can release their work through "open source." The problem has grown so serious that some top computer programmers question whether the Internet would even exist today if its development had occurred under the restrictive proprietary ethos that pervades academia today.[84]

———

Given how frequently they seem to be behaving like their counterparts in industry, might courts begin to view universities less as nonprofit educational institutions than as for-profit commercial outfits? In fact, as a federal appeals court ruling in *Madey v. Duke University* shows, this is already happening.

In 1998, John Madey, an internationally renowned physicist, sued his former employer, Duke University, for patent infringement, seeking to retain control over free electron laser equipment he had invented, patented, and partially financed himself (together with more than $40 million in federal funding). Madey's lawsuit was filed shortly after Duke removed him as the principal investigator on a federal research grant that involved use of this laser. In its defense, Duke maintained that although Madey did hold patents to the technology, the school was using the equipment "under the authority of a government research grant" and should continue to enjoy free access under what is commonly known as a research exemption for experimental uses.[85]

For decades, universities and their professors have successfully invoked this experimental use defense when conducting "pure" academic research, based on a long line of court decisions dating back to 1813 that permitted investigators to experiment with patented technologies provided their research was "for amusement, to satisfy idle curiosity, or for strictly philosophical inquiry," not commercial use. Yet in October 2002, a federal appeals court rejected Duke's "experimental use defense," noting that the school was no different from a business-like enterprise, particularly where intellectual property issues were concerned. "Duke . . . like other major research institutions of higher learning, is not shy in pursuing an aggressive patent licensing program from which it derives a not insubstantial revenue stream," observed the appeals court in a revealing footnote to its decision.

Many university leaders expressed shock at the ruling, and promptly filed a joint appeal to the U.S. Supreme Court. But was the ruling really so surprising? In an editorial published in *Science*, the legal scholar Rebecca Eisenberg rightly pointed out that on the contrary, the decision was perfectly logical in light of recent trends. "As universities have become increasingly aggressive as patent owners," Eisenberg observed, "they have compromised their claim to disinterested stewardship of knowledge in the public interest, leaving themselves more vulnerable to patent infringement claims as defendants." The university leadership certainly should have known better than to take the "research exception" for granted, Eisenberg pointed out, since its legal foundation was always extremely fragile. Instead, these universities exercised little restraint: They had been "in the vanguard of claimants seeking patents on 'upstream' research discoveries," and extremely aggressive when it came to enforcing their own patent claims in court.[86]

The problem with such an aggressive posture, of course, is that it compromises the university's legitimacy when one of its own academic investigators needs access to a particular patented technology. How can the same university that has been aggressively prosecuting others for patent infringement suddenly turn around and expect others to honor its "research exemption" privilege?[87] Once again, it appears that money has blinded most universities to this rather obvious inconsistency in commercial versus academic aims. Many schools have succeeded in generating impressive windfalls from their patent-infringement suits—the University of California won a $200-million settlement from Genentech; the University of Minnesota settled a suit against Glaxo-Wellcome for $300 million—emboldening numerous other schools to try and do the same.[88]

Even when these lawsuits are glaringly out of sync with their stated public mission, many universities have refused to back down. Recently, MIT, Harvard, and ARIAD Pharmaceuticals, Inc., a spin-off firm, were roundly criticized for their decision to aggressively enforce an extremely broad patent on the NF-kB messenger protein, a key biological trigger that was already in widespread use based on published papers. The claim is so broad as to cover treatments for *all* diseases that work through the NF-kB pathway, including cancer, osteoporosis, and rheumatoid arthritis. Immediately after the patent was issued in June 2002, MIT and its partners filed a lawsuit against Eli Lilly, alleging that two of its most valuable drugs worked in a way that violated their new patent. They also sent out warning letters to fifty additional companies with products either on the market or in development, demanding that they pay royalties. All of which prompted many academic scientists to worry about the precedent these universities might be setting. "I feel that [the patent] is overly broad," said Sankar Ghosh, a professor in Yale's School of Medicine. "A lot of the science we do is for the purpose of finding new drugs. And if this prevents research in this area, it seems to be not in the best interest of the science."[89]

Putting the Public Interest Last

Back in the early 1900s, when Frederick Cottrell embraced patenting at U.C. Berkeley, he hardly could have fathomed that it would one day lead to the levels of commercialism we see on university campuses today. Indeed, in 1932, as mentioned earlier, Cottrell cautioned that "a danger was involved" should Berkeley's patenting experiment "prove highly profitable to the university and lead to a general emulation of the plan." That danger, he warned, "was the possibility of growing commercialism and competition between institutions and an accompanying tendency for secrecy in scientific work."[90] Several decades later, when government patent reform was surfacing as a contested issue in Congress, Joshua Lederberg, a geneticist and Nobel laureate, wrote a letter to Senator Gaylord Nelson of Wisconsin strongly opposing any direct profiteering by the university. "My gravest concern is not unjust enrichment," Lederberg asserted. "Rather, I do not believe the pursuit of proprietary gains to be the proper business of the university. The possibility of profit—especially when other funding is so tight—will be a distorting influence on open communication and on the pursuit of basic scholarship." Lederberg acknowledged that patenting *was* an important vehicle for commercializing some academic inventions, but like Cottrell, he believed this activity should be conducted at arm's length from the university. Using Cottrell's Research Corporation as a model, he proposed that all publicly financed inventions that had commercial promise should be transferred to a national, nonprofit R&D foundation, which would license this research at "arm's length" and use the resulting proceeds to finance additional public research.[91]

Today, Lederberg's recommendation still holds enormous appeal. And the broader concerns that he and Cottrell expressed have continuing resonance. For the new gold rush mentality sweeping our nation's campuses has placed universities on a collision course with many of their own stated goals and ideals: the ability to nurture basic science and public-good research; the willingness to protect the public domain; and the capacity to expand, through publications and teaching, public access to knowledge.

Consider the impact on the developing world, for example, where global knowledge sharing is critically important to public health and economic advancement. In the summer of 2003, the Rockefeller Foundation, together with the heads of numerous prominent U.S. agricultural centers and universities—North Carolina State, University of California, Ohio State, Rutgers, Michigan State, Cornell, and others—published an editorial in *Science* warning that the rapid escalation of public-sector patenting and licensing was threatening the future of plant research—especially research on subsistence crops so vital to the developing world. "Our institutions have found," the authors wrote, that the nonprofit sector "is increasingly restricted when wishing to develop new crops with the technologies *it has itself invented*, including so-called 'enabling technologies'—the research tools necessary for further experimentation and innovation" (emphasis added). The source of the problem? The proliferation of intellectual property restrictions in both the public and the private research sectors. In the case of Golden Rice, a genetically engineered plant designed to alleviate vitamin A deficiency, for example, scientists had to navigate "more than 40 patents or contractual obligations associated with material transfer agreements" in order to move their research forward. The university presidents and researchers did not mince words concerning their own culpability: Roughly *one-fourth* of the patented inventions in agricultural biotechnology—including many of the "technologies that are necessary to conduct basic biological research"—originated at public-sector institutions but are now tied up under restrictive commercial agreements. The time has come, they announced, for universities and other taxpayer-financed institutions to explore new ways of keeping more of this public knowledge broadly accessible.[92]

This statement is a clear indication of how serious the threat to the knowledge commons has become. Yet the crisis it addresses extends far beyond agricultural research. At a time when the gap between rich and poor nations is greater than ever, and the human and technological capacity exists to combat many of the problems now plaguing the developing world—poverty, disease, lack of education—knowledge sharing has become a vital tool. As students, professors, and administrators at one prominent U.S. university learned recently, it can even mean, literally, the difference between life and death.

The AIDS Crisis in Africa—and at Yale

In the summer of 2000, prior to beginning her first year at Yale law school, Amy Kapczynski, a petite twenty-six-year-old woman with an athletic build, short-cropped hair, and dark eyes, traveled to Durban, South Africa, to attend the World AIDS Conference. There, she and fellow AIDS activists met to strategize about how the world community could successfully combat a deadly disease that had already infected 35 million people. Out in the streets, Kapczynski and her colleagues were greeted by five thousand demonstrators protesting their lack of access to the latest HIV-AIDS drugs capable of prolonging or saving lives, which were already in widespread use in the United States and Europe. When she returned to New Haven to start law school later that fall, Kapczynski tried to immerse herself in textbooks on constitutional law and torts. However, her scholarly pursuits were soon interrupted when she received a call from the South African chapter of Doctors Without Borders (DWB), the Nobel Prize–winning health organization. DWB was planning to launch a campaign exposing Yale's complicity in the AIDS crisis, and it wanted Kapczynski's help.[93]

Longtime AIDS activists had known for some time that Yale owned the patent to d4T (stavudine), a powerful antiretroviral drug sold under the brand name Zerit. In February 2001, DWB wrote a letter to Yale requesting that the university refrain from enforcing its patent in South Africa so the government there could begin importing or producing low-cost generic copies of d4T to meet the needs of its 4.7 million HIV-positive citizens. By supporting DWB's request, Yale not only would be acknowledging the gravity of the global AIDS crisis but also affirming the right of underdeveloped nations to access generic medicines during national health emergencies. Weeks later, however, Jon Soderstrom, managing director of Yale's technology licensing office, wrote back to say that although the university sympathized with DWB's concerns, it had licensed its d4T patent *exclusively* to Bristol-Myers Squibb (BMS) and therefore its hands were tied.[94] Independent efforts to raise these issues with the company were equally unsuccessful.

Kapczynski and other student activists were hopeful that Yale, a nonprofit educational institution—and the recipient of more than $250 million in annual federal research funding—could be persuaded to change its mind, particularly as the existing consumer market in South Africa for drugs in stavudine's class was pitifully small.[95] After extensive research and digging—much of it leaked to reporters at the *Yale Daily News*—they helped expose the fact that from 1994 to 2000, Yale had netted $262 million in royalties on sales of d4T. When Yale erected a new medical building on campus, one-third of the $176-million price tag had been paid for with stavudine royalties. (BMS had also provided large grants for several major research projects on campus.[96])

Yale insisted it had no choice but to issue an exclusive license to d4T, as no pharmaceutical company would have been willing to test and commercialize the drug without monopoly control over the invention. Whether this was true or not, Kapczynski and DWB were firmly convinced the school had an obligation to disseminate its medical research in a manner consistent with the public interest, particularly considering that nearly all the original research on the d4T compound had been funded by the federal government. In their view, Soderstrom's position also failed to accord with Yale's own written principles and guidelines, many of which were posted on the technology-transfer office's own official Web site. Yale's patent policy, for example, stated, "As a general policy, the University wishes to grant non-exclusive licenses to its inventions to insure the broadest availability to the public." Another document affirmed that a central objective was to commercialize research for "the benefit of the society in general." Therefore, the students asked, why hadn't Yale been more vigilant in drawing up its licensing agreement with BMS? For example, Yale could have stipulated in the contract that in the case of a national health emergency, the school retained the right to issue voluntary licenses to poor countries permitting them to import low-cost or generic versions of the drug. If Yale was truly committed to commercializing its research "for the benefit of the society in general," why were the vast majority of HIV-AIDS patients—95 percent of whom live in the developing world—unable to access the school's publicly financed drug?

Yale continued to insist it had no legal authority to intervene. Meanwhile, the pharmaceutical industry argued that South Africa lacked the necessary health infrastructure to properly administer these drugs, and that any release of generics in the developing world would cut into industry profits and stifle new drug research. Yet the more publicity the students generated, the more uncomfortable Yale's public relations situation grew. By mid-March, hundreds of Yale professors, graduate students, technicians, and postdocs had signed a petition calling on Yale and BMS to permit the release of a generic version of stavudine in South Africa. "I became a scientist because I wanted to help create new cures for diseases around the world," declared Fran Balamuth, a Yale immunologist quoted in a student press release. "Now I find that Yale is turning results of publicly funded research into corporate profit."[97]

The activists' biggest break came when an article appeared on March 11, 2001 in the *New York Times*, quoting Yale's own William Prusoff, the inventor of d4T. Although Prusoff had personally profited from Zerit sales—and had used a large portion of the royalty income to fund new research in his lab—he was deeply perturbed to learn that millions of South Africans were unable to access his discovery. Prusoff told the *Times* he "strongly supported" the students' campaign to permit broader distribution of d4T in South Africa. "I wish they would either supply the drug for free," he said, "or allow India or Brazil to produce it cheaply for underdeveloped countries. But the problem is, the big drug houses are not altruistic organizations. Their only purpose is to make money."[98]

Prusoff's comments greatly embarrassed Yale. The school immediately grew fearful that its financial interest in d4T might tarnish its academic reputation, and it started carefully weighing its next move. Halfway across the country, students at the University of Michigan, inspired by the actions at Yale, had started to expose their own institution's financial interest in Ziagen, another important AIDS drug, which had been developed at the university and licensed to Glaxo Wellcome (now GlaxoSmithKline) and which was also inaccessible to poor patients in the developing world. On March 15, Bristol-Myers announced a massive reduction in prices in South Africa and promised not to prosecute any generic producer. Although the company later told the *Wall Street Journal* its decision had had nothing to do with mounting student pressure, the timing clearly suggested otherwise.[99]

If intellectual property disputes like these appear to be out of keeping with the university's nonprofit research mission, that's because they are. In a provocative 1996 article in the *University of Pennsylvania Law Review*, Peter Blumberg, then a law student, argued that much of the commercial activity emanating from university tech-transfer offices is so far removed from academia's public mission that it "could be treated as unrelated business income for tax purposes." Universities, Blumberg wrote, "enjoy their tax exemption because of a belief that they are producing research that no other market actor would produce absent a public subsidy; basic research, publishable research, research that educates students and . . . is usable by the whole society." Thus far, the SEC has not chosen to challenge the universities' tax exemption, because commercial profits are plowed back into the cost of operating their tech-transfer offices and into research.[100] However, the question of whether such aggressive, market-oriented behavior is consistent with the university's nonprofit mission, and truly warrants public subsidy, is an important one.

In the end, what was at stake for Yale in the AIDS controversy was not just a few hundred million dollars in royalties but something far more valuable: its reputation. However much universities may wish to mimic the business world, they are ultimately beholden to the public for support. Would alumni continue to give so generously to their alma maters if they perceived them as increasingly motivated by profit rather than serving the public good? Would politicians and taxpayers continue to issue tens of billions of dollars annually to colleges and universities in the form of grants, tax exemptions, and student financial aid? Isn't it time for university administrators to consider such questions as they weigh how to balance commercial interests with their commitment to the public good?

AUTM Goes to Disney World

In early February 2003, I traveled to the Association of University Technology Managers' annual meeting in Orlando, Florida, to see how much had changed in the tech-transfer world since I'd last visited Stanford's tech-licensing office. The conference—"Partnering for Prosperity"—was held in the heart of Disney World, a colorful capitalist dreamscape about as far removed from the ivy-covered halls of academe as one can imagine. In search of affordable accommodations, I put myself up at Disney's Animal Kingdom, in the economy-class All-Star Sports Resort, a ten-year-old boy's fantasy motel with gargantuan basketball hoops looming overhead; sports stars and iconography covering the walls; and a large blue pool surrounded by palm trees.[101]

Inside the convention center, the atmosphere was considerably more toned down, though it was hardly what you'd expect at your typical academic conference. The names of the conference rooms reminded us that we were still at Disney: Nutcracker 1 and 2; Fantasia K and N. And most of the panels listed in the AUTM program were unabashedly commercial:

- "Football! Physiology! Sports Stars! Marketing! The Gatorade Story"

- "Advanced Topics in Equity: What Your Mama Never Told You About Equity Deals"
- "Dirty Little Tricks in Licensing"
- "Make $10 Million with No Money Down!"
- "Creating an Enterprise Environment"

The most intriguing panel of all, given our location in Disney World, was titled "Getting Value Out of Mice." Held in a narrow, generic-looking conference room, the panel was packed with university tech-transfer officers eager to learn more about extracting profits from transgenic mice. Two of the featured speakers were none other than Joyce Brinton of Harvard and Lynne Schaefer of Baylor College of Medicine, administrators who had been extensively involved in the oncomouse and p53 mouse controversies, respectively. Brinton and Schaefer both tried to impress upon their audience that they should not have unreasonable expectations: Although some mice are highly profitable, they emphasized, most are not great moneymakers. David Einhorn, a tall man with a mane of black hair and a crumpled suit, struck a different note. General counsel at the Jackson Laboratory—the repository formed shortly after the p53 mouse controversy to protect open access to transgenic mice—Einhorn reminded the audience members to think hard about their academic obligations and consider whether squeezing profits out of mice was in the best interest of science. He observed, with studied calm, that he now frequently found it more difficult to work with universities than with corporations, because of the academic community's fierce reluctance to surrender proprietary rights.

Following his presentation, most of the tech-transfer officers directed their questions to the technical details and financial feasibility of mouse licensing. There was, in fact, little discussion throughout the conference of the potential downsides of commercialization. Academic commercialism stimulates entrepreneurship! It fosters economic growth! Best of all, many speakers noted, it provides universities with "unrestricted funding"—that is, money that institutions can spend however they wish (as opposed to it being earmarked for a specific purpose). As I roamed from one panel to the next, these themes were sounded again and again. One professor spoke enthusiastically about an entrepreneurship course he taught, noting that several of his students had already gone off to start their own companies. In Florida alone, the revenue figures were impressive: Florida State University's total income from its cancer-fighting drug Taxol now topped $200 million; the University of Florida had pulled in $94 million from selling the rights to Gatorade. In 2002, the University of Florida struck it rich again when it sold its stake in Regeneration Technologies, a start-up venture based on a patented process for harvesting bone and tissue from cadavers, for $60 million.[102]

Amid all the cheerleading, however, one important fact was missing— a fact easily discernable to anyone who bothered to examine AUTM's licensing surveys: Few universities actually make any money from their tech-transfer operations. In 2002, universities collected an impressive $959 million from the commercialization of drugs, software, and other academic inventions. But the lion's share of the revenue—two-thirds— went to just thirteen institutions, and largely stemmed from a small number of "big hit" inventions, like those at Florida State and the University of Florida.[103] Once this aggregate figure is broken down, it becomes apparent that more than half the nation's academic tech-transfer offices very likely *do not break even.*[104]

Part of the reason is that the cost of running a tech-transfer office—a complex operation that involves sifting through new invention disclosures, filing patent claims, hiring attorneys, negotiating industry licenses, and seeking out venture-capital funds—is considerable. AUTM doesn't publish any data on these operational costs or factor them into its own revenue calculations. However in 2003, Cornell University economist Ronald G. Ehrenberg decided to take a closer look, examining data from the year 2000, when AUTM reported $1 billion in university tech-licensing revenue. That year, Ehrenberg estimated that academic tech-transfer offices employed approximately 480 full-time-equivalent licensing administrators. Assuming the fully loaded cost of each of these employees (salaries, benefits, office space, etc.) was $100,000, this was an expense of $161.5 million dollars. Another drain on the balance sheet was legal fees: Patent defense costs, patent infringement costs, and attorney fees are very high. (In 2002, the University of Rochester established an "eight-figure" legal fund to go after billions of dollars in back royalties that the school contended it was owed by companies that manufacture and market Celebrex, the blockbuster arthritis drug.[105]) In 2000, AUTM reported that universities had incurred a total of $117 million in legal expenses; after subtraction of reimbursements from third parties, the costs amounted to $64 million.

Add to this the fact that most of the truly big earnings went to a small number of schools and, according to Ehrenberg, the typical (median) university ended up with a mere $343,952 in net revenues from its tech-licensing activities. Even this amount overstates their true earnings, since 30 to 50 percent of these revenues actually go to the inventors, not to the tech-transfer office. Of the 138 institutions, 51 actually lost money that year, Ehrenberg estimated. When all was said and done, he concluded, "it seems clear that commercialization of research has yet to provide most universities with large amounts of *net* income."[106]

If most university tech-transfer offices are not, in fact, profitable, does it make sense for so many institutions to be pouring resources into these commercial operations? At a time when many schools are bleeding red ink, cutting courses, downsizing full-time teaching, and increasing class size, is this really a wise investment? When one factors in the other costs—the conflict-of-interest entanglements, the threat to academic freedom, and the enclosure of the scientific commons—is the investment justified?

Many of the schools on the losing side of this tech-transfer business are "catch-up schools" or "wannabes": universities that are striving mightily to join the ranks of Duke, Stanford, and Columbia but are still at the bottom of the heap. Rather than abandon this costly gambit, however, they seem eager to throw their fate to the winds by building impressive new academic-industrial research centers, luring talented young entrepreneurial faculty to their campuses with impressive pay packages, and plowing resources into business incubators, technology parks, and venture-capital funds in the hopes of seeding new companies.

It would be too easy to blame the employees who toil away inside these university tech-transfer offices for this seemingly irrational behavior. Yet, to a large extent, they are merely responding to the financial incentives and imperatives coming from other, more powerful quarters. For in recent years, nearly every university president, dean, or provost has felt enormous pressure from federal legislators, state governors, and regents to turn his or her institution into an engine of economic growth, capable of spawning the next Silicon Valley.

7

Dreaming of Silicon Valley

When Wisconsin governor Tommy Thompson delivered his State of the State address on January 26, 2000, he spelled out his desire to make the University of Wisconsin a central player in the "long-term economic vitality of our state," a knowledge factory capable of spawning cutting-edge ideas, high-tech corridors, spin-off companies, and jobs. Holding up a vial that contained a strand of DNA, Thompson told the state legislature, "The face of our future economy lies in this little tube and many others like it in laboratories across Wisconsin. The race is on to see which state will create the Silicon Valley of 2000."

Thompson's plan involved building on the much-celebrated Wisconsin Idea of the early twentieth century—when the University of Wisconsin (UW) engaged in a concerted effort to reach out to the state's constituencies, including private industry, to provide research, training, extension courses, and other practical advice and service. Now, he said, the state's university system needed to push this utilitarian mission further: "New discoveries in science and technology will create high-skill, high-paying jobs in Wisconsin. These jobs will provide a higher quality of life for our families and a brain gain for our state. A driving force behind this new economy will be the *New* Wisconsin Idea, a bold new partnership between the University of Wisconsin and the private sector."[1] Before closing his speech, Thompson sealed his commitment to this new economic growth strategy by pledging $317 million in state funding for the UW-Madison "Biostar" program over the next ten years to fund four state-of-the-art biotech research facilities, a biotechnology master's program, and the recruitment of a hundred world-class faculty.

Thompson was by no means the first state governor to champion such an ambitious educational agenda. Arizona governor Jane Hull had recently announced plans to pump an extra $75 million a year into her own state's higher-education system to boost workforce development and technology transfer to industry. Without this money, she declared, "10 or 15 years down the line, we're not going to be positioned anywhere for the New Economy. We're not going to be players."[2] Numerous other states have launched similar economic development strategies, designed to exploit the commercial high-tech potential of their public universities.[3]

Culminating Thompson's year-long effort to advance his new educational agenda was the Wisconsin Economic Summit, held the following winter in downtown Milwaukee. Academic leaders from across the state, ever vigilant about the need to justify ongoing state support for higher education, gathered en masse to show their support. The event itself was hosted and organized by UW-Milwaukee, and by the regents for the entire UW system.[4]

Not everyone in the academic community looked on these developments so favorably, however.

On November 29, the opening day of the summit, a group of undergraduate students from UW campuses across the state gathered outside the Midwest Express Center to show their disapproval. It was a rainy, miserable day, cold and blustery—the kind of weather for which Milwaukee is famous in the early winter. The downtown streets were deserted, save for a wet, bedraggled-looking band of protesters holding aloft a banner that read, *"Students are not products. Teachers are not tools. The University is not a factory."* One student, dressed from head to toe in blue recycling bags, with two googly eyes pasted on top of his head—calling himself the Corporate Cookie Monster—led a group chant by marking out a steady rhythmic beat on his drum. "The University . . . Is Not . . . for Sale," the students cried out in unison, jumping up and down to fight off the cold.

Shortly after the guests began arriving in their business suits and overcoats, Dana Churness, a young woman with fair skin and sopping wet hair, peeled away from the student group to pass out flyers. "Are you going to sell off another piece of our university?" she asked them as they passed, her eyes barely visible behind her foggy, rain-covered glasses. She bitterly informed me that there weren't going to be many UW students attending the summit itself. The event had been scheduled in the middle of the school week, during work hours, and cost anywhere from $119 to $149 per person. The only reason she and a handful of other students had been able to come was that the chancellor of UW-Stevens Point had granted them a special fee waiver. Just before I pushed through the doors of the convention center, with its shiny marble floors and red Christmas poinsettias visible through the glass, she blurted out, "There aren't any students represented on any of the panels either!"

The summit was just beginning when I entered the main auditorium and found a seat. Churness had been right about the guest list. The large, cavernous room was filled nearly to capacity with some nine hundred university administrators, statewide business leaders, politicians, and the CEOs of major corporations, including Kimberly Clark, Scient, Harley Davidson, and Cisco Systems. Studying the program, I saw that the list of speakers and panelists was much the same. With only two UW faculty listed, even the professoriate seemed strangely underrepresented.

At the front of the auditorium, the UW chancellors spoke about their "regional listening sessions" and the need to strengthen the UW's ties with private industry, enhance workforce development, and leverage the university's knowledge assets to create new high-tech, high-wage jobs. Numerous references were made to Silicon Valley and Route 128, where schools like Stanford and MIT had helped to stimulate remarkable clusters of high-tech growth right in their own backyards. As each chancellor rose to stand at the podium, a huge blown-up image of his or her face was projected on a large white screen facing the audience. UW-Eau Claire chancellor Donald Mash spoke enthusiastically about using his university's resources to "build economic growth and entrepreneurship in the Chippewa Valley." Nancy Zimpher, the chancellor at UW-Milwaukee, spoke of her determination to raise Milwaukee's academic stature and turn her campus into Wisconsin's second great flagship institution, replete with its own regional biotech hub and spin-off companies. Many of the speakers bemoaned the fact that Wisconsin was still known more for its breweries, manufacturing, dairy farming, and those funny-looking "cheesehead hats" worn at football games than for its promise as a gateway to the new economy. The time had come, they proclaimed, for the state university system and political leaders to cultivate a "new brand image" for the state.

There were legitimate reasons for Wisconsin to be concerned about its economic future. The state had suffered badly during the 1980s, losing some 134,000 jobs and watching its unemployment rate soar to nearly 9 percent. By 2000, the picture looked brighter, as several hundred thousand new jobs created during the 1990s had pushed unemployment back down to just 3 percent. Yet the state's economic future remained uncertain.[5] Wisconsin faced stiff regional competition, and the "brain drain" that continued to afflict so many of the nation's midwestern, southern, and rural regions remained a source of widespread concern. As soon as the state's young people graduated from college, many complained, the "best and brightest" moved out of the state in search of greater opportunities and better-paying jobs. "What we plant," noted one frustrated state representative who spoke at the conference, "other states harvest."

But would attempting to transform the state's higher-education system into a jobs-and-product mill actually solve this problem—or merely erode the value of its education? The flyer Churness had stuffed into my hand earlier asserted the latter was more likely:

> As state funding for higher education decreases, the UW System is having to rely more heavily upon private corporate funding sources. This will jeopardize the balanced liberal arts education that students require for critical thinking. As the UW System schools move further away from a non-profit, unbiased endeavor, the foundation of what higher-education was built upon continues to crumble.

The students were certainly right that most public universities now receive a shrinking portion of their funding from the state, even as governors and local elected officials have been imposing heavy new economic-development demands on their universities.[6] Was it reasonable to ask the UW system to secure Wisconsin's economic competitiveness while simultaneously continuing to deliver quality education? Or might it simply wind up failing miserably at both? To be sure, UW-Madison, the state's flagship university (which routinely draws in around $300 million in federal research funding) did possess the resources and scientific expertise to help contribute to the regional economy.[7] But were the state's other campuses in, for example, Milwaukee, Eau Claire, Oshkosh, and Green Bay—with a tiny fraction of this funding and cutting-edge science—really up to such a task?

Such questions were never raised during the three-day summit, where the atmosphere was boosterish. A lone dissenting voice came, somewhat unexpectedly, from Arthur Rolnick, senior vice president of the Federal Reserve Bank of Minneapolis, who spoke during a lunchtime banquet for esteemed guests. A middle-aged man with dark, receding hair, Rolnick strongly questioned the wisdom of asking the state's university system to drive economic development and productivity in the state. States weren't good at picking "winners and losers," he said, and neither were universities. If the university system was pushed to expend more resources and energy consulting with businesses and doing commercially oriented research, it would inevitably devote less attention to educating students and generating high-quality, basic, exploratory science—two public goods that were of vital importance in the new knowledge-driven economy. "I can't stress enough, you shouldn't train people for industry," he said. "You should educate them."

Follow the Leader: Emulating Stanford and MIT

The notion of using the university as a vehicle for fostering state-level economic growth was an idea that grew out of the same bleak economic realities that had led Congress to pass Bayh-Dole. In the 1970s and early 1980s, many older industrial regions seized on university-industry relationships as a way to spur growth. Eager to emulate the high-tech successes of Boston's Route 128 region, California's Silicon Valley, and North Carolina's Research Triangle Park, each of which had grown up near prominent research universities, state planners launched a series of new science and technology initiatives.[8] Pennsylvania founded the Ben Franklin Partnership; Ohio created the Thomas Edison program; Colorado, New York, Florida, and numerous other states followed with university-technology initiatives of their own.[9] This heightened interest in technology was triggered by new opportunities to match state funds with federal research grants, and by shifting priorities in Washington, which sent a strong signal that future competition for federal research money would require demonstrated links to industry.[10] By 1994, there were some 390 technology-diffusion programs spread across all fifty states, with expenditures of $385 million. The actual success rate of these ventures, however, wasn't impressive.[11] "State policymakers felt they had invested significant sums of money, and were not seeing the economic returns they expected," explained Dan Berglund, president and CEO of the State Sciences and Technology Institute (SSTI), an advocacy and research group.[12] The money for such initiatives started to dry up.

But not for long. The emergence of the Internet in the mid-1990s, followed by the dot-com boom and the rise of biotechnology, sent a powerful message to state economic planners: Invest in science and technology, or be left behind. With unprecedented zeal, governors and political leaders across the country raced, once again, to emulate places like Route 128 and Silicon Valley. The logic was straightforward: If it worked in Silicon Valley, why not here?

But this was precisely the problem: State after state rushed to emulate the Silicon Valley paradigm without understanding the complex array of factors that accounted for its success. Because nearly every one of the nation's celebrated "technopoles" had arisen near a major research center, it was assumed that the university must be the main driver for all this postindustrial growth.[13] As Richard Florida, an expert on regional economic development at George Mason University, explained to me, state planners watched one cutting-edge idea after another emerge from the ivory tower during the 1990s and assumed that the logical way to get a piece of the action was to embark on a "giant technology-push experiment."[14] The idea was simple. "If you create certain incentives for pumping out technologies, either in the form of intellectual property ownership, business incubation, or venture capital," Florida explained, "that will somehow magically turn into economic growth."

In reality, however, regional economic development is far more complicated than this. Universities can churn out lots of creative talent and technology, but if the surrounding region doesn't have a rich, dynamic infrastructure capable of absorbing and nurturing these knowledge assets, the benefits are likely to prove fleeting.[15] When Carnegie Mellon succeeded in spinning off the Internet search-engine company Lycos, for example, during the early days of the Internet boom, both the university and the surrounding Pittsburgh community were elated. America's long-suffering former steel town embraced this exciting high-tech venture with open arms, while Carnegie Mellon sold off its initial equity stake in the company and pocketed roughly $25 million. Yet, in 1998, Pittsburgh's luck suddenly turned: Lycos announced it was relocating all of its business operations to Boston. Nothing personal, of course; it was just that Pittsburgh lacked Boston's deep pools of skilled managers and talented technologists, which the company felt it needed.[16]

As this example illustrates, universities are only one of several components necessary for high-tech regional growth to be successful. Equally important is the vitality of the local infrastructure and the business support systems that surround the university. Indeed, scholars who have studied the rise of high-tech clusters in places like Route 128, Research Triangle Park, and Silicon Valley all seem to agree that the larger regional ecosystem is of equal if not greater significance.

MIT and Harvard did, of course, play a vital role in nurturing the aerospace, electronics, and mini-computing industries that grew up along Boston's vibrant Route 128 highway. Yet their influence was more indirect than most people assume. The development was "largely indigenous and spontaneous, rather than the result of a concerted effort to attract industry," wrote the historian Nancy Dorfman. "Neither Harvard nor MIT in the Boston area have involved themselves seriously as institutions in the local technical economy. Nevertheless, the graduates and staff of MIT have provided the single most important source of entrepreneurs to the region."[17] Because Boston's business, investment, and legal infrastructure was so strong, it was able to capture these universities' valuable outputs, their talent and ideas; incubate embryonic technologies; and support the growth of new high-tech companies.

The history of Research Triangle Park (RTP) is similar in this regard. According to Al Link, the author of two books on the park, North Carolina's three universities—which occupy the corners of this high-tech growth region—were *not* the principal drivers of RTP's development, despite myths to the contrary. Bankers, industrialists, and land developers conceived of and drew up the initial plans and provided the necessary momentum to keep the project moving forward, prompting Link to describe RTP as "North Carolina's finest example of civic entrepreneurship." According to Link, particular care was taken to respect the universities' academic priorities and their aversion to becoming mere research arms of industry: "The universities saw themselves as magnets to attract research companies to the area, not as participants in those companies' research efforts."[18]

The role that Stanford University played in driving regional economic growth in the Santa Clara Valley was certainly, by comparison, more direct. Frederick Terman, the man who "did more to propel Silicon Valley's rise than any other individual," according to the historian Annalee Saxenian, was a supremely confident, hard-edged electrical engineer who came to Stanford from MIT and rose to become dean of its School of Engineering. Shortly after his arrival, in the mid-1920s, he set his sights on building an industrial center in the Santa Clara Valley similar to the one that surrounded MIT. "Such a community," he wrote, "is composed of industries using highly sophisticated technologies, together with a strong university that is sensitive to the creative activities of the surrounding industry. This pattern appears to be the wave of the future."[19]

Because the San Francisco peninsula lacked the economic infrastructure that existed in Boston, Saxenian observed, Terman promoted "more open and reciprocal ties between Stanford and local industry than existed in the Rt. 128 region."[20] However, far more than today, these efforts were conducted at arm's length, with an eye toward protecting the core research and teaching functions of the university: Professors consulted with industry and encouraged their students to start up companies, but they didn't try to go into business or become CEOs themselves, nor did they assume any direct financial stake in the companies funding their academic work. The university, for its part, accepted funding from industry, but for the most part, it assiduously avoided having any direct profit interest in campus-based research.

Terman's true passion was encouraging Stanford graduates—including now famous entrepreneurs such as William Hewlett and David Packard— to found their own companies. On occasion, Terman and the university even worked to raise seed funding to help these young firms get off the ground. Other Terman-inspired innovations included the Stanford Research Institute, a defense-related research center that lent assistance to West Coast businesses; the Honors Cooperative Program, a graduate-level teaching initiative designed for engineers working at local electronics companies; and the Stanford Industrial Park, one of the first such parks in the nation.[21] As important as these industrial outreach efforts were, however, they were not sufficient to explain the valley's phenomenal high-tech growth. "Stanford didn't turn the Silicon Valley area into a high-tech powerhouse on its own," Florida told me. "Regional actors played an important role in building up the local infrastructure that this kind of economy needed."

Indeed, quite independently of the university, a unique infrastructure of interlocking support systems emerged in the valley that were critical to the region's success. These included professional management and business capabilities, venture-capital funding, legal and banking services, marketing and advertising talent—all of which served to nurture and sustain the high-tech businesses that were locating in the region. According to the historian Stuart Leslie, the valley's growth was also highly dependent on the military, which he has referred to as the region's "biggest angel investor" because of the large numbers of companies that relied on military procurement contracts to get off the ground before moving into more civilian-based production.[22]

These case studies should make any university president leery of assuming responsibility for driving high-tech regional economic growth, as academic-industry partnerships alone are unlikely to succeed without a broader, functioning, regional business ecology. As John Seely-Brown, chief scientist at the Xerox Corporation and former director of its Palo Alto Research Center, explained, "Bootstrapping an ecology, especially a knowledge ecology, is simply hard—very hard," no matter where it is being tried.[23] In Florida's view, shifting the economic development burden onto the shoulders of university presidents is only a recipe for failure. Instead, he told me, state governors, legislators, and regional planners should work with local business leaders to bring together the venture-capital funding, managerial talent, legal expertise, and vital services needed to sustain high-tech growth. Florida contended that states also need to invest in the human and cultural infrastructure surrounding the university, with the aim of capturing its most highly prized asset of all: high-skilled, creative talent. In his book *The Rise of the Creative Class*, Florida argued persuasively that any high-tech regional initiative must include the development of vibrant communities—revival of downtown business districts, support for culture and the arts, creation of public space and outdoor amenities—as these are the kinds of places that knowledge workers who drive the new economy gravitate toward and prefer to live in. Dan Berglund of the State Science and Technology Institute is equally blunt about keeping universities out of the driver's seat. When I asked him what factors were most critical for university-led economic growth initiatives to succeed, he said: "For them *not* to be university-driven.

"When local industry and the economic development community are the originators and the managers of these programs, rather than the universities, it's probably better for all involved," he asserted.[24]

In Pursuit of Prestige

Judging by the recent wave of state-led technology initiatives, heeding this advice and reflecting on historical lessons are rare among elected officials these days. In addition to the $317-million Biostar program at UW-Madison, numerous other states have launched major university-driven biotechnology initiatives of their own, many of them funded out of the state tobacco-settlement reserves. Michigan led the way by pledging $50 million a year, over twenty years, to building the Michigan Life Sciences Corridor; Pennsylvania allocated $100 million to create new Life Sciences Greenhouses in three separate regions of the state; Ohio promised an initial $4.4 million, rising incrementally to $24 million a year over a five-year period, to create a biomedical research and technology-transfer fund. California governor Gray Davis spearheaded three new high-tech centers of excellence, including the QB3 project discussed in Chapter 1, costing $300 million in joint public-private funding. New York steered $250 million into six Strategically Targeted Academic Research (or STAR) Centers, four of which have a strong bioscience focus. Florida's governor Jeb Bush launched a total of five university-based "centers of excellence" costing $50 million.[25] Other states, including Colorado, Connecticut, Illinois, Kansas, Louisiana, Massachusetts, Maryland, Minnesota, Missouri, New Jersey, New Mexico, and Utah, have also invested hefty sums hoping to jump onboard the biotech bandwagon.[26]

Although biotechnology has been far and away the most popular field for states to fund, other targets include information technology, telecommunications, microelectronics, nanotechnology, and just plain talent. Kentucky, for example, launched a $250-million "Bucks for Brains" initiative, to recruit eminent scholars to the University of Kentucky and the University of Louisville. Dozens of other states have poured taxpayer money into university-affiliated venture-capital firms, seed funds for creating prototype products, industrial parks, and start-up incubators. According to the National Science Foundation, in 1995 state and local governments spent $1.6 billion on research and development at universities; by 2002, that figure shot up to roughly $2.4 billion.[27] Meanwhile, the share of the states' budgets going to fund general higher education continues to decline.

This targeted state spending is not occurring in a vacuum. It comes at a time when elected officials are anxious to demonstrate to their constituents that they are serious about capturing the benefits of the new knowledge-driven economy. It also comes at a time when many universities, including many lower-tier institutions, are betting that marketing themselves as "engines of economic growth" will win them more prestige—and money—in an academic environment where competition has grown extremely fierce.

Today's higher-education marketplace is often likened to an "arms race" in which the nation's colleges and universities continuously scramble to raise their national rankings by avidly pursuing more research dollars, better faculty, brighter students, new amenities, winning sports teams, and whatever else it may take to grow their national prestige. Each school aspires to make it into the top fifty, or top twenty, or top ten, according to any number of ranking systems, including those released by the National Research Council, the Carnegie Foundation for the Advancement of Teaching, and the ever-popular *U.S. News & World Report*. Because these national ranking systems are mostly relative, no school is ever really secure: For every school that rises up a notch, another school must fall. The top ten compete against one another as ferociously as the bottom hundred do.

The *U.S. News & World Report* special issues on "America's Best Colleges" and "America's Best Graduate Schools," widely considered "must-reads" for parents and students, have played a central role in fueling this competitive frenzy. First launched in 1983, the *U.S. News* analyses popularized the use of national rankings as a way of determining top-performing schools and guiding students' application decisions as never before. The result was that any small change in an institution's statistical *U.S. News* ranking suddenly had enormous consequences in terms of its application pool, acceptance rates, and average student GPA—which, in turn, had enormous financial and academic repercussions in terms of faculty hiring and funding. "The competition is intense," one president at a leading university recently complained. "[It is] driven by our boards, by the states, and by the applicants (they all have copies of *U.S. News & World Report*). The state government considers what our position is. And it is pushed by the craziness about lists: who is in the top ten, who is in the bottom ten."[28] In addition to reinforcing the obsession with rankings, *U.S. News*'s analyses have been sharply criticized for methodological flaws and for encouraging schools to use a variety of gimmicks and accounting tricks to manipulate their statistical data in ways that may be contrary to the public interest. By accepting more students under a binding "early-decision plan," for example—where students agree in advance to attend a school if admitted—a university can instantly improve both its selectivity (the percentage of applicants who get admitted) and its yield (the percentage of those admitted who actually attend), and thus also its national ranking, without having to do anything to actually improve its educational quality. The most important problem with these rankings is that they don't measure learning or the quality of instruction at all.[29]

It is impossible to comprehend the commercialization of academia today without situating it in this broader, über-competitive higher-education landscape. The typical university administrator essentially makes the following calculation: By becoming more business-friendly and amassing industry dollars, my institution can increase the amount of research it performs, raise its national ranking, and attract more star professors and high-performing students. This will enable my school to win a larger share of federal research grants and lead to more cutting-edge science and commercial spin-offs, which will in turn create new revenue streams and curry favor with local politicians and industry leaders, who will reward the institution with greater financial support.

To many educational leaders, this looks like a winning strategy, particularly given the number of authoritative state and federal bodies, such as the National Academy of Sciences and the National Governors Association, that have issued reports promoting enhanced university-industry ties as a vehicle for promoting economic growth. The federal grant-making agencies also now increasingly place a premium on research that has demonstrable commercial application. As a result, more and more institutions—often referred to as "catch-up schools"—are trying to ascend into the big leagues of the national research-oriented universities, leading some to worry that a one-size-fits-all paradigm is being reinforced. "Zeroing in on graduate level research programs . . . can distract an institution from fulfilling its traditional role in the region," explained Michael Arnone of the *Chronicle of Higher Education*. "The competition is fierce against better-known rivals, both private and public, with more money and talent. The wannabes have to hit a moving target, as the best universities continue to raise the bar for what constitutes a top-ranked institution."[30]

The number of catch-up schools—including many second- and third-tier institutions—that are now aggressively pursuing a research orientation and striving to become engines of economic growth is startling. Schools think nothing now of spending astronomical sums to lure a star professor to their campus, as the University of Arizona (UA) recently did when it hired Rod Wing, an internationally renowned geneticist, by offering him a $122,500 annual salary (plus an additional 10 percent for serving as director of a new plant genomics institute) and $2.5 million over three years to underwrite his laboratory and computer equipment.[31] UA's hope, of course, is that Wing's ultimate value to the school—in terms of prestige, research dollars, and commercial growth—will be worth far more. The school has already announced it expects Wing's biotech institute to spin off two to three new companies every year.[32] Even a growing number of liberal arts schools are making gestures in this direction. Marlboro College in Vermont, for example, opened an incubator in the fall of 2000 to help boost regional economic development. "It's an unusual move for a small liberal arts college but a logical one," Marlboro college president Paul LeBlanc told *University Business.* "The presence of our faculty and the influx of new graduates, combined with Brattleboro's progressive culture, make Brattleboro a great place to be if you're a technology business." At the Claremont Colleges, a cluster of private liberal arts schools in Southern California, a new Masters institute, known as the Keck Graduate Institute, has been launched that features "a curriculum focused on the needs of the industrial sector," a faculty without tenure, and an educational mandate to train students for "professional careers in emerging fields at the intersection of life sciences and engineering."[33]

A majority of these catch-up schools, however, are public institutions that receive a shrinking percentage of their funding from state taxpayers. Indeed, as Irwin Feller, an emeritus economist at Penn State, explained, many states are trying to do "technology-based economic development on the cheap" by reducing public support for their universities' general funds, while boosting spending on targeted high-tech initiatives—a substitution policy that clearly runs the risk of eroding the universities' core research and teaching capacities over the long term.[34]

The more catch-up institutions strive to attain national research stature—and emulate the high-tech commercial successes of MIT and Stanford—the more acute the competition becomes. Texas Tech, a "wannabe" school currently ranking 146th in the number of federal research dollars it pulls in, is competing against the University of Texas at Austin and other prominent state institutions to become a "top 50 public research university" by 2005. The University of Houston—currently ranked 234th in federal R&D money—is avidly trying to join the University of Texas at Austin and Texas A&M to become the state's third prominent flagship institution. In Kentucky, meanwhile, the legislature recently ordered the University of Kentucky to become a top-twenty research university by 2020.[35]

Some would argue that this frenzy of activity is a good thing—a healthy sign that the nation's research infrastructure is growing. After all, competition has long been one of the hallmarks of American higher education, helping to distinguish it from its European and Asian counterparts. Whereas in Europe and Asia most universities are public and wholly rely on the national government for funding, U.S. colleges and universities are highly heterogeneous (public, private, and for-profit), decentralized (many of the public institutions have strong regional identities and loyalties), and dependent on diverse sources of funding (tuition, federal grants, state appropriations, foundations, private industry, and alumni). Even in the case of federal appropriations, the U.S. system is far more competitive, as research funds are disbursed by individual agencies without centralized coordination and largely according to a peer-review process. Many scholars believe this institutional rivalry explains why so many U.S. universities are ranked among the best in the world.[36]

In recent years, however, the combination of increased competition and diminished public support has begun to prove debilitating. Because federal research spending has not grown anywhere near as rapidly as the number and types of new institutions now seeking federal support (including many liberal arts, technical, two-year, and other nonresearch schools), professors applying for federal grants now face much stiffer competition.[37] According to the National Science Board, the concentration of academic R&D funds among the top research universities diminished between the mid-1980s and the mid-1990s: Specifically, the group below the top one hundred saw their share of federal support rise from 17 to 20 percent, balanced by a decline in the top twenty institutions' share.[38] This has caused some experts to worry the nation's research budget is becoming spread too thin. Feller recently warned that "the R&D capacities of the system may be overextended, with the number of institutions now committed to a research orientation . . . exceeding realistic projections of external support likely to come from government and industry."[39] The danger in such an overextended system is that scarce federal research dollars get diverted from prestigious institutions with the most qualified scientists to schools with far fewer capabilities, thereby decreasing the efficiency and the productivity of the system as a whole.

One early sign of dysfunction is the dramatic rise in federal research spending that now takes the form of congressional "earmarks"—otherwise known as academic pork—which is disbursed outside the federal government's competitive peer-review system. Any university hoping to raise its national research stature and prestige needs money to do it—lots of money. So, beginning in the early 1980s, a growing number of catch-up schools began aggressively lobbying friendly members of Congress for direct appropriations. John R. Silber, the former president of Boston University who helped pioneer this practice, justified it by claiming it was a way for less prestigious schools to raise their research standing. But soon, as the competition intensified, this lobbying grew out of hand. By 2003, universities were actually spending more on lobbying than their counterparts in the defense industry.[40] That year, the amount of noncompetitively awarded money in the federal research budget, farmed out to more than seven hundred universities, topped $2 billion—up from $1 billion in 2000.[41]

The problem with these earmarks and other forms of academic pork—known as carve-outs and set-asides—is that they undermine the competitive peer-review system that Vannevar Bush and the scientific leadership took pains to implement after World War II. The original vision was simple but its consequence profound: By insisting that grant applications be judged and selected by independent scholars—rather than political appointees—the system helped to ensure a highly efficient, meritocratic allocation of federal research money. Most important of all, it limited the potential for science to fall victim to political manipulation. Today, university lobbyists frequently justify academic pork as a vehicle for enhancing regional economic growth. In the long run, however, Congress's willingness to indulge these lobbyists is likely to do far more harm than good. First, it will steadily erode a federal peer-review system that has propelled American higher education to great heights.[42] Second, it will encourage universities to continue to refashion themselves as "engines of economic growth," a mission that few institutions are actually equipped to undertake.

Can Everyone Be a Winner?

Not long ago, I visited Michael Crow, who was then still serving out the end of his term as Columbia University's executive vice provost in charge of technology-transfer operations. A stocky man with a broad, ruddy face and straight brown hair carefully parted on the side, Crow is widely regarded as one of the most successful tech-transfer officers in the country, not least thanks to the aggressive campaign he launched to extend the life of Columbia's lucrative cotransformation patent—first through a failed lobbying initiative in Washington, and later through a second, altered patent on the same invention.

We met in a conference room attached to his office on the third floor of the Low Memorial Library, a majestic, nineteenth-century building that evokes the noble, scholarly pursuits of the mind far more than it does the commercial exploitation of academic knowledge. On entering the building's spacious rotunda, with its exquisitely detailed marble floors, you are greeted by a large statue of Columbia's alma mater, a woman draped in flowing robes with her left hand stretched up, cupping the sky, and a large book open on her lap. In striking contrast, when I entered Crow's office of Science and Technology Ventures, one of the first things I noticed was a white chalkboard with the following words scribbled on it: "Academic Content," "Products," "Market Lead," "E Services."

This seemed fitting, for Crow is a man who frequently speaks of knowledge as "a form of venture capital" and refers to himself as an "academic entrepreneur." At the time of my visit, he was preparing to leave Columbia after eleven years of service to become president of Arizona State University (ASU), an emerging research institution that, as Crow readily acknowledged, was still a long ways away from being a top-tier "Research I" institution.

I arrived expecting to hear Crow lay out ambitious plans for how to catapult ASU into the ranks of the academic tech-transfer elite. But his remarks surprised me. It would be a grave mistake for ASU to model itself after Columbia, Crow said. "The situation is just too different, the dynamic is too different," he observed, noting the vast gulf between the institutions' respective resources and scientific expertise. At Columbia, he explained, "the faculty that have been most successful commercially are the best scientists that we have. Not, you know, among the best, but *the* best—those who've made the most fundamental research breakthroughs. At places like ASU, Case Western, and Georgia, they may have a few of those cutting-edge scientists, but they don't have as many as UC, Columbia, Stanford, and MIT." Compounding the problem, he said, is the limited managerial talent at such schools: "When I staffed this office [at Columbia], I could interview fifty people who lived within fifty miles of New York City to potentially be a part of this operation, people who had run pharmaceutical businesses, who had run venture-capital firms. There was a high concentration of talent."[43]

Crow believes passionately in the virtue of translating academic knowledge into commercial products for the public's benefit. He is clearly proud of having led Columbia to becoming one the nation's top academic royalty earners, and he's quick to boast about the many commercial linkages he helped to build there. But when it comes to the catch-up schools, he told me, he has little patience with their misguided attempts to emulate the successes of the star research institutions.

"It drives me crazy sometimes," he said, speaking more quickly and animatedly now. "I mean, I'll give you a story. While I was here at Columbia's tech-transfer office, this guy that I know down at the University of Mississippi said, 'Come on down. We'll hire you for a day as a consultant. . . . We need you to look at this technology transfer deal we've got going on down here.'" Crow agreed to make the trip—and was deeply troubled by what he saw. "They wanted to build this lab; they wanted to put a company in the lab; and they wanted this company to be *on the university's campus*," he said. After returning to New York, he explained, "I wrote them this report that said, 'You know, listen, the whole way you're approaching technology transfer is stupid. . . . It's not the way you should do it; you're gonna wreck the university.'" Evidently, the message didn't go over terribly well. "These guys were so pissed off at me," Crow explained, "they wouldn't even pay me my airfare until I bugged them, because they . . . were looking for me to endorse this idea."

Crow told me he'd spoken with administrators all over the country—even internationally—and was often frustrated by their simplistic view of tech-transfer activities. "I'm sure I haven't been a hundred percent successful," he admitted, "but one of the things I've tried to do here [at Columbia] is to stay true to the academic mission, which is to let these faculty members do what their noses tell them to do. Don't interfere with them." A lot of places, he continued, "they're just hell-bent on trying to get these commercial operations going. They get all messed up, because all of a sudden the universities have to start thinking like companies and they're bad at that."

"The second-, third-, and fourth-tier schools," he added, "they're going to destroy themselves."

Strong words, particularly from a man who was about to head off to lead a catch-up school himself, and who had clearly given the matter a lot of careful thought. "I worry a little bit about ASU in that regard," he said, noting that, like so many state schools, the university was under enormous pressure to spearhead economic growth. "The university can be a driving force," said Crow, "if it's a great center for science—*not* if it's a great center for technology transfer. Technology transfer is . . . a secondary objective at best, probably even a third-level objective. Anybody that moves it to a higher-level objective than that is foolhardy. Because they will corrupt the university for sure."

It was a bit jarring to hear Crow speak so candidly about the misapplication of a commercial model he had done so much to cultivate himself. What he feared most, he said, was "the emergence of universities that are basically 'job shops.' They just become marginal, industrially driven, technology-transfer-driven enterprises." Some schools, he added, are already well on their way. "These institutions need to be very, very careful because what they will turn into, in the end, won't be a university."

At the close of our conversation, I asked Crow how many of the nation's universities possessed the cutting-edge science needed to run an effective tech-transfer office. "Look at the list of top university royalty earners that AUTM [the Association of University Technology Managers] publishes," he responded, without hesitation. Any school whose tech-transfer activities "rank below fifteenth" on that list, he said, doesn't have the research capacity, talent, or resources it takes to do commercialization successfully. "They're basically getting nothing out of it, except a lot of economic development rhetoric."

False Expectations

If the capacity of the catch-up schools to run successful tech-transfer operations is limited, their ability to deliver on jobs and economic growth is even more remote. In a 2003 report, "Signs of Life," the Brookings Institution noted that in the biotechnology sector in particular, the likelihood of coming out a winner is slim indeed. After surveying fifty-one of the largest U.S. metropolitan areas, Brookings found that only nine have the demonstrated "entrepreneurial and financial capacity" needed "for consistently generating significant numbers of new biotechnology-related businesses." More sobering still, considering the size of current state investments in university-based biotech initiatives, was the report's final conclusion that "to date, even successful biotechnology industry clusters have produced only modest returns to their regional economies" (emphasis added).[44]

According to the report, most biotech companies are small (only forty-four have more than a thousand employees), so new job creation tends to be limited. Another problem states face is that most biotech start-ups, even the successful ones, do not grow into large pharmaceutical firms. Instead, they tend to license their technologies to larger, established drug companies, to form joint ventures, or to sell off their entire companies, so that whatever commercial activity they generate locally may actually be quite short-lived.[45] Furthermore, many biotech start-ups actually lose money, and precious few achieve long-term profitability. In 2000, one study estimated that half of the biotech firms formed since the 1970s had folded or had merged into other companies.[46] "A strong research presence appears to be a necessary condition for biotechnology commercialization," the Brookings authors concluded, "but it does not seem to be sufficient." Chicago, Detroit, Houston, and St. Louis all "have very high levels of research but below-average values of commercialization activity."[47]

What has the track record been for other university-led commercial initiatives—incubators, research parks, venture-capital funds—in terms of new job creation? When I called numerous leading experts and economists to find out, virtually all of them noted a dearth of serious analytic research in this area. Occasionally, a state will commission a study showing that a new university-affiliated research park has produced an impressive array of jobs and businesses. But most experts say these studies often employ poor methodologies and are inadequate as a basis for broader generalization. Al Link, an expert on research parks, told me there's been "no systemic research nationally" on this topic. "The bottom line is that no good studies have been done other than case-by-case studies, and the data that are out there are pretty bad."[48]

Anecdotally, of course, there are plenty of success stories, such as the business incubator at Rensselaer Polytechnic and Stanford Research Park, but there are also plenty of failures.[49] In the 1980s, dozens of state universities invested sizable sums to purchase land and develop research parks in the hope of luring big companies and spurring economic growth. By the early 1990s, there was a widespread consensus that this "research park fad" was driven more by grandiose dreams than sound economics (although, interestingly, this opinion did little to diminish the launching of new university-affiliated research parks).[50] More recently, in 2002, the University of Southern California was forced to shut down an incubator program designed to hatch new companies, known as Egg Company 2, which at an annual cost of $1.5 million was never profitable.[51]

Some of the more reputable published studies on this subject suggest that most schools that choose to go down this commercial development path are engaged in a high-stakes gamble, where the actual payoff may in fact be limited. A 2002 study by Scott Shane and Dante DiGregorio, for example, examined the reasons some universities generate more start-ups than others and found that the effects of university-affiliated incubators and venture-capital funds were "insignificant." The intellectual eminence of the institution had a far greater effect. The authors speculated that the existence of an incubator may merely shift the location of start-ups (to the incubator from outside), and the availability of university-financed venture-capital funds "may merely substitute for, rather than add to, external venture capital in its effect on start-up activity." Joshua Lerner, a Harvard scholar, wrote that although numerous universities were attempting to "duplicate the activities of independent venture funds," the available case studies and empirical evidence raised "serious questions about whether such efforts are likely to be sustainable." Most schools, he said, would do better to cultivate stronger ties with existing, private-sector venture capitalists.[52]

Perhaps the biggest danger of all, then, in marketing the university as an "engine of economic growth" is the risk of creating false expectations that will only serve to disappoint. If large numbers of catch-up schools find that they can't deliver the economic growth they've promised their political patrons, couldn't this undermine these institutions' chances of obtaining future public support? "Absolutely," Dan Berglund replied, when I posed the question. "In every presentation I give, I discuss the fact that there are universities across the country trying to make the basic argument that if you give us more money, economic development will result. All they are doing is setting themselves up for retribution down the road." In the long run, he added, these tactics are likely to produce only "heavy skepticism among legislators and governors: 'Well, why should we put more money into this when you said five years ago, or ten years ago, that if we gave you lots of money, there would be an economic dividend—and we still haven't seen it?' This could be a repeat of what happened in the 1980s," Berglund warned, "except much more severe."

Industry Speaks

You might think at least one sector of society would voice unequivocal support for turning universities into engines of economic growth: the business community. But you would be wrong.

Although plenty of industry representatives do support the Bayh-Dole Act and the broader trend toward commercializing higher education, a surprising number are more wary, as I discovered when I attended an industry-led panel at the 2003 AUTM conference. The panel was chaired by Peter Kramer, director of External Science and Technology Licensing at Bristol-Myers Squibb, and included several other prominent industry representatives. In contrast to the platitudes that dominated most of the AUTM proceedings, these industry leaders did not mince words about the deleterious effects that academic commercialism may be having on the nation's innovation system. Thomas Burger, vice president for corporate development at Genta Incorporated, a small up-and-coming biotech firm that is traded on the stock exchange, began by observing that there was a lot of grumbling about industry's increasingly contentious dealings with universities.

"I've gotten pretty much complete consensus on this," he said, referring to his colleagues in the biotech sector. "[The universities'] motivations have become more focused on *near-term* returns on investment, rather than on more traditional thoughts of the public good. I think the public good, quite frankly, has gone out the window, and it's now turning into something more predatory." Elaborating on this point, he noted a striking shift in recent years away from "the dissemination of information, education, and technology to being focused on money, money, money. And I find that disturbing."

In one case—involving an exciting new cancer drug then in clinical trials—Burger claimed the university that had licensed out the original research demanded such high royalties that when it came time to license the drug to a third party for marketing, "the majority of the revenues gained from the sublicensee were actually owed to the university," even though Genta had invested some $250 million over the previous eight years to develop the drug into a viable product. Such "profit-maximizing behavior" on the part of universities was hard to stomach, said Burger. "They want the big payoff . . . but they don't want to take any risk."

Jack DeForrest, director of technology licensing at Amersham Health, echoed this concern, complaining of "greedy" university tech-licensing officers that put maximizing revenue above all else: "The more money they bring in, the more they get [paid]. And I think that's a fundamental flaw in the system." But the most acerbic comments of all came from an audience member, Jim Duley, director of technology programs and university relations at Hewlett Packard. "HP spends about

$20 million on university-based R&D for sponsored research," Duley announced, "but increasingly universities are demanding unreasonable terms." Tech-transfer officers have become so focused on short-term revenue, he said, that they are destroying long-term sponsored-research relationships with industry. "We're trying to optimize the wrong thing here," Duley argued. "HP has found that it simply can't afford to make a product if universities demand such steep royalties on all the pieces of technology it needs to build that product. It's increasingly looking to universities overseas that don't impose such costly licensing agreements."

This was not the first time industry representatives had voiced such concerns. When the President's Council of Advisors on Science and Technology (PCAST) held a forum devoted to technology transfer on December 12, 2002, many of the industry representatives on hand expressed similar views. Five months prior to the AUTM meeting, moreover, R. Stanley Williams, an esteemed senior fellow at Hewlett Packard, delivered a shockingly blunt critique of Bayh-Dole to an influential congressional subcommittee, chaired by Senators Ron Wyden (Democrat of Oregon) and George Allen (Republican of Virginia). The hearing was devoted to the subject of nanotechnology, a highly promising, cutting-edge field in which scientists build electronic circuits and devices from single atoms and molecules. (Already, nanoscale particles are being used to develop pin-sized biosensors that can signal the presence of biotoxins; they are also used in antimicrobial dressings for battlefield wounds designed to prevent infection.) Hewlett Packard was investing heavily in this path-breaking science, Williams testified, but was finding it increasingly difficult to work with universities. "Relations between large corporations and American universities have never been worse," he declared. "Severe disagreements have arisen over conflicting interpretations of the Bayh-Dole Act." In his written testimony Williams elaborated: "Large US-based corporations have become so disheartened and disgusted with the situation, they are now working with foreign universities, especially the elite institutions in France, Russia and China" where academic administrators are "more than willing to offer extremely favorable intellectual property terms."[53]

At the heart of Williams's concern was the proliferation of exclusive licensing deals. "The thing that Bayh-Dole does not really recognize is that there is a difference between an exclusive and a nonexclusive license." It was clear from Williams's testimony that much of the academic research Hewlett Packard wants to access is nonrival and can be licensed nonexclusively to multiple companies without its value being eroded. Yet many university tech-transfer officers prefer to license their research exclusively, Williams noted, often to a start-up company founded by one of the university's own professors, the result being an unnecessary monopoly that stifles broad commercial use of the technology.

These complaints from industry are by no means limited to intellectual property disputes. Others in the business world worry that by focusing too much on churning out jobs and products, universities risk shortchanging the most important economic functions they perform, namely teaching and basic research.

Back in 1991, the Government-University-Industry Research Roundtable published a survey, "Industry Perspectives on Innovation and Interactions with Universities," based on interviews with seventeen senior research managers from a variety of companies. When corporate managers were asked how successful their partnerships with universities had been thus far (roughly ten years after Bayh-Dole), their responses were overwhelmingly critical. Many said fewer benefits had been achieved from these partnerships than anticipated; they also sharply criticized universities for overestimating the commercial value of their inventions, and for their aggressive stance in licensing negotiations. Yet the most frequent complaints were more general. Again and again, the survey report stated, industry representatives stressed two points:

- The primary role for universities is as educator and provider of talent. This function is the universities' greatest contribution to the process of innovation.
- Universities should not attempt to orient their research more closely to product discovery. This is not an appropriate role for universities, nor is it a task for which they are generally well suited. Rather, they must continue to teach, to foster creativity, and to advance the frontiers of knowledge through long-term basic research.[54]

Two years after this survey was completed, John Armstrong, IBM's former vice president for science and technology, published a similar critique warning that universities should steer clear of commercial activities that pull them away from their core teaching function. As Armstrong pointed out, universities "lack deep understanding of products or markets, have no responsibility for development or manufacturing, and tend to overestimate the importance of science in technological competitiveness." The most effective technology transfer from universities, Armstrong emphasized, "is well-trained technical and scientific workers."

The True Value of Academic Science

It's not that businesspeople like Armstrong don't care about enhancing the industrial competitiveness of the United States and creating high-tech jobs. It's that many believe these goals can't be achieved unless universities stay true to their traditional missions. After all, without top-notch professors, cutting-edge academic science, and an abundance of creative young minds, the nation's scientific and technological innovation system will inevitably atrophy.[55] What many companies want from universities, moreover, is access to ideas and innovative paths of inquiry that they themselves would be unlikely to undertake because the research is too speculative or expensive. In other words, what they value most is the *distinctiveness* of the academic research culture.

In the late 1980s and early 1990s, Partha Dasgupta and Paul David, prominent economists at Cambridge and Stanford, respectively, wrote a series of influential essays explaining why it is essential to keep the nation's academic and industrial research cultures distinct. According to Dasgupta and David, the most important difference between the two cultures is not the frequently discussed division between "basic" and "applied" research. (Contrary to popular belief, a lot of scientific inquiry, both in academia and in industry, does not fit neatly into *either* of these two categories. Instead, it falls into a hybrid realm of "use-oriented basic research," known as *Pasteur's quadrant*, a term coined by Donald Stokes in his 1997 book of the same name, where research is undertaken with a quest for both practical application *and* fundamental knowledge.[56]) "For our purposes, what fundamentally distinguishes the two communities of researchers is not their methods of inquiry, nor the nature of the knowledge obtained, nor the resources of their support," wrote Dasgupta and David. "What matters is the socio-economic rule structures under which the research takes place and, most importantly, what the researchers do with their findings."[57]

In other words, most important are the distinctive cultural norms, customs, and reward systems that govern the behavior of the scientists who work in these two spheres—one an *open science* culture, the other *proprietary*. "In order to ensure a reasonably efficient allocation of resources in the production of knowledge," these authors argued, "modern societies need to have both communities firmly in place," as each has special capabilities that complement each other and sustain the pace of innovation.[58]

Today, it is fashionable to criticize academic culture for its inefficiency and failure to move ideas more rapidly from the laboratory to the marketplace. What's forgotten is how effective this same culture has been in furnishing society with valuable public goods that markets do a poor job of producing on their own: a reliable and ever-expanding body of scientific and technological knowledge; a well-trained cadre of students and workers; a richly endowed public information commons; and an educated citizenry. Historically, the vitality of this academic research culture has always stemmed from its nonmarket reward structure, a system predicated not on money, but on "priority of discovery," where professors are continuously racing against one another to be the *first* to unearth and publish new inventions and theories that advance the state of knowledge in their fields of expertise. This system does a remarkably good job of speeding the creation of new discoveries, hastening public disclosure, and enabling peers to evaluate and replicate new research findings to ensure their accuracy—all of which helps to broaden the stock of reliable public knowledge that is available for future research and innovation. Academic investigators have traditionally enjoyed a high degree of intellectual freedom and autonomy—and also collegiality, because academic publication requires them to disclose what they are working on publicly, including their raw data and methodologies. In industry, by contrast, results are often closely guarded and judged by narrow, short-term commercial and production criteria. Industry scientists also tend to conduct their work in a far more regulated, hierarchical environment.

It is the very flexibility and freedom of the academic research culture that has made it so innovative. Even when academic research is more "use-oriented," or applied, in nature, the direction of the investigator's research can change markedly, opportunistically, as new possibilities emerge. "Some of the most striking scientific breakthroughs have resulted from research projects that started with quite different ends in mind," noted the economist Richard Nelson, pointing to everything from X-ray and radio communication to high-yield hybrid corn and nylon production.[59]

The emergence of a utilitarian, market-model university, combined with a loud drumbeat calling on schools to spur national and regional economic growth, now threatens to obliterate the distinctiveness of this academic research culture.

Over the course of a generation, there has already been a profound shift in the cultural norms of the academy: the reward structures professors follow; their perceptions of the intrinsic value and relative importance of various types of research; and the appropriateness of putting their research into the public domain. According to Irwin Feller, over time the emphasis on patenting and generating royalties alters the "signals as to what constitutes productive allocation of faculty time," encouraging professors to pursue research that has patentable commercial ends. This proprietary orientation also threatens to tear apart the delicate fabric of an academic culture that has long rewarded cooperation and collaboration. As Paul David noted in a speech at the National Academy of Sciences, "Cooperative relationships are readily undermined by alternative systems of exchange based on the ownership and control of property." The two communities of open and proprietary science work best, he said, when "they are separate, but imbedded in a larger system. When you try to put the two reward systems together within one institution, one either takes over and destroys the other, or it corrupts its functioning."[60]

This transformation comes at an extremely unfortunate time. In recent decades the private sector has steadily curtailed its own long-term exploratory science programs of the kind that Bell Laboratories once famously carried out, making the universities' traditional blue-sky, nondirected research all the more important. Also, as the old Fordist model of industrial development has given way to a more knowledge-driven economy, the nation's ability to generate truly novel ideas is more important than ever before. What matters most in the information era is a nation's ability to sustain its competitive edge in science and technology so that its industries will be well positioned to exploit the next big commercial breakthrough. This is precisely what our nation's universities did when they launched the computer and biotechnology revolutions, giving U.S. firms a decisive global advantage. And it is precisely what business leaders need

U.S. universities—which have long outperformed industry in risk-taking experimentation and boundary-breaking thinking—to continue doing in the decades to come.

"The university has an environment which is constantly, not only pushing the frontier, but allowing experimental work to go on at the fringes," noted Richard Florida in our interview. "So I think the university itself actually gives you a very good handle on the dynamics of this new stage of capitalism. Instead of making the university fit the old stage of capitalism and trying to shoehorn it in there, we should be making the university an example of how to reorganize other economic institutions. In a sense, what we're doing now is going in reverse, and that's very frustrating."

8

Paying More for Less

The Commercial Squeeze
on Teaching & the Humanities

When the typical middle-class family—let's call them the Smiths—agree to pay $30,095 in undergraduate tuition (plus another $13,000 for room and board, books, and other expenses) per year to send their eldest daughter, Jane, to New York University, they understandably expect a good return on their investment.[1] Footing the bill for such an education is, after all, an enormous strain on most families—even those with two incomes. To afford it, the Smiths very likely had to set aside money for years, and their daughter had to take out a substantial student loan to cover the remainder.

And yet, on paper at least, the Smith's investment will be well worth it. In 2003, New York University ranked a respectable thirty-fifth in *U.S. News & World Report*'s ratings of the nation's top colleges and universities, ahead of competitors like Boston College. Though not an Ivy League institution, NYU's location—in the heart of New York City's Greenwich Village—has long made it a popular destination. In recent years, moreover, the university has added numerous star professors to boost its research profile and cachet. In 1996, it recruited Ned Block, an acclaimed philosopher from MIT, to enhance the prestige of its philosophy department.

Shortly after, it snatched up two more luminaries, Hartry Field and Stephen Schiffer, to join that same department. In 2002, NYU also recruited eight prestigious economists thought to command salaries of $200,000 to $300,000 each, a coup that even made a splash in the popular news media.[2] A year later, NYU offered a $500,000 salary to lure Andrei Shleifer from Harvard and paid an undisclosed amount to woo Niall Ferguson, a young British historian from Oxford. (A mere six months later, however, Ferguson accepted an even better offer from Harvard).[3] NYU currently pays at least four professors of obstetrics salaries well over $1.5 million.[4]

In reality, however, if her experience is typical, Jane Smith will not interact much with any of these star professors. In fact, she'll be lucky if she gets any real time with them at all: NYU recruited these academic heavyweights with an explicit promise to keep their teaching loads to a bare minimum. As an undergraduate, Jane's courses will more likely be taught by NYU graduate students and professors like Ward Regan.

Regan is a thirty-six-year-old adjunct professor who has been teaching NYU undergraduates for the past twelve years. NYU employs roughly 3,277 part-timers like Regan per year. Together, they teach roughly 50 to 60 percent of NYU's classes and outnumber the 3,083 full-time faculty that the school employs. When I met Regan on a sunny afternoon in Central Park in April 2004, I might easily have mistaken him for a graduate student. Dressed in khaki cargo pants, a T-shirt, and sneakers, Regan has a boyish face and a thick head of brown hair that he wears slightly spiked on top. Born on Long Island, he grew up in a highly literate working-class family and earned his bachelor's degree from NYU. Later, he received a fellowship to attend the State University of New York (SUNY) at Stonybrook, where he completed a master's degree in eighteenth- and nineteenth-century European intellectual history, followed by a Ph.D. in modern American labor and cultural history.

Gobbling down a late lunch—a deli sandwich overstuffed with egg salad—Regan tried to explain why he is so passionate about teaching. "I believe the process of education, wherever it occurs, is a transformative event," he said. "It changes people's lives. If your students go out of the classroom thinking the same way they did when they came in, you haven't succeeded as a teacher. That's what I believe."[5] In his own case, Regan added, "I had professors who cared deeply about teaching, who believed that these lessons they delivered on philosophy, morality, ethics, social interaction, art, and beauty were tremendously important. They helped to create a society of intelligent, thinking human beings, instead of passive subjects." Regan said he still enjoys teaching, and his student evaluations are always "top drawer." But, he told me, the twelve years he's spent at NYU have mostly served to reinforce one hard lesson: Teaching is not really a valued part of the university enterprise.

Throughout his career at NYU, Regan has mostly been teaching traditional college-age undergraduates in the General Studies Program, a two-year liberal arts program housed in the School of Continuing and Professional Studies. Back in 1993, when Regan first began teaching, he was still completing his graduate studies at SUNY, working as a teaching assistant, and supplementing his income with a part-time teaching gig at NYU. His starting salary was $2,700 per course (roughly the average pay for NYU adjuncts in 2003). Later his compensation rose to $3,900 per course, the highest adjunct rate in his department. Yet his financial situation remained precarious. "Just to survive" during these years, he explained, "I was forced to cobble together multiple part-time teaching positions, at multiple institutions, to make ends meet." Some semesters Regan taught three NYU courses, others fewer. For the most part, these were introductory survey courses—"Modern Roots of Twentieth Century Politics and Philosophy," "Topics in Modern Culture," "Western Civilization" (spanning from the Renaissance to the mid-nineteenth century)—which he preferred to teach with primary texts "to keep it interesting." Whenever he could, he also picked up courses in history and architecture at Pratt Institute and Bard College. His life as a "road scholar" was hectic as he raced by subway from his home on the Upper West Side, down to the Village, out to Brooklyn, and back again, lugging a heavy pile of books and papers on his back. In his most flush years, he earned $35,000–$40,000 a year, but he never had any job security or benefits. In a city with a famously high cost of living, he paid $3,700 for his health insurance alone.

"I did everything not only that my department asked of me, but that was possible to do," he told me between bites of his sandwich. In addition to teaching up to five and six classes per semester, Regan often advised 40 NYU students—which meant that at any one time, between courses and advisory duties, he might be responsible for knowing the names of some 150 students. Regan ran two student clubs, including a theater group; served as a writing tutor; and oversaw students doing independent studies. He even conducted admissions interviews. The extra income didn't hurt, though the pay was lousy—an extra $1,000 for each

group of 20 undergraduates he advised, for example. But the more troubling thing to Regan was that from semester to semester, he never knew
whether he would have work or not—or how much. "Just this past summer," he said, "I got a call from my dean at NYU, and he said, 'We're
really sorry, we had two courses for you but now we only have one.' So
literally a month before my classes were scheduled to start, I had one less
paying job." In 1997, Regan received an excellence-in-teaching award
from NYU. But no matter how many times he applied, he was invariably
turned down for a full-time teaching position.

"I was stupid," Regan admitted, reflecting back on his academic career. "You know, I figured years of service at NYU would help me
whenever a full-time job became available in my department. . . . I had
seen other adjuncts move into full-time positions. No one told me that the
rules had somehow changed. I mean, you start to get this stink of an adjunct. I kept applying, and I kept being told, 'Well, next time, next time.'"
Regan insisted that despite all of this, he has never let down his students
as a teacher. Although he was never given a private office at NYU in
which to hold student office hours, he told me, "I am always available to
talk to my students by phone."

Downsizing the Professoriate

If the Smiths knew that many of their daughter's courses would be taught
by overworked, underpaid adjuncts like Ward Regan, would they be as
quick to fork over $36,000 in annual tuition? To date, few parents have
voiced much opposition to this trend. Yet it's possible their silence is a
product more of ignorance than of apathy: Most parents, after all, very
likely assume that a first-class college education means just that.

Unfortunately, this is increasingly *not* the case—and not just at NYU.
More and more of the teaching at top-notch universities is being farmed
out to adjuncts like Regan. Much like their counterparts in other service
industries, this growing army of temp workers increasingly view themselves as part of an exploited class—the hamburger flippers of the
academic world. A study of ten social science and humanities disciplines,
conducted by the Coalition on the Academic Workforce in 2000, found
that with the exception of history and art history, graduate students and
contingent faculty now teach more than half the courses offered in these
disciplines.[6] As of 2001, the most recent year for which Department of

Education statistics are available, 44.5 percent of all faculty in higher education were employed part-time.[7] At many schools, it is now taken for granted that only seniors, who have settled on their majors and are close to graduating, will actually get to interact with the top professors in their fields. In 1999, a commission for the Carnegie Foundation for the Advancement of Teaching concluded that "freshmen—the students who need the very best teaching—may actually receive the worst."[8] So, you might think that parents deserve a tuition *discount*, but this obviously isn't happening. The spiraling cost of higher education has begun to generate outrage. From 1980 to 2004, tuition and related charges at public universities have increased at three times the rate of inflation, rising over 50 percent in real terms since the early 1990s alone. At private colleges, again since the early 1990s, tuition and fees rose by a comparable 36 percent.[9] But few have noted the disturbing paradox of universities simultaneously raising tuition fees and cutting full-time professorships—a process that began in roughly the mid-1970s, proceeded through the bounty years of the 1990s, and is ongoing today.

By shifting to part-timers, colleges have clearly sought to extract more labor from their faculty at a lower per pupil cost. But at what cost to the quality of instruction? Adjunct and other contingent professors are often highly dedicated, talented teachers. But usually this is true *in spite of*, not because of, their university employers. Frequently these contingent faculty lack the resources they need to do their jobs well, including such basics as office space and administrative support. Their lives are hectic; they're perpetually overworked—all of which could compel reasonable people to look for ways to cut corners and reduce their workloads. One study found that liberal arts adjuncts are 50 percent less likely to require essay exams than full-time faculty, presumably because of the extra time required to read and grade them.[10] The temptation to pander to one's students is another chronic problem. Because part-time and contingent faculty (unlike their tenured counterparts) are usually evaluated only by students rather than by their professional peers, there is a strong incentive for them to "go easy" on their students and engage in grade inflation, depriving these students of an honest evaluation of their work. One assistant professor of creative writing at Columbia University told *Time* magazine that the best way to ensure favorable student evaluations was to flatter one's students.

As he put it, "Submitting students to the rigors of learning seemed only to incur the wrath of many of them, which entered the record as my teacherly shortcoming. . . . The business model has taught me that the customer is always right. But maybe a few more dissatisfied customers would mean a better learning experience."[11] An even more serious problem, in the view of Gwendolyn Bradley of the American Association of University Professors (AAUP), is the "silent self-censorship of thousands of professors holding temporary, insecure appointments."[12] When so many faculty lack long-term job security and are afraid of losing their jobs, there is a powerful disincentive for them to discuss controversial issues in the classroom or express unorthodox views, a troubling prospect for those who care about academic freedom and the intellectual vitality of the university culture. Finally, excessive reliance on part-time and contingent faculty reduces the amount of time that talented, full-time professors will actually devote to teaching undergraduates and passing on their intellectual passions and expertise.

The rapid growth of this part-time academic workforce is part of a conscious administrative strategy to lower the cost of instruction and eliminate tenure, though most academic leaders know better than to state that as an explicit goal. The preferred approach is to make as many new appointments as possible *off the tenure track*; that is, professors are hired with no opportunity to earn tenure, even as the older, tenured faculty gradually move into retirement. At NYU, for example, President John Sexton has started giving faculty one-year full-time positions that pay just $25,000 a year. Nationally, between 1998 and 2001, the number of full-time appointments off the tenure track rose by a whopping 35.5 percent. Today, as a consequence, more than 60 percent of all college and university faculty hold non-tenure-track appointments. The speed of the transformation has been remarkable: Only a generation ago, such positions were virtually unheard of. In 1969, a mere 3.3 percent of all full-time faculty appointments were non-tenure-track.[13]

There are, to be sure, cases where getting rid of deadweight tenured faculty members, who neglect their teaching and research, is in the best interests of both students and the university. But those who would like to do away with tenure—as if it were a pestilence to be eradicated—seem oblivious of the important role it has played, historically, in insulating universities from outside influence and thus helping to safeguard intellectual freedom. When Arthur O. Lovejoy, John Dewey, and others spearheaded the academic freedom movement in the late nineteenth and early twentieth centuries (as discussed in Chapter 2), they did so in response to flagrant abuses. Often, professors were fired simply for expressing controversial views that diverged from those of the mainstream, or for offending corporate interests and wealthy benefactors. The leaders of the academic freedom movement came to realize that without secure working conditions, due process, and faculty control over academic affairs—including the hiring and firing of professors and the capacity to judge scholarship through peer review—academic freedom was meaningless. By dismantling this system, universities risk not only diminishing the quality of instruction but imperiling this ideal. As Louis Menand wrote:

> At the heart of the political and economic battles over the future of the university is the concept of academic freedom. Academic freedom is not simply some kind of bonus enjoyed by workers within a system, a philosophical luxury universities could function just as effectively, and much more efficiently, without. It is the key legitimating concept of the entire enterprise. . . . The alternative is a political free-for-all, in which the decisions about curricula, funding, employment, classroom practice, and scholarly merit are arrived at through a process of negotiation among competing interests. The power in such negotiations will not be wielded by the professors.[14]

If the administrators running universities today seem unmindful of such matters, it is perhaps not so surprising. For increasingly these administrators come directly from industry or are recruited for their corporate know-how, *not* their educational experience. Even university presidents are chosen on the basis of their ability to raise money and their close ties to the corporate sector: a growing number of them are former business school deans and even CEOs. Most also sit on the boards of directors of large corporations and not uncommonly earn executive-level salaries—a practice that has grown increasingly controversial at a time when tuition fees are skyrocketing and the teaching force is being downsized.[15] In 2002, the presidents of four private universities received salaries over $800,000, not including their pay for serving on corporate boards, which raised their annual compensation to well over $1 million. In the public sector, the number of university presidents paid over half a million dollars doubled in 2003–2004, from six to twelve. In the private sector, that number rose from twenty-seven to forty-two. When university presidents take seats on company boards, as large numbers of them do these days, they acquire fiduciary duties to advance the interests of the shareholders they represent—interests that may *not* always line up with those of the university. At state schools, many university presidents receive a substantial share of their salaries not from taxpayers but from private sources, a circumstance raising troubling questions about whether they are ultimately accountable to public or private interests.[16] In November 2003, for example, a powerful private foundation paying *more than half* of University of Georgia president Michael F. Adams's salary challenged the authority of the state's board of regents by demanding Adams's resignation. Angered by the president's decision not to renew a former football coach's employment contract, the foundation threatened to cut back the $320,365 contribution it was making to Adams's $559,468 annual compensation. After battling the foundation for nearly a year, the university was finally forced to take the unprecedented step of terminating its relationship with its own private fund-raising arm in May 2004, vowing to end all private supplements to the president's pay.[17]

Given their business backgrounds, is it any surprise these new university leaders are intent on adopting a more corporate style of management? Granted, the institutions these leaders run *do* face serious financial challenges. The cost of maintaining modern laboratories and research facilities continues to mount. Competition for talented faculty (and students) is fierce. And the need to raise money is never-ending, particularly at public universities, where the portion of the budget funded by the state has been shrinking. In addressing such challenges, however, administrators need to respect the distinctive intellectual values of the university and its nonmarket culture. The emergence of a multitiered, highly contingent academic labor force unravels the fabric of this culture. When faculty are split between those who have tenure and those who don't, and between a variety of new part-time and full-time teaching positions (each with different pay scales and benefit packages), it becomes far more difficult for professors to speak in a unified voice or to exercise effective control over internal academic affairs. Part-timers rarely hold seats on academic committees, are shut out of faculty governance, and lack loyalty to any one institution because of their multiple places of employment and their high rates of turnover. As a result, the faculty's power to shape academic policy—including crucial decisions regarding the establishment, expansion, or elimination of departments and programs; the hiring and dismissal of professors; class size; teaching workloads; and assignment of deanships and other leadership positions—erodes. At the same time, the power of administrators to set priorities and push schools in a more commercial direction increases. As Richard Moser of AAUP explained, bringing in large numbers of adjuncts and contingent workers "weakens the group within the university that has the most power to act as a counterweight to corporate values."[18]

"Show Me the Money"

That schools like New York University are willing to pay top dollar to attract star professors while leaving more and more of the actual teaching to temp workers and grad students is hardly surprising if viewed in the context of today's hypercompetitive—and increasingly commercial—academic environment. The star professors, after all, are able to bring in large federal grants, enhance the institution's prestige, and raise its national profile. In the sciences and engineering, they may also produce path-breaking discoveries that will one day be converted into lucrative, royalty-generating commercial products. Teaching, by contrast, is a net drain on the bottom line—and it is not measured in any of the major national ranking surveys.[19] The reason is partly that unlike a suit that can be easily inspected for how well it fits and how well it is made, the quality of pedagogy is more illusive and challenging to evaluate. Assessments of teaching and learning can generally be made only while the process is going on, or decades later, when the actual benefits of higher education to the individual (employment, higher lifetime wages, and other achievements) and society (enlightened citizens and higher productivity) are realized. To a disturbing extent, university administrators have simply concluded that they need not concern themselves with the quality of undergraduate instruction or the salaries paid to instructors. As Rand economists Dominic Brewer, Susan Gates, and Charles Goldman, explained, "Prestige seeking promotes excellence on the one hand but can lead to excessive expenditures and unresponsive schools that neglect the needs of some undergraduate students and other customers who don't contribute to institutional prestige. . . . Further, competition for prestige in the student market does not encourage institutions to improve the quality of educational delivery."[20] Many have long suspected that the research universities may in fact subsidize their graduate research operations with undergraduate tuition.

These same pressures have begun to alter the provision of financial aid. In recent years, a growing number of universities have started to divert their student aid money (traditionally reserved for low-income, needy students) into "merit scholarships" designed to attract more high-performing, high-scoring students, most of whom are financially better off. Their goal is to raise their national prestige and *U.S. News* rankings, and to discourage talented students from moving out of state. But as it turns out, using student aid in this way can be extremely expensive, forcing schools to raise their base tuition price. To compensate, Brewer and his colleagues explained, "Many institutions are beginning to adopt two-tiered admission programs, essentially lowering admission standards for students who can pay the full tuition but offering generous scholarships and 'financial aid' to bright students, often regardless of their financial need."[21] Needless to say, when financial aid is used in such a self-serving manner, the students who suffer most are those from low-income families, whose decision to go to college is often entirely dependent on access to financial aid. This diversion of aid away from those with the greatest need is all the more disturbing when one considers that the income gap in college attendance is growing. Today, at the nation's top 146 colleges and universities, 75 percent of the students come from the top income quartile of families, and just 3 percent hail from the bottom quartile.[22]

That the quest for money and prestige has come to supplant teaching—and other traditional priorities, such as educational equity—is no secret, although many professors, evidently fearing it might harm their careers, were reluctant to speak with me on the record about this situation. Donald Stein was an exception. A professor of neuroscience at Emory University, Stein served for more than thirteen years as an academic administrator, most recently as vice provost and dean of Emory's Graduate School of Arts and Sciences. He is also a distinguished scientist who for years brought in large NIH grants—and a fair amount of industry funding—to underwrite his studies of the brain.

An energetic man with thinning gray hair and a warm demeanor, Stein is concerned about how profoundly the stress on money and commercialization has transformed the incentive structure and culture of the university. "At the time I came into academia," he told me over coffee at a noisy café in New York City, "most people believed that they were doing what they were doing—generating ideas and discoveries—because of the public good. . . . It was a calling. The pressures on you were *not* to produce a product."[23] These days, he said, the atmosphere could not be more different: "Now when you go and look at university business plans, as they are called, students are seen as clients; parents are seen as customers. . . . The question has now become 'What is going to sell?' as opposed to 'What is the right thing to teach?' Once things take on commercial, monetary value, the whole academic decisionmaking structure becomes impacted."

Academic administrators have, indeed, embraced the language of the business world, referring to students as consumers and to courses and ideas as products. They strategize about the university's brand name and niche market, its competitive edge and pricing strategies. Administrators say these trends are driven by economic necessity, but Stein doesn't buy it, pointing out that the emphasis on research and commercialization is a reflection of the values and priorities that now govern academic life. "It's like going for the most valuable player in the sports world," he said of the trend toward recruiting high-status professors and investing in multi-million-dollar research facilities. "I mean, all of these things require tremendous investments in infrastructure that require everybody else to support that. If you are going to keep bringing in star professors who have to have state-of-the-art labs, you have to have everyone else killing themselves to provide the resources and indirect costs to support that. So everybody gets caught up in it and feels pressured to do that."

Where does all this leave teaching? Stein did not mince words. "There's this whole myth about the importance of teaching," he said in a wistful tone, a troubled look in his eyes. "All university administrators, everybody pays lip service to it—especially at the research universities that have a substantial undergraduate component, where the students are paying a large amount of money. But the fact is, it is more honored in the breach; the real commitment is to the research scholarship—and the generation of indirect costs. I mean, it couldn't be more clear, especially in the sciences. Space allocation is dependent upon it, status within the university, reduced teaching loads, reduced committee assignments. All of the reward structures: higher salaries, merit increases, travel to scientific and professional meetings. . . . You have to be deprived of all your sensory apparatus not to see what is going on."

Adjuncts and Graduate
Students of the World, Unite!

In fact, a growing number of adjunct faculty and grad students *do* realize what's going on, which is perhaps why, in recent years, so many campuses have found themselves embroiled in aggressive union organizing battles. In 2000, the teaching assistants and research assistants at NYU were the first private-university graduate students to win approval from the National Labor Relations Board (NLRB) to form a union. (At state schools, graduate student unions have existed for some time.) In 2004, however, a new Republican-dominated NLRB rejected a union petition filed by students at Brown University, dealing a major blow to grad-student organizing in the private sector, but not to faculty organizing overall.[24] Shortly after the grad students at NYU led the charge, the school's adjuncts followed suit, forming a union of their own in the summer of 2002. Several days before I met with Ward Regan, the adjuncts' union had successfully negotiated their first contract, granting instructors with sufficient teaching hours new guaranteed pay increases, enhanced job security, and health benefits.[25]

Such organizing drives have spread like wildfire in recent years—a sign that a backlash is brewing among the growing army of part-time instructors on whom universities increasingly rely. In New York State alone, adjunct faculty at New School University, Cornell, Pratt, Long Island University, and Pace have attempted to form unions to improve their employment conditions. At Columbia University, the graduate students went on strike just before exam period to protest the administration's refusal to allow the votes to be counted from their own union election two years earlier.[26] Elsewhere, graduate teaching assistants at Harvard, Yale, the University of Pennsylvania, and Tufts have been rallying to form unions, arguing that the only way to compel universities to value teaching and stop eliminating full-time, tenure-track positions is through contract negotiations, just as workers in the industrial world have done for decades. (Fittingly, one of the largest unions representing part-time professors today is the United Auto Workers.)

In response, academic administrators have taken pains to emphasize that universities are *not* like most industrial workplaces. At hearings and in press releases, leaders have consistently maintained that the university is a collegial institution where internal policies have traditionally been formulated through committees and negotiation, not pressure by outside interest groups. As NYU spokesperson John Beckman explained, questions such as "who is taught, what is taught, how it is taught, and who does the teaching . . . are central to the mission of institutions of higher education; no university rightfully should accede to handing over such responsibilities to a union."[27] What's more, administrators say, graduate students are *not* employees in the traditional sense of the term. Most have a large portion of their expenses paid by the institution or federal grants. As University of Pennsylvania president Judith Rodin recently explained to the *New York Times Magazine*, "We don't think our students are employees. We think they're our protégés. We think we're nurturing and nourishing them, and the first time a student files a union grievance against a faculty member, it will transform the relationship forever."[28]

Rodin has a point. Graduate students are, first and foremost, apprentice scholars and teachers who have traditionally worked under the tutelage of a faculty mentor, a relationship radically different than that of a worker and a corporate manager. Historically, the mentoring relationship between professor and student has played a crucial role in preparing young scholars for advanced study, with mentors helping their protégés select a dissertation subject and guiding their course of study. The relationship is intended to be cooperative, not antagonistic, with graduate students regarding their mentors as allies, even role models. Because this guild tradition has many virtues, it is worth considering whether a union is the most appropriate vehicle for expressing graduate students' grievances—especially in an age of growing academic commercialism.

Yet the problem, in the eyes of many graduate students, is that this noble guild tradition is rapidly breaking down. When graduate students were true apprentices who could look forward to honorable, full-time careers, their heavy teaching loads and low pay were tolerable. Now, however, they simply feel exploited: Most know that their teaching assistantships will only prolong the time it takes to complete their Ph.D.s, and that their chances of landing a full-time teaching position when they graduate, particularly in the humanities, are slim indeed. Worse, they are keenly aware that by allowing universities to exploit their cheap labor, they are helping to eliminate the very full-time positions for which they are purportedly being trained. Thus, is it any wonder that so many graduate students are flocking to unions for help? To some, joining unions is less about improving their own working conditions than about preventing the perpetuation of an unjust system that imperils the future of higher education.

Many colleges insist that if the adjuncts and graduate students succeed, universities will simply be forced to raise their undergraduate tuitions even higher. At some schools, however, the undergraduates seem more troubled by the deteriorating quality of their own education and have forged alliances with their professors. At the New School University—where 85 percent of the faculty work part-time—undergraduates at one of the smaller liberal arts colleges, Eugene Lang, launched a student organization, the Student Labor Union Group, or SLUG, to champion better working conditions for their professors. The group gathered more than a thousand signatures on statements expressing solidarity with the adjuncts' organizing drive. Karen Bray, a twenty-one-year-old member of SLUG, said that many of her professors at Lang have been good, dedicated teachers. But the students aren't stupid, she said: They understand that their professors are overworked and distracted. "They're holding down multiple part-time jobs at multiple institutions throughout the city," she explained. "They don't have their own offices, and it's hard for students to schedule office hours." SLUG's motto? "Their teaching conditions are our learning conditions."[29]

Can Chaucer Pay the Bills?

The commercialization of higher education is not only transforming who does the teaching at many universities. Slowly but surely, it is also changing what is being taught. For as schools pour money into commercially promising lines of research like biotechnology and computer science, many are scaling back course offerings—particularly in the humanities and the social science fields—where the economic payoffs are less direct.

Not long ago, a graduation ceremony at George Mason University (GMU), a state school located in the leafy suburbs of Fairfax County, Virginia, erupted in protest as hundreds of students attached to their caps and gowns bright pink buttons bearing the slogan *"Stop Dis-Engaging Our Future."* The buttons, which were distributed by a group called Students for Quality Education, were a pointed reference to a George Mason mission statement, *"Engaging the Future,"* which calls for boosting investment in information technology and tightening relations between the university and northern Virginia's booming technology industry.

This initiative came after James S. Gilmore, the governor of Virginia, promised in the late 1990s to increase state funds for GMU by as much as $25 million a year if the university better served the region's high-tech businesses. GMU's president, Alan G. Merten, a computer scientist and former dean of the business school at Cornell, hardly needed urging. "We must accept that we have a new mandate, and a new reason for being in existence," Merten announced at the World Congress on Information Technology, a gathering of industry executives hosted by GMU. "The mandate is to be *networked*."[30] Soon, Merten set about adding new degree programs in information technology and computer science to the curriculum. He poured money into the 125-acre Prince William campus, whose focus is biosciences, bioinformatics, biotechnology, and computer and information technology, and suggested that all students would be trained to pass a "technology literacy" test.

Amid this whirlwind of change, however, other areas fared less well. Degree programs in classics, German, French, and several other humanities departments were eliminated.

"I'm pissed off as hell," said Monica McTyre, an honors student at GMU who majored in English and minored in an interdisciplinary program called "Study of the Americas," which was among those eliminated. When I met with McTyre and other founding members of Students for a Quality Education (SQE) shortly after the cuts went through, they were still fuming. We met inside GMU's brand-new student center, a mall-like structure replete with a Taco Bell, a Cinnabun, a campus bookstore run by Barnes and Noble, and a movie theater. "High-tech corporate interests are being allowed to manipulate the curriculum and dictate the content of our education," exclaimed McTyre, as we settled into lounge chairs. When SQE's members circulated a petition protesting the cuts, they gathered seventeen hundred signatures. But according to Alexander Milas, a heavy-set anthropology student, the petition didn't do much good; neither GMU's board nor the president ever responded. Mocking the university's efforts to cater to the surrounding high-tech industry, Milas said, "This is not going to produce a generation of enlightened, informed people. I'm quite certain that if we were surrounded by bakeries, we'd be sacrificing the arts and humanities so we could put out more bakers."[31]

In defending the changes, President Merten spoke as a realist—and, it's impossible not to notice, as someone versed in the language of the business world. "There was a time when universities weren't held accountable for anything—people just threw money at them," he told me in an interview, just shortly after I met with the students.[32] Today, "people with money are more likely to give you money if you have restructured and repositioned yourself, got rid of stuff that you don't need to have. They take a very dim view of giving you money to run an inefficient organization." The process of making GMU more efficient was, he conceded, "a little bloody at times," but there was a logic to it. "We have a commitment to produce people who are employable in today's technology workforce," he said. Students at GMU are "good consumers" who want degrees in areas where there are robust job opportunities, and the university has an obligation to cater to that demand.

But should meeting the demand come at the expense of providing a well-rounded education? In response to GMU's cuts in the humanities, 180 professors in the College of Arts and Sciences sent a letter to Merten arguing that although training students for the job market was a legitimate goal, "precisely in the face of such an emphasis on jobs and technology, it is more necessary than ever to educate students beyond technological proficiency. . . . The central mission of George Mason University should be to educate self-reflective, knowledgeable, critically thinking and responsible citizens upon whom a humane society depends." Kevin Avruch, a GMU anthropologist who signed the letter, explained, "My concern is that we are turning the university into a subcontractor for local industry. . . . A university should teach people to read and write and think critically. And my guess is that, ironically, that's what corporations really want as well. If they need to teach them Lotus, they can do that after they graduate."[33]

Avruch is not alone in thinking that a liberal arts education has value not only for the individual and society but for industry as well. In a recent speech defending a liberal education, Federal Reserve chairman Alan Greenspan observed that as we move into a knowledge-based economy, "the ability to think abstractly will be increasingly important across a broad range of professions." There is still controversy regarding how the human mind innovates, he explained, "yet, even without hard indisputable evidence, a remarkable and broad presumption is that the ability to think conceptually is fostered through exposure to philosophy, literature, music, art and languages. Most great conceptual advances are interdisciplinary and involve synergies of different specialties." However, he emphasized, "The liberal arts embody more than a means of increasing technical intellectual efficiency. They encourage the appreciation of life experiences that reach beyond material well-being and, indeed, are comparable and mutually reinforcing. The intense pleasure many experience from listening to Mozart's great D Minor Piano Concerto has much in common with the deep satisfaction of solving a complex mathematical problem."[34] Judging from the high levels of professional achievement of students who have graduated from the nation's elite liberal arts colleges (Amherst, Williams, Swarthmore, Bryn Mawr), there is indeed reason to believe that broadening access to a liberal education, beyond producing a more enlightened citizenry, is also a wise investment.

———————

Unfortunately, what happened at GMU appears to be part of a national trend. Across the country, schools looking to trim their budgets are targeting programs in history, foreign languages, and journalism or are combining disciplines like philosophy, religion, and political science into one pared-down department. Of course, it is important to acknowledge that throughout academic history, the various academic degree programs have often been in a state of flux. At one time, classics and religion were de rigeur for everyone. What's striking about the changes today, however, is the degree to which they are being driven not by intellectual concerns but by financial considerations and pure market demand. *Business Week* reported that at the University of Florida and other schools, the administrations' approach to management and cost cutting has taken on a distinctly corporate cast: "Defying traditional academic notions, departments now vie openly for resources. English professors must demonstrate, in essence, that Chaucer pays the bills as effectively as engineering or business classes. . . . Professors worry that creative writing and other courses requiring very small classes will cost their department funding under a system that strictly measures productivity."[35]

When the criteria for judging an academic discipline centers on how much money faculty can generate through grants and corporate sponsorship, most humanities departments invariably find it difficult to compete. Yet this is precisely what many are being asked to do. In a recent essay, "Franchising the University," Jeffrey Williams, an English professor and editor at the *Minnesota Review*, reported that while he was teaching at East Carolina University, one of the larger schools within the North Carolina state system, the dean of the College of Arts and Sciences announced one day that he was amending the criteria for professors' yearly evaluations (determining salary raises) to emphasize the importance of bringing in grants. Even though English has never been a great revenue generator, the faculty were told that from now on, submitting four grants would equal publishing one article in their evaluations. "Not to put too fine a point on it," wrote Williams, "the dean by fiat seemed to rewrite our professional self-definition, from scholarship to salesmanship."[36] At the New School University, meanwhile, Kenneth Prewitt, the dean of the Graduate Faculty of Political and Social Science, abruptly resigned from his position because, as he disclosed at a public forum, he believed the administration's policies risked subordinating academic values to market values. In one instance, Prewitt explained, the school's provost had proposed issuing "private bonuses" to deans who boosted the tuition-paying enrollment of their divisions—the size of each bonus corresponding to the number of paying students a dean could bring in. To Prewitt, this looked dangerously like admitting students based on their "cash value" to the university—this crass bottom-line imperative surfacing at an institution that was once home to such illustrious scholars as John Dewey, Claude Lévi-Strauss, and Hannah Arendt.

As Prewitt explained to me shortly before he departed for Columbia University, when he arrived at the New School, he believed he had been hired to enhance the university's renowned graduate division, which because of its focus on disciplines with little commercial or market application had long relied on subsidies from other divisions to stay afloat. "It wasn't realistic to expect a small graduate school specializing in the social sciences and humanities to be entirely self-sufficient," Prewitt explained. But shortly after his arrival, he was told that each unit of the university was expected to be self-sustaining. "Everything revolved around the budget, not around talent," he told me. "I felt it was always chip away here, save a dollar there. The irony is you end up achieving less that way. There were trustees who could have gotten excited about raising the academic prestige of the graduate faculty. This would have greatly benefited the whole university. However, it's extremely difficult to generate prestige on an eroded foundation."[37]

Accurate statistics on the state of the humanities—in terms of funding, enrollment, degrees, and so on—are surprisingly difficult to find.[38] The data that we do have, however, suggest that the prognosis is not good. According to Steven Brint, a sociologist at the University of California at Riverside, over the period 1970–2000, "almost every field which constituted the old arts and sciences core of the undergraduate college was in absolute decline." These included all of the humanities and social sciences (except philosophy and economics), as well as the physical sciences and mathematics. What makes these declines especially striking is that over this same period, the number of bachelor's degrees awarded to undergraduates actually rose by

50 percent. Brint found that at the same time the humanities had been declining, there had been a corresponding rise in the prominence of the "practical arts," which, by his definition, included business, engineering, computer science, nursing, education, and other fields focused on preparing students for occupational careers. In the late 1960s, the majority of undergraduates who attended four-year colleges graduated with traditional arts-and-sciences degrees; if they wanted to pursue an occupational or professional degree, these students waited until after their undergraduate studies were over. By 1998, Brint found that these numbers had reversed, a strong majority of undergraduates now pursuing occupational degrees.[39] "A century ago, liberal arts colleges were a dominant force in American higher education," wrote David L. Kirp in his compelling 2003 book *Shakespeare, Einstein, and the Bottom Line*. "Now these schools educate fewer than 4 percent of all undergraduates, and they are at risk of becoming an endangered species."[40]

To some degree, of course, these shifts are simply a reflection of changes in student demand. But the increasing commercial orientation of universities has also played a role. In an article published in *Harvard Magazine*, based on a two-year national study of the humanities, James Engell, a professor of English and comparative literature at Harvard, and Anthony Dangerfield, a graduate of Cornell, concluded that the real threat to the future of the humanities stemmed from the rise of a new "market-model university," in which subjects that either make money, study money, or attract money are given priority. "Test what you will— majors, salaries, graduate programs. . . . the results will come back the same," they wrote. "Since the late 1960s the humanities have been neglected, downgraded, and forced to retrench, all as other areas of higher education have grown in numbers, wealth, and influence."[41]

David Hollinger, a prominent historian at U.C. Berkeley, agreed with Engel and Dangerfield that these new market pressures threaten to do considerable harm. In a recent essay, he pointed to contemporary university salary policies, where, he said, "we find compelling evidence that the gap is closing between what universities value and what is valued in the commercial marketplace." Traditionally, universities sought to keep professors' salary levels relatively equal across all disciplines, explained Hollinger, with certain exceptions for the faculty in the medical schools. Today, it is not uncommon for an entering assistant professor of business administration to be paid $100,000, whereas a comparably qualified recruit in mathematics or history is paid $45,000 or even less.

Administrators say these stark salary differentials are unavoidable because talented young faculty, with marketable skills, simply won't enter academia unless a university can offer a salary commensurate with those in the private sector. (So much for the traditional view that a modest salary, adequate to provide a comfortable standard of living, is sufficient, because what the professor gains through an academic appointment—time to pursue research, true intellectual freedom, prestige, and respect—is worth far more.) What troubles Hollinger is that true academic achievement has no value under this new market reward system, so that "a young economist only a few years beyond the Ph.D. who has published but a handful of papers may be awarded a higher annual salary than a distinguished midcareer mathematician who has won the Field Medal or a senior humanist who has served as poet laureate of the United States."[42]

Such trends have received surprisingly little attention. During the 1980s and early 1990s, after all, U.S. culture was consumed by the seemingly endless debate over the content of the Western canon—the question of whether Shakespeare or Toni Morrison, European history or Latin American history, should be taught to undergraduates. In the decades to come, the more pressing issue may be whether undergraduates are taught any meaningful literature or history at all. Kevin Avruch told me that the recent restructuring at GMU had brought home that lesson. "It actually united professors on the left and the right," said Avruch. "This faculty is often characterized as overly liberal, but we discovered that, in at least one sense, most of us are tremendously conservative: We share a nineteenth-century view that our job is to educate well-rounded citizens."[43]

Higherlearning.com

While humanities professors at some schools have been battling to save their departments from being scaled back or eliminated, others have discovered that university administrators have taken a newfound interest in their course material because of its potential to be marketed online. Seemingly overnight the computer revolution transformed "courseware" into a valuable piece of "content" that could be packaged and sold over the Internet. The spectacular growth in virtual education that followed—and the problems encountered by many of the schools that rushed to leap on board—illustrates the perils that can arise when education is viewed as a mere commodity.

In the late 1990s, NYU, Temple, and Cornell raced to set up their own for-profit subsidiaries—NYUonline, eCornell, Virtual Temple—to tap into the seemingly limitless new market in online learning. "The market is global," exclaimed Jack Seely in an NYUonline press release. "I can sell to someone in Bayonne, and I can sell to someone in Beirut."[44] At Columbia, Michael Crow, the head of technology transfer, spun off a for-profit subsidiary called Fathom and hired Ann Kirschner, whose previous job had involved launching the National Football League's commercial Web site, to be its CEO. At a conference on online learning held at Columbia—where panelists discussed topics such as "The Business of Education: Growing Minds and Bottom Lines"—Kirschner explained that her own experience at the NFL had provided her with a useful model: "What I learned is that you could take an important brand and use a new technology to extend its range"; like sports franchises, she asserted, universities "need to extend their resources in as many ways as they can."[45]

In the public sector, anticipating a boost in demand for postsecondary degrees as a result of the "baby boom echo"—but loath to raise taxes to pay for it—many state institutions eagerly embraced distance learning as a way to expand on the cheap. "Just building campuses is a very expensive proposition," Jeffrey Livingston, associate commissioner for the Utah System of Higher Education, explained. "Governors see [online education] as a way to not spend as much money in the future to meet growth."[46]

Not all of the enthusiasm behind such ventures was financially motivated. When the concept of distance education—or virtual learning—first took hold in the mid-1990s, many professors were genuinely enthusiastic about its pedagogical possibilities. Geometry and calculus classes could be enhanced with the aid of computer-generated visual imagery; statistics courses could be taught with interactive, self-paced online tutorials. Students taking a survey course on early American history could tap into digital archives with extensive primary source materials on the drafting of the U.S. Constitution, early slave history, and the Civil War. Others welcomed the power of this revolutionary technology to expand access to higher education, enabling working mothers and professionals to earn degrees from home, according to their own schedule and at their own pace.

From the beginning, however, it was clear that the dream of using information technology to enhance teaching and learning risked being subordinated to other, less noble goals, namely, the desire to make money, cut costs, and further reduce the need for full-time professors. In a 1995 paper, prepared under the auspices of Educause—a consortium of 1,700 universities and more than 170 corporations seeking to enhance academic "productivity"—William Massy and Robert Zemsky, two prominent education scholars, compared traditional classroom instruction to an inefficient "handicraft" industry, in which each professor creates his or her own highly individualized course and teaches it to a small number of students. Enhancing productivity, they baldly asserted, required replacing many of these faculty activities with digital technology. "With labor accounting for 70 percent or more of current operating costs, there is simply no other way."[47] In a 1998 report, the consulting firm Coopers and Lybrand echoed this viewpoint, noting that online technology could eliminate two significant cost factors: "The first is the need for bricks and mortar; traditional campuses are not necessary. The second is fulltime faculty. [Online] learning involves only a small number of professors, but has the potential to reach a huge market of students."[48]

Among the faculty's principal concerns was that management might try to disaggregate professors from their own intellectual and creative works—that is, their courses—thereby turning them into mere "content providers" and robbing them of any professional control over their teaching craft. Such a scenario was not difficult to imagine: Pay a prestigious professor a flat fee to design an online course, copyright it, and then hire low-paid, part-time instructors to administer the class over the Internet (including all the online discussion groups and grading). And indeed, many online education advocates endorsed just such a goal. "In today's academic culture, responsibility for content rests with the faculty," explained Carol A. Twigg, one of the nation's foremost authorities on virtual education. "But a shift is occurring in higher education where increasingly the institution is, in a sense, buying content which it can control. We are seeing tremendous growth in the number of courses taught by untenured, part-time, adjunct, or temporary instructors."[49]

At first, much of what drove the frenzied pace of online education—in addition to the quest for profits—was the fear of falling behind in the tech revolution. In an article that reflected this mood, Arthur Levine, the president of Columbia's Teachers College, predicted that the traditional college degree would soon be supplanted by an "educational passport" cataloging "the specific information that the student knows or the skills that he or she can perform." Those skills, he predicted, could be taught by any number of institutions: "Why should a credential from Microsoft University . . . be less prestigious than one from a regional state college?" Schools that failed to adapt to the market's need for "lifelong learning" and high-tech convenience, Levine warned, could quickly find themselves beaten out by for-profit competitors, much as traditional booksellers had been overtaken by Amazon.com.[50]

Indeed, some schools were so afraid of being left behind that they jumped into bed with their for-profit challengers. After Michael Milken, the former junk-bond trader, served a prison term for securities fraud in the early 1990s, he turned to the online education business and launched a company called UNext.com, which quickly signed valuable partnerships with many of the nation's most prestigious "brand-name" schools. These included the University of Chicago, Stanford, Carnegie Mellon, the London School of Economics, and Columbia's business school, each of which reportedly stood to make upwards of $20 million over five years. UNext's deals were not without controversy, particularly in the case of its first academic partner, the University of Chicago. Andrew Rosenfield, the head of UNext and a close friend of Milken's, happened to be a member of the school's board of trustees, which approved the deal. At least three other university employees also had direct financial interests in UNext, among them Daniel Fischel, dean of the law school (and the author of a favorable book about Milken), and Gary Becker and Merton Miller, two Nobel Prize–winning economists.[51]

So preoccupied were many institutions with "keeping up," however, that they failed to grasp how to run an effective online enterprise. With dizzying speed, many of these ventures crashed and burned. Virtual Temple closed its doors in July 2001. David Adamany, the school's president, said the decision was a simple one: "I didn't see any profit potential here."[52] Four months later, NYUonline shut down, this after gobbling up roughly $25 million—a figure that came to light just when the school's adjuncts were beginning to organize. When Fathom folded in 2003, it, too, had failed to turn a profit and had burned through nearly $30 million. As one student reporter at Columbia commented, "It is very ironic that a university that claims never to have enough money for clearly needed academic enhancements—i.e., more faculty for an increased number of undergraduates—would be so willing to throw money at something whose benefits are unlikely, if ever, to materialize."[53]

Of course this was not the first time that a distance learning experiment had yielded disappointing returns. As David Noble, a historian at York University in Toronto, noted in a fascinating essay series, titled "Digital Diploma Mills," the online learning craze of recent years has eerie parallels with the rise—and fall—of correspondence schools in the late nineteenth and early twentieth centuries. Back in 1885, William Rainey Harper, an early pioneer of distance education who went on to become president of the University of Chicago, predicted that "the day is coming when the work done by correspondence will be greater in amount than that done in the classrooms of our academies and colleges." By 1919, more than 70 universities had launched correspondence programs that actively competed against some 300 for-profit correspondence schools, with a combined income of more than $70 million. Much like the promoters of online learning, the correspondence schools emphasized the benefits of learning in the comfort of one's home, at one's own pace. But although universities initially promised high-quality courses taught by regular professors, they soon resorted to an assortment of poorly paid "readers" and associate instructors to offset their spiraling administrative costs. Schools like Columbia and U.C. Berkeley experienced dropout rates from their correspondence programs of 70 to 80 percent, and critics began to assail the practice of inducing students to enroll under a no-refund policy and providing shoddy instruction in return. "The whole thing is business, not education," wrote the distinguished scholar Abraham Flexner in a scathing 1930 critique of the correspondence schools that marked the beginning of their eventual demise.[54]

Whether history will repeat itself, however, remains to be seen. For although the collapse of many online learning ventures diminished some of the hype, the virtual revolution in higher education is far from over. According to the most recent available data, enrollment in distance-education courses at postsecondary institutions more than doubled from 1997 to 2001, when it hit the 3 million mark. (Remarkably, 82 percent of those students were enrolled in undergraduate-level courses.) Nearly 80 percent of this online enrollment has occurred at the nation's public colleges and universities, which are under enormous pressure, because of declining state support, to cut costs.[55] From 2000 to 2003, for example, online enrollment at the University of Maryland University College grew from 39,865 to 110,423 students.[56]

Though few academic leaders still see the virtual university as a "get-rich-quick scheme"—in part because there is no evidence thus far that quality online education is actually any cheaper than classroom instruction—the possibility of using online technology to cut costs continues to prove alluring. At Florida Gulf Coast University (FGCU), a new public college, one-quarter of the students are enrolled online and there is no tenure. FGCU keeps its costs low by limiting the amount of time the full professors actually spend with their students online. Instead, the school hires "coordinators" to handle all the administrative aspects of the course, as well as a group of "preceptors," each of whom is paid $1,800 to work with a cohort of sixty students. These preceptors are "responsible for interacting with students, monitoring student progress, overseeing four Web board discussions, and grading critical analysis essays"—in other words, they are responsible for nearly all the work traditionally performed by full-time professors.[57]

Carol Twigg, who now heads an $8.8-million center for virtual learning at Rensselaer Polytechnic, believes that schools like FGCU offer a model for the future. In 2003, Twigg lamented the fact that on many campuses "new technologies represent a black hole of additional expense." The problem, she complained, is that most campuses "have simply bolted new technologies onto a fixed plant, a fixed faculty, and a fixed notion of classroom instruction."[58] In a paper titled "Expanding Access to Learning," Twigg reminded administrators that "an important avenue for reducing costs in a labor-intensive industry like higher education is to substitute capital—in the form of technology—for labor." There are various ways to do this, she suggested. First, abandon the popular "small-class model," which "assumes that the instructor must be responsible for all interactions by answering every inquiry, dealing with every comment, and participating in every discussion personally." Second, combine multiple small sections of a course into one large section with anywhere from 800 to 1,500 students; use automatic grading of tests wherever possible. Third, and perhaps most important, employ a "differentiated personnel strategy," just as FGCU has done, to reduce the amount of time that full-time professors have to spend with students.[59]

Needless to say, despite its cost-saving appeal, this is not a vision of American higher education that most parents, students, and teachers would endorse.

9

The Path Forward

Preserving Our Public Domain

Although I have argued throughout this book that the commercialization of higher education is undermining the strength and vitality of our nation's universities, I do not believe it is realistic to demand that these institutions simply wall themselves off from private industry. On the rare occasions when the issue has been discussed, the question of how to structure academic-industry relations has frequently deteriorated into an us-versus-them debate, with the advocates of commercialization lined up on one side and academic traditionalists on the other. In my view, this division is artificial and counterproductive. Universities can make vital contributions to scientific and technological innovation and collaborate productively with industry *without* having to sacrifice their core scholarly principle and essential autonomy. But if this is to happen, fundamental changes are needed. Among those changes are a series of reforms at the federal level, including a revision of the Bayh-Dole Act, a revamped set of conflict-of-interest regulations, and stronger federal oversight of clinical drug research. Most important of all, universities themselves need to make a renewed commitment to defending the values and ideals they have long claimed to stand for.

By and large, as I've shown, the reformers of the late 1970s who pressed for closer academic-industry ties were motivated by noble intentions. They genuinely wanted to improve the transfer of academic technology to industry and to stimulate the U.S. economy. At the time, academics across a range of disciplines had also come to feel that universities were overly insular and cut off from the real world. There was some truth to this assessment. Years of generous federal funding had helped foster a culture at many schools that reflexively held researchers who collaborated with industry in disdain; applied research was often seen as uninspired and unsuitable for the academy, even when it had scientific merit and the potential to expand knowledge frontiers.[1] Similarly, scholars who aspired to be public intellectuals and engage with contemporary issues were frequently discouraged from doing so—as, indeed, they sometimes still are.[2] Thus, in the minds of many reformers, the Bayh-Dole Act seemed to offer a tantalizing new opportunity to revitalize the academy by bringing knowledge into practical use. As Donald Stein, a neuroscientist at Emory University who initially championed Bayh-Dole, explained to me, "It seemed to us that there was a lot of opportunity outside of traditional academic research for the business community to play a role in shaping research and putting new ideas into practical use, particularly in the realm of biotechnology and computer science. The idea of actually translating this work into real-world applications was very, very exciting."[3]

Few people would disagree with this goal. Universities should have mechanisms in place for effectively transferring commercially promising new ideas to industry. They should be places that encourage scholars to grapple with contemporary problems and engage with the outside world; they should support entrepreneurial thinking and hands-on problem solving and should offer courses and internship opportunities to students interested in starting new companies, nonprofit groups, and other vital social organizations.

Since the mid-1980s, however, the pendulum has swung too far in the opposite direction, to the point where universities have increasingly come to resemble commercial enterprises and professors, businesspeople. Almost immediately after the Bayh-Dole Act passed, it was interpreted as a mandate from Congress to convert "knowledge assets" into "commercial assets" on the rather narrow premise that federally funded research was valuable to the public *only* if it could be translated into useful, marketable products. Soon, the interests of the academic and commercial sectors converged around a mutual desire to extract profits from campus-based research, and administrators were led to equate serving the "public interest" with serving the needs of private industry. Traditionally, the university's public-interest mission was far more expansive: to open new scientific frontiers, to educate and train the next generation of scholars and world leaders, to advance technological and industrial development, to perform disinterested research, to preserve humankind's greatest intellectual and cultural achievements, to provide expert advice and public service, to protect the public domain of knowledge, and to serve as a critic and conscience of society. "Public service" meant providing service not only to powerful constituencies—industry, state legislatures, Congress, and the military—but also to farmers, laborers, the poor, and the disaffected.

Universities cannot perform all of these functions and simultaneously seek to profit from campus-based research. When universities become interested parties, with financial profits at stake, not surprisingly they begin to behave like any other business enterprise. In the intellectual property sphere, as we've seen, schools today all too frequently put their own financial concerns ahead of the public interest in advancing science and innovation. In medicine, faculty financial interests often interfere with both patient care and public health. In the classroom, deans and provosts are concerned less with the quality of instruction than with how much grant money their professors bring in. As universities have become commercial entities, the space to perform research that is critical of industry or that challenges conventional market ideology—research on environmental pollution, poverty alleviation, occupational health hazards—has gradually diminished, as has the willingness of universities to defend professors whose findings conflict with the interests of their corporate sponsors. Will universities stand up for academic freedom in these situations, or will they bow to commercial pressure out of a fear of alienating donors? As the cases of David Kern, Nancy Olivieri, and David Healy reveal, the answer, too often of late, has been the latter. To the extent that universities view themselves first as drivers of economic development, and only second as educational institutions, their priorities will be skewed, and they will neglect their commitment to the life of the mind. The quest for profits crowds out the space for undirected research, social criticism, fundamental inquiry, unconventional thought, and boundary-breaking experimentation. Teaching, mentoring, and the cultivation of young people's intellectual talents gradually become little more than second- or third-order activities.

The utilitarian movement in American higher education has a proud history. In the past, however, this movement was always counterbalanced by other forces within the academy that rose up to champion pure research, teaching, and the ideal of a well-rounded education that encompassed the humanities and the arts. The biggest problem today is that these countervailing forces are missing. Academic administrators are so focused on maximizing revenue and prestige that they have become blind to the deleterious effects of commercialization. Similarly, professors who straddle the academic and business worlds often fail to perceive that anything is amiss, because many of them are profiting handsomely from these collaborations and drawing much-needed revenue into their labs. Faculty who are not involved in such ventures, meanwhile, are often so consumed by their own narrow disciplines, internal politics, grant writing, and the increasingly competitive quest for tenure that they, too, have tended to stand aside as their universities are drawn into a whirlwind of dizzying commercialism. Although many are concerned about these trends—including former university presidents, Nobel Prize–winning scholars, and other academic leaders—few have translated their growing unease into a forceful call for the kinds of changes needed to safeguard the universities' integrity and autonomy.

Four federal reforms lie at the core of my own proposal for change. Some in the academic world will bristle at this level of federal regulation. However, the reason I believe federal involvement is important—indeed, essential—is that in recent years, universities have proven unwilling or unable to address these concerns collectively themselves because of the ceaseless competition for better rankings, money, and prestige that pits each university against the others. My four proposals are, in brief, (1) the creation of independent third-party licensing bodies (loosely modeled after the Research Corporation) that would assume control over university techtransfer and commercialization activities nationwide; (2) an amendment to the Bayh-Dole Act clarifying that the true intent of the legislation is to promote widespread use of taxpayer-financed research, not to maximize short-term profits; (3) new requirements that all federally funded university scholars comply with strict conflict-of-interest laws; and (4) the creation of a new federal agency to administer and monitor industry-sponsored clinical drug trials submitted to the Food and Drug Administration.

Independent, Third-Party Licensing

In 1912, as you may recall, when Berkeley professor Frederick Cottrell was looking to patent his pollution control invention, he rejected the idea of having the University of California handle this commercial activity directly. "A danger was involved," he cautioned some years later, noting that direct profiteering by the university could lead to "growing commercialism and competition between institutions and an accompanying tendency for secrecy in scientific work."[4] Instead, Cottrell established an independent nonprofit—the Research Corporation—to handle these patenting and licensing activities on behalf of the university and its scientists. By the mid-1960s, the corporation was servicing nearly two-thirds of the nation's leading research universities.[5]

In my view, both to safeguard universities' autonomy and to remove the profit motive and conflicts of interest that too often distort their behavior, a return to this third-party licensing model is in order. Only this time, the federal government should take the initiative by establishing a series of nonprofit technology-transfer hubs, located in different regions of the country, which would handle the patenting and licensing needs of all the nation's universities and colleges. These offices—let's call them academic tech-transfer agencies (or ATTAs)—would operate under a federal mandate to carry out the provisions of the Bayh-Dole Act. They would probably function best if they were chartered, pseudogovernmental organizations that enjoyed considerable independence and flexibility. An amended version of the Bayh-Dole Act would spell out the ATTAs' functions and clearly state that their purpose is to facilitate the commercialization of federally sponsored research *while preserving academic autonomy*. To achieve this, one provision of the act would prohibit universities from taking equity or making any direct financial investments in companies that spin out of federally funded research. All commercialization activities of this kind would be handled instead by the regional ATTAs in conjunction with the private sector.

These offices would be staffed with highly skilled tech-transfer professionals, people with extensive expertise across a range of scientific, technological, business, and industrial-research areas. In addition to filing patents and overseeing licensing, the ATTAs would operate their own seed funds to develop embryonic inventions into prototype products. They would also work closely with private-sector venture capitalists and investors to commercialize promising academic discoveries. Revenues generated by the ATTAs would go first toward covering their own operational expenses; the remainder of the profits could then be split three ways: one-third to the inventor; one-third to the federal government (for reinvestment in peer-reviewed research grants); and one-third to the inventor's university (in the form of unrestricted grant money).

For the vast majority of the three hundred or so schools currently engaged in tech-transfer activities, contracting out these commercial functions to the ATTAs would offer innumerable advantages. Currently, most of these tech-transfer offices are understaffed, overworked, poorly financed, and lacking in the expertise needed to handle many of the complex patenting and licensing deals they are trying to negotiate. As we saw, the quality of these offices is often so poor that industry leaders complain they are obstructing, rather than facilitating, the successful commercialization of academic research. What's more, as Michael Crow, the former head of technology transfer at Columbia University, noted, the vast majority of these schools do not have the requisite science base needed to make these offices commercially successful. Most campuses are not making any significant profits off their tech-transfer activities; many are losing money. So relieving schools of these commercial functions would be a win-win situation: It would enable schools to refocus their attention and resources on their core teaching and research responsibilities. It would eliminate their now-pervasive institutional conflicts of interest. And it would also improve the overall efficiency and performance of the tech-transfer system nationally.

Funneling invention disclosures from around the country into a small number of regional ATTAs would make it far easier for industry to keep track of any new academic technologies that became available for licensing. It would also facilitate smoother, less contentious licensing negotiations with industry, because the ATTAs would have an interest in successfully licensing a broad portfolio of inventions, rather than trying to maximize profits from any one discovery (as the individual campuses often do), a goal that can stymie widespread utilization of taxpayer-funded research.

Should some universities—namely, those with high-performing tech-transfer operations—be allowed to opt out of such a system? Although I would prefer not to see any universities opt out (because their withdrawal would erode the quality of the ATTAs' invention portfolios and leave many of the old institutional conflicts in place), for practical reasons this option may become necessary to stop the most politically powerful universities from attempting to block efforts at reform. As a condition, however, any university that wishes to apply for a federal waiver to continue operating its own tech-transfer office should be required to demonstrate that its internal tech-transfer capabilities are equivalent to those of the regional ATTAs. This idea has antecedents in the earlier Institutional Patent Agreements (IPAs), which required federal agencies to ascertain that universities had the necessary expertise to handle a particular class of inventions, before the federal government would grant them blanket authority to own and license taxpayer-financed research. I would propose that these waivers, like the older IPAs, be renewed every five years to verify that individual university tech-transfer offices are continuing to maintain high standards of quality and professionalism—which include, of course, not allowing their quest for profits to interfere with their obligation to disseminate new inventions and ideas as broadly as possible. After all, permission to license taxpayer-financed research on behalf of the public is a privilege, not a right.

Amending Bayh-Dole

It is important for Congress to revisit and revise the Bayh-Dole Act not only to safeguard the university's autonomy but also to protect the dynamism of our national innovation system. As currently written, the Bayh-Dole Act has several problems. First, it encourages universities to pursue the most restrictive licenses possible because they maximize the short-term profits flowing to the institution even as they often impede broad use of the invention. Second, the act does not adequately protect the public domain for fundamental knowledge—the wellspring for all future scientific and technological discovery. If the U.S. Patent Office enforced its utility and nonobviousness standards more forcefully, as many have been calling for, it would certainly help to obviate many of these problems, but Bayh-Dole's incentive structure also needs revising.

The Bayh-Dole Act did bring about some positive reforms. It created a uniform federal policy governing the patenting and licensing of federally funded research that proved far easier for universities and industry to navigate. It also made universities more aware of the need to usher promising new inventions out of the ivory tower into the marketplace. The problem today is not that universities are indifferent to patenting and commercialization, but that they have become so eager to extract income from their research that they are slapping overly restrictive proprietary claims on a wide array of taxpayer-financed discoveries. As opposed to enhancing technology transfer, these ownership claims often impose high rents on creators, stifle competition, and clog the pipeline for future innovation. Already in patent-sensitive fields like pharmaceuticals, computer electronics, and software, prominent industry leaders and scholars have urged universities and the federal government to keep more of this knowledge broadly available in the public domain.

In 2003, prominent scholars of innovation put forward two proposals for revising the language of Bayh-Dole. In my view, both are eminently sensible and would go a long way toward solving the problems I've outlined above. The first proposal, made by Columbia University's Richard Nelson, would revise the language of Bayh-Dole to emphasize that the principal objective of the act is to promote "the widest possible use" of taxpayer-financed inventions. In most cases, this would mean that an exclusive or highly restrictive license is not appropriate because it "may deter widespread use at considerable economic and social cost."

Currently, the Bayh-Dole Act *does* state that one of its objectives is "to ensure that inventions made by nonprofit organizations . . . are used in a manner to promote free competition and enterprise *without unduly encumbering future research and discovery*" (emphasis added). But as Nelson observed, this clause currently has no teeth, and universities frequently flout it. As a remedy, Nelson would revise Bayh-Dole's language to clarify that exclusive licensing should be the exception, not the norm. "Exclusive or narrow licensing by a university should require an explicit rationale," he wrote. "Willingness of firms to take up university research results without an exclusive license should be regarded as evidence that an exclusive license is not appropriate."[6] To ensure compliance, I would suggest that any university or regional ATTA interested in imposing a more restrictive license be required to provide written documentation to the funding agency explaining why such a license was deemed necessary. This documentation would provide the government with a useful window onto internal licensing decisions, and with a paper record should concerns arise later that this more restrictive license was impeding effective use of the technology.

A second proposal, put forward by legal scholars Arti Rai and Rebecca Eisenberg, would safeguard the information commons by making it easier for the National Institutes of Health to intervene in situations where university licensing decisions were *not* promoting widespread use of publicly funded research. Currently, as we saw with the p53 mouse at Baylor and stem cells at the University of Wisconsin, the federal government can only intervene in university licensing decisions in "exceptional circumstances." Rai and Eisenberg proposed removing this clause and streamlining the judicial review process, thus making it far easier for the NIH to intercede when access to taxpayer-financed research is being thwarted unnecessarily.[7] In my view, we should extend these same powers to all federal grant-making agencies.

Federal Conflict-of-Interest Regulations

Today, it increasingly seems there is no branch of science that is not riddled with conflicts of interest. In December 2003, the *Los Angeles Times* revealed that top scientists and directors at the National Institutes of Health—many of them in charge of disbursing federal research grants, or of overseeing human subject research—were padding their government salaries with tens, and sometimes hundreds, of thousands of dollars by moonlighting as consultants for private drug companies, the same companies that rely on NIH research to endorse their products. One-quarter of these agency officials also received stock or stock options in drug and biotech firms.[8] Shortly after, in May 2004, it came to light that a top scientist at the Food and Drug Administration was also consulting for a pharmaceutical corporation that would have been affected by his research, prompting a congressional inquiry into moonlighting by senior FDA officials as well.[9] Meanwhile, also in 2004, the editors of prestigious medical journals continued to warn about the pervasive manipulation of academic science by industry sponsors. "Academics have a choice," asserted *The Lancet*, "to develop their entrepreneurial skills or to maintain a commitment to public-interest science—and we do not accept that the two options are mutually compatible."[10]

Congress's response to the NIH scandal was swift and forceful, resulting in several days of explosive hearings at which senators and representatives on both sides of the aisle lambasted the agency for its abuse of the public trust. When the NIH's own blue-ribbon panel recommended that its financial conflicts simply be better "managed," many members were dissatisfied and called for their outright elimination instead. "It is clear . . . that some NIH scientists are either very close to the line or have crossed the line" of ethical conduct, said Representative James Greenwood, a Republican from Pennsylvania who chaired one of the hearings. "If we are serious about upholding the highest ethical standards at the NIH, then [these] scientists should not even be close to the line."[11]

The urgent need to address these conflicts of interest in science, as well as the political momentum for doing so, appears to be growing. In late September 2004, the NIH grudgingly announced plans to impose a one-year ban on researchers engaging in any outside paid consulting activities for industry, until the agency could devise a more rigorous oversight system. However, in an earlier interview, NIH director Elias Zerhouni expressed the concern that if he imposed such a ban, many of his best researchers might simply leave for greener pastures: "My scientists can walk across the street [to a university] and do the exact same job with less restrictions."[12] All of which raises an obvious question: Why isn't Congress trying to eliminate these pervasive financial conflicts of interest not only in government labs but in academic ones as well, where 60 percent of all research is paid for by U.S. taxpayers?

As long as federal conflict-of-interest rules remain lax, competitive pressures will continue to create a dangerous race to the bottom in standards. Current federal laws (which apply exclusively to academic investigators receiving grants from Health and Human Services and the National Science Foundation) require universities only to internally "manage" their professors' financial conflicts of interest; no financial ties are prohibited outright. Whenever a grantee receives salary, consulting fees, honoraria, stock holdings, or intellectual-property rights valued at $10,000 or more per year from a for-profit entity, as well as any corporate equity interests greater than 5 percent, he or she is required to disclose those financial interests to the university employer—which must, in turn, report to the funding agency. None of these disclosures are made public, however, and the university is free to manage its professors' financial conflicts however it sees fit—thereby leaving the fox to guard the henhouse.

It has been clear for some time now—even to federal authorities—that these regulations are inadequate. As we saw in Chapters 4 and 5, both in 1989 and again in 2001 the federal government attempted to push through stricter conflict-of-interest guidelines after serious academic research abuses came to light. Both times, however, university leaders vigorously rejected any federal intervention in their affairs, promising to rein in the conflicts of interest themselves. To this day, these promises have yet to be fulfilled. Nationally, as we've seen, universities' conflict-of-interest policies remain weak and inconsistent. Given all of this, isn't it time for the federal government—which spends more than $20 billion annually on science and engineering at the nation's academic and non-profit research institutions—to hold these institutions and their scientists publicly accountable?[13]

Let's not forgot that one of the principal reasons U.S. taxpayers subsidize academic science so generously is to preserve a unique public research culture, where scholars are free to conduct investigations far removed from any immediate commercial application, such as blue-sky inquiry, risky experimentation, disinterested science, and public good research. As a society, we depend on this public research sphere to stimulate innovation and provide us with an impartial source of knowledge and expertise we can trust. If universities choose to have looser conflict-of-interest laws for faculty members performing research *not funded by the federal government*, that's their prerogative of course. But in the case of taxpayer-funded research, the federal government should insist that all academic investigators—across all disciplines—abide by mandatory federal conflict-of-interest regulations.

In my view, these rules should prohibit anyone in a key research, consulting, or management role (as well as his or her spouse and dependent children) from having any *personal financial ties* to (or equity interests and options in) any company that would be *affected* by the outcome of his or her government-sponsored research—or that produced a product or a piece of equipment being evaluated in the research project. Prohibited financial ties should include such compensation as grants, consulting fees, gifts of equipment, salaries, and honoraria. The new federal rules should also prohibit grant recipients (and their academic collaborators) from holding executive positions or sitting on the scientific advisory boards of companies that might stand to profit from their federally funded research. This ban should be enforced not only during the period when the research is undertaken, but for *one or two years following the publication of the research results* to ensure that this divestiture of outside commercial interests and relationships is not mere window-dressing. Finally, the new rules should cap the amount of money that academic researchers can earn from outside consulting (whether for industry or other special interest groups) to no more than 25 percent of their annual university salaries.

Some might question whether strengthening the rules for federally funded research would still leave unaddressed the bigger problem, namely, the growing amount of corporate money that flows into universities with strings attached. Under these proposed rules, professors would still be free to consult for industry and perform industry-sponsored research, provided that the companies paying for their work did not stand to profit or benefit from the professors' other federally funded research projects in any way. Although it is true industry collaborations would not be prohibited under these rules, there can be little doubt that academic-industry relations would change significantly. First and most important, the new rules would prevent much of the current commingling of public and private funding, so that federally financed research would be truly public, impartial, and free of commercial conflicts of interest. Many of the most troubling sponsored-research arrangements—like the U.C. Berkeley–Novartis deal—would have been avoided were such rules in place at that time, because the College of Natural Resources could not have mixed Novartis money and federal-grant money as loosely and freely as it did, and the company also could not have received first rights to license *all* the most valuable research in Berkeley's lab, regardless of its funding source.

Currently, a large portion of the federal government's academic grant money is directly tied to matching grants from industry or requires applicants to show that their research has explicit commercial applications.[14] This blending of industrial and academic research support dilutes the federal government's capacity to preserve an independent, public research sphere that operates according to its own distinctive academic norms and customs. There is nothing wrong, of course, with the federal government's choosing to subsidize commercial research as part of an industrial policy, for example. But this funding should be kept separate from the money it provides to academic institutions for public-interest research.

Second, it is quite possible that the new rules would reduce the overall amount of corporate money now flowing into universities. The reason is quite simple. What corporations often covet most when they sponsor academic scholars is not only their talents but all of the other publicly subsidized assets they bring with them: access (often exclusive) to other federally financed research projects and discoveries, brilliant (and cheap) graduate students and postdocs, and cutting-edge laboratories and equipment. These additional assets give the company a remarkably high return on its investment. If this substantial subsidy isn't there—or is limited by the new rules—it is possible that corporate funding will decline, though certainly not completely because most companies will want to preserve their connection to university scientists and path-breaking academic science.

To further safeguard the public sphere, the federal government should require all researchers who receive public money to disclose *all* their sources of financial support and financial interests (including any patents or patent options) on an easily accessible public Web site. Whenever these professors are treating patients, writing in scholarly journals, or testifying before Congress, they should also be required to report any *related* financial interests (including patents and patent options) that might represent a potential conflict of interest. When it comes to sitting on federal advisory committees—which not only provide expert advice but also directly shape public-policy decisions—academic scholars should be required to have no financial interests whatsoever in the companies or interest groups that stand to be affected. At present, as we've seen, federal officials frequently claim they cannot find qualified academics to sit on these committees who do not have financial conflicts. Insisting that both the federal-grant system and the advisory system abide by the same conflict-of-interest rules would create a strong incentive for academics who want to play an active role in public policy to avoid financial relationships that could compromise their independence. Scholars who are caught violating any of these rules should be barred from receiving any additional federal-grant money for three years. Because oversight in this area is minimal, a stiff penalty is necessary to ensure compliance.

The purpose of these regulations, as I've said, is not to ban industry funding of academic research. Most universities have charters that require them to provide expert advice and service not only to the government and the broader public but to the commercial sector as well, as they should. The purpose is to preserve a public research sphere that is distinct from that of industry.

Federal Oversight of Clinical Research

I cannot conclude these recommendations without addressing the particularly pervasive conflicts of interest that exist in our nation's academic medical colleges. Here I take my cue from various experts, including Marcia Angell, Sheldon Krimsky, and Merrill Goozner, all of whom have written books calling on the federal government to play a more direct role in administering and overseeing drug trials.[15] The need for special federal oversight in this area is, as I've shown, extremely well documented. Eighty percent of the nation's clinical drug trials are paid for by the pharmaceutical industry.[16] Whereas in the past, academic investigators operated at arm's length from their industry sponsors, today corporations exert enormous direct influence over the research process—including everything from study design and patient recruitment to the control of raw data and publication—thereby destroying the scientific integrity and trustworthiness of these studies, and often compromising public health.

Under Sheldon Krimsky's proposal, which holds great promise as a way to clean up industry-sponsored drug and medical-device trials, the federal government would mandate that any pharmaceutical firm wishing to submit a new-drug application to the Food and Drug Administration be required to have all of the clinical research it submits *independently administered* by a new federal agency, the National Institute for Drug Testing (NIDT). Pharmaceutical firms would be free to conduct their own preliminary research and testing, explained Krimsky, but "only data coming from the NIDT [could] be used to gain drug approval." The NIDT would work with the industry sponsor to design the research protocol and approve a budget. After issuing a request for proposals, the agency would contract out the research to an array of academic medical centers and private clinical research firms, which would carry out the trials independent of the sponsor.

Under my version of this plan, only research centers and investigators who could meet the federal government's conflict-of-interest rules (outlined above) would be eligible. Furthermore, the NIDT would contract out clinical trials only to institutions with written policies in place that met the NIDT's strict certification standards—policies that would have to apply to *all of the institutions' clinical research trials*, not only those contracted out by the NIDT. By functioning as a credentialing agency and insisting on these written policies, the NIDT would raise clinical research standards communitywide, since most prestigious medical centers would want to be NIDT-certified.

NIDT certification standards would require that institutions be able to guarantee that all their clinical trials met the following criteria: (1) The lead investigators (and other subordinates) have no financial interests in the outcome of their research; (2) the investigators have complete access to *the raw data from the entire study* (i.e., from all the clinical trial sites, not only their own); (3) the investigators have the right to publish their research findings without interference from the sponsor (corporate proprietary secrets will be protected); (4) a group of independent experts (i.e., independent of the sponsor and the host institution) will be appointed to continually monitor the study, overseeing the informed-consent process, tracking adverse events, and guaranteeing the accuracy of the final published results; and (5) whatever the study outcome (and regardless of whether it is published or not), the investigators will write up a complete abstract and enter it into the NIDT's clinical trial registry. (Currently, as we saw in the case of Paxil and other antidepressants, drug manufacturers frequently seek to bury their negative findings, the consequence being a highly distorted picture of a drug's effectiveness, wasteful duplication of dead-end research, and abuse of the human subjects who have risked their lives for the advancement of science.)

Any proposal that seeks to protect medical science by breaking the drug industry's stranglehold on clinical testing is sure to face stiff resistance from the pharmaceutical lobby. However, it is an idea whose time has clearly come.

As I hope I've demonstrated, economic growth and academic scholarship need not be in conflict. But if the two are going to be compatible, academic entrepreneurship needs to be radically reconceived. Instead of allowing faculty to become CEOs, who often wind up shirking their academic duties and neglecting their students, schools might consider adopting a more flexible sabbatical policy. Professors of engineering, computer science, or chemistry who wanted to keep up with new technological advancements and industrial practices relevant to their fields could take periodic sabbaticals to work in the private sector. In special circumstances, a molecular biologist might be granted an extended two- to three-year leave to join a biotech start-up, if his or her understanding of a particular invention was deemed to be so critical that commercialization would not occur without this active participation. Whatever the arrangements might be, the line dividing academia and business would be clear, and the university's academic values and teaching priorities would be protected.

It is quite possible that the reforms I've suggested will reduce the total amount of corporate funding that universities receive—money that the federal government should be prepared to make up, so that academic science continues to thrive. Some star entrepreneurial professors who don't want to give up their commercial gains may also choose to leave academia for industry. But there will be plenty of highly talented faculty who stay on because of the exceptional freedoms they enjoy in academia, and truly important collaborations that benefit both academia and industry will, in all likelihood, continue much as they did before. When the university isn't trying to maximize its own profits, moreover, it will be able to support student entrepreneurship in a manner far more in keeping with its educational responsibilities. Instead of suing its students (as the University of Illinois did when Marc Andreesen, a 1993 graduate, founded Netscape Communications),[17] or competing with its students over the rights to commercially promising discoveries (as the University of South Florida did when it accused Petr Taborsky of stealing university property); or betraying its students' trust (as Stanford did when it failed to properly monitor Garry Nolan's academic lab and its relationship with Rigel Pharmaceuticals, Inc.), the university would be able to dedicate itself to truly nurturing the intellectual, creative, and entrepreneurial talents of its students—who are, after all, the university's most valuable and important "assets."

Knowledge for Knowledge's Sake

The reforms I have proposed above will, I believe, go a long way toward safeguarding the universities' autonomy. However, equally crucial is the willingness of our nation's academic leaders, administrators, and faculty to stand up and defend traditional academic values. The university has many important "uses," but the source of its great strength lies not in its ability to generate commercial products, but in its capacity to appreciate the intrinsic value of intellectual discovery, human creativity, knowledge, and ideas.

"It has been the fate of American higher education to develop in a preeminently businesslike culture," the historian Richard Hofstadter wrote in 1952. Throughout the modern era, Hofstadter acknowledged, U.S. universities helped to fuel technological and economic development. But too often, he lamented, higher education in the United States was judged on purely pragmatic grounds. "Education is justified apologetically as a useful instrument in attaining *other* ends: it is good for business or professional careers," he complained. "Rarely, however, does anyone presume to say that it is good for man."[18]

Some would argue that Hofstadter's vision of higher education is an unaffordable luxury. In today's information age, ideas have become prized commodities. Still, even on the utilitarian grounds that traditionalists like Hofstadter might scorn, preserving the distinction between higher education and business is vitally important.

For if commercial criteria are allowed to prevail, schools not only risk shrinking their educational mission, but they also risk ceasing to be centers of technological innovation. When I met with Paul Berg, a Nobel Prize–winning biologist at Stanford, he told a story that dramatically illustrates why.

Berg, an energetic scientist in his late seventies, is a seminal figure in the biotech revolution, having laid the early groundwork for splicing DNA to make hybrid molecules. (Stanley Cohen and Herbert Boyer built on Berg's work to create the first recombinant DNA clone.) His discovery propelled the billion-dollar industry that is now hailed as a model of university-industry relations. But Berg pointed to an underlying irony: "The biotech revolution itself would not have happened had the whole thing been left up to industry. Venture-capital people steered clear of anything that didn't have obvious commercial value or short-term impact. They didn't fund the basic research that made biotechnology possible." Indeed, nearly all of this research was paid for by U.S. taxpayers. Berg recalled that shortly after his own path-breaking discovery, he gave a seminar at the Merck pharmaceutical company, where he met a young scientist who had been pursuing the same research idea. When this scientist encountered some obstacles after six or seven months, Merck prevented him from continuing to work on the project. "Even though Merck was widely championed for its support of research, they wouldn't let him go beyond a certain point," Berg said, "and that is just one of the limitations of corporate research."

The freedom of universities from market constraints is precisely what allowed them in the past to nurture the type of open-ended fundamental research that led to some of the most important (and least expected) discoveries in history. Today, as the line between academic and commercial science dissolves, as the openness of the academic culture gives way to a proprietary one, as professors are encouraged to think more and more like entrepreneurs, a question arises: Will the Paul Bergs of the future have the freedom to explore ideas that have no obvious and immediate commercial value? Only, it seems, if universities cling to their traditional ideals and maintain their independence from the marketplace. Only, that is, if higher education is appreciated not only for its potential use value but for its intrinsic worth. This will not be easy in an age of dwindling public support for higher education, but the university is simply too important a public institution to be surrendered to the narrow dictates of the market. "The best reason for supporting the college and the university," wrote Hofstadter, "lies not in the services they can perform, vital though such services may be, but in the values they represent. The ultimate criterion of the place of higher learning in America will be the extent to which it is esteemed not as a necessary instrument of external ends, but as an end in itself."

Acknowledgments

The idea for this book began to take shape roughly 6 years ago when I was working with Bill Hartung at the World Policy Institute. In 1998, we both teamed up to write an article about Lockheed Martin, the U.S. defense contractor, and its bid to take over the administration of Texas's public welfare system. The notion that the nation's largest military contractor was vying to take over an essential governmental function (one where it clearly had no previous expertise and would be dealing with a highly vulnerable population), seemed extraordinary to me, and soon sparked my deeper inquiry into America's growing fascination with privatizing the public sphere—including everything from prisons and governmental services, to public schools and universities.

I am grateful to Bill for being a wonderful friend, mentor, and early source of inspiration. I also thank Jack Beatty, my first editor at the *Atlantic Monthly*, and the late Michael Kelly, the magazine's former editor in chief, for publishing my article, "The Kept University," coauthored with Eyal Press in 2000, which was the genesis of this book. Other vital support during these early years came from the Open Society Institute, which awarded me an Individual Project Fellowship to facilitate my investigative journalism. I am grateful to George Soros, Gara LaMarche, Gail Goodman, and Jo-Ann Mort for providing this seed money to help me get started.

Having now completed my book, I feel an enormous debt of gratitude to many people, and many organizations. I greatly appreciate the intellectual and financial support that I received over the past four years from the New America Foundation in Washington, D.C. In particular, I want to thank Ted Halstead and Sherle Schwenninger for encouraging me to embark on what initially seemed like an impossibly ambitious book project, and for remaining true allies throughout the process.

Grateful thanks also go to Janet Maughan and her colleagues at the Rockefeller Foundation for taking a keen interest in my work and for stepping in to provide additional support at a time when it was critical to my being able to finish the manuscript.

Writing this book would not have been possible—especially for an outsider like myself—were it not for the many thoughtful people inside of academia who consented to speak to me, shared their stories, and opened my eyes to the complex challenges and threats that the United States' universities now face. In the course of our conversations, each of these people passionately conveyed their concerns about the future of the university and its importance to the intellectual life of this nation. As such, all of them were an inspiration to me. I cannot list each person by name, but I would like to single out a few: Paul Berg, Clark Kerr, Bhaven Sampat, Donald Stein, Ignacio Chapela, Mildred Cho, Christopher Scott, Nancy Olivieri, David Kern, and David Hollinger. Although these sources did influence my thinking, the views I express in my book are, of course, wholly my own.

New America's bright and spirited research associates—Joe Dempsey, John Mangin, Richard So, John Gravois, Louise Feld, Louisa Lombard, Mark Goldberg, Kartik Ramachandran—provided indispensable help tracking down articles, transcribing interviews, and gathering statistical data, among other things. I am especially grateful to Kartik, who devoted long days and nights to helping me complete the final research, fact-checking, and editing of the manuscript—and who did so with remarkable aplomb under pressure. Thanks to Eddie Dobson at my local copy shop in Brooklyn for always being there with a hug. Grateful thanks also go to Chris Calhoun, my agent, for his enduring faith in this project. At Basic Books, I thank Jo Ann Miller, Ellen Garrison, Iris Richmond, and Margaret Ritchie for their care in getting this book into print.

My writing career has been kept alive by many wonderful fellow journalists, writers, editors, and friends, some of whom I also want to gratefully acknowledge: Adam Haslett, Alice Vogt, Rudy Wurlitzer, Bill Berkeley, Glenn Frankel, Tina Rosenberg, Bob Kuttner, Laura Secor, Adam Shatz, Nick Thompson, Glenn Frankel, David Bollier, Karen Rothmyer, Monika Bauerlein, Ruth Baldwin, and Robin Dutcher. My deepest and most heartfelt thanks go to Eyal Press, whose love and friendship have nourished and sustained me, and whose confidence in me and my abilities has made me stronger.

To all my family and friends, thank you for your patience and for standing by me through these long years of writing. I am, and will always remain, deeply grateful to you for your love and support.

Notes

Introduction

1. Jeffrey Brainard, "Lobbying to Bring Home the Bacon," *Chronicle of Higher Education*, October 22, 2004, p. A26.

2. Rhonda L. Rundle, "A New Name in Skin Care: Johns Hopkins," *Wall Street Journal*, April 5, 2006, B1; Rhonda L. Rundle, "Johns Hopkins Backs Off Pact For Skin Care," *Wall Street Journal*, April 11, 2006, B1.

3. In 2005 and 2006, numerous academic associations debated this issue at conferences and symposia, including the Council on Government Relations, the Association of American Universities, the Association of University Technology Managers, the American Federation of Teachers, the Social Science Research Council, and the American Sociology Association. See also "Baying for Blood or Doling out Cash? A Landmark Law Has Allowed American Universities to Profit by Patenting Their Innovations. But the Costs Are Adding Up," *The Economist*, December 20, 2005.

4. Robert Zemsky, Gregory R. Wegner, William F. Massy, *Remaking the American University: Market-Smart and Mission Centered* (New Brunswick, NJ: Rutgers University Press, 2005), p. 195.

5. Quoted in John Rothfork, "Remaking the American University: Open for Business," *Education Review*, 9(3), March 27, 2006, http://edrev.asu.edu/essays/v9n3/; Original source: Anne Marie Cox, "Phoenix Ascending," *In These Times*, May 13, 2002.

6. Zemsky et al., pp. 186, 191.

7. Anne Wilson, "U. Parties Settle Dispute on Cancer-Gene Patent," *Salt Lake City Tribune*, February 16, 1995, p. B1.

8. Eliot Marshall, "NIH Gets a Share of BRCA1 Patent," *Science*, 267(5201), February 24, 1995: p. 1086.

9. Ronald Kotulak, "Taking License with Your Genes," *Chicago Tribune*, September 12, 1999, p. 1. Allen Bale of Yale University also reported being forced to drop out of a large NIH study on early-stage breast cancer because Myriad refused to let him conduct the sequencing of

the BRCA1 breast cancer gene himself. See: Kimberly Blanton, "Corporate Takeover Exploiting the US Patent System: A Single Company Has Gained Control over Genetic Research and Testing for Breast Cancer and Scientists and Doctors Have to Play by Its Rules," *Boston Globe*, February 24, 2002, p. 10.

10. Gregory K. Sobolski, John H. Barton, Ezekiel J. Emanuel, "Technology Licensing: Lessons from the US Experience," *Journal of the American Medical Association*, 294, pp. 3137–3140, 2005; Association of University Technology Managers, "AUTM Licensing Surveys," 1996–2004.

11. Figures are drawn from College Board, "Trends in College Pricing, 2005," Trends in Education Series, www.collegeboard.com.

12. Calculations, by the Project on Student Debt, come from the National Center for Education Statistics (NCES), National Postsecondary Student Aid Study (NPSAS), 2004 undergraduates and 1993 undergraduates, Data Analysis System.

13. Remarks by Edward B. Cohen, vice president of government and industry relations at Honda, "The Tuition Spiral: High Cost vs. Higher Education," a forum hosted by the *Atlantic Monthly* magazine, Washington, DC, October 5, 2004.

14. State Higher Education Executive Officers, "State Higher Education Finance FY 2005," http://www.sheeo.org/.

15. Irwin Feller, "Virtuous and Vicious Cycles in the Contributions of Public Research Universities to State Economic Development Objectives," *Economic Development Quarterly*, 18(2), May 2004: 138–150, available at: http://edq.sagepub.com/cgi/reprint/18/2/138.pdf.

16. Keith H. Hammonds, Susan Jackson, et al., "The New U," *Business Week*, December 22, 1997.

17. James Engell, Anthony Dangerfield, "The Market-Model University: Humanities in the Age of Money," *Harvard Magazine*, May–June 1998. Available online at: http://www.harvard-magazine.com/.

18. Lynne Rudder Baker, "Should the Humanities Be Saved?" *UMass*, alumni magazine, Winter 1999: 18–23, p. 22.

19. Howard Kurtz, "Reading Between the Lines," *Washington Post*, April 2, 2001; Jonathan H. Esensten, "Mixing Science and Politics: Graham Faces Opposition," *Harvard Crimson*, April 17, 2001.

20. G. D. Curfman, S. Morrissey, and J. M. Drazen, "Expression of Concern: Bombardier et al. . . . " *New England Journal of Medicine*, December 29, 2005; 353: 2813–2814; Curfman et al., "Expression of Concern Reaffirmed," *New England Journal of Medicine*, March 16, 2006; 354: 1193.

21. General Accounting Office, "EPA's Science Advisory Board Panels," GAO–01–536, June 2001, available at: http://www.gao.gov/new.items/d01536.pdf.

22. Dennis Cauchon, "FDA Advisors Tied to Industry," *USA Today,* September 25, 2000; Gardiner Harris and Alex Berenson, "10 Voters on Panel Backing Pain Pills Had Industry Ties,"

New York Times, February 25, 2005; "FDA Advisers Shouldn't Have Ties to Industry, Groups Say," *Washington Post*, March 11, 2005, A6; "House Approves Rep. Hinchey Restriction for FDA Boards," *Associated Press State and Local Wire*, June 8, 2005.

23. Shannon Brownlee, "Doctors Without Borders," *Washington Monthly*, April 1, 2004. See also: Melody Peterson, "Undisclosed Financial Ties Prompt Reproval of Doctor," *New York Times*, August 3, 2003.

24. Sheldon Rampton, John Stauber, *Trust Us, We're Experts* (New York: Penguin Putnam, 2001), p. 199.

25. Lee Hancock, Mark Curriden, "UT-Tyler's Tobacco Ties Questioned; School Officials Say Relationship Uneasy," *Dallas Morning News*, November 15, 1997, p. 1A.

26. "Deregulation Deception," a report by HarvardWatch, Cambridge, MA, May 21, 2002, pp. 8–13, 17–18. For an example of Hogan's lobbying see: William W. Hogan, "An Efficient Bilateral Market Needs a Pool," Hearings, California Public Utilities Commission, San Francisco, August 4, 1994. The two reports Hogan wrote downplaying Enron's role in price manipulation and the need for reregulation are: Scott M. Harvey, William W. Hogan, "Identifying the Exercise of Market Power in California," Law and Economic Consulting Group (LECG), LLC, Cambridge, MA, December 28, 2001; Scott M. Harvey, William W. Hogan, "Further Analysis of the Exercise of Market Power in the California Electricity Market," LECG, LLC, Cambridge, MA, November 21, 2001. See also: Marcy Gordon, "Enron Directors Spread Blame Around," *Associated Press*, May 8, 2002; Nella Banerjee, David Barboza, et al., "Will It Be California Redux?" *New York Times*, May 12, 2002; Tim Reiterman, Nancy Rivera Brooks, "Enron Memos Fuel Inquiry of Power Pricing; Energy Documents Lend Credence to Claims the State's Crisis Was at Least Partly Manufactured," *Los Angeles Times*, May 12, 2002; Ricardo Alonso-Zaldivar, Richard Simon, "Power Firms Are Ordered to Turn Over Trading Data; Energy Regulators Seek to Determine If Sellers Tried to Manipulate the California Market," *Los Angeles Times*, May 9, 2002.

27. The Harvard Business School reports are posted on Enron's Web site at: http://universityaffairs.enron.com/case_studies.asp (accessed on June 4, 2002).

28. "Deregulation Deception," HarvardWatch, p. 5.

29. Robert Kuttner, *Everything for Sale: The Virtues and Limits of Markets* (New York: Knopf, 1997), pp. 361–362.

30. Brian O'Reilly, "Why Edison Doesn't Work," *Fortune*, December 9, 2002; Eyal Press, Jennifer Washburn, "The At-Risk-Youth Industry," *Atlantic Monthly*, 290(5), December 2002; Eyal Press, Jennifer Washburn, "Neglect for Sale," *American Prospect*, 11(12), May 8, 2000.

31. Francis Narin, Kimberly S. Hamilton, et al., "The Increasing Linkage Between U.S. Technology and Public Science," *Research Policy*, 26(3), October 1997: 317–330; William J. Broad, "Study Finds Public Science Is Pillar of Industry," *New York Times*, May 13, 1997.

32. Iain Cockburn, Rebecca Henderson, "Public-Private Interaction in Pharmaceutical Research," *Proceedings of the National Academy of Sciences* 93, November 1996: 12725–12730.

33. William J. Broad, "U.S. Is Losing Its Dominance in the Sciences," *New York Times*, May 3, 2004, p. A1; "Going Global: The New Shape of American Innovation," Council on Competitiveness, 1999, available at: http://www.compete.org/publications/ competitiveness_reports.asp.

34. Martha C. Nussbaum, *Cultivating Humanity: A Classical Defense of Reform in Liberal Education* (Cambridge, MA: Harvard University Press, 1997), pp. 8–9.

35. According to NSF estimates, the federal government contributed $21.7 billion to universities and colleges for R&D in 2003. See: National Science Foundation, Division of Science Resources Statistics, "Table 1A: Federal Obligations to Universities and Colleges for Total Research, by Detailed Field of Science and Engineering: All Agencies, Fiscal Years 1973–2003," *Federal Funds for Research and Development, Research to Universities and Colleges by Agency and Field of Science: Fiscal Years 1973–2003* (Arlington, VA: 2004), NSF 04–332, available at: http://www.nsf.gov/sbe/srs/nsf04332/start.htm. For the student loans and grants figure, see: Stephen Burd, "Bush's Next Target?" *Chronicle of Higher Education*, July 11, 2003, p. A18.

36. Paul E. Lingenfelter, Hans P. L'Orange, et al., "State Higher Education Finance: FY 2003," State Higher Education Executive Officers, Denver, 2004, available at: http://www.sheeo.org/finance/shef.pdf.

Chapter 1. A New Kind of Uprising at Berkeley

1. Clark Kerr, "Shock Wave II: An Introduction to the Twenty-First Century," in Steven Brint, Ed., *The Future of the City of Intellect* (Stanford: Stanford University Press, 2002), p. 17.

2. Clark Kerr, *The Uses of the University* (Cambridge, MA: Harvard University Press, 1963).

3. David L. Goines, *The Free Speech Movement: Coming of Age in the 1960s* (Berkeley, CA: Ten Speed Press, 1993).

4. Personal interview with Clark Kerr, April 17, 2001.

5. Kerr's most forceful criticism of the U.C. Berkeley–Novartis deal appears in his essay "Shock Wave II," cited above (see p. 17 and endnote 1).

6. Much of this next section first appeared in an article I coauthored. See: Eyal Press, Jennifer Washburn, "The Kept University," *Atlantic Monthly*, 285(3), March 2000.

7. The November 1998 agreement between U.C. Berkeley and Novartis was officially signed with the Novartis Agricultural Discovery Institute, Inc. (NADII), a research institute under the corporate umbrella of Novartis AG. Subsequently, in early 2001 Novartis and Astra Zeneca combined their respective agricultural divisions to create a new company, Syngenta, one

of the world's largest agrochemical corporations. After this, NADII was renamed the Torrey Mesa Research Institute.

8. Julianne Basinger, "Increase in Number of Chairs Endowed by Corporations Prompts New Concerns," *Chronicle of Higher Education*, April 24, 1998, p. A51.

9. Most experts agree that giving Novartis an up-front, exclusive license to one-third of the department's research effectively gave the company the right to cherry-pick all of the Department of Plant and Microbial Biology's most commercially valuable inventions, as it was highly unlikely that more than one-third of the discoveries would have commercial promise. In effect, this arrangement gave Novartis monopoly control over the department's output.

10. "Is the University-Industrial Complex Out of Control?" editorial, *Nature*, 409(6817), January 11, 2001: p. 119.

11. Letter to the PMB faculty signed by twenty-three PMB graduate students, December 14, 1998.

12. Personal interview with Donald Dahlsten, April 19, 1999.

13. Personal interview with Andy Gutierrez, April 16, 1999.

14. Rausser's consulting group—the Law and Economic Consulting Group, Inc. (LECG, Inc.)—was the subject of much controversy on campus. First, there were concerns that the company, which employs many U.C. professors, had improperly exploited and capitalized on its prestigious association with the U.C. system. Robert Berring, "Is Berkeley Off Course?" *California Monthly*, February 1999: 18–20. Second, there were concerns that Rausser's LECG association represented a conflict of interest, since its client list included biotech firms. In 1996, Rausser also made $1.3 million from LECG, significantly more than his salary as dean. Jonathan Marshall, "Group of UC Economists Hope to Cash In on IPO," *San Francisco Chronicle*, October 30, 1997, p. C1; Securities and Exchange Commission 1998, cited in Lawrence Busch, Richard Allison, et al., *External Review of the Collaborative Research Agreement Between Novartis Agricultural Discovery Institute, Inc. and the Regents of the University of California*, Institute for Food and Agricultural Standards, Michigan State University, July 13, 2004. The quote is from my personal interview with Gordon Rausser, April 15, 1999.

15. Gordon Rausser, "Fueling the Research Engine," *California Monthly*, April 1999: 24–26, p. 26.

16. Personal interview with Gordon Rausser, April 15, 1999.

17. According to National Science Foundation (NSF) estimates, the federal government contributed $21.7 billion to universities and colleges for R&D in 2003. See: National Science Foundation, Division of Science Resources Statistics, "Table 1A: Federal Obligations to Universities and Colleges for Total Research, by Detailed Field of Science and Engineering: All Agencies, Fiscal Years 1973–2003," *Federal Funds for Research and Development, Research to Universities and Colleges by Agency and Field of Science: Fiscal Years 1973–2003* (Arlington, VA: National Science Foundation, 2004), NSF 04–332, available at: http://www.nsf.gov/sbe/srs/nsf04332/start.htm. Other statistics come from: National Science

Board, *Science and Engineering Indicators—2004* (Arlington, VA: National Science Foundation, May 2004), NSB 04–1, NSB 04–1A; and National Science Board, *Science and Engineering Indicators—2002* "Appendix Table 5–2: Support for Academic R&D, by Sector: 1953–2000," (Arlington, VA: National Science Foundation, 2002), NSB–02–1, available at: http://www.nsf.gov/sbe/srs/seind02/start.htm.

18. All the figures used here were computed with data from: Ronald Meeks, *Federal Funds for Research and Development, Research to Universities and Colleges by Agency and Field of Science: Fiscal Years 1973–2003,* Tables 1A, 2A, 3A (Arlington, VA: National Science Foundation, 2004), NSF 04–332.

19. The figures on U.C. Berkeley came from the chancellor's office; the national figures came from: Ronald G. Ehrenberg, Michael J. Rizzo, "Financial Forces and the Future of American Higher Education," *Academe,* July-August 2004: 28–31, p. 29.

20. National Science Board, *Science and Engineering Indicators—2004* "Appendix Table 5–2: Support for Academic R&D, by Sector: 1972–2001," (Arlington, VA: National Science Foundation, May 2004), NSB 04–1A.

21. Ibid., Chapter 5: "Academic Research and Development," p. 6, and "Appendix Table 5–2: Support for Academic R&D, by Sector: 1972–2001."

22. E-mail correspondence with Denis O. Gray, August 16, 2004. See also: Denis O. Gray, Mark Lindblad, Joseph Rudolph, "Industry-University Research Centers: A Multivariate Analysis of Member Retention," *Journal of Technology Transfer,* 26(3), June 2001: 247–254. The authors wrote, "According to research by Cohen and his colleagues (1994), industry-university research centers in the U.S. had research expenditures of $2.53 billion, accounting for roughly 15% of university research funding. Add to this support for traditional cooperative activities like consulting and contract research and industry-sponsored and industry-leveraged government research probably accounts for 20–25% of university R&D," p. 247.

23. Gordon Rausser made these arguments on numerous occasions, including during my interview with him on April 15, 1999. See: Gordon Rausser, "Public/Private Alliances," *AgBioForum,* 2(1), April 1999; Gordon Rausser, "Complimentarities," College of Natural Resources, University of California, Berkeley; Gordon Rausser's testimony before the California State Senate, "Impacts of Genetic Engineering on California's Environment: Examining the Role of Research at Public Universities (Novartis/UC Berkeley Agreement)," Joint Hearing, Committee on Natural Resources and Wildlife, Senate Select Committee on Higher Education, California State Legislature, Sacramento, May 15, 2000, pp. 44–46.

24. The University of California Student Association is made up of undergraduates and graduates from every U.C. campus.

25. Margaret Eaton, "Novartis-UC Berkeley Research Collaboration," *Ethics and the Business of Bioscience* (Stanford: Stanford University Press, 2004): 161–195.

26. In 1999, for example, about 45 percent of U.S. university plant breeders reported that the difficulty they had obtaining seeds from private companies had interfered with their

research (Steven C. Price, "Public and Private Plant Breeding," *Nature Biotechnology*, 17, October 1999: 938, available at: http://biotech.nature.com). See also: Ken Frey, "National Plant Breeding Study-I: Human and Financial Resources Devoted to Plant Breeding Research and Development in the United States in 1994," Iowa Agriculture and Home Economics Experiment Station, Iowa State University, 1996; Andrew Pollack, "The Green Revolution Yields to the Bottom Line," *New York Times*, May 15, 2001; W. R. Coffman, W. H. Lesser et al., "Commercialization and the Scientific Research Process: The Example of Plant Breeding," paper presented at the Cornell Higher Education Research Institute conference titled "Science and the University," May 20–21, 2003, available at: www.ilr.cornell.edu/cheri/conf/cheri-conf2003-may.html; Jonathan Knight, "Crop Improvement: A Dying Breed," *Nature*, 421(6923), February 6, 2003: 568–570.

27. California State Legislature, Senate, "Impacts of Genetic Engineering on California's Environment: Examining the Role of Research at Public Universities (Novartis/UC Berkeley Agreement)," Joint Hearing, Committee on Natural Resources and Wildlife, Senate Select Committee on Higher Education, California State Legislature, Sacramento, May 15, 2000, p. 50. (Hereinafter California Senate Hearing.)

28. Ibid., p. 54.

29. Ibid., p. 55.

30. Ibid., p. 57.

31. Ibid., pp. 61, 63.

32. This section is based on a comprehensive review of all the correspondence between the Academic Senate and the U.C. Berkeley administration between October 6, 1998, and November 23, 1998, as well as personal interviews with various principal members of the Academic Senate at that time, including: Todd LaPorte, chair of the Ad Hoc Committee on the CNR-Novartis Proposal, and of the Committee on Research (January 21, 2002); and Robert Spear, vice chair of the Division Council of the Academic Senate (May 14, 2002).

33. Letter to Carol Christ, executive vice chancellor and provost, from Robert Brentano, chair of the Academic Senate, October 6, 1998. Attached to this letter is a memorandum addressed to Brentano (September 30, 1998) from five Academic Senate chairs and vice chairs laying out their concerns regarding the U.C. Berkeley–Novartis alliance.

34. Letter from Robert J. Brentano to Carol Christ, November 18, 1998.

35. Personal interviews with Todd LaPorte and Robert Spear, cited above.

36. Busch et al., *External Review*, p. 77, see footnote 36.

37. Robert M. Price, Laurie Goldman, "The Novartis Agreement: An Appraisal," *Administrative Review*, University of California, Berkeley, October 4, 2002, p. 40; Andrew Lawler, "Last of the Big Time Spenders," *Science*, 299, January 17, 2003: 330–333, p. 332.

38. Quoted in Robert Sanders, "Closing the Book on the Novartis Deal?" *Berkeleyan*, U.C. Berkeley's public affairs newsletter, January 29, 2003.

39. Busch et al., *External Review*, p. 152, (for complete cite see endnote 14).

40. Goldie Blumenstyk, "Peer Reviewers Give Thumbs Down to Berkeley-Novartis Deal," *Chronicle of Higher Education*, July 30, 2004.

41. Busch et al., *External Review*, pp. 61–62.

42. Ibid., p. 13.

43. Ibid., p. 17.

44. It is worth noting that many professors apparently did change their research orientation somewhat, in order to take advantage of the company's proprietary databases, thus removing much of the department's work from the public domain. See: Busch et al., *External Review*, p. 95.

45. Busch et al., *External Review*, pp. 127–129. Both research perspectives were vitally important, noted the reviewers, but "in practice not all points of view have been treated equally by the administration of UCB [U.C. Berkeley]. For a number of reasons the UC system and UCB administration have committed themselves to certain areas of research more than other areas, and to greater relations with industry."

46. Busch et al., *External Review*, p. 42. Busch was also quoted in the media saying that the agreement "played a very clear role and an unsatisfactory role in the tenure process" of Chapela (Blumenstyk, "Peer Reviewers").

47. David Quist, Ignacio Chapela, "Transgenic DNA Introgressed into Traditional Maize Landraces in Oaxaca, Mexico," *Nature*, 414, 2001: 541–543.

48. Marc Kaufman, "The Biotech Corn Debate Grows Hot in Mexico," *Washington Post*, March 25, 2002, p. A9.

49. Much of the debate surrounding the Quist-Chapela papers got played out on a biotechnology listserver used by more than three thousand scientists called AgBioWorld. The listserver circulated a petition calling on Nature and Chapela to retract the study. *The Guardian* newspaper reported finding a number of suspicious connections between the critics who posted messages on this site and a PR firm called the Bivings Group, which specializes in Internet lobbying for biotech firms. An article on the PR firm's Web site explains that "there are some campaigns where it would be undesirable or even disastrous to let the audience know that your organization is directly involved. . . . It simply is not an intelligent PR move. . . . Once you are plugged into this world it is possible to make postings to these outlets that present your position as an uninvolved third party. . . . Perhaps the greatest advantage of viral marketing is that your message is placed into a context where it is likely to be considered seriously." See: George Monbiot, "The Fake Persuaders," *The Guardian*, May 14, 2002.

50. John E. Losey, Linda S. Rayor, et. al., "Scientific Correspondence: Transgenic Pollen Harms Monarch Larvae," *Nature*, 399(6733), May 20, 1999: 214. For further discussion of Losey's case and others, see: "The Pulse of Scientific Freedom in the Age of the Biotech Industry," a public conversation sponsored by the Knight Center for Science and Environmental Journalism, U.C. Berkeley School of Journalism, Berkeley, CA, December 10, 2003, available at: http://nature.berkeley.edu/pulseofscience.

51. Matthew Metz*, Johannes Fütterer, "Suspect Evidence of Transgenic Contamination," *Nature*, 416(6881), April 11, 2002; Nick Kaplinsky*, David Braun*, Damon Lisch*, Angela Hay*, Sarah Hake*, Michael Freeling*, "Maize Transgene Results in Mexico Are Artefacts," *Nature*, 416(6881), April 11, 2002: 600–601. All authors marked with an asterisk are or were working in U.C. Berkeley's Department of Plant and Microbiology.

52. Ayala Ochert, "Food Fight," *California Monthly*, June 2002.

53. Charles C. Mann, "Has GM Corn 'Invaded' Mexico?" *Science*, 295, March 1, 2002: pp. 1617, 1619; Marc Kaufman, "The Biotech Corn Debate," p. A9.

54. Carol Kaesuk Yoon, "Journal Raises Doubts on Biotech Study," *New York Times*, April 5, 2002; Russell Schoch, "Novartis: Gone but Not Forgotten," *California Monthly*, April 13, 2004.

55. Busch et al., *External Review*, p. 143.

56. Daniel Zoll, "The Selling of the U.C. System," *San Francisco Bay Guardian*, 35(25), March 21–27, 2001.

57. Martin Van De Werf, "California Names 3 University-Industry Research Projects to Receive State Funds," *Chronicle of Higher Education*, January 12, 2001; Diane Ainsworth, "The Start of Something Big," *Berkeleyan*, U.C. Berkeley public affairs newsletter, December 8, 2001, available at: www.berkeley.edu/news/berkeleyan; and Daniel Zoll, "The Selling of the U.C. System," p. 12.

58. Christopher Scott, "University of California at San Francisco and Mission Bay: Innovative Strategies for 21st Century Bioventures," draft essay provided by author, April 2001.

59. Robert C. Dynes, U.C. President, "Statement on Proposed Mid-Year Budget Cuts," U.C. Office of the President, November 25, 2003.

60. Data for years 1993 to 2002: National Science Foundation, "NSF Survey of R&D Expenditures at Universities and Colleges," WebCASPAR Database, available at: http://webcaspar.nsf.gov/; data for 2003: University of California, Office of the President, "National Science Foundation: Survey of Research and Development Expenditures," available at: http://www.ucop.edu/irc/projects/nsf/survey.htm.

61. Drummond Rennie, "Thyroid Storm," *Journal of the American Medical Association*, 277(15), April 16, 1997: 1238–1243.

62. Ralph T. King, Jr., "Bitter Pill: How a Drug Firm Paid for University Study, Then Undermined It," *Wall Street Journal*, April 25, 1996, p. A1.

63. David Shenk, "Money & Science = Ethics Problems on Campus," *The Nation*, May 12, 1999: 11–18.

64. Betty J. Dong, Walter W. Hauck, et al., "Bioequivalence of Generic and Brand-Name Levothyroxine Products in the Treatment of Hypothyroidism," *Journal of the American Medical Association*, 277(15), April 16, 1997: 1205–1213.

65. David Shook, "Synthroid's Maker to Pay $41 M to Settle States Charges," *The Record* (Bergen County, NJ), July 30, 1999, p. B1; "Judge Gives Final Approval to Synthroid Settlement," *Associated Press*, August 8, 2000.

66. Glennda Chui, "Study: Herbicide Wrecks Frog Sex Organs; Report May Explain Population Decline Among Amphibians," *San Jose Mercury News*, April 16, 2002.

67. Goldie Blumenstyk, "The Price of Research," *Chronicle of Higher Education*, October 31, 2003.

68. Jennifer Lee, "Popular Pesticide Faulted for Frogs' Sexual Abnormalities," *New York Times*, June 19, 2003.

69. Robert Sanders, "Popular Weed Killer Demasculinizes Frogs, Disrupts Their Sexual Development, U.C. Berkeley Study Shows," *Berkeleyan*, U.C. Berkeley public affairs newsletter, April 4, 2002.

70. James A. Carr, Angie Gentles, et al., "Response of Larval Xenopus Laevis to Atrazine: Assessment of Growth, Metamorphosis, and Gonadal and Laryngeal Morphology," *Environmental Toxicology and Chemistry*, 22(2), February 2003: 396–405.

71. Ecorisk Press Release, "Frog Research on Atrazine Casts Doubt on Earlier Studies," *PR Newswire*, June 20, 2002.

72. Blumenstyk, "The Price of Research."

73. Tyrone Hayes, Kelly Haston, et al., "Atrazine-Induced Hermaphroditism at 0.1 PPB in American Leopard Frogs (Rana Pipiens): Laboratory and Field Evidence," *Environmental Health Perspectives*, 111(4), April 2003.

74. Lee, "Popular Pesticide."

75. Alison Pierce, "Bioscience Warfare," *San Francisco Weekly*, June 2, 2004.

76. Robert M. Berdahl, "The Privatization of Public Universities," a speech delivered at Erfurt University, Erfurt, Germany, May 23, 2000.

77. Jeff Nesmith, "A Sweet Finding on Possible Benefit of Chocolate," *Atlanta Journal and Constitution*, February 19, 2000. In 2002, Keen presented additional research on the health benefits of chocolate; again the research was funded by Mars. See: Michael Lasalandra, "Study's Sweet News: Chocolate's Healthy," *Boston Herald*, February 16, 2002.

Chapter 2. The Lessons of History

1. Quoted in Lawrence Veysey, *The Emergence of the American University* (Chicago: University of Chicago Press, 1965), pp. 13–14.

2. Gordon C. Rausser, "Fueling the Research Engine," *California Monthly*, April 1999: 24–26.

3. John S. Brubacher, Willis Rudy, *Higher Education in Transition*. (New York: Harper & Row, 1976), p. 151. The Jefferson quote comes from Garry Wills, *Mr. Jefferson's University* (Washington, DC: National Geographic, 2002), p. 117.

4. The Commanger quote appears in Richard Hofstadter, *Anti-Intellectualism in American Life* (New York: Vintage Books, 1963), p. 299.

5. Edwin D. Duryea, *The Academic Corporation* (New York: Falmer Press, 2000), p. 85.

6. Quoted in Frederick Rudolph, *The American College and University: A History* (Athens: University of Georgia Press, 1962), p. 3. Also available from the *Collections of the Massachusetts Historical Society*, 1792, Vol. 1, pp. 242–248.

7. Richard Hofstadter, C. DeWitt Hardy, *The Development and Scope of Higher Education in the United States* (New York: Columbia University Press, 1952), p. 4.

8. Ibid., p. 5.

9. Ibid., p. 9.

10. Ibid., p. 11; Veysey, *Emergence of the American University*, p. 9.

11. Ibid., p. 55; Hofstadter, Hardy, *Development and Scope*, pp. 53–56.

12. Richard Hofstadter, Walter P. Metzger, *The Development of Academic Freedom in the United States* (New York: Columbia University Press, 1955), pp. 5–9; Jean Porter, "Misplaced Nostalgia," *Commonweal*, 128(8), April 20, 2001.

13. Hofstadter, Metzger, *Development of Academic Freedom*, p. 6.

14. Ibid., pp. 126–134.

15. Hofstadter, Hardy, *Development and Scope*, p. 129.

16. Hofstadter, Metzger, *Development of Academic Freedom*, pp. 123, 128.

17. Hofstadter, Hardy, *Development and Scope*, p. 130; Abraham Flexner, *Universities: American, English, German* (New York: Oxford University Press, 1930), p. 180.

18. Brubacher, Rudy, *Higher Education*, p. 154.

19. The First Morrill Act, 1862. Available from the U.S. National Archives and Records Administration's Web site: http://www.ourdocuments.gov/doc.php?doc=33.

20. Hofstadter, Hardy, *Development and Scope*, pp. 24–25; Veysey, *Emergence of the American University*, Chapter 2, pp. 57–120.

21. Hofstadter, Hardy, *Development and Scope*, pp. 26–27.

22. Ibid., pp. 31–32.

23. David A. Hollinger, "Money and Academic Freedom a Half-Century after McCarthyism: Universities amid the Force Fields of Capital," in Peggie J. Hollingsworth, Ed., *Unfettered Expression* (Ann Arbor: University of Michigan Press, 2000), pp. 171–173.

24. Veysey, *Emergence of the American University*, pp. 60, 64–66, quote on p. 66.

25. Hofstadter, Hardy, *Development and Scope*, p. 43. The federal experiment stations were created under the Hatch Act (1887). However, according to Hofstadter and Hardy, it was not until the Smith-Lever Act of 1914 that a system of extension demonstrations brought to farmers the results of experimental work that bore directly on their problems.

26. Ibid., p. 46.

27. Brubacher, Rudy, *Higher Education*, p. 165.

28. Veysey, *Emergence of the American University*, p. 108. Interestingly, winning financial support from the legislature never proved easy, despite these goodwill efforts. Even during La Follette's reign, explained Veysey, the legislature restricted university funding and investigated whether university professors were "wasting" too much time on their own research.

29. Richard Hofstadter, *Anti-Intellectualism*.

30. Veysey, *Emergence of the American University*, p. 78.

31. Ibid., p. 186; Russell Jacoby, *The End of Utopia: Politics and Culture in an Age of Apathy* (New York: Basic Books, 1999), pp. 89–99.

32. Quoted in Veysey, *Emergence of the American University*, p. 255.

33. Hofstadter, Hardy, *Development and Scope*, pp. 53–56.

34. Hofstadter, Metzger, *Development of Academic Freedom*, pp. 373, 376, 381.

35. Ibid., pp. 386–387, quote on p. 393.

36. Veysey, *Emergence of the American University*, pp. 158–159; Hofstadter, Metzger, *Development of Academic Freedom*, pp. 377–378.

37. Ibid., p. 381.

38. David F. Noble, *America by Design: Science, Technology, and the Rise of Corporate Capitalism* (New York: Knopf, 1977), see Chapters 2, 3, 7; Nathan Rosenberg, Richard R. Nelson, "American Universities and Technical Advance in Industry," *Research Policy*, 23, 1994: 323–348.

39. Roger L. Geiger, *To Advance Knowledge* (New York: Oxford University Press, 1986), p. 177.

40. David C. Mowery, Bhaven N. Sampat, "Patenting and Licensing University Inventions: Lessons from the History of the Research Corporation," *Industrial and Corporate Change*, 10(2), 2001: 317–355.

41. Nathan Rosenberg, Richard R. Nelson, "American Universities and Technical Advance in Industry," p. 326.

42. Ibid., p. 326. "Until the 1920s or so," the writers noted, "for better or for worse, a large share of American university research was very much 'hands-on' problem-solving," (p. 324). See also: Robert V. Bruce, *The Launching of Modern American Science, 1846–1876* (New York: Knopf, distributed by Random House, 1987).

43. David Dickson, *The New Politics of Science* (New York: Pantheon Books, 1984), pp. 61–62. Gray's quote comes from: U.S. Congress Hearings, House Committee on Science and Technology, Subcommittee on Investigations and Oversight and Subcommittee on Science, Research, and Technology, *Commercialization of Academic Biomedical Research*, 97th Congress, 1st Session, June 8–9, 1981, p. 33.

44. Hofstadter, Metzger, *Development of Academic Freedom*, pp. 380–381.

45. Ibid., p. 413.

46. Dickson, *New Politics*, p. 63. Even as late as the Depression, when President Franklin D. Roosevelt considered providing federal funding for university research, two-thirds of his

Scientific Advisory Board argued that the risk of political interference was too great, and the idea was dropped.

47. Veysey, *Emergence of the American University*, pp. 348–349.

48. Hofstadter, Metzger, *Development of Academic Freedom*, p. 419.

49. Ibid., p. 415.

50. Ibid., p. 416.

51. Ibid., p. 459.

52. Ibid., p. 459.

53. Roger Geiger, *To Advance Knowledge*, pp. 96, 188–191.

54. Rebecca S. Lowen, "Transforming the University: Administrators, Physicists, and Industrial and Federal Patronage at Stanford, 1935–49," *History of Education Quarterly*, 31(3), Autumn 1991: 365–388.

55. John W. Servos, "The Industrial Relations of Science: Chemical Engineering at MIT, 1900–1939," Isis, 71(259), 1980: 531–549; Geiger, *To Advance Knowledge*, pp. 177–178.

56. Ibid., *Knowledge*, p. 179. Noyes's dismissal aroused considerable controversy on campus both because of his national stature as a scientist and because he had been a past acting president of MIT.

57. Servos, "Industrial Relations," pp. 540–542.

58. Geiger, *To Advance Knowledge*, p. 180.

59. Servos, "Industrial Relations of Science," p. 546.

60. Both quotes come from Veysey, *Emergence of the American University*, p. 346.

61. Thorstein Veblen, *The Higher Learning in America* (New York: B. W. Huebsch, 1918), p. 139; Noble, *America by Design*, p. 244.

62. Hofstadter, Metzger, *Development of Academic Freedom*, pp. 420–421.

63. Industrial interests were by no means the only threat to academic freedom during these years, even though they bore the brunt of faculty ire. Metzger pointed to several state institutions where the demand for economic conformity and violations of academic freedom arose from the populist "left" instead. Ibid., pp. 423–425.

64. Ibid., pp. 436–439.

65. Daniel H. Pollitt and Jordan E. Kurland, "Entering the Academic Freedom Arena Running: The AAUP's First Year," *Academe*, July-August 1998: 45–52.

66. Hofstadter, Metzger, *Development of Academic Freedom*, pp. 464–466.

67. Clyde W. Barrow, *Universities and the Capitalist State: Corporate Liberalism and the Reconstruction of American Higher Education, 1894–1928* (Madison: University of Wisconsin Press, 1990), p. 219.

68. Ibid., p. 241.

69. G. Pascal Zachary, *Endless Frontier: Vannevar Bush, Engineer of the American Century* (New York: Free Press, 1997).

70. Geiger, *Research and Relevant Knowledge: American Research Universities Since World War II* (New York: Oxford University Press, 1993), p. 8. Scientific work on the Manhattan Project continued to be based at the nation's universities for the first twelve months. The principal research groups were based at Berkeley at Columbia, Chicago, and at Berkeley. In addition, vital experimental data were being accumulated from cyclotron experiments at Minnesota, Wisconsin, Harvard, and Cornell. Later this research became increasingly centered at Los Alamos.

71. Ibid., pp. 12–13.

72. "Science: The Endless Frontier," a report to the president by Vannevar Bush, director of the Office of Scientific Research and Development (Washington, DC: U.S. Government Printing Office, July 1945).

73. Linda Marsa, *Prescription for Profits* (New York: Scribner, 1997), p. 24.

74. Geiger, *Research and Relevant Knowledge*, p. 16.

75. Ibid., pp. 16–18.

76. National Institutes of Health, "The NIH Almanac—Appropriations," available at: http://www.nih.gov/about/almanac/appropriations/part2.htm.

77. Geiger, *Research and Relevant Knowledge*, p. 157. (This figure includes the federal contract research centers.)

78. Stuart W. Leslie, *The Cold War and American Science: The Military-Industrial-Academic Complex at MIT and Stanford* (New York: Columbia University Press, 1993), Introduction, p. 2.

79. Leslie, *Cold War*, pp. 27, 37–38, 241–242. At Stanford, for example, even after faculty and students protested against classified research on campus, a special subcommittee of the academic council issued a report in 1967 that defended full student participation in classified research. Anything less, it argued, "constitutes a most objectionable form of paternalism that forces upon students a priority by which the faculty is unwilling to live."

80. Bruce Cummings, "Boundary Displacement," in Christopher Simpson, Ed., *Universities and Empire* (New York: New Press, 1998), pp. 159–188. See also: Sigmund Diamond, *Compromised Campus: The Collaboration of Universities with the Intelligence Community* (New York: Oxford University Press, 1992).

81. Leslie, *Cold War*, Introduction, pp. 2, 13; J. William Fulbright, "The War and Its Effects: The Military-Industrial-Academic Complex," pp. 171–178, see p. 34 in Herbert I. Schiller, Ed., *Super-State: Readings in the Military-Industrial Complex* (Urbana: University of Illinois Press, 1970).

82. Leslie, Cold War, Introduction, p. 8.

83. Geiger, *Research and Relevant Knowledge*, p. 56.

84. Leslie, *Cold War*, pp. 42–43.

85. Geiger, *Research and Relevant Knowledge*, p. 38.

86. Ibid., pp. 37–40. For an excellent history of this period, see also: Ellen W. Schrecker, *No Ivory Tower: McCarthyism and the Universities* (New York: Oxford University Press, 1986).

87. Ibid., p. 162.

88. Ibid., pp. 160, 174.

89. Ibid., p. 173.

90. Ibid., p. 181.

91. Ibid., pp. 164–165. See also: Brubacher, Rudy, *Higher Education*, p. 236.

92. National Endowment for the Humanities Web site: www.heh.gov/whoeweare/timeline.html.

93. James T. Patterson, *America in the Twentieth Century: A History* (San Diego: Harcourt Brace Jovanovich, 1989), p. 419. Original source: Andrew Hacker, Ed., *A Statistical Portrait of the American People* (New York: Viking, 1983), p. 251.

94. Geiger, *Research and Relevant Knowledge*, p. 195; Michael S. McPherson, Morton Owen Shapiro, *Keeping College Affordable: Government and Educational Opportunity* (Washington, DC: Brookings Institution, 1991), pp. 37–38.

95. Geiger, *Research and Relevant Knowledge*, p. 166.

96. Leslie, *Cold War*, pp. 233–234.

97. Ibid., p. 241.

98. Ibid., p. 235; Geiger, *Research and Relevant Knowledge*, p. 239.

99. Leslie, *Cold War*, Chapter 9, pp. 233–249.

100. Geiger, *Research and Relevant Knowledge*, pp. 193–195. According to Geiger, because this Pentagon funding was not shifted to the NSF, many areas of basic research—aeronautical engineering, optics, underwater acoustics, and numerous other specialties—suffered a loss of funding as a result of the restrictions imposed by the Mansfield Amendment.

Chapter 3. The Rise of the Market-Model University

1. Linda Marsa, *Prescription for Profits* (New York: Scribner, 1997), p. 87; Edmund L. Andrews, "Biotechnology Dispute Is Rekindled," *New York Times*, August 31, 1988, p. D1.

2. Niels Reimers, interview with Sally Smith Hughes, "Stanford's Office of Technology Licensing and the Cohen/Boyer Cloning Patents," Regional Oral History Office, University of California, Berkeley, 1997, available at: http://ark.cdlib.org/ark:/13030/kt4b69n6sc. See also: Linda Marsa, *Prescription for Profits*, p. 63; Marilyn Chase, "Designer Genes: Universities to Wield Power in DNA Field via Patent on Processes," *Wall Street Journal*, December 31, 1980, p. A1; "How Two Genies at Stanford and Cal Evoked Science of Recombinant DNA," *Wall Street Journal*, December 31, 1980, p. 12.

3. Quote from Daniel J. Kevles, *The Physicists: The History of a Scientific Community in Modern America* (Cambridge, MA: Harvard University Press, 1995), p. 268. For the early

history of the Wisconsin Alumni Research Foundation, see: David Blumenthal, Sherrie Epstein, et. al., "Commercializing University Research: Lessons from the Experience of the Wisconsin Alumni Research Foundation," *New England Journal of Medicine*, 314(25), June 19, 1986: 1621–1626. According to Blumenthal et al., the Steenbock patent generated $14 million in royalty and investment income over the lifetime of the patent.

4. David C. Mowery, Bhaven N. Sampat, "Patenting and Licensing University Inventions: Lessons from the History of the Research Corporation," *Industrial and Corporate Change*, 10(2), 2001: 317–355, Cottrell's quote appears on p. 321.

5. Charles Weiner, "Universities, Professors, and Patents: A Continuing Controversy," *Technology Review*, February-March 1986: 33–43; Albert Q. Maisel, "Combination in Restraint of Health," *Reader's Digest*, February 1948, pp. 42–45; David Blumenthal, et. al., "Commercializing University Research."

6. David C. Mowery, "The Evolving Structure of University-Industry Collaboration in the United States: Three Cases," in *Research Teams and Partnerships: Trends in the Chemical Sciences*, a report of a workshop, Chemical Sciences Roundtable, National Research Council (Washington, DC: National Academy Press, 1999), pp. 7–20, see p. 9.

7. Reimers, interview with Sally Smith Hughes. For further evidence of faculty opposition, see: Paul Berg, interview with Sally Smith Hughes, "A Stanford Professor's Career in Biochemistry, Science Politics, and the Biotechnology Industry," Regional Oral History Office, University of California, Berkeley, 1997, available at: http://ark.cdlib.org/ark:/13030/kt1c6001df; Herbert W. Boyer, interview with Sally Smith Hughes, "Recombinant DNA Research at UCSF and Commercial Application at Genentech," Regional Oral History Office, University of California, Berkeley, 1994, available at: http://ark.cdlib.org/ark:/13030/kt5d5nb0zs. Last, for the scientific community's reaction to the Cohen-Boyer patent, see: Linda Marsa, *Prescription for Profits*, pp. 64–66.

8. This anonymous scientist is quoted in: Reimers, interview with Sally Smith Hughes.

9. Weiner, "Universities, Professors, and Patents," pp. 33–43. See also: David C. Mowery, Richard R. Nelson, et al., *Ivory Tower and Industrial Innovation: University-Industry Technology Transfer Before and After the Bayh-Dole Act* (Stanford: Stanford University Press, 2004), p. 38.

10. Quoted in Seth Shulman, *Owning the Future* (Boston, New York: Houghton Mifflin, 1999), p. 54.

11. Mowery et al., *Ivory Tower*, p. 43.

12. Stanley N. Cohen, "The Stanford DNA Cloning Patent," in William J. Whelan, Sandra Black, Eds., *From Genetic Experimentation to Biotechnology—The Critical Transition: Proceedings of a Symposium* (Sussex, NY: Wiley, 1982), p. 215.

13. Reimers, interview with Sally Smith Hughes.

14. Ibid.

15. Ibid.

16. This estimate comes from Arti K. Rai, Rebecca S. Eisenberg, "Bayh-Dole Reform and the Progress of Biomedicine," *American Scientist*, 91(1), January-February 2003: 52–59, p. 57. Although the Cohen-Boyer technology is often referred to as the most successful patent in university licensing history, it is actually composed of three patents. For more details, see: "Intellectual Property Rights and Research Tools in Molecular Biology," summary of a workshop held at the National Academy of Sciences, National Research Council (Washington, DC: National Academy Press, 1997), pp. 40–42.

17. Reimers, interview with Sally Smith Hughes.

18. In a May 1975 MIT Archives interview, Herbert Boyer remarked, "We're in the process of having a look at the expression of this material in bacteria. I think this has a lot of implications for utilizing the technology in a commercial sense— that is, one could get bacteria to make hormones" (Linda Marsa, *Prescription for Profits*, p. 83).

19. Boyer, interview with Sally Smith Hughes; Jim Doyle, "UC Sues Genentech Over Patent," *San Francisco Chronicle*, August 8, 1990, p. B12.

20. Linda Marsa, *Prescription for Profits*, p. 85.

21. Roger L. Geiger, *Research and Relevant Knowledge: American Research Universities Since World War II* (New York: Oxford University Press, 1993), pp. 302–303; Martin Kenney, *Biotechnology: The University-Industrial Complex* (New Haven: Yale University Press, 1986), pp. 4–5, 93–95; Linda Marsa, *Prescription for Profits*, pp. 86, 90.

22. Interview with Sally Smith Hughes.

23. Ibid.

24. Linda Marsa, *Prescription for Profits*, pp. 89–90.

25. David Dickson, *The New Politics of Science* (New York: Pantheon Books, 1984), p. 78.

26. Linda Marsa, *Prescription for Profits*, pp. 88–93.

27. Philip J. Hilts, "The Gold Rush of Companies into Biotechnology Is Waning"; "Brave New Science: Monks in the Lab Cloning Dollars, Part 3," *Washington Post*, November 3, 1981, p. A1.

28. Martin Kenney, Biotechnology, pp. 94, 96–97; Gene Bylinksy, "DNA Can Build Companies, Too," *Fortune*, June 16, 1980, p. 144.

29. Kenney, *Biotechnology*, 1986; Sheldon Krimsky, *Biotechnics and Society: The Rise of Industrial Genetics* (New York: Praeger, 1991).

30. Philip J. Hilts, "Brave New Science."

31. Robert Weissman, "Public Finance, Private Gain: The Emerging University-Business-Government Alliance and the New U.S. Technological Order," dissertation, Committee on Degrees in Social Studies, Harvard College, March 1989, p. 18. After this sharp dip, growth in federal funding for academic research and development rose only slightly during the period 1974–1978 to 4 percent.

32. Ibid.

33. National Science Board, "University-Industry Research Relationships: Myths, Realities and Potentials," National Science Foundation, Washington, DC, October 1, 1982, pp. 1–32, quote on p. 15. These early NSF programs included the University-Industry Cooperative Research Centers Experiments and the Innovation Centers Experiments.

34. U.S. Congress, House Committee on Science and Technology, Subcommittee on Science, Research and Technology, *Government and Innovation: University-Industry Relations*, 96th Congress, 1st Session, July 31, August 1, 2, 1979, see Richard Atkinson's testimony, p. 77.

35. Quote from Henry Etzkowitz, Andrew Webster, "Science as Intellectual Property," in Sheila Jasanoff et al., Eds., *Handbook of Science and Technology Studies* (Thousand Oaks, CA: Sage, 1995), p. 481. This shift to a knowledge-based economy has been noted by many observers: Peter Drucker, *Post Capitalist Society* (New York: HarperBusiness, 1993); Ikujuro Nonaka, Hirotaka Takeuchi, *The Knowledge-Creating Company* (Oxford, UK: Oxford University Press, 1996); Richard Florida, "Toward the Learning Region," *Futures*, 27(5), 1995: 527–536; Paul Romer, "Ideas and Things," *The Economist*, September 11, 1993, 1995; Paul Romer, "Beyond the Knowledge Worker," *World Link*, January-February 1995: 56–60; Dorothy Leonard-Barton, *Wellsprings of Knowledge: Building and Sustaining the Sources of Innovation* (Boston: Harvard Business School Press, 1995).

36. National Science Board, "University-Industry Research Relationships," pp. 4–6. See Chart 3, p. 6, showing that between 1960 and 1970, basic research done in industrial laboratories shrank significantly from nearly one-third to about one-sixth of total basic research activity.

37. Kenney, *Biotechnology*, p. 94.

38. Lewis Branscomb, "America's Rising Research Alliance," *American Education*, April 1984: 46.

39. Dickson, *New Politics*, p. 65, quoted in Weissman, "Public Finance," p. 12.

40. Walter W. Powell, Jason Owen-Smith, "Universities and the Market for Intellectual Property in the Life Sciences," *Journal of Policy Analysis and Management*, 17(2), 1998: 253–277, p. 257.

41. Edward E. David, Jr., "Science Futures: The Industrial Connection," *Science*, 203(4383), March 2, 1979: 837.

42. See: Dickson, *New Politics*, pp. 56–106, for an overview of these early university-industry alliances. For more on joint university-industry lobbying, see: Rochelle L. Stanfield, "Campuses and Corporations: Industry Offers Money, but Not Without Strings," *National Journal*, November 29, 1980: 2021–2024; Timothy B. Clark, "Campuses and the Feds: Dancing to Washington's Regulatory Tune," *National Journal*, November 29, 1980: 2016–2020; Jack Magarrell, "Academe and Industry Weigh a New Alliance," *Chronicle of Higher Education*, February 5, 1979, p. 1. See also: Paul Seabury, Ed., *Bureaucrats and Brainpower: Government Regulation of Universities* (San Francisco: Institute for Contemporary Studies, 1979). In this book, Nathan Glazer, Richard W. Lyman, Casper

Weinberger, and other contributors complain about excessive government regulation of universities and find common cause with private industry.

43. Act of December 12, 1980, Public Law 96–517, 94 Stat. 3015–3028 (codified as amended at 35 U.S.C. §§ 200–211, 301–307 (1994)).

44. U.S. Congress, Senate Committee on the Judiciary, *The University and Small Business Patent Procedures Act*; Hearings on S. 414, 96th Congress, May 16 and June 6, 1979, CIS NO: 79-S521–57, see: Bob Dole, Opening Statement p. 28.

45. See: Bradley Graham, "Patent Bill Seeks Shift to Bolster Innovation," *Washington Post*, April 8, 1979, reprinted in U.S. Congress, Senate Hearings, *The University and Small Business Patent Procedures Act*, Hearing on S. 1215, pp. 28–31.

46. U.S. Congress, Senate Committee on Commerce, Science, and Transportation, Subcommittee on Science, Technology, and Space, Patent Policy, Part 1, 96th Congress, 1st Session, July 23 and 27, and October 25, 1979, CIS-NO: 80-S261–19. For quote, see: U.S. Congress, Senate Hearings, *The University and Small Business Patent Procedures Act*, p. 181.

47. Dickson, *New Politics*, pp. 91, 93. Quote comes from Russell Long, "Dear Colleague" letter, U.S. Senate, February 21, 1980. See also: Celia W. Dugger, "House Panel Votes Patent Law Change," *Washington Post*, July 25, 1980, p. A9.

48. U.S. Congress, Senate Hearings, *The University and Small Business Patent Procedures Act*. See: prepared statement of Admiral H. G. Rickover, director of the Division of Naval Reactors, Department of Energy, p. 175.

49. Kenneth J. Arrow, "Economic Welfare and the Allocation of Resources for Invention," in Richard Nelson, Ed., *The Rate and Direction of Inventive Activity* (Princeton: Princeton University Press, 1962), pp. 609–626; Richard R. Nelson, "The Simple Economics of Basic Scientific Research," *Journal of Political Economy*, 67, 1959: 297–306. Both of these papers are reprinted in Philip Mirowski, Esther-Mirjam Sent, Eds., *Science Bought and Sold: Essays in the Economics of Science* (Chicago: University of Chicago Press, 2002). This analysis also draws heavily from: David C. Mowery, Richard R. Nelson, et al., "The Growth of Patenting and Licensing by U.S. Universities: An Assessment of the Effects of the Bayh-Dole Act of 1980," *Research Policy*, 30, 2001: 99–119, pp. 103, 117.

50. Quoted in Lawrence Lessig, *Code and Other Laws of Cyberspace* (New York: Basic Books, 1999), p. 132.

51. Quoted in Stephen M. Mauer, "Promoting and Disseminating Knowledge: The Public/Private Interface," a paper prepared for the U.S. National Research Council's Symposium on the Role of Scientific and Technical Data and Information in the Public Domain, Washington, DC, September 5–6, 2002, p. 5.

52. Mowery et al., *Ivory Tower*, p. 87 (complete citation appears at endnote 9); Rebecca S. Eisenberg, "Public Research and Private Development: Patents and Technology Transfer in Government-Sponsored Research," *Virginia Law Review*, 82(8), November 1996: 1671–1679.

53. Eisenberg, "Public Research," p. 1664.

54. Ibid., pp. 1688–1689; William J. Broad, "Patent Bill Returns Bright Idea to Inventor," *Science*, 205(4405), August 3, 1979: 473–476, p. 474.

55. Although the bill did pass with large majorities, its passage was hardly assured. For an interesting political history, discussing the role played by Joseph Allen, a staffer in Birch Bayh's office, and others, see Ashley J. Stevens, "The Enactment of Bayh-Dole," *Journal of Technology*, 29, 2004: 93–99. See also: Mowery et al., *Ivory Tower*, p. 91.

56. U.S. Congress, Senate Hearings, *The University and Small Business Patent Procedures Act*; U.S. Congress, House Committee on the Judiciary, *Amending the Patent and Trademark Laws*, 96th Congress, 2nd Session, Report, September 9, 1980, CIS-NO: 80-H523–34. See also: Eisenberg, "Public Research," p. 1667.

57. Weissman, "Public Finance," p. 75, see footnote 103. In particular, see Admiral Hyman Rickover's jumbled testimony in his exchange with Senator Birch Bayh in U.S. Congress, Senate Hearings, *The University and Small Business Patent Procedures Act*, pp. 155–168.

58. Federal Council on Science and Technology, "Report on Government Patent Policy, 1973–1976," Washington, DC, USGPA, 1978.

59. Harbridge House, Government Patent Policy Study, Final Report for the FCST Committee on Government Patent Policy, 1968.

60. Eisenberg, "Public Research," pp. 1680–1681, 1702–1704, quote on pp. 1703–1704. See also: Mowery et al., *Ivory Tower*, p. 91.

61. Broad, "Patent Bill," pp. 473, 474. Ashley J. Stevens (in "The Enactment of Bayh-Dole," cited earlier) noted that the legislation would not have made it through the Congress in the waning days of the session if, in a magnanimous gesture of respect for Senator Birch Bayh, who had just been defeated in the 1980 election, Senator Russell Long had not withheld his opposition and allowed the legislation to win approval.

62. This section draws heavily from my personal interviews with Norman Latker, managing attorney, Browdy and Niemark, March 13, 2003, and Howard Bremer, former patent attorney at the University of Wisconsin's Alumni Research Foundation, March 6, 2003. All of Latker's direct quotes come from this interview.

63. The IPA program was first introduced 1953, but the program remained small. By 1958, when the agency stopped accepting any new requests for admission, only eighteen universities had been granted IPAs. The reason HEW decided, in 1968, to allow Latker to revamp its IPA program was due to the release of two reports that year—one from the General Accounting Office ("Problem Areas Affecting Usefulness of Results of Government-Sponsored Research in Medicinal Chemistry") and the other from the Harbridge House consulting firm— that criticized the agency for imposing excessive restrictions on university patenting. During the 1940s and 1950s, drug companies routinely screened compounds developed by academic investigators to see if they were biologically active. In some cases, depending on the school's policy, a company could exclusively license a compound in order to develop it into a drug. However,

in 1962, these collaborations abruptly ceased when HEW notified universities that any firm performing such screenings would now be required to sign a formal agreement that prohibited the firm from obtaining patent rights to any technologies that were developed with NIH funding, or that were in the "field of research work" supported by an NIH grant. The public outcry generated by these reports enabled Latker to revitalize the IPA program to strengthen the universities' ability to retain title to agency-sponsored inventions (Mowery et al., *Ivory Tower*, pp. 87–88; Weissman, "Public Finance," pp. 45–46).

64. From 1971 to 1978, Latker served as chair of the Subcommittee on University Patent Policy of the Federal Council for Science, Engineering and Technology. From 1974 to 1978, he also served as the vice chair of this body's Subcommittee on Intellectual Property. From these positions, he actively worked to develop a uniform federal patent policy, similar to the IPA program at HEW. In addition to NSF and HEW, the Department of Defense administered its own version of an IPA program for universities. By the mid-1960s, the Department of Defense (DOD) also had a "special situations" exemption, which gave universities with approved patent policies the right to retain the title to federally funded research. As a "license" agency, the DOD already routinely granted government title to commercial contractors.

65. Personal interview with Latker, 2003.

66. Weissman, "Public Finance," pp. 74–75; personal interview with Latker, 2003.

67. While this review was under way, HEW deferred decisions on thirty waiver petitions for rights to agency-sponsored inventions, and three requests for IPAs.

68. Personal interviews with Latker, 2003, and Bremer, 2003. See also: Mowery et al., *Ivory Tower*, p. 89. According to Latker, HEW's decision to slow down patent waivers and order a review of its patent policy "added up to a decision by [myself and the university patent administrators] that there was no way we could attempt to get to where we wanted to go through an administrative policy. It had to be a legislative process."

69. Nancy K. Eskridge, "Dole Blasts HEW for 'stonewalling' Patent Applications," *BioScience*, 28(9): 605–606.

70. Mowery et al., *Ivory Tower*; Robin Marantz Henig, "New Patent Policy Bill Gathers Congressional Support," *BioScience*, 29(5), May 1979: 281–284, p. 282. According to this contemporaneous *BioScience* article, the decision to leave big business out of the bill was "a tactical exclusion taken to assure the bill's liberal support."

71. The recoupment fee was important to Republicans as well as to Democrats. In his testimony, Senator Strom Thurmond said, "Perhaps the most significant feature of this bill is the recoupment provision. Under this provision, the Government would be able to recoup its original investment once the inventor either surpasses $250,000 in after tax profits or receives over $2 million in sales of related products" (U.S. Congress, *The University and Small Business Patent Procedures Act*, p. 34).

72. "(c) The Grantee shall administer those subject inventions to which it elects to retain title in the public interest and shall, except as provided in paragraph (d) below, make them

available through licensing on a nonexclusive, royalty-free or reasonable royalty basis to qualified applicants. (d) The Grantee may license a subject invention on an exclusive basis if it determines that nonexclusive licensing will not be effective in bringing such inventions to the commercial market in a satisfactory manner. Exclusive licenses should be issued only after reasonable efforts have been made to license on a nonexclusive basis, or where the grantee has determined that an exclusive license is necessary as an incentive for development of the invention or where market conditions are such as to require licensing on an exclusive basis" (HEW IPA agreement, August 26, 1968).

73. Personal interview with Bremer, 2003. See also Robert Weissman's account of this "tacit agreement" with big-business groups, as related to him by Niels Reimers in an interview on January 5, 1989, in Weissman, "Public Finance," pp. 39, 77.

74. Personal interview with Latker, 2003; Weissman, "Public Finance," pp. 77–78; and Eisenberg, "Public Research," p. 1704.

75. Memorandum to the Heads of Executive Agencies: Government Patent Policy, Pub. Papers 252 (February 18, 1983), and Executive Order 12591 (April 10, 1987), codified at 3 C.F.R. 221.

76. A partial listing of these programs includes the Economic Recovery Tax Act (1981), the Cooperative Research Act PL 98–462 (1984), the Small Business Innovation Research Program (1982), the NSF Engineering Research and Science and Technology Centers (mid-1980s), the NSF State/Industry University Cooperative Research Centers (1990), and the Small Business Technology Transfer Program (1992). For more details, see: Norman E. Bowie, *University-Business Partnerships* (London: Rowman & Littlefield, 1994), pp. 16–17; Wesley Cohen, Richard Florida, et. al., "University-Industry Research Centers in the United States" (Pittsburgh: Carnegie Mellon University, Center for Economic Development, 1994); and General Accounting Office, "Small Business Technology Transfer Program," GAO–01–766R, June 4, 2001.

77. For a good overview of the various federal laws and executive orders that extended patenting and licensing to all government-owned and -operated laboratories, see: S. Yong Lee, "Technology Transfer and Public Policy in an Age of Global Economic Competition: Introduction to the Symposium," *Policy Studies Journal*, 22(2), Summer 1994: 260–266.

78. Sheila Slaughter, Larry L. Leslie, Academic *Capitalism: Politics, Policies, and the Entrepreneurial University* (Baltimore: Johns Hopkins University Press, 1997); Henry Etzkowitz, "Entrepreneurial Scientists and Entrepreneurial Universities in American Academic Science," *Minerva*, 21, 1983: 198–233; Derek Bok, Universities *in the Marketplace* (Princeton: Princeton University Press, 2003).

79. Bhaven Sampat, "Patenting and U.S. Academic Research in the Twentieth Century: The World Before and After Bayh-Dole," working paper forthcoming in *Research Policy*, 2004.

80. Stanford University Press Office, report, Committee on Research meeting of March 11, 1981, quoted in Dickson, *New Politics*, p. 76.

81. Richard Nelson, "Observations on the Post-Bayh-Dole Rise of Patenting at American Universities," *Journal of Technology Transfer*, 26(1/2), January 2001: 13–19, p. 13.

82. Arti Rai and Rebecca Eisenberg observed that this dramatic jump in academic patenting "was significantly greater than the twofold increase in overall rates of patenting during the same period and also exceeded growth in university research spending" (Rai, Eisenberg, "Bayh-Dole Reform," pp. 52–59). Figures cited come from Rai and Eisenberg (above) and National Science Board, Science and Engineering Indicators—2004 (Arlington, VA: National Science Foundation, 2004), NSB–04–1, available at: http://www.nsf.gov/sbe/srs/seind04/toc.htm.

83. One of the first large-scale academic-industry partnerships—a $23.3-million contract between Monsanto and Harvard—was signed in 1974, the same year Stanford filed a patent on the Cohen-Boyer technique.

84. Kenney, *Biotechnology*, 1986, pp. 55–56; Ann Crittenden, "Industry's Role in Academia," *New York Times*, July 22, 1981, p. D1.

85. Geiger, *Research and Relevant Knowledge*, p. 320.

Chapter 4. The Republic of Science in Turmoil

1. Robert Merton, "The Normative Structure of Science," *The Sociology of Science* (Chicago: University of Chicago Press, 1973), quoted in David Dickson, *The New Politics of Science* (New York: Pantheon Books, 1984), p. 90.

2. Partha Dasgupta, Paul David, "Toward a New Economics of Science" (originally published in *Research Policy*, 23, 1994: 487–521), reprinted in Philip Mirowski, Esther-Mirjam Sent, Eds., *Science Bought and Sold: Essays in the Economics of Science* (Chicago: University of Chicago Press, 2002), pp. 219–248.

3. Michael Polanyi, "The Republic of Science: Its Political and Economic Theory," in Michael Polanyi, *Knowing and Being* (Chicago: University of Chicago Press, 1969), pp. 49–72. Reprinted in Mirowski, *Sent, Science Bought and Sold*.

4. David Blumenthal, NancyAnne Causino, et al., "Relationships Between Academic Institutions and Industry in the Life Sciences—An Industry Survey," *New England Journal of Medicine*, 334(6), February 8, 1996: 368–373. For National Institutes of Health recommendation, see: "Developing Sponsored Research Agreements: Considerations for Recipients of NIH Research Grants and Contracts," *Federal Register*, 59(215), 1994: 55674–55678.

5. Eyal Press, Jennifer Washburn, "The Kept University," *Atlantic Monthly*, 285(3), March 2000.

6. David Blumenthal, Eric G. Campbell, et al., "Withholding Research Results in Academic Life Science: Evidence from a National Survey of Faculty," *Journal of the American Medical Association*, 277(15), April 16, 1997: 1224–1228.

7. Ibid., p. 1228

8. Wesley Cohen, Richard Florida, et. al., "University-Industry Research Centers in the United States" (Pittsburgh, PA: Carnegie Mellon University, Center for Economic Development, July 1994).

9. This section is based on personal interviews with David Kern and a review of numerous internal university documents and records, journal articles, and media stories. Key sources include: internal Brown University committee report, "Investigation of Alleged Interference with Academic Freedom of David Kern, M.D.," conducted by Deans Peter Shank, Peder Estrup, and Lois Monteiro for Donald J. Marsh, Dean of Medicine and Biological Sciences, May 6, 1997, pp. 1–6; David Kern, "The Unexpected Result of an Investigation of an Outbreak of Occupational Lung Disease," *International Journal of Occupational and Environmental Health*, 4(1), January-March 1998; letter from Francis R. Dietz, president of Memorial Hospital, to "Constituents of Memorial Hospital of Rhode Island," July 10, 1997, pp. 1–7, summarizing the hospital's position on Dr. Kern's dismissal and his academic freedom case; Frank Davidoff, "New Disease, Old Story," editorial, *Annals of Internal Medicine*, 129(4), August 15, 1998: 327–328.

10. Letter from Peter R. Shank, associate dean of medicine and research, to David G. Kern, November 18, 1996.

11. Kern, "Unexpected Result."

12. Memorandum from Francis R. Dietz, president of Memorial Hospital, to David Kern, December 23, 1996.

13. The university received roughly sixty to seventy letters calling on the university to defend Kern's academic freedom. Many members of the Brown faculty also raised their objections; see letter from Kim Boekelheide, Lundy Braun, Dan Brock, Charles Sherman, Harold Ward, and Sally Zierler to the Faculty Executive Committee, April 21, 1997.

14. Letter from Howard Frumkin to Donald J. Marsh, April 11, 1997.

15. Letter from Donald J. Marsh, Brown University School of Medicine, to Frank Dietz, president and CEO of Memorial Hospital, April 30, 1997; Felice J. Freyer, "Doctor: Hospital Tried to Silence Health-Risk Findings," *Providence Journal*, April 25, 1997; Richard A. Knox, "R.I. Firm Wanted Doctor Silent on Lung Research," *Boston Globe*, May 12, 1997.

16. "Dear Faculty Colleague" letter from Donald J. Marsh, May 14, 1997, summarizing the findings from Brown's internal committee investigation of David Kern's case. See also: letter from David S. Greer, dean of medicine emeritus, to Donald Marsh, May 19, 1997, and letter from Paul Calabresi, M.D., former chairman of the Department of Medicine, to Donald Marsh, May 30, 1997.

17. Kern provided alternative documentation, such as grant applications and Brown University reference manuals that suggest that the Program for Occupational Medicine was indeed treated as a program of the Brown University Department of Medicine.

18. See internal Brown University committee report. Five of the committee's seven recommendations center on the need to better clarify the lines of authority in order to protect the educational and research interests of the Brown faculty working at affiliated hospitals.

19. David G. Kern, Robert S. Crausman, et al., "Flock Worker's Lung: Chronic Interstitial Lung Disease in the Nylon Flocking Industry," *Annals of Internal Medicine*, 129(4), August 15, 1998: 261–272.

20. "Brown University Supports the Academic Freedom of Dr. David Kern," press release from the Brown University News Bureau, distributed May 21, 1997, and "An Expression of Support and Praise for Dr. David Kern," press release, Brown University News Bureau, May 21, 1997.

21. "Dear Faculty Colleague," letter from Donald J. Marsh, May 14, 1997, summarizing the findings from Brown's internal committee investigation of David Kern's case; see p. 2.

22. Felice J. Freyer, "Doctor: Hospital." See also letter from Francis R. Dietz, president of Memorial Hospital, to "Constituents of Memorial Hospital of Rhode Island," July 10, 1997, pp. 1–7, in which Dietz acknowledged meeting with Microfibres representatives in November 1996 to discuss a donation to the primary-care center's capital campaign.

23. Annual Report, Memorial Hospital of Rhode Island, 1996.

24. Brian C. Jones, "Technology: The Engine of Economic Growth," *Providence Journal-Bulletin*, May 26, 1996, p. 1A.

25. *Brown Medicine*, 2(1), Spring 1998.

26. Gilbert Geis, Alan Mobley, David Shichor, "Private Prisons, Criminological Research, and Conflicts of Interest: A Case Study," *Crime and Delinquency*, 45(3), July 1999: 372–388; Chris Bryson, "Crime Pays for Those in the Prison Business," *National Times*, September-October 1996: 28–35.

27. Steve Bousquet, "Ethics Panel Rejects Fine on UF Professor as Too Low," *Miami Herald*, June 4, 1999, p. 6B.

28. Marcia Angell, "Is Academic Medicine for Sale?" *New England Journal of Medicine*, 342(20), May 18, 2000: 1516–1518.

29. Douglas Jehl, "Regulations Czar Prefers New Path," *New York Times*, March 25, 2001; Anne Barnard, "Nominee's Funding at Issue," *Boston Globe*, March 18, 2001, p. A7.

30. At one point, Graham even invited Philip Morris to review a draft of a chapter the center produced concerning the surgeon general's report on smoking. See testimony, correspondence, and other supporting documents in U.S. Congress, Senate Committee on Governmental Affairs, *Nominations of Angela B. Styles, Stephen A. Perry, and John D. Graham*, 107th Congress, 1st Session, May 17, 2001 (Washington, DC: Government Printing Office, 2002), pp. 255–302. See also: Anne Barnard, "Nominee's Funding at Issue," *Boston Globe*, March 18, 2001, p. A7; David Corn, "The Loyal Opposition: Harvard University's Gift to the Nation," TomPaine.com, June 1, 2001.

31. Peter J. Howe, "Harvard Downplays Risk of Cell Phone Use by Drivers," *Boston Globe*, July 24, 2000, p. A3; Dick Durban, "Graham Flunks the Cost-Benefit Test," opinion editorial, *Washington Post*, July 16, 2001, p. A15; "Safeguards at Risk: John Graham and Corporate America's Back Door to the Bush White House," a report by Public Citizen, Washington, DC, March 2001, pp. 1–130; and other documents posted at: www.citizen.org/congress/regulations/graham.html.

32. Ibid., p. 109. Numerous prominent groups, including the EPA, the International Agency for Research on Cancer (part of the World Health Organization), and the U.S. National Toxicology Program, have designated many dioxin and furan chemicals as "known human carcinogens."

33. Ross Gelbspan, *The Heat Is On: The High Stakes Battle over Earth's Threatened Climate* (Reading, MA: Addison-Wesley, 1997).

34. Jeffrey Short, chief chemist, Exxon *Valdez* oil spill, National Marine Fisheries Service, National Oceanic and Atmospheric Administration, in a presentation delivered at the Center for Science in the Public Interest's "Conflicted Science" conference, Washington, DC, July 11, 2003.

35. Goldie Blumenstyk, "Greening the World or 'Greenwashing' a Reputation?" *Chronicle of Higher Education*, January 10, 2003.

36. After this event, the *Des Moines Register* managed to obtain a list of subjects the university-affiliated lab prohibited its scientists from pursuing without approval from national headquarters. Agricultural pollution of air, water, or soil, *and antibiotic-resistant bacteria* topped the list (Perry Beeman, "Ag Scientists Feel the Heat," Des Moines Register, December 1, 2002, p. 1A). See also Beeman's discussion of the cases of Phillip Baumel at Iowa State University, James Russell at Cornell University, and JoAnn Burkholder at North Carolina State University.

37. Presentation by Steven Wing, associate professor, Department of Epidemiology, University of North Carolina, Chapel Hill, at the Center for Science in the Public Interest's conference on "Conflicted Science," Washington, DC, July 11, 2003.

38. Richard Darling, president and CEO of the FAIR (Fair Allocations in Research) Foundation, Palm Springs, Florida.

39. David A. Hollinger, "Money and Academic Freedom a Half-Century After McCarthyism: Universities amid the Force Fields of Capital," in Peggie J. Hollingsworth, Ed., *Unfettered Expression: Freedom in American Intellectual Life* (Ann Arbor: University of Michigan Press, 2000), pp. 161–184; Robert M. Rosenzweig, president emeritus, Association of American Universities, "What's for Sale These Days in Higher Education: Two Stories," Center for Studies in Higher Education, University of California, Berkeley, October 26, 1999.

40. Mildred K. Cho, Lisa A. Bero, "The Quality of Drug Studies Published in Symposium Proceedings," *Annals from Internal Medicine*, 124(5), March 1, 1996: 485–489.

41. Mark Friedberg, Bernard Saffran, et al., "Evaluation of Conflict of Interest in Economic Analyses of New Drugs Used in Oncology," *Journal of the American Medical Association*, 282(15), October 20, 1999: 1453–1457.

42. Deborah E. Barnes, Lisa A. Bero, "Why Review Articles on the Health Effects of Passive Smoking Reach Different Conclusions," *Journal of the American Medical Association*, 279(19), May 20, 1998: 1566–1570.

43. J. E. Bekelman et al., "Scope and Impact of Financial Conflicts of Interest in Biomedical Research," *Journal of the American Medical Association*, 289(4), January 22, 2003: 454–465. See also: Joel Lexchin, Lisa A. Bero, et al., "Pharmaceutical Industry Sponsorship and Research Outcome and Quality: Systematic Review," *British Medical Journal*, 326(7400), May 31, 2003: 1167–1170.

44. Marc Ballon, "Professors Profiting from Practicing What They Teach," *Los Angeles Times*, July 16, 2000, p. C1.

45. Goldie Blumenstyk, "SEC Says Columbia U. Scientist Profited from Insider Knowledge of Drug Trials," *Chronicle of Higher Education*, September 29, 1997. For other cases see: Lisa Guernsey, "S.E.C. Sues 2 Researchers and 11 Others for 'Insider Trading' on Drug Stocks," *Chronicle of Higher Education*, April 14, 1997; Kathleen Day, "Cold Researcher Made Profit on Quigley Shares: Stock Soared After Release of Study Favorable to Lozenges," *Washington Post*, January 31, 1997, p. G1; Eliot Marshall, "Disclosing Data Can Get You in Trouble," *Science*, 276, May 2, 1997: 671–672, David J. Morrow, "Drug Researchers in Rare Position to Exploit Stocks," *New York Times*, April 11, 1998, p. B1; Katherine S. Mangan, "U. of Michigan Business Dean Forbids Use of School's Research Data for Personal Gain," *Chronicle of Higher Education*, February 20, 2003.

46. David H. Guston, "Mentorship and the Research Training Experience," in *Responsible Science: Ensuring the Integrity of the Research Process*, vol. 2 (Washington, DC: National Academy of Science, 1993): 52–53.

47. Chris Woolston, "When a Mentor Becomes a Thief," *Chronicle of Higher Education*, April 1, 2002.

48. Press, Washburn, "Kept University."

49. "Request to Secure Theses and Dissertations," Brigham Young University, available at: http://www.byu.edu/gradstudies/resources/forms/form-RequestToSecureETD.pdf.

50. From an unpublished 1995 survey by David Blumenthal, cited in Eric G. Campbell, David Blumenthal, "Academic Industry Relationships in Biotechnology: A Primer on Policy and Practice," *Cloning*, 2(3), 2000: 129–135.

51. Blumenthal et al., "Relationships Between Academic Institutions."

52. Personal interview with Eric Campbell, instructor in Healthcare Policy, Harvard Institute for Health Policy at Harvard Medical School, August 21, 2002.

53. Personal interview with David Zapol, June 10, 2002.

54. "Special Edition: 2000 In Review," *Brainstorm*, the newsletter of Stanford University's Office of Technology Licensing, 10(1), Winter 2001. Press release, "Rigel Receives U.S. Patent for Unique Method of Genomic Screening," PR Newswire, December 4, 2000.

55. Richard Popp, written reply to interview questions, September 9, 2004.

56. In July 1996, Nolan gave a local newspaper a short synopsis of Zapol's project: "A researcher in our lab, David Zapol, will most likely be applying our intracellular peptide libraries against the new receptor. He hopes to block HIV binding or fusion to immune cells" (Jeff Getty, "HIV Puzzle Pieces Fit Together," *Bay Area Reporter*, July 23, 1996, available at: http://www.aegis.com/news/bar/1996/BR960704.html).

57. Personal interview with David Zapol, July 26, 2002.

58. Garry Nolan's written reply to interview questions, August 24, 2004.

59. E-mail from Michael Rothenberg to Garry Nolan, "Re: Meet with Mike R. tomorrow?" August 3, 1997.

60. E-mail from Garry Nolan to Michael Rothenberg, "A lengthy followup to yesterday," August 3, 1997.

61. Written responses to interview questions from Garry Nolan (August 24, 2004) and Richard Popp (September 9, 2004).

62. "Rigel Inc. Completes First Financing; Broad-Based Technology Couples Genomics with Rapid Drug Discovery," *Business Wire*, March 6, 1997.

63. Michael Rothenberg's written reply to interview questions, September 30, 2004, and follow-up interview on October 17, 2004.

64. E-mail from Donald Payan to Michael Rothenberg, April 25, 1997.

65. E-mail from Garry P. Nolan to Michael Rothenberg, May 4, 1997.

66. Michael Rothenberg, written reply to interview questions, September 30, 2004.

67. E-mail from David Zapol to David Botstein, "Meeting with Garner [sic] and Nolan," June 23, 1998.

68. Phyllis Gardner's written reply to interview questions, August 31, 2004. See also written replies from Richard Popp (September 9, 2004) and Garry Nolan (August 24, 2004), cited earlier.

69. Michael Rothenberg's written reply to interview questions, September 30, 2004.

70. Letter from Warren M. Zapol to Margaret Dale, administrative liaison to the Committee on Conflicts of Interest and Commitment, Harvard Medical School, January 21, 1999.

71. Office of Technology Licensing, Stanford University, Annual Report, 2000–2001, p. 3.

72. Office of Technology Licensing, Stanford University, Annual Report, 2001–2002, p. 10.

73. News release, Joseph B. Martin to members of the Harvard Faculty of Medicine, May 25, 2000, available at: www.hms.harvard.edu/news/releases/0500conflict.html.

74. The Valentine controversy is discussed in detail in U.S. Congress, House Committee on Science and Technology, Subcommittee on Investigations and Oversight, Subcommittee on

Science, Research and Technology, *University-Industry Cooperation in Biotechnology*, 97th Congress, 2nd Session, June 16, 17, 1982. See in particular the testimony of Albert H. Meyerhoff, senior attorney, Natural Resources Defense Council, and Charles Hess, dean of the College of Agricultural and Environmental Sciences at the University of California at Davis, pp. 9–89.

75. The Manning memo is reprinted in U.S. Congress, House Hearing, *University-Industry Cooperation in Biotechnology*, p. 82. See also: William Boly, "The Gene Merchants," *California* magazine, September 1982, also reprinted in these hearings at pp. 171–175.

76. Amy Dockser Marcus, "Class Struggle: MIT Students, Lured to New Tech Firms, Get Caught in a Bind," *Wall Street Journal*, June 24, 1999, p. A1.

77. Lisa Guernsey, "M.I.T. Media Lab at 15: Big Ideas, Big Money," *New York Times*, November 9, 2000.

78. Eliot Marshall, "Appeals Court Clears Way for Academic Suit," *Science*, 293(5529), July 20, 2001: 411–413; Eliot Marshall, "Patent Suit Pits Postdoc Against Former Mentor," *Science*, 287(5462), March 31, 2000: p. 2399.

79. *Chou v. University of Chicago*, 2000 WL 222638, *1 (N.D. Ill. 2000), rev'd 254 F.3d 1347 (Fed. Cir. 2001).

80. "Ethical Challenges for Graduate Education," Fifty-seventh Annual Meeting, Midwestern Association of Graduate Schools, St. Louis, Missouri, April 17–20, 2001.

81. For a discussion of the meeting, see: Kenney, *Biotechnology*, p. 85.

82. U.S. Congress, House Committee on Science and Technology, Subcommittee on Investigations and Oversight, Subcommittee on Science, Research and Technology, *Commercialization of Academic Biomedical Research*, 97th Congress, 1st Session, June 8–9, p. 90.

83. Pajaro Dunes Biotechnology Statement, 1982, quoted in Kenney, *Biotechnology*, p. 88. See also: Barbara J. Culliton, "Pajaro Dunes: The Search for Consensus," *Science*, 216(4542), April 9, 1982: 155–156, p. 158.

84. See, for example, the case of Scheffer Tseng and Spectra Pharmaceutical Services at Harvard, and the case of Nicholas Bodor and Pharmatec at the University of Florida, discussed in Claire Turcotte Maatz, "University Physician-Researcher Conflict of Interest: The Inadequacy of Current Controls and Proposed Reform," *High Technology Law Journal*, 7, 1992: 137–188, and Peter Gosselin, "Flawed Study Helps Doctors Profit on Drug," *Boston Globe*, October 19, 1988, p. A1.

85. U.S. Congress, House Committee on Government Operations, *Federal Response to Misconduct in Science: Are Conflicts of Interest Hazardous to Our Health?* 100th Congress, 2nd Session, September 29, 1988; U.S. Congress, House Committee on Government Operations, *Is Science for Sale? Conflicts of Interest vs. the Public Interest*, 100th Congress, 1st Session, June 13, 1989; U.S. Congress, House Committee on Government Relations, *Are Scientific Misconduct and Conflicts of Interest Hazardous to Our Health?*, House Report

101–688, 100th Congress, 2nd Session (Washington, DC: Government Printing Office, September 20, 1990).

86. "Request for Comment on Proposed Guidelines for Policies on Conflicts of Interest," National Institutes of Health and the Alcohol, Drug Abuse, and Mental Health Administration, U.S. Department of Health and Human Services, September 15, 1989.

87. Deborah Mesce, "NIH Scrapping Conflict-of-Interest Guidelines," *Associated Press*, December 29, 1989.

88. Mark S. Frankel, "Perception, Reality, and the Political Context of Conflict of Interest in University-Industry Relationships," *Academic Medicine*, 71(12), December 1996; Robert Weissman, "The Front," *Multinational Monitor*, 11(12), December 1989; Deborah Mesce, "NIH Scrapping Conflict-of-Interest Guidelines," *Associated Press*, December 29, 1989.

89. On July 11, 1995, the Department of Health and Human Services, which includes NIH, promulgated new regulations (42 C.F.R. Part 50 and 45 C.F.R. Part 94), and NSF revised its Investigator Financial Disclosure Policy to establish largely consistent requirements for universities and other grantees (General Accounting Office, "University Research: Most Federal Agencies Need to Better Protect Against Financial Conflicts of Interest," GAO–04–31, November 2003, pp. 28–29). For a discussion of the comparative weakness of the new policy, see Mark S. Frankel, "Perception, Reality, and the Political Context of Conflict of Interest in University-Industry Relationships," *Academic Medicine*, 71(12), December 1996: 1297–1304.

90. Mildred K. Cho, Ryo Shohara, et al., "Policies on Faculty Conflicts of Interest at US Universities," *Journal of the American Medical Association*, 284(17), November 1, 2000: 2203–2208.

91. Katherine Mangan, "Harvard Weighs a Change in Conflict-of-Interest Rules," *Chronicle of Higher Education*, May 19, 2000.

92. S. Krimsky, L. S. Rothenberg, "Conflicts of Interest Policies in Science and Medical Journals: Editorial Practices and Author Disclosure," *Science and Engineering Ethics*, 7, 2001: 205–218; Merrill Goozner, "Unrevealed: Non-Disclosure of Conflicts of Interest in Four Leading Medical and Scientific Journals," a study by the Center for Science in the Public Interest, Washington, DC, July 12, 2004.

93. Kenneth J. Rothman, "Conflict of Interest: The New McCarthyism in Science," *Journal of the American Medical Association*, 269(21), June 2, 1993: 2782–2784.

94. Dennis F. Thompson, "Understanding Financial Conflicts of Interest," *New England Journal of Medicine*, 329(8), August 19, 1993: 573–576.

Chapter 5. Are Conflicts of Interest Hazardous to Our Health?

1. David Brown, "Scientists Report Bid to Block Publication of an AIDS Study," *Washington Post*, November 1, 2000, p. A10; Thomas M. Burton, "Unfavorable Drug Study Sparks Battle Over Publication of Results," *Wall Street Journal*, November 1, 2000, p. B1.

2. Personal interview with James O. Kahn, April 17, 2001. All direct quotes come from this interview with Kahn.

3. Letter (via facsimile) from Ronald B. Moss, vice president of medical affairs at the Immune Response Corporation, to James Kahn (San Francisco General Hospital), Kenneth Mayer (Memorial Hospital of Rhode Island), Stephen Lagakos (Harvard School of Public Health), Henry Murray (Cornell University Medical College), January 17, 2000; e-mail from James Kahn to Ronald Moss, January 18, 2000; e-mail from Stephen Lagakos to Ronald Moss, January 18, 2000; letter (via facsimile) from Dennis J. Carlo, president and CEO, Immune Response Corporation and R. Moss to J. Kahn, K. Mayer, S. Lagakos, and H. Murray, January 26, 2000.

4. Carol C. Morton, "Company, Researchers Battle over Data Access," *Science*, 290(5494), November 10, 2001: p. 1063.

5. Research and Investigational Site Agreements between the regents of the University of California and the Immune Response Corporation, "HIV–1 Immunogen Study No. 806," obtained from Chris Patti, University of California counsel handling the Kahn/Immune Response Corporation case. See also: "The Immune Response Corporation Announces Arbitration Proceedings and Dispute over Exclusion of Clinical Investigators and Sponsor Comments in the Publication of Clinical Trial Data of Remune HIV-1 Immunogen," PR Newswire, Carlsbad, CA, October 31, 2000; Karen Young Kreeger, Paula Park, "When Corporations Pay for Research," *The Scientist*, 15(11), May 28, 2001: p. 29.

6. James O. Kahn, D. W. Cherng, et al., "Evaluation of HIV–1 Immunogen, an Immunologic Modifier, Administered to Patients Infected with HIV," *Journal of the American Medical Association*, 284(17), November 1, 2000: 2193–2202. "The dispute was settled on September 11, 2001, with the company dropping its claim for damages and agreeing to release the data" (Bruce Mirken, "Science, Money, and Industry: Is Commerce Corrupting AIDS Research?" *Bulletin of Experimental Treatments for AIDS*, San Francisco AIDS Foundation, Spring 2002, available at: www.sfaf.org/treatment/beta/b50/b50commerce.html).

7. Catherine DeAngelis, "Conflict of Interest and the Public Trust," *Journal of the American Medical Association*, 284(17), November 1, 2000: 2237–2238, p. 2238.

8. S. Krimsky, L. S. Rothenberg, et al., "Financial Interests of Authors in Scientific Journals: A Pilot Study of 14 Publications," Science *and Engineering Ethics*, 2(4), 1996: 395–410.

9. Michael McCarthy, an editor at *The Lancet*, told the *Seattle Post-Intelligencer* such links are now so common that he "often can't find anyone who doesn't have a financial interest" in a drug or therapy the journal would like to review (Tom Paulson, "Who's Paying the Bill for Public Research?" *Seattle Post-Intelligencer*, February 13, 1997, p. A1). Marcia Angell, while editor in chief of the *New England Journal of Medicine*, noted that when she and her coeditors attempted to find a psychiatrist to write an editorial on the treatment of depression, "we found very few who did not have financial ties to drug companies that make antidepressants. . . . The

problem is by no means unique to psychiatry. We routinely encounter similar difficulties in finding editorialists in other specialties, particularly those that involve the heavy use of expensive drugs and devices" (Marcia Angell, "Is Academic Medicine for Sale?" *New England Journal of Medicine*, 342(20), May 18, 2000: 1516–1518). Since 1999, the *New England Journal of Medicine* reported, it has been unable to find qualified authors free of financial conflicts to write reviews of therapy-specific drug studies that address important conditions like ulcerative colitis, rheumatoid arthritis, and multiple sclerosis (David Blumenthal, "Financial Conflict of Interest in Academic Medicine: How Much and Who?" presentation delivered at the Institute of Medicine Annual Meeting, available at: http://www.iom.edu/file.asp?id=8954, see p. 19).

10. "Changing Patterns of Pharmaceutical Innovation," a report by the National Institute for Health Care Management, Washington, DC, May 2002; Peter Lansbury, "An Innovative Drug Industry? Well, No," opinion editorial, *Washington Post*, November 16, 2003, p. B2.

11. Iain Cockburn, Rebecca Henderson, "Public-Private Interaction in Pharmaceutical Research," *Proceedings of the National Academy of Sciences*, 93, November 1996: 12725–12730.

12. Personal interview with Marcia Angell, January 8, 2001.

13. Frank Davidoff, Catherine D. DeAngelis, et al., "Sponsorship, Authorship, and Accountability," editorial, Canadian *Medical Association Journal*, 165(6), September 18, 2001: 786–788; Susan Okie, "A Stand for Scientific Independence: Medical Journals Aim to Curtail Drug Companies' Influence," *Washington Post*, August 5, 2001, p. A1.

14. Thomas Bodenheimer, "Uneasy Alliance—Clinical Investigators and the Pharmaceutical Industry," *New England Journal of Medicine*, 342(20), May 18, 2000: 1539–1544.

15. Ibid., p. 1541; Thomas Bodenheimer, "Conflict of Interest in Clinical Drug Trials: A Risk Factor for Scientific Misconduct," plenary presentation, Conference on Human Subject Protection and Financial Conflicts of Interest, National Institutes of Health, Washington, DC, August 15–16, 2000; Gerhard Levy, "Publication Bias: Its Implications for Clinical Pharmacology," *Clinical Pharmacology and Therapeutics*, 52(2), August 1992: 115–119.

16. Paula A. Rochon, Jerry H. Gurwitz, et al., "A Study of Manufacturer-Supported Trials of Nonsteroidal Anti-inflammatory Drugs in the Treatment of Arthritis," *Archives of Internal Medicine*, 154(2), January 24, 1994: 157–163. See also: Helle K. Johansen, Peter C Gotzsche, "Problems in the Design and Reporting of Trials of Antifungal Agents Encountered During Meta-Analysis, *Journal of the American Medical Association*, 282(18), 1999: 1752–1759; Thomas Bodenheimer, Ronald Collins, "The Ethical Dilemmas of Drugs, Money, Medicine," opinion, *Seattle Times*, March 15, 2001, p. B7.

17. "Ghost with a Chance in Publishing Undergrowth," editorial, *The Lancet*, 342(8886–8887), December 18–25, 1993: 1498–1499.

18. George Blackburn of Harvard, Albert Stunkard of the University of Pennsylvania, and others also signed ghostwritten papers authored by this company; see: Alicia Mundy, *Dispensing with the Truth* (New York: St. Martin's Press, 2001), pp. 163–164.

19. Sharyl Attkisson, "Ghostwriting Articles for Medical Journals," *CBS News HealthWatch*, April 5, 2001.

20. Troyen A. Brennan, "Buying Editorials," editorial, *New England Journal of Medicine*, 331(10), September 8, 1994: 673–675.

21. Drummond Rennie, Veronica Yank, et al., "When Authorship Fails: A Proposal to Make Contributors Accountable," *Journal of the American Medical Association*, 278(7), August 20, 1997: 579–585; Annette Flanagin et al, "Prevalence of Articles with Honorary Authors and Ghost Authors in Peer-Reviewed Medical Journals," *Journal of the American Medical Association*, 280, July 15, 1998: 222–224; Drummond Rennie, Annette Flanagin, "Authorship! Authorship! Guests, Ghosts, Grafters, and Two-Sided Coin," *Journal of the American Medical Association*, 271(6), February 9, 1994: 469–471; Antony Barnett, "Revealed: How Drug Companies 'Hoodwink' Medical Journals," The Observer, December 7, 2003; Sarah Boseley, "Scandal of Scientists Who Take Money for Papers Ghostwritten by Drug Companies," *The Guardian* (London), February 7, 2002.

22. Richard Horton, "The Dawn of McScience," *New York Review of Books*, March 11, 2004, p. 9.

23. Bodenheimer, "Conflict of Interest." For an interesting case see: K. Lauritsen, T. Havelund, et al., "Withholding Unfavorable Results in Drug Company Sponsored Clinical Trials," *The Lancet*, 1, May 9, 1987, p. 1091.

24. Fred E. Silverstein, Gerald Faich, et al., "Gastrointestinal Toxicity with Celecoxib vs. Nonsteroidal Anti-Inflammatory Drugs for Osteoarthritis and Rheumatoid Arthritis," *Journal of the American Medical Association*, 284(10), September 13, 2000: 1247–1255. See also: Susan Okie, "Missing Data on Celebrex; Full Study Altered Picture of Drug," *Washington Post*, August 5, 2001, p. A11.

25. I would like to thank Vera Hassner Sharav at the Alliance for Human Research Protections and Shannon Brownlee at the New America Foundation for their generous assistance in pulling together the various pieces of this story on the SSRIs and the suppression of negative data.

26. Express Scripts, "Preschoolers Lead Growth of Antidepressant Use, Study Reveals," news release, April 2, 2004, available at: http://www.expressscripts.com/other/news_views/outcomes_research.htm; Thomas J. Moore "Medical Use of Antidepressant Drugs in Children and Adults: 1998–2001," Drug Safety Research, Washington, DC, January 26, 2004.

27. Craig J. Whittington, Tim Kendall, et al., "Selective Serotonin Reuptake Inhibitors in Childhood Depression: Systematic Review of Published Versus Unpublished Data," *The Lancet*, 363, April 24, 2004: 1341–1345.

28. Thomas P. Laughren, "Background on Suicidality Associated with Antidepressant Drug Treatment," memorandum for February 2, 2004, meeting of Psychopharmacological Drugs Advisory Committee, January 5, 2004, available at: http://www.fda.gov/ohrms/dockets/ac/04/briefing/4006B1_03_Background%Memo%2001–05–04.htm.

29. See: Eliot Spitzer, New York attorney general, complaint, "The People of the State of New York vs. GlaxoSmithKline & SmithKline Beecham Corporation," Supreme Court of New York, June 2, 2004, pp. 6–7, available at: www.oag.state.ny/press/2004/jun/jun2b_04.html.

30. Gardiner Harris, "Expert Kept from Speaking at Antidepressant Hearing," New York Times, April 16, 2004, p. A16; Gardiner Harris, "Antidepressant Study Seen to Back Expert," New York Times, August 20, 2004. The FDA initially tried to silence its own expert medical officer, Mosholder, by preventing him from reporting his analysis of the unpublished data and his recommendations before a public hearing on February 2, 2004 (Rob Waters, "Drug Report Barred by FDA; Scientist Links Antidepressants to Suicide in Kids," San Francisco Chronicle, February 1, 2004).

31. Jon N. Jureidini, Christopher J. Doecke, et al., "Efficacy and Safety of Antidepressants for Children and Adolescents," British Medical Journal, 328, April 10, 2004: 879–883, p. 881.

32. Martin B. Keller, Neal D. Ryan, et al., "Efficacy of Paroxetine in the Treatment of Adolescent Major Depression: A Randomized, Controlled Trial," Child and Adolescent Psychiatry, 40(7), July 2001: 762–772.

33. See: Spitzer, "People of the State of New York."

34. Laughren, "Background on Suicidality." See also: Jon Jureidini, Anne Tonkin, "Paroxetine in Major Depression," letter, Journal of the American Academy of Child and Adolescent Psychiatry," 42(5), May 2003: p. 514.

35. Jureidini et al., "Efficacy and Safety," p. 880.

36. Dolores Kong, Alison Bass, "Case at Brown Leads to Review; NIMH Studies Tighter Rules on Conflicts," Boston Globe, October 8, 1999.

37. Martin B. Keller, ISI Author Publication A0390–2003-H, last updated June 24, 2003, Thompson Scientific ISIHighlyCited.com, Philadelphia, available at: http:hcr3.isiknowledge.com/.

38. Karen Dineen Wagner, Paul Ambrosini, et al., "Efficacy of Sertraline in the Treatment of Children and Adolescents with Major Depressive Disorder," Journal of the American Medical Association, 2900(8), August 27, 2003: 1033–1041; Laughren, "Background on Suicidality"; Jureidini et al., "Efficacy and Safety," p. 880.

39. Craig J. Whittington, Tim Kendall, et al., "Selective Serotonin Reuptake Inhibitors in Childhood Depression: Systematic Review of Published Versus Unpublished Data," The Lancet, 363, April 24, 2004: 1341–1345, p. 1344.

40. Disclosure statement from Wagner et al., "Efficacy of Sertraline."

41. A statistical review by the FDA concluded that the sponsor, Eli Lilly, "did not win on these two pediatric depression studies. . . . The evidence for efficacy based on the pre-specified endpoint is not convincing." See: Food and Drug Administration, Center for Drug Evaluation and Research, "Statistical Review of Prozac for Pediatric OCD and Depression," available at: www.fda.gov/cder/foi/nda/2003/18936S064_Prozac%20Pulvules_statr.pdf, p. 36. Cited in: Jureidini et al., "Efficacy and Safety."

42. "Preliminary Report of the Task Force on SSRIs and Suicidal Behavior in Youth," American College of Neuropsychopharmacology, January 21, 2004, p. 16; "Experience in the Use of SSRIs and Other Antidepressants in Children and Teens," *Child and Adolescent Psychiatry*, disclosure notes from a conference convened by the College of Physicians and Surgeons of Columbia University, April 2003, Washington, DC; both documents on file at Center for Science in the Public Interest, http://www.cspinet.org/.

43. The FDA advisory on the use of antidepressants in children and teens is available at: http://www.fda.gov/bbs/topics/news/2004/NEW01124.html.

44. For Rezulin, see David Willman's extensive investigative reporting in the *Los Angeles Times*; for Redux, see Mundy, *Dispensing with the Truth*; for Retin-A, which was hyped as a wrinkle cure by university scientists (with financial ties to the manufacturer) on the basis of weak evidence, see Leslie N. Vreeland, "The Selling of Retin-A," *Money*, April 1, 1989; for Neurontin, an epilepsy drug marketed by the manufacturer and promoted by big-name physicians (paid by the drug maker) for some twelve non-FDA-approved conditions on the basis of weak or nonexistent evidence of effectiveness, see: Melody Peterson, "Whistle-Blower Says Marketers Broke the Rules to Push a Drug," *New York Times*, March 14, 2002, p. C1; David Armstrong, Anna Wilde Mathews, "Pfizer Case Signals Tougher Action on Off-Label Drug Use," *Wall Street Journal*, May 14, 2004, p. B1; and Gardiner Harris, "Pfizer to Pay $430 Million over Promoting of Drug to Doctors," *New York Times*, May 14, 2004, p. C1.

45. Another dramatic example involves Joseph Osterling, chief of urology at the University of Michigan Medical Center, who widely promoted a procedure used to treat prostate disorders in which he had financial interest. His peers accused him of misrepresenting the accuracy of his test results in a conference presentation. Eventually he pled no contest to a felony charge after it was discovered that he had been double and triple billing for his trips and had not reported his income to the university (Thomas M. Burton, "Urodollars: A Prostate Researcher Tested Firm's Product and Sat on Its Board," *Wall Street Journal*, March 19, 1998, p. A1).

46. Mundy, *Dispensing with the Truth*, pp. 52–85, 121–126, 156–157.

47. Marcia Angell, Jerome P. Kassirer, "Editorials and Conflicts of Interest," editorial, *New England Journal of Medicine*, 335(14): 1055–1056.

48. Goldie Blumenstyk, "Conflict-of-Interest Fears Rise as Universities Chase Industry Support," *Chronicle of Higher Education*, May 22, 1998, p. A41.

49. Matthew Kauffman, Andrew Julien, "Medical Research: Can We Trust It? Scientists Helped Industry to Push Diet Drug," second of three parts, *Hartford Courant*, April 10, 2000, p. A1.

50. Mundy, *Dispensing with the Truth*, p. 164.

51. David Willman, "Risk Was Known as FDA OK'd Fatal Drug," *Los Angeles Times*, March 11, 2001, p. A1; David Willman, "How a New Policy Led to Seven Deadly Drugs," *Los Angeles Times*, December 20, 2000, p. A1; Matthew Kauffman, Andrew Julien, "Medical Research: Can We Trust It? Surge in Corporate Cash Taints Integrity of Academic Science," first of three parts, p. A1.

52. Paul Starr, *The Social Transformation of American Medicine* (New York: Basic Books, 1982), p. 214.

53. Ibid., pp. 31, 45, 81–102; Christopher Jencks, David Riesman, *The Academic Revolution* (Chicago: University of Chicago Press, 1968, 1977), pp. 213–214.

54. Starr, *Social Transformation*, p. 22.

55. Ibid.

56. Ibid.

57. Richard Hofstadter, *The Development and Scope of Higher Education in the United States* (New York: Columbia University Press, 1952), p. 82. Jencks, Riesman, *Academic Revolution*, p. 212.

58. Ibid., p. 213.

59. Thomas E. Malone, "The Moral Imperative of Biomedical Research," pp. 10–11, in Roger J. Porter, Thomas E. Malone, Eds., *Biomedical Research* (Baltimore: Johns Hopkins University Press, 1992).

60. Starr, *Social Transformation*, p. 113.

61. Hofstadter, *Development and Scope*, p. 82; Starr, *Social Transformation*, pp. 43–47.

62. Hofstadter, *Development and Scope*, p. 83.

63. M. Gregg Bloche, "Corporate Takeover of Teaching Hospitals," *University of Southern California Law Review*, 65(3), March 1992: p. 1076; Starr, *Social Transformation*, pp. 116–121.

64. Ibid., p. 121.

65. Arnold S. Relman, "What Market Values Are Doing to Medicine," *Atlantic Monthly*, March 1992.

66. Marc A. Rodwin, *Medicine, Money, and Morals* (New York: Oxford University Press, 1993), p. 21.

67. Ibid., pp. 22, 28–29.

68. Starr, *Social Transformation*, p. 343.

69. Bloche, "Corporate Takeover," pp. 1049–1050; Rodwin, *Medicine, Money*, p. 13; Arnold Relman, "Who Will Pay for Medical Education in Our Teaching Hospitals?" *Science*, 226, October 5, 1984: 20–23, p. 21.

70. Starr, *Social Transformation*, p. 347.

71. Ibid., p. 361.

72. Ibid., p. 335.

73. Bloche, "Corporate Takeover," p. 1060.

74. Between 1974 and 1984, NIH funding for academic research grew by an average annual rate of just 2.6 percent, compared to 17.5 percent during the period 1970–1974. See: National Science Board, *Science and Engineering Indicators—2004*, "Federal Obligations for Academic Research, by Agency: 1970–2003 (constant dollars), 2004," Table 5–9 (Arlington, VA: National Science Foundation, May 2004).

75. Insurers now often reviewed the clinical decisions of physicians, required preauthorization for hospitalization or other costly services, and stopped reimbursements when services were deemed inappropriate. Many plans even used financial bonuses to induce doctors to limit referrals.

76. Arnold S. Relman, "The New Medical-Industrial Complex," *New England Journal of Medicine*, 303(17), October 23, 1980: 963–970. For other A. Relman articles, see: "Who Will Pay for Medical Education in Our Teaching Hospitals?" *Science*, 226(4670), October 5, 1984: 20–23; "Practicing Medicine in the New Business Climate," *New England Journal of Medicine*, 316(18), April 30, 1987; "Economic Incentives in Clinical Investigation," *New England Journal of Medicine*, 320(14), April 6, 1989: 933–934.

77. E-mail from David Goldbloom to David Healy, December 7, 2000, available at: www.healyprozac.com/AcademicFreedom /default.htm.

78. Carl Elliot, "Parma Buys a Conscience," *American Prospect*, 12(17), September 24–October 8, 2001; David Healy, "Conflicting Interests in Toronto: Anatomy of a Controversy at the Interface of Academia and Industry," *Perspectives in Biology and Medicine*, Johns Hopkins University Press, 45(2), Spring 2002: 250–263.

79. Nicholas Keung, "MD Settles Lawsuit with U of T Over Job," *Toronto Star*, May 1, 2002, p. A23.

80. Nancy F. Olivieri, Gary M. Brittenham, et al., "Iron-Chelation Therapy with Oral Deferiprone in Patients with Thalassemia Major," *New England Journal of Medicine*, 332(14), April 6, 1995: 918–922.

81. For a comprehensive review of this case, see: Jon Thompson, Patricia Baird, et al., *The Olivieri Report: The Complete Text of the Report of the Independent Inquiry Commissioned by the Canadian Association of University Teachers* (Toronto: James Lorimer, 2001). See also: the December 19, 2001, Complaints Committee report written by the College of Physicians and Surgeons of Ontario in response to a formal complaint filed by Lawrence Becker, chair of the Medical Advisory Committee at the College, which found no basis to the allegations made against Olivieri.

82. Thompson et al., *Olivieri Report*, p. 98.

83. Robert A. Phillips, John Hoey, "Constraints of Interest: Lessons at the Hospital for Sick Children," editorial, *Canadian Medical Association Journal*, 159(8), October 20, 1998: 955–957.

84. Personal interview with Nancy Olivieri, July 10, 2003.

85. Miriam Shuchman, "Legal Issues Surrounding Privately Funded Research Cause Furore in Toronto," *Canadian Medical Association Journal*, 159(8), October 20, 1998: 983–986; Thompson et al., *Olivieri Report*, p. 94.

86. Ibid., pp. 10, 94.

87. John Deverell, "U of T Appeals to Ottowa to Help Generic Drug Firms," *Toronto Star*, September 4, 1999.

88. Portions of the rest of this chapter originally appeared in: Jennifer Washburn, "Informed Consent," *Washington Post Magazine*, December 30, 2001.

89. Personal interview with Paul Gelsinger, April 3, 2001.

90. Food and Drug Administration, Public Health Service, Inspector's Report, investigating James W. Wilson, director, Institute for Human Gene Therapy, University of Pennsylvania Health System, November 30, 1999–January 19, 2000; Rick Weiss, Deborah Nelson, "Gene Researchers Apologize for Lapses in Teen's Fatal Treatment," *Washington Post*, December 10, 1999, p. A6.

91. Food and Drug Administration, Inspector's Report; Rick Weiss, Deborah Nelson, "FDA Lists Violations by Gene Therapy Director at U-Penn," *Washington Post*, March 4, 2000, p. A4.

92. Rick Weiss, Deborah Nelson, "Methods Faulted in Gene Test Death: Teen Too Ill for Therapy, Probe Finds," *Washington Post*, December 8, 1999, p. A1; Jesse A. Goldner, "Dealing with Conflicts of Interest in Biomedical Research," *Journal of Law, Medicine, and Ethics*, 28(4), December 22, 2000.

93. Deborah Nelson, Rick Weiss, "Penn Researchers Sued in Gene Therapy Death," *Washington Post*, September 19, 2000, p. A3.

94. Deborah Nelson, Rick Weiss, "Hasty Decisions in the Race to a Cure?" *Washington Post*, November 21, 1999, p. A1.

95. Nelson, Weiss, "Penn Researchers"; S. Hensley, "Targeted Genetics' Genovo Deal Leads to Windfall for Researcher," *Wall Street Journal*, August 10, 2000, p. B12.

96. Washburn, "Informed Consent."

97. Alice Dembner, "Doctor Stirs Questions on Genetics' Frontier," *Boston Globe*, May 21, 2000, p. A1; Liz Kowalczyk, "Group Hits Hub Doctor Facing FDA Scrutiny: Possible Financial Conflict Is Seen," *Boston Globe*, May 13, 2000, p. C1.

98. Rick Weiss, "Gene Therapy Firms Resist Publicity; U.S. Regulators, Researchers Are Divided on Releasing Information About Adverse Effects," *Washington Post*, December 11, 1999, p. A2.

99. Donna Shalala, "Protecting Research Subjects—What Must Be Done," *New England Journal of Medicine*, 343(11), September 14, 2000: 808–810.

100. "How Are Experimental Drugs Tested in Humans?" *Centerwatch*, available at: http://www.centerwatch.com/patient/backgrnd.html#Section2. See also: "Is the Media Portrayal of Clinical Research Causing Negative Perceptions That Endanger Medical Advances?" white paper, Association of Clinical Research Professionals, Washington, DC, April 23, 2001.

101. Personal interview with George Annas, June 25, 2001. For more evidence of IRBs' losing their independence, see: General Accounting Office, "Scientific Research: Continued Vigilance Critical to Protecting Human Subjects," GAO/HEHS–96–72, March 8, 1996, available at: www.gao.gov/.

102. "Protecting Human Research Subjects: Status of Recommendations," Department of Health and Human Services, Office of Inspector General, OEI–01–97–00197, pp. 22, 3.

103. In 1998, the Office of Inspector General (OIG) at the Department of Health and Human Services (HHS) issued four reports addressing the IRBs and the urgent need for reform of the oversight system ("Institutional Review Boards: Their Role in Reviewing Approved Research," OEI–01–9700190, 1980; "Institutional Review Boards: Promising Approaches," OEI–01–91–00191, 1998; "Institutional Review Boards: The Emergence of Independence Boards," OEI–01–97–00192, 1998; "Institutional Review Boards: A Time for Reform," OEI–01–97–00193, 1998). In April 2000, the OIG examined the IRB problem again and found that HHS had taken little action to improve oversight and adopt its recommendations ("Protecting Human Research Subjects: Status of Recommendations," OEI–01–97–00197, p. 11).

104. "FDA Oversight of Clinical Investigators," Department of Health and Human Services, Office of the Inspector General, OEI–05–99–00350, June 2000, p. 3; General Accounting Office, "Scientific Research: Continued Vigilance Critical to Protecting Human Subjects," GAO/HEHS–96–72, March 8, 1996, p. 24, available at: www.gao.gov/. Even after the heightened attention generated by Jesse Gelsinger's death, the General Accounting Office found that in the first two-thirds of fiscal year 2001, the Office of Human Research Protections (OHRP) failed to make a single unannounced spot-check of research sites (General Accounting Office, "Human Subjects Research: HHS Takes Steps to Strengthen Protections, but Concerns Remain," GAO–01–775T, May 2001, p. 12).

105. National Bioethics Advisory Commission, *Ethical and Policy Issues in Research Involving Human Participants*, Summary and Volume 1, Bethesda, MD, August 2001, see Summary, pp. 5–6; "Institutional Review Boards: The Emergence of Independent Boards," Department of Health and Human Services, Office of the Inspector General, OEI–01–97–00192, June 1998.

106. In 2002, total grant spending for clinical trials involving human subjects was approximately $5.6 billion, with more than 70 percent provided by the biopharmaceutical industry. If device manufacturers are included, the total fraction of grant support rises to 80 percent, with

the remainder ($1.1 billion) supplied primarily by the National Institutes of Health (Ken Getz, "Clinical Grants Market Decelerates," *CenterWatch*, 10(4), 2003; "Grant Market to Exceed $4 Billion in 2000," *CenterWatch*, 7(11), November 2000. Both available at: http://www.center-watch.com/bookstore/pubs_profs_periodicals.html).

107. Bodenheimer, "Uneasy Alliance"; Jennifer Washburn, "Undue Influence: How the Drug Industry's Power Goes Unchecked," *American Prospect*, 12(4), August 13, 2001: 16–22.

108. Ken Getz, "Grant Market to Exceed $4 Billion in 2000," *CenterWatch*, 7(11), November 2000, available at:
http://www.centerwatch.com/bookstore/pubs_profs_periodicals.html.

109. Kurt Eichenwald, Gina Kolata, "A Doctor's Drug Trials Turn into Fraud," *New York Times*, May 17, 1999, p. A1. See also: Larkin Marilynn, "Clinical Trials: What Price Progress?" *The Lancet*, 354(9189), October 30, 1999: 1534.

110. This quote from Timothy G. Wighton of the Vaxgen Company appears in the Research Roundtable newsletter, April 2001, pp. 8–9, available at:
www.ResearchRountable.com.

111. "Recruiting Human Subjects: Pressures in Industry-Sponsored Clinical Research," Office of the Inspector General, Department of Health and Human Services, OEI–01–97–00195, June 2000.

112. Personal interview with Michael Leahey, May 7, 2001.

113. Quoted in Gary D. Lightfoot, Kenneth A. Getz, et al., "Faster Time to Market," white paper, Association of Clinical Research Professionals, Washington, DC, 1997, p. 11, available at: http://onlineethics.org/reseth/nbac/h1ref.html.

114. "Clinical Research: Harvard Launches Clinical Research Institute," Focus, news from Harvard Medical, Dental, and Public Health Schools, July 14, 2000; Liz Kowalczyk, "Medical Schools Join Forces: Harvard, Others Aim to Give Drug Firms Faster OKs on Clinical Trials," *Boston Globe*, July 28, 2000.

115. This section on Alan Milstein is drawn from previous reporting. See: Washburn, "Informed Consent."

116. Draft minutes from Conflict of Interest Standing Committee (CISC) meetings, Center for Technology Transfer, University of Pennsylvania, December 15, 1994–July 12, 1995.

117. Washburn, "Informed Consent."

118. Duff Wilson, David Heath, "The Blood-Cancer Experiment," *Seattle Times*, March 11, 2001, p. A1. Many of the primary documents on which this story was based are posted on-line at: http://seattletimes.nwsource.com/uninformed_consent/documents.html.

119. G. F. Gjerset, P. J. Martin, et al., "Immunologic Status of Hemophilia Patients Treated with Cryoprecipitate or Lyophilized Concentrate," *Blood*, 64(3), September 1984: 715–720.

120. Alice Dembner, "Research Integrity Declines," *Boston Globe*, August 22, 2000, p. E2.

121. *Journal of the American Medical Association*, 284(17), November 1, 2000; *New England Journal of Medicine*, 343(22), November 30, 2000.

122. David Korn, "Conflicts of Interest in Biomedical Research," *Journal of the American Medical Association*, 284(17), November 1, 2000: 2234–2237, p. 2236.

123. "Financial Relationships in Clinical Research: Draft Interim Guidance," January 10, 2001, Department of Health and Human Services, available at: http://ohrp.osophs.dhhs.gov/humansubjects/finreltn/finguid.html.

124. Eliot Marshall, "Financial Conflict: Universities Puncture Modest Regulatory Trial Balloon," *Science*, 291(5511), March 16 2001: 2060.

125. See Letters of Comment to the Office of Human Research Protections from these four organizations and others. Available online at: ohrp.osophs.dhhs.gov/nhrpac/mtg12–00/finguid.htm.

126. David Korn, "Letter: Conflicts of Interest," *Science*, 292(5517), April 27, 2001: 639.

127. Personal interview with Arthur Caplan, April 11, 2001.

128. Donna Shalala, "Protecting Research Subjects," *Ethical and Policy Issues in Research Involving Human Participants*, Summary and Volume 1, National Bioethics Advisory Commission, Bethesda, MD, August 2001; Jeffrey Brainard, "Panel Proposes New Guidelines for Research with Human Subjects," *Chronicle of Higher Education*, January 12, 2001.

129. "Report on Individual and Institutional Financial Conflict of Interest," Task Force on Research Accountability, American Association of Universities, October 2001; "Protecting Subjects, Preserving Trust, Promoting Progress—Policy and Guidelines for the Oversight of Individual Financial Interests in Human Subject Research," Task Force on Financial Conflicts of Interest in Clinical Research, Association of American Medical Colleges, December, 2001.

130. Eric C. Campbell, Joel S. Weissman, et al., "Characteristics of Medical School Faculty Members Serving on Institutional Review Boards: Results of a National Survey," Academic Medicine, 78(8), August 2003: 831–836.

131. Kevin A. Schulman, Damon M. Seils, et al., "A National Survey of Provisions in Clinical-Trial Agreements Between Medical Schools and Industry Sponsors," New England Journal of Medicine, 347(17), October 24, 2002: 1335–1341.

Chapter 6. The University as Business

1. Derek Bok, "Business and the Academy," Harvard Magazine, May-June 1981.

2. Goldie Blumenstyk, "Inventions Produced Almost $1 Billion for Universities in 2002," Chronicle of Higher Education, December 19, 2003, p. A28. Original source: Association of University Technology Managers, *AUTM Licensing Survey: FY 2002* (Northbrook, IL: AUTM, 2003).

3. This section dealing with Stanford's Office of Technology Licensing draws from Eyal Press, Jennifer Washburn, "The Kept University," *Atlantic Monthly*, 285(3), March 2000.

4. "Funding: Making Ideas, People and Things Happen," *Brainstorm*, newsletter of Stanford University's Office of Technology Licensing, 7(3), Fall 1998.

5. Presentation by Christopher Scott, director of industry collaborations at the University of California at San Francisco's Mission Bay campus, Chemical Sciences Roundtable, National Academy of Sciences, Washington DC, May 22, 2000.

6. Wesley Cohen, Richard Florida, et. al., "University-Industry Research Centers in the United States," a report from Carnegie Mellon University, Center for Economic Development, Pittsburgh, 1994.

7. Seth Shulman, "Trouble on the 'The Endless Frontier': Science, Invention and the Erosion of the Technological Commons," a report from New America Foundation and Public Knowledge, Washington, DC, 2002, p. 16.

8. Louis G. Tornatzky, Paul G. Waugaman, Denis O. Gray, "Innovation U.: New University Roles in a Knowledge Economy," a report from Southern Growth Policies Board, Research Triangle Park, NC, 2002, p. 138.

9. National Science Board, "Appendix Table 5-2: Support for academic R&D, by sector: 1972–2001," Science and Engineering Indicators—2004 (Arlington, VA: National Science Foundation, May 2004), NSB 04–1A.

10. Sheldon Krimsky, *Science in the Private Interest* (Oxford, UK: Rowman & Littlefield, 2003), pp. 80–81.

11. Paul Desruisseaux, "Universities Venture into Venture Capitalism," *Chronicle of Higher Education*, May 26, 2000, p. A44. For an excellent overview of the university as venture capitalist, see: Gary W. Matkin, *Technology Transfer and the University, a report from the American Council on Education* (New York: Macmillan, 1990), pp. 148–177.

12. Karen Robinson-Jacobs, "USC to Shutter High-Tech Incubator," *Los Angeles Times*, June 6, 2002.

13. ARCH Development Corporation serves the Argonne National Laboratory and the University of Chicago, thus the acronym ARCH.

14. Richard Melcher, "An Old University Hits the High-Tech Road," *Business Week*, August 31, 1998, p. 94.

15. Arti K. Rai, "Regulating Scientific Research: Intellectual Property and the Norms of Science," *Northwestern University Law Review*, 94(1), Fall 1999: p. 110, see footnote 186.

16. Editorial, "Profit—and Losses—at Harvard," *New York Times*, November 13, 1980, p. A34, quoted in Martin Kenney, *Biotechnology: The University-Industrial Complex*, p. 80.

17. Joseph R. Perone, "Phi Beta Capitalism," *Star-Ledger* (Newark, NJ), February 25, 2001, Business Section, p. 1.

18. Carolyn Said, "Mining Gold in the Ivory Tower: How US Universities' Licensing Offices Bring Great Ideas to Market," San *Francisco Chronicle*, August 29, 2004, p. J1.

19. Eyal Press, Jennifer Washburn, "The Kept University," *Atlantic Monthly*, 285(3), March 2000.

20. Mark Pitsch, "U of L to Create For-Profit Venture to Boost Revenue," *Courier-Journal* (Louisville, KY), March 30, 2001. This article reported that once the new for-profit, Minerva

Ventures, was launched, the "U of L will join a select group of other universities—no more than about 20 according to national estimates—that have created for-profit businesses, mostly in the past 18 months." For information on the University of Pittsburgh deal, see: Yudhijit Bhattacharjee, "Pitt Takes over a Struggling Genetic Technology Firm," Science, 303, March 5, 2004: 1449. For more examples of universities becoming directly involved in commercial-development activities formerly performed only in the private sector, see: "Trustees Establish a Life Sciences Research Center," WMU News press release, Western Michigan University, Office of University Relations, July 30, 2003; Andrew Pollack, "Three Universities Join Researcher to Develop Drugs," New York Times, July 31, 2003.

21. "Yamaha and Stanford Make Beautiful Music Together," Brainstorm, newsletter of Stanford University's Office of Technology Licensing, 6(2), Summer 1997; Press, Washburn, "Kept University."

22. Association of University Technology Managers, AUTM Licensing Survey: FY2002 (Northbrook, IL: AUTM, 2003).

23. Jerry G. Thursby, Marie C. Thursby, "Industry Perspectives on Licensing University Technologies: Sources and Problems," Journal of the Association of University Technology Managers, 12, 2000. See also: Jerry G. Thursby, Marie C. Thursby, "University Licensing Under Bayh-Dole: What Are the Issues and Evidence?" February 2002, available at: www.gtrc.gatech.edu/thursbylicensing2.htm.

24. Association of University Technology Managers, "AUTM Commemorates 30 Years of Advancing the Academic Technology Transfer Profession," press release, June 16, 2003, available at: www.autm.net/media/PressReleases/PR_AUTM 30thAnniversary.htm.

25. Thursby, Thursby, "University Licensing," p. 1052.

26. James A. Severson, hearing testimony, oversight hearing on "Gene Patents and Other Genomic Inventions," House Committee on the Judiciary, Subcommittee on Courts and Intellectual Property, July 13, 2000. Reprinted in the Journal of the Association of University Technology Managers, 12, 2000, available at: www.autm.net/pubs/journal/00/testimony.html.

27. "Innovation's Golden Goose," editorial, The Economist, December 14, 2002.

28. Personal interview with Bhaven Sampat, January 27, 2004.

29. Amy Docser Marcus, "Bose and Arrows: MIT Seeds Inventions but Wants a Nice Cut of Profits They Yield," Wall Street Journal, July 20, 1999, p. A1.

30. Richard Nelson, "Observations on the Post-Bayh-Dole Rise of Patenting at American Universities," Journal of Technology Transfer, 26(1/2), 2001: 13–19, p. 16.

31. "[The Association of University Technology Managers] believes that the activities involving inventions have added to the economy in general," the GAO noted. But "no independent verification or validation of the data is provided . . . in interpreting the data, it is not possible to isolate the impact of inventions related to Bayh-Dole" (emphasis added). See: General Accounting Office, "Technology Transfer: Administration of the Bayh-Dole Act by Research Universities," GAO/RCED-98-126, May 1998, pp. 1–17.

32. "New Cures to Highest Bidders," editorial, *Los Angeles Times*, December 22, 2001, p. B20.

33. Paul Elias, "Schools Patent, Profit from Publicly Funded Research," *Associated Press*, April 28, 2003.

34. Nathan Rosenberg, Richard R. Nelson, "American Universities and Technical Advance in Industry," *Research Policy*, 23, 1994: 323–348; Nathan Rosenberg, "American Universities as Endogenous Institutions," in Nathan Rosenberg, Ed., *Schumpeter and the Endogeneity of Technology: Some American Perspectives* (London and New York: Routledge, 2000); N. Rosenberg, "Scientific Instrumentation and University Research," *Research Policy*, 21, 1992: 381–390.

35. Richard Nelson, "Observations on the Post-Bayh-Dole," p. 16.

36. Wesley M. Cohen, Richard R. Nelson, et. al., "Links and Impacts: The Influence of Public Research on Industrial R&D," pp. 1–23, and Ajay Agrawal, Rebecca Henderson, "Putting Patents in Context: Exploring Knowledge Transfer from MIT," pp. 44–60, both published in *Management Science*, 48(1), January 2002. See also: Wesley Cohen, Richard Florida, et al., "Industry and the Academy: Uneasy Partners in the Cause of Technological Advance," pp. 171–200, in Roger G. Noll, Ed., *Challenges to Research Universities* (Washington, DC: Brookings Institution Press, 1998). Patents and licenses tend to be considerably more important in the pharmaceutical sector than in other industries, but even in the development of pharmaceutical products, open channels of technology transfer have historically been very important; see Alfonso Gambardella, *Science and Innovation* (Cambridge, UK: Cambridge University Press, 1995).

37. Nelson, "Observations on the Post-Bayh-Dole," p. 16; Rebecca Eisenberg, Richard R. Nelson, "Public vs. Proprietary Science: A Fruitful Tension?" *Daedalus*, 131(2), 2002: 89–101.

38. The NIH was surprised to learn that the legal restraints universities now impose on their research tools, through their technology-transfer offices, "present just about every type of clause that universities site as problematic in the [contracts] they receive from industry" ("Report of the National Institute of Health Working Group on Research Tools," presented to the Advisory Committee to the Director, June 4, 1998, available at: www.nih.gov/news/researchtools/).

39. Ibid.

40. Sheldon Krimsky, Science *in the Private Interest: Has the Lure of Profits Corrupted Biomedical Research?* (Lanham, MD: Rowman & Littlefield, 2003), p. 30.

41. Quoted in "The Ethics of Patenting DNA: A Discussion Paper," Nuffield Council on Bioethics, London, July 2002, p. 26, available at: www.nuffieldbioethics.org.

42. Bhaven Sampat, "Patenting and U.S. Academic Research in the Twentieth Century: The World Before and After Bayh-Dole," draft working paper, forthcoming in *Research Policy*, 2004.

43. Arti K. Rai, Rebecca S. Eisenberg, "Bayh-Dole Reform and the Progress of Biomedicine," *American Scientist*, 91(1), January-February 2003: 52–58.

44. Seth Shulman, *Owning the Future* (Boston, New York: Houghton Mifflin, 1999), p. 8.

45. Seth Shulman, "Trouble on the 'The Endless Frontier,'" p. 14.

46. Eliot Marshall, "Patent on HIV Receptor Provokes an Outcry," *Science*, 287(5457), February 25, 2000: 1375–1377; "Ethics of Patenting DNA."

47. James Boyle, "Sold Out," editorial, *New York Times*, March 31, 1996, Section 4, p. 15.

48. Rebecca Eisenberg, "Intellectual Property Issues in Genomics," *Trends in Biotechnology*, 14(8), August 1996: 302–307, p. 304.

49. Hamilton Moses III, Joseph B. Martin, "Academic Relationships with Industry: A New Model for Biomedical Research," *Journal of the American Medical Association*, 285(7), February 21, 2001: 933–935. Original source: "From Serendipity to Strategy: The Pharmaceutical Industry in 2000," Boston Consulting Group, Boston, 1999. See also: "Ethics of Patenting DNA."

50. Rebecca S. Eisenberg, Richard R. Nelson, "Public vs. Proprietary Science: A Fruitful Tension?" *Daedalus*, Spring 2002: 89–101, p. 96. Although ESTs still are not in principle excluded from eligibility for patenting, under the U.S. Patent Office's revised Utility Guidelines (January 5, 2001), most experts agree that it is very unlikely that further patents on ESTs will be granted because they would not meet this new utility requirement ("Ethics of Patenting DNA," pp. 32–33, 87).

51. Jeannette Colyvas, Michael Crow, et al., "How Do University Inventions Get into Practice?" *Management Science*, 48(1), January 2002: 61–72.

52. This point was made by Richard Nelson, one of the Colyvas study's authors, in "Observations on the Post-Bayh-Dole," pp. 15–16.

53. Richard Nelson, "The Simple Economics of Basic Research," 1959, pp. 151–164, reprinted in Philip Mirowski, Esther-Mirjam Sent, Eds., *Science Bought and Sold: Essays in the Economics of Science* (Chicago: University of Chicago Press, 2002), pp. 152–153, 158.

54. Marylynn Marchione, "Foundation Amends Stem Cell Suit," *Milwaukee Journal-Sentinel*, September 25, 2001, p. 1D.

55. Sheryl G. Stolberg, "Patent on Human Stem Cell Puts U.S. Officials in Bind," *New York Times*, August 17, 2001, p. A1; Rai, Eisenberg, "Bayh-Dole Reform," p. 54.

56. Professor James A. Thomson's initial research on rhesus monkeys and macaques, which led to the UW patent (issued in December 1998) claiming broad rights to all primate embryonic stem cells, including those of humans, was funded by the NIH. However, later, when Thomson went on to do research on human embryonic stem cells, which the federal government then was refusing to fund, he received support from the Geron Corporation. It was under this sponsored-research agreement that UW agreed to give Geron exclusive rights to these six types of differentiated cells.

57. Tim Friend, "Half of Stem-Cell Money Could Go to Royalties, Panel Is Told," *USA Today*, August 2, 2001, p. 7A.

58. Sheryl G. Stolberg, "Patent Laws May Determine Shape of Stem Cell Research," *New York Times*, August 17, 2001. Dr. Melton was not the only doctor who found these licensing restrictions objectionable. In congressional testimony in September 2002, Dr. Curt I. Civin, a prominent Johns Hopkins oncologist, complained that these growing proprietary claims threatened to impede scientific research: "Many of the owners of [preexisting] lines . . . are not anxious to share them with other researchers. Those that are willing to share the lines are not willing to do so without getting a piece of the profits of future discoveries made using the lines. The owners also expect an up-front fee. The going rate is $5,000—an amount 50–100 times greater than the $50–$100 we are accustomed to paying for a cell line" (quoted in Christopher Scott, Tom Maeder, "No Cure for Alzheimer's: The Consequences of the Stem Cell Ban," *Acumen Journal of Sciences*, 1(1), May-June 2003: 36–45, p. 40).

59. Rai, Eisenberg, "Bayh-Dole Reform," p. 54. For another interesting case, where the government was restricted in its ability to intervene in an intellectual property dispute because of the provisions of Bayh-Dole, see: Avital Bar-Shalom, Robert Cook-Deegan, "Patents and Innovation in Cancer Therapeutics: Lessons from CellPro," *Milbank Quarterly*, 80(4), December 2002.

60. Antonio Regalado, "Research, Red Ink: An Academic Group Seeks Balance," *Wall Street Journal*, January 14, 2002, p. B4; "Stem Cell Patent Issues Resolved," *Associated Press*, September 5, 2001; Wisconsin Alumni Foundation, "WARF and Geron Resolve Lawsuit and Sign New License Agreement," press release, January 9, 2002.

61. Christopher Anderson, "Researchers Win Decision on Knockout Mouse Pricing," *Science*, 260(5104), April 2, 1993: 23–24

62. Eliot Marshall, "A Deluge of Patents Creates Legal Hassles for Research," *Science*, 288(5464), April 14, 2000: 255–257; Eliot Marshall, "NIH Cuts Deal on Use of OncoMouse," *Science*, 287(5453), January 28, 2000: p. 567; Eliot Marshall, "DuPont Ups Ante on Use of Harvard's OncoMouse," *Science*, 296, May 17, 2002: 1212–1213; Peg Brickley, "Mouse Patent Fails in Canada," *The Scientist*, 17(1), January 13, 2003.

63. Presentation delivered by Lynne Schaefer, director, Office of Technology Administration, Baylor College of Medicine, at the Association of University Technology Managers' Annual Meeting, *Partnering for Prosperity*, Disney World, FL, February 8, 2003.

64. Presentation given by David Einhorn, legal counsel at Jackson Laboratory, Bar Harbor, Maine, at the Association of University Technology Managers' Annual Meeting, ibid.; Eliot Marshall, "Deluge of Patents"; David L. Wheeler, "Biologists Discuss Ways to 'Share' Mice," *Chronicle of Higher Education*, April 7, 1993.

65. "Intellectual Property Rights and Research Tools in Molecular Biology," summary of a workshop held at the National Academy of Sciences, February 15–16, 1996, National Research Council, National Academy Press, Washington, DC, 1997. See also "Report of the National Institute of Health Working Group on Research Tools," June 4, 1998, cited earlier.

66. Department of Health and Human Services, National Institutes of Health, "Principles and Guidelines for Recipients of NIH Research Grants and Contracts on Obtaining and Disseminating Biomedical Research Resources: Final Notice," Federal Register Notice, 64 FR 72090, December 23, 1999, available at: http//ott.nih.gov/NewPages/RTguide_final.html.

67. David C. Mowery, Richard R. Nelson, et al., *Ivory Tower and Industrial Innovation: University-Industry Technology Transfer Before and After the Bayh-Dole Act* (Stanford: Stanford University Press, 2004), p. 112.

68. Eliot Marshall, "Deluge of Patents."

69. "Keeping Science Open: The Effects of Intellectual Property Policy on the Conduct of Science," Royal Society, London, April 2003; Jennifer Couzin, "Royal Society: Report Deplores Growth in Academic Patenting," *Science*, 300(5618), April 18, 2003.

70. Letter from Alan Asher, K. Balasubramaniam, Konrad Becker, et al., to Kamil Idris, director general, World Intellectual Property Organization, July 7, 2003. Related documents may be obtained through the Web site of Public Citizen's Consumer Project on Technology: www.cptech.org/ip/wipo/openwipo.html. See also: Declan Butler, "Drive for Patent-Free Innovation Gathers Pace," *Nature*, 424(6945), July 10, 2003: p. 118; Andrea L. Foster, "Who Should Own Science?" *Chronical of Higher Education*, October 1, 2004, p. A33.

71. Richard R. Nelson, "The Market Economy, and the Scientific Commons," Laboratory of Economics and Management Working Paper Series 2003/24, November 2003, available at: http://www.lem.sssup.it/WPLem/files/2003-24.pdf.

72. Michael A. Heller, Rebecca S. Eisenberg, "Can Patents Deter Innovation? The Anticommons in Biomedical Research," *Science*, 280, May 1, 1998: 698–701. See also: Michael A. Heller, "The Tragedy of the Anticommons: Property in the Transition from Marx to Markets," *Harvard Law Review*, 111(3), January 1998: 621–688.

73. Personal interview with Bhaven Sampat, Georgia Institute of Technology, March 12, 2002.

74. James A. Severson, hearing testimony, July 13, 2000.

75. Rai, Eisenberg, "Bayh-Dole Reform," pp. 56–57.

76. Jerry Thursby, Richard Jensen, Marie Thursby, "Objectives, Characteristics and Outcomes of University Licensing: A Survey of Major U.S. Universities," *Journal of Technology Transfer*, 26(1/2), January 2001: 59–72.

77. Goldie Blumenstyk, "How One University Pursued Profit from Science—and Won," *Chronicle of Higher Education*, February 12, 1999, p. A39.

78. The judge's opinion in this case contained confidential information and, accordingly, was filed under seal. The quote used here comes from the official order from the U.S. District Court of New Jersey, Civ. No. 97–2836 (GEB), which is dated October 21, 1999. See also: "American Pharmaceutical Partners Announces Exclusive Cisplatin Launch; Bristol's Cisplatin Patent Rules Invalid," PR Newswire, November 3, 1999.

79. Ted Agres, "Columbia Patents Under Attack: Latest Lawsuits Allege the University Misled the Patent Office to Extend Cotransformation Revenue," *The Scientist*, July 25, 2003; Mowery et al., *Ivory Tower*, Chapter 8, pp. 155–159.

80. Sen. Gregg unsuccessfully tried to argue that the Hatch-Waxman Act, which allows pharmaceutical companies to extend their patent terms when the drug approval process is delayed by the FDA, should also apply to the Axel patents.

81. Ted Agres, "Columbia Patents"; Andrew Pollack, "3 More Biotech Firms File Suit Against Columbia over Patent," *New York Times*, July 16, 2003, p. B2.

82. For detailed discussions of this case, see: Seth Shulman, *Owning the Future*, pp. 106–111; Mirowski, Sent, Eds., *Science Bought and Sold*, pp. 3–8. Some important original sources include: Claudio Sanchez, "Disputes Rise over Intellectual Property Rights," report aired on National Public Radio, September 30, 1996; a series of reports in the student newspaper, *The Oracle*, available at http://www.usforacle.co; "Ex-Student Sent to Chain Gang," *Associated Press*, June 18, 1996; and documents and chronologies posted on the Web by the Student Coalition for Handling Intellectual Property, run by Petr Taborsky, available at: http://web.archive.web/19990428155527.

83. A sampling of some recent legal cases involving universities, professors, and students includes: "Lawsuit Between Purdue University, Biotech Firm Continues," *Indianapolis Star*, January 12, 2004; Goldie Blumenstyk, "Universities Try to Keep Inventions from Going 'Out the Back Door,'" *Chronicle of Higher Education*, May 17, 2002; Philip Hilts, "University Forced to Pay $1.6 Million to Researcher," *New York Times*, August 10, 1997, p. A13; Philip Hilts, "Jury Award Voided in Scientific Research Case," *New York Times*, February 2, 1997; Julie L. Nicklin, "Where Some Colleges See a Potential Donor, Others See a Target for a Lawsuit," *Chronicle of Higher Education*, July 17, 1998.

84. For a discussion of the cases of Johnson, Brenner, and many others, see: Annalee Newitz, "Genome Liberation," *Salon.com*, February 26, 2002, and Jeffrey Benner, "Public Money, Private Code," *Salon.com*, January 8, 2002. In August 2000, the University of California's Office of Technology Transfer implemented a three-year pilot program permitting research in electrical engineering and computer science to be licensed more flexibly and nonexclusively, recognizing that in these industries exclusive licensing often impedes rather than enhances commercial use of university inventions. See: http://patron.ucop.edu/ottmemos/docs/ott00–02.html.

85. *Madey v. Duke University*, 307 F.3d 1351 (October 3, 2002).

86. Rebecca S. Eisenberg, "Patent Swords and Shields," *Science*, 299, February 14, 2003: 1018–1019.

87. Universities still often vehemently protest when outside companies demand payment of royalties on their patented technologies. Recently, for example, Inproteo, a company partly owned by Indiana and Purdue Universities and also by Eli Lilly and Co., sent out hundreds of letters to universities that were using its patented "His-tag" technique, a common research

technique for separating proteins. When the universities received these letters, warning that they could be liable for patent infringement unless they obtained a license from Inproteo, they mounted such a strong protest that Eli Lilly stepped in and got Inproteo to back down. However, when universities tried to protest similar patent-infringement letters from Test Central, Inc. and Acacia, both of which hold patents to technologies important for the delivery of online courses, their objections proved less successful. (Test Central's patents cover various types of online testing, and Acacia's patent covers streaming video technology.) For more details on these cases, see: Dan Carnevale, "Company Claims to Own Online Testing," *Chronicle of Higher Education*, March 26, 2004, and Scott Carlson, "A Patent Claim That May Cost Millions," *Chronicle of Higher Education*, November 7, 2003.

88. Margaret Cronin Fisk, "Ivory Towers Fire Back over Patents," *National Law Journal*, August 28, 2002.

89. Quoted in: Peg Brickley, "New Patent Worries Professors," *The Scientist*, 16(15), July 22, 2002. See also: Sharon Begley, Laura Johannes, "Ariad Patent Spurs Legal Battle Between Biotech Firm, Eli Lilly," *Wall Street Journal*, June 26, 2002.

90. Quoted in David C. Mowery, Bhaven N. Sampat, "Patenting and Licensing University Inventions: Lessons from the History of the Research Corporation," *Industrial and Corporate Change*, 10(2), 2001: 317–355, p. 321. Original source: Frederick Cottrell, "Patent Experience of the Research Corporation," *Transactions of the American Institute of Chemical Engineers*, 1932: 222–225.

91. Letter from Joshua Lederberg, professor of genetics at Stanford University's School of Medicine, to Gaylord Nelson, U.S. Senate, May 22, 1978, in the "Joshua Lederberg Papers," National Library of Medicine. Available at: http://profiles.nlm.nih.gov/BB/A/N/V/I/_/bbanvi.pdf.

92. Richard C. Atkinson, Roger N. Beachy, et al., "Public Sector Collaboration for Agricultural IP Management," *Science*, 301, July 11, 2003: 174–175.

93. Personal interview with Amy Kapczynski, February 7, 2002; Daryl Lindsey, "Amy and Goliath," *Salon.com*, May 1, 2001.

94. Letter from Eric Goemaere, South African representative of Médecins Sans Frontières, to Jon Soderstrom, in Yale University's Office of Cooperative Research, February 14, 2001.

95. In 1998, for example, according to Doctors Without Borders, sales of all drugs belonging to the staduvine class were a mere $600,000 in 1998. Therefore, the group argued, "the income foregone by a loss of market exclusivity in the country would be small. It would certainly pale in comparison to the $40 million Yale earned in royalties from the stavudine license" in 1999 alone. (See letter from Goemaere to Soderstrom, cited above.)

96. Philippe Dement, "Yale Shares Profits from AIDS Drugs," *Le Monde Diplomatique*, translated by Malcolm Greenwood, February 2002. See also: Lindsey, "Amy and Goliath"; Marc Wortman, "A Neighborhood for Cures," *Yale Alumni Magazine*, March 2003, available at: http://www.yalealumnimagazine.com/issues/03_03/medbuilding.html.

97. Graduate Employee and Students Organization, "Yale Researchers Demand That University, Bristol-Myers Squibb Give Up Patent Rights to AIDS Drug," press release, March 16, 2001; Janice D'Arcy, "AIDS Drug Debate Intensifies," *Hartford Courant*, March 20, 2001, p. A3.

98. Donald G. McNeil, Jr., "Yale Pressed to Help Cut Drug Costs in Africa," *New York Times*, March 12, 2001.

99. Lindsey, "Amy and Goliath."

100. Peter D. Blumberg, "From 'Publish or Perish' to 'Profit or Perish': Revenues from University Technology Transfer and the § 501 (c) (3) Tax Exemption," *University of Pennsylvania Law Review*, 145(89), 1996: 89–147. See also: James T. Y. Yang, "Collaboration Between Nonprofit Universities and Commercial Enterprises: The Rationale for Exempting Nonprofit Universities from Federal Income Taxation," *Yale Law Journal*, 95, July 1986: p. 1857.

101. "Partnering for Prosperity," 2003 annual meeting, Association of University Technology Managers, Disney World, FL, February 6–8, 2003.

102. Frank Stephenson, "A Tale of Taxol," *Research in Review*, Florida State University, Fall 2002: 13–37; Jim Hopkins, "Google Shows How Schools Turn Research into Big Bucks," *USA Today*, May 13, 2004.

103. Association of University Technology Licensing Managers, *AUTM Licensing Survey: FY 2002* (Northbrook, IL: AUTM, 2003). See also: Blumenstyk, "Inventions Produced," p. A28.

104. For various estimates, see: Bhaven Sampat, "Patenting and U.S. Academic Research." See also: Dennis R. Trune, Lewis N. Goslin, "University Technology Transfer Programs: A Profit/Loss Analysis," Technology *Forecasting and Social Change*, 57(3), March 1998: 197–204; Rebecca S. Eisenberg, "Public Research and Private Development: Patents and Technology Transfer in Government-Sponsored Research," *Virginia Law Review*, 82(8), November 1996: 1663–1727, pp. 1712–1713.

105. Goldie Blumenstyck, "Taking on Goliath: U. of Rochester Risks Millions in Patent Fight with Pharmaceutical Giants," *Chronicle of Higher Education*, September 20, 2002, p. A27.

106. Ronald G. Ehrenberg, Michael J. Rizzon, George H. Jakubson, "Who Bears the Growing Cost of Science at Universities?" *NBER Working Papers*, 9627, April 2003.

Chapter 7. Dreaming of Silicon Valley

1. Louis G. Tornatzky, Paul G. Waugaman, et. al., "Innovation U.: New University Roles in a Knowledge Economy," a report from Southern Growth Policies Board, Research Triangle Park, NC, 2002, p. 106; Peter Schmidt, "Public Universities Get Money to Attract High-Tech Industry," *Chronicle of Higher Education*, February 25, 2000.

2. Beverly Medlyn, "Hull Tax Plan Finds Receptive Audience; Governor Seeks Educator's Support," *Arizona Republic*, March 24, 2000, p. 6B.

3. Schmidt, "Public Universities."

4. The Wisconsin Economic Summit was held from November 29 to December 1, 2000, in Milwaukee, Wisconsin.

5. "Report of the Wisconsin Economic Summit," November 29–December 1, 2000, Milwaukee, Wisconsin, p. 15, available at: www.wisconsin.edu/summit.

6. Irwin Feller, "Virtuous and Vicious Cycles in the Contributions of Public Research Universities to State Economic Development Objectives," *Economic Development Quarterly*, 18(2), May 2004: 138–150, available at: http://edq.sagepub.com/cgi/reprint/18/2/138.pdf. See also: T. Reindl, D. Bower, "Financing State Colleges and Universities: What Is Happening to the Public in Public Higher Education?" paper presented at the Cornell Higher Education Research Institute's conference on "Financing Higher Education Institutions in the 21st Century," Cornell University, May 22–23, 2001.

7. John V. Lombardi et al., "The Top American Research Universities," Annual Report from the Lombardi Program on Measuring University Performance, University of Florida, November 2003.

8. Michael S. Fogarty, Amit K. Sinha, "Why Older Regions Can't Generalize from Route 128 and Silicon Valley: University-Industry Relationships and Regional Innovation Systems," in Louis M. Branscomb, Fumio Kodama, Richard Florida, Eds., *Industrializing Knowledge: University Industry Linkages in Japan and the United States* (Cambridge, MA: MIT Press, 1999), pp. 3–19.

9. Dan Berglund, Christopher Coburn, *Partnerships: A Compendium of State and Federal Cooperative Technology Programs* (Columbus, OH: Battelle Press, 1995), Table 10, p. 51; Richard Florida, Martin Kenney, *The Breakthrough Illusion* (New York: Basic Books, 1990), p. 186.

10. These included the Bayh-Dole Act and Stevenson-Wydler Act of 1980; various new programs at the National Science Foundation, including the Engineering Research Centers, Science and Technology Centers, and State-Industry University Cooperative Research Centers; and the 1982 Small Business Innovation Research (SBIR) program, which required federal agencies to set aside a specific percentage of R&D money for small business, much of which went to small technology firms. In 1988, Congress also established the Manufacturing Technology Centers (MTC) program in the National Bureau of Standards to help firms adopt the latest manufacturing methods, as well as the Advanced Technology Program, providing federal R&D grants to companies and consortia for use in commercial technology development. See: Berglund, Coburn, *Partnerships*, pp. 8–11.

11. Ibid., p. 9.

12. Personal Interview with Dan Berglund, January 28, 2003.

13. The term *technopole* was coined by: Manuel Castells, Peter Hall, *Technopoles of the World: The Making of Twenty-First-Century Industrial Complexes* (UK: Routledge, 1994).

14. Personal interview with Richard Florida, then based at Carnegie Mellon University, May 12, 2003.

15. Fogarty, Sinha, "Why Older Regions." See also: Goldie Blumenstyk, "Study Says South Is 'Net Exporter' of Academic Inventions," *Chronicle of Higher Education*, May 26, 1995, which references a report by the Southern Technology Council discussing the South's trouble in holding on to its own university-generated inventions and technologies and keeping them from being developed outside the region.

16. Richard Florida, *The Rise of the Creative Class* (New York: Basic Books, 2002), pp. x, 216–217; Richard Florida, "The Role of the University: Leveraging Talent, Not Technology," *Issues in Science and Technology*, National Academy of Sciences, Summer 1999, available at: www.nap.edu/issues/15.4/florida.htm.

17. Nancy S. Dorfman, "Route 128: The Development of a Regional High-Technology Economy," *Research Policy*, 12, 1983: 299–316, p. 301.

18. Al Link, *A Generosity of Spirit: The Early History of the Research Triangle Park* (North Carolina: Research Triangle Foundation of North Carolina, 1995), p. 29. See also: Al Link, *From Seed to Harvest: The Growth of Research Triangle Park* (North Carolina: Research Triangle Foundation of North Carolina, 2002).

19. Annalee Saxenian, Regional Advantage: Culture and Competition in Silicon Valley and Route 128 (Cambridge, MA: Harvard University Press, 1994, 1996), p. 22.

20. Ibid., p. 27.

21. SRI was charged with "pursuing science for practical purposes [which] might not be fully compatible with the traditional roles of the university" (ibid., p. 23).

22. Stuart W. Leslie, "The Biggest 'Angel' of Them All: The Military and the Making of Silicon Valley," in Martin Kenney, Ed., *Understanding Silicon Valley* (Stanford: Stanford University Press, 2000), pp. 48–67.

23. John Seely-Brown, "Foreword," in Kenney, *Understanding Silicon Valley*, p. xvi.

24. Personal interview with Dan Berglund, January 28, 2003.

25. *Weekly Digest*, a publication of the State Science and Technology Institute, issues dated May 16, 2003, and January 30, 2004.

26. "State Government Initiatives in Biotechnology 2001," a report prepared for the Biotechnology Industry Organization (BIO) by Technology Partnership Practice, Battelle Memorial Institute, and State Science and Technology Institute, September 2001, available at: http://www.bio.org/news/newsitem.asp?id=2001_1001_01.

27. National Science Foundation, "Table B–25: State and Local Government-Financed R&D Expenditures at Doctorate-Granting Institutions, by Geographic Division and State: Fiscal Years 1995–2002," *Academic Research and Development Expenditures: FY 2002: Detailed Statistical Tables* (Arlington, VA: National Science Foundation, 2004), NSF 04–330,

available at: http://www.nsf.gov/sbe/srs/nsf04330/. A detailed study conducted by the State Science and Technology Institute (SSTI) in 1995 found the amount of state-financed research and development expenditures at universities to be even higher, at about $2 billion. For a summary of the results, see: National Science Board, "What Is the State Government's Role in the R&D Enterprise?" (Arlington, VA: National Science Foundation, 1999), NSF 99–348, available at: http://www.nsf.gov/sbe/srs/nsf99348/htmstart.htm.

28. John Immerwahr, "Meeting the Competition: College and University Presidents, Faculty, and State Legislators View the New Competitive Academic Arena," a report by Public Agenda for the Futures Project: Policy for Higher Education in a Changing World, Brown University, Providence, RI, October 2002, quote on p. 7.

29. James Fallows, "The Early-Decision Racket," Atlantic Monthly, 288(2), September 2001; Amy Graham, Nick Thompson, "Broken Ranks," *Washington Monthly*, September 2001; Nick Thompson, "Playing with Numbers," *Washington Monthly*, September 2000.

30. Michael Arnone, "The Wannabes: More Public Universities Are Striving to Squeeze into the Top Tier. Can States Afford These Dreams?" Chronicle of Higher Education, January 3, 2003, p. A18.

31. Mari N. Jensen, "Geneticist Aims to Feed World, Lift UA Research," *Tucson Citizen*, January 9, 2002, p. 1A.

32. Blake Morlock, "UA Jumps into Race for Research Money," *Tucson Citizen*, October 14, 2003, p. 1A.

33. Nicole Rivard, "Opportunity Knocks," *University Business*, February 2001, available at: www.universitybusiness.com.

34. Feller, "Virtuous and Vicious Cycles," pp. 143, 147, available at: http://edq.sagepub.com/cgi/reprint/18/2/138.pdf; Eyal Press, Jennifer Washburn, "The Kept University," *Atlantic Monthly*, 285(3), March 2000.

35. Arnone, "The Wannabes," p. A18.

36. Irwin Feller, "The American University System as a Performer of Basic and Applied Research," in Branscomb et al., *Industrializing Knowledge*.

37. According to the National Science Board, the number of nonresearch and non-doctorate-granting institutions (such as technical, liberal arts, and two-year community colleges) receiving federal research support more than doubled between 1973 and 1994, rising from 315 to 680, leveling off at 587 in 2000 (National Science Board, *Science and Engineering Indicators—2004* "Chapter 5: Academic Research and Development," (Arlington, VA: National Science Foundation, 2004), NSB–04–1, pp. 5–5, 17–18, available at: http://www.nsf.gov/sbe/srs/seind04/toc.htm. Also from 1979 to 1991, although the absolute level of federal spending on university research increased, federal support per full-time academic researcher declined by roughly 9.4 percent in real terms; see: Wesley M. Cohen, Richard Florida, et al., "Industry and the Academy: Uneasy Partners in the Cause of Technological

Advance," in Roger A. Noll, Ed., *Challenges to Research Universities* (Washington, DC: Brookings Institution Press, 1998), pp. 171–199, at p. 184.

38. National Science Board, "Chapter 5," p. 5.

39. Feller, "American University System," p. 93. See also: Irwin Feller, "Research Subverted by Academic Greed," *Chronicle of Higher Education*, January 16, 2004, p. B6, where he wrote, "We must clarify the federal interest in supporting academic research. . . . One part of the examination should be an explicit discussion of the number and geographic distribution of research universities that the United States needs and is willing to support."

40. Jeffrey Brainard, "Lobbying to Bring Home the Bacon," *Chronicle of Higher Education*, October 22, 2004, p. A26.

41. See Feller, "Research Subverted," pp. B6–7; these figures come from a survey conducted by the *Chronicle*.

42. Ibid.; Jeffrey Brainard, Anne Marie Borrego, "Academic Pork Tops $2-Billion for the First Time," *Chronicle of Higher Education*, September 26, 2003; "Real Money," editorial, *Washington Post*, August 16, 2001, p. A24.

43. Personal interview with Michael Crow, May 1, 2002.

44. Joseph Cortright, Heike Mayer, "Signs of Life: The Growth of Biotechnology Centers in the U.S.," Brookings Institution, Center on Urban and Metropolitan Policy, 2002, p. 35, available at: http://www.brookings.edu/es/urban/publications/biotech.htm.

45. Ibid., p. 7.

46. Ibid., p. 8.

47. Ibid., p. 33.

48. Personal interview with Al Link, January 24, 2003.

49. Martin Van Der Werf, Goldie Blumenstyk, "A Fertile Place to Breed Business," *Chronicle of Higher Education*, March 2, 2001.

50. Karen Grassmuck, "Wariness Dampens 1980's Craze for Building Technology Parks," *Chronicle of Higher Education*, June 27, 1990; Goldie Blumenstyk, "Pitfalls of Research Parks Lead Universities and States to Reassess Their Expectations," *Chronicle of Higher Education*, July 5, 1990; Michael Luger, Harvey Goldstein, "Technology in the Garden: Research Parks and Regional Economic Development," First Report to the Ford Foundation, 1990. Studies suggest that university research parks, business incubators, and other commercial ventures have had limited success for some time. See: General Accounting Office, "The Federal Role in Fostering University-Industry Cooperation," (GAO/PAD–83–22), 1983, p. 10; Victor J. Danilov, "The Research Park Shakeout," *Industrial Research*, May 1971, p. 45; and Gary W. Matkin, *Technology Transfer and the University* (New York: American Council on Education and Macmillan, 1990), pp. 240–274.

51. Karen Robinson-Jacobs, "USC to Shutter High-Tech Incubator," *Los Angeles Times*, June 6, 2002.

52. Josh Lerner, "Venture Capital and the Commercialization of Academic Technology: Symbiosis and Paradox," in Branscomb et al., Eds., *Industrializing Knowledge*, pp. 385–409.

53. U.S. Congress, Senate Committee on Commerce, Science and Transportation, Subcommittee on Science, Technology and Space, Hearing, Nanotechnology, September, 17, 2002, Washington, DC, pp. 36, 56–57. See also: R. Stanley Williams's "Extended Written Remarks" to the committee, p. 5, available at: http://commerce.senate.gov/hearings/091702williams.pdf.

54. "Government-University-Industry Research Roundtable: Industrial Perspectives on Innovation and Interactions with Universities (1991)," reprinted in Norman E. Bowie, Ed., *University-Business Partnerships* (London: Rowman & Littlefield, 1994), pp. 208–219, at pp. 214–215, 219.

55. For more industry criticism, see: Dan Dimancescu, James Botkin, *The New Alliance* (Cambridge, MA: Ballinger, 1986), pp. 90–91.

56. Donald Stokes, *Pasteur's Quadrant* (Washington, DC: Brookings Institution, 1997).

57. Partha Dasgupta, Paul David, "Toward a New Economics of Science," *Research Policy*, 23, 1994: 487–521, reprinted in Philip Mirowski, Esther-Mirjam Sent, Eds., *Science Bought and Sold: Essays in the Economics of Science* (Chicago: University of Chicago Press, 2002), pp. 219–248, p. 228.

58. Ibid., p. 229. This idea is further elaborated on by Paul David in "The Political Economy of Public Science," a contribution to Helen Lawton Smith, Ed., *The Regulation of Science and Technology* (London: Palgrave Macmillan, 2002), pp. 33–57.

59. Richard R. Nelson, "Simple Economics of Basic Scientific Research," Journal *of Political Economy*, 67, 1959: 297–306, reprinted in Mirowski, Sent, *Science Bought*, p. 159.

60. Remarks by Paul David, "Symposium on the Role of Scientific and Technical Data and Information in the Public Domain," National Academy of Sciences, Washington, DC, September 5–6, 2002.

Chapter 8. Paying More for Less

1. New York University, "Tuition, Fees, and Expenses," New York University: Office of Financial Aid, available at: http://www.nyu.edu/financial.aid/tuition.html. Tuition is about $3,000 more for NYU's Tisch School of the Arts.

2. David L. Kirp, *Shakespeare, Einstein, and the Bottom Line* (Cambridge, MA: Harvard University Press, 2003), pp. 77–78; Jon E. Hilsenrath, "More Economists Love New York as NYU Lures Eight Academics," *Wall Street Journal*, September 16, 2002, p. A2.

3. Robin Wilson, Piper Fogg, "Half a Million Reasons to Leave Harvard," *Chronicle of Higher Education*, January 10, 2003, p. 7; Patrick Healy, "College Rivalry," *Boston Globe Magazine*, June 29, 2003, p. 13; David L. Kirp, "How Much for That Professor?" editorial, *New York Times*, October 27, 2003, p. A21.

4. "Executive Compensation," a supplement to the *Chronicle of Higher Education*, November 14, 2003, p. S15.

5. Personal interview with Ward Regan, April 29, 2004.

6. Ana Marie Cox, "Report Details Colleges' Heavy Reliance on Part-Time Instructors," *Chronicle of Higher Education*, November 22, 2000.

7. Gwendolyn Bradley, "Contingent Faculty and the New Academic Labor System," *Academe*, 90(1), January-February 2004; American Association of University Professors, "Contingent Faculty Appointments," last updated April 2004, available at: www.aaup.org/Issues/part-time/index.html; "AAUP Policy Statement: Contingent Appointments and the Academic Profession," adopted by the national Council on November 9, 2003, available at: www.aaup.org/statements/SpchState/contingent.htm.

8. Robert W. Kenny, "Reinventing Undergraduate Education: A Blueprint for America's Research Universities," Boyer Commission on Educating Undergraduates in the Research University, 1998, available at: http://naples.cc.sunysb.edu/Pres/boyer.nsf/

9. College Board, "Trends in College Pricing 2004," *Trends in Higher Education Series*, (New York: College Board Publications, 2004), p. 3., available at: http://www.collegeboard.com/prod_downloads/press/cost04/041264TrendsPricing2004_FINAL.pdf.

10. Richard Moser, "The New Academic Labor System: Corporatization and the Renewal of Academic Citizenship," American Association of University Professors, June 12, 2001, available at: www.aaup.org/Issues/part-time/cewmose.htm.

11. Quoted in Jane Buck, "The President's Report: Successes, Setbacks, and Contingent Labor," *Academe*, 87(5), September-October 2001.

12. Bradley, "Contingent Faculty."

13. Martin Finkelstein, Jack Schuster, "Assessing the Silent Revolution: How Changing Demographics Are Reshaping the Academic Profession," American Association of Higher Education Bulletin, October 2001.

14. Louis Menand, "The Limits of Academic Freedom," in Louis Menand, Ed., *The Future of Academic Freedom* (Chicago: University of Chicago Press, 1996), pp. 3–20, p. 4.

15. Mark Pitsch, "Todd Chosen to Lead UK: Trustees Turn to Businessman to Help Boost School's Rating," *Courier-Journal* (Louisville, KY), January 24, 2001; Katherine S. Mangan, "Corporate Know-How Lands Presidencies for a Growing Number of Business Deans," *Chronicle of Higher Education*, March 27, 1998, p. A43; Julianne Basinger, Sarah H. Henderson, "Hidden Costs of High Public Pay," *Chronicle of Higher Education*, November 14, 2003, p. 3.

16. For a national overview of university president salaries, see: "Executive Compensation," a supplement to the *Chronicle of Higher Education*, November 14, 2003; Sam Dillon, "Ivory Tower Executive Suite Gets CEO-Level Salaries," *New York Times*, November 15, 2004, A17.

17. Julianne Basinger, "Georgia Battle Pits Board Against Board," *Chronicle of Higher Education*, November 28, 2003, p. 1; Julianne Basinger, "U. of Georgia Breaks Ties to Its

Fund-Raising Arm, a Split Unprecedented in Academe," *Chronicle of Higher Education*, May 27, 2004.

18. Moser, "New Academic Labor System."

19. Amy Graham, Nick Thompson, "Broken Ranks," *Washington Monthly*, September 2001; Nick Thompson, "Playing with Numbers," *Washington Monthly*, September 2000.

20. Dominic J. Brewer, Susan M. Gates, Charles A. Goldman, *In Pursuit of Prestige: Strategy and Competition in U.S. Higher Education* (New Brunswick, NJ: Transaction, 2002), pp. 147–148.

21. Ibid., p. 148.

22. Anthony P. Carnevale, Stephen J. Rose, "Socioeconomic Status, Race/Ethnicity, and Selective College Admissions," in Richard D. Kahlenberg, Ed., *America's Untapped Resource: Low-Income Students in Higher Education* (New York, Century Foundation Press, 2004), pp. 101–156.

23. Personal interview with Donald Stein, November 20, 2001.

24. Steven Greenhouse, Karen W. Arenson, "Labor Board Says Graduate Students at Private Universities Have No Right to Unionize," *New York Times*, July 16, 2004, p. A14.

25. New York University press release, "Part-time Faculty Unionization Issues," April 21, 2004, available at: http://www.nyu.edu/adjunct.issues/; Karen W. Arenson, "Benefits Outlined for Adjuncts at NYU," *New York Times*, May 8, 2004, p. B3.

26. The election was held in March 2002. Scott Smallwood, "Graduate-Student Unions Play a Waiting Game," *Chronicle of Higher Education*, November 28, 2003, p. 21; Karen W. Arenson, "Protest Seeks Union Rights at Columbia," *New York Times*, April 20, 2004, p. B3.

27. New York University press release, "Statement by NYU Spokesman John Beckman on Strike Vote by United Auto Workers," April 15, 2004.

28. Daniel Duane, "Eggheads Unite," *New York Times Magazine*, May 4, 2003.

29. Personal interview with Karen Bray, a student at the New School University's Eugene Lang College, April 27, 2004.

30. Alan G. Merten, "Universities in the Information Age: Changing Roles, Responsibilities, and Relationships," 1998 World Congress on Information Technology, June 24, 1998.

31. Personal interviews with GMU students, originally reported in Eyal Press, Jennifer Washburn, "The Kept University," *Atlantic Monthly*, 285(3), March 2000.

32. Personal interview, originally reported in ibid.

33. "A Statement of Principle," signed by more than 180 College of Arts and Sciences faculty members and presented to President Merten on March 3, 1998, available at: http://www.gmu.edu/artsciences/principles.html. Personal interview with Kevin Avruch, originally reported in Press, Washburn, "Kept University."

34. Alan Greenspan, remarks delivered at the International Understanding Award Dinner, Institute of International Education, New York City, October 29, 2002, available at: http://www.federalreserve.gov/boarddocs/speeches/2002/20021029/default.htm.

35. Keith H. Hammonds, Susan Jackson, et al., "The New U.," *Business Week,* December 22, 1997.

36. Jeffrey J. Williams, "Franchising the University," p. 16.

37. Personal interview with Kenneth Prewitt, dean of the Graduate Faculty at the New School University, June 24, 2002.

38. In a recent report, the American Academy of Arts and Sciences noted that "the human-ities are, at present, lagging behind the sciences and engineering in developing the systems of data resources needed to monitor *even the most basic trends* in the number, activity levels, pro-ductivity of, and the future prospects for, practitioners in humanities fields at all degree levels" (emphasis added) ("Making the Humanities Count," April 15, 2002).

39. Steven Brint, "The Rise of the Practical Arts," in Steven Brint, Ed., *The Future of the City of Intellect: The Changing American University* (Stanford: Stanford University Press, 2002), pp. 231–259; for statistics, see pp. 232, 235.

40. Kirp, *Shakespeare, Einstein*, p. 53.

41. James Engell, Anthony Dangerfield, "The Market-Model University: Humanities in the Age of Money, *Harvard Magazine*, May-June 1998, available at: http://www.harvard-magazine.com/.

42. David A. Hollinger, "Money and Academic Freedom a Half-Century after McCarthyism: Universities amid the Force Fields of Capital," in Peggie J. Hollingsworth, Ed., *Unfettered Expression* (Ann Arbor: University of Michigan Press, 2000), pp. 171–173.

43. Personal interview, originally reported in Press, Washburn, "Kept University."

44. NYU press release, "NYUonline and McGraw-Hill Announce Strategic Partnership for Corporate Learning," May 16, 2000.

45. Interview with Ann Kirschner, quoted in Eyal Press, Jennifer Washburn, "Digital Diplomas," *Mother Jones*, January-February 2001.

46. Quoted in Press, Washburn, "Kept University."

47. William F. Massy, Robert Zemsky, "Using Technology to Enhance Academic Productivity," June 1995. This paper is part of a series produced in connection with Educause's National Learning Infrastructure Initiative and is available at: http://www.educause.edu.nlii/keydocs/massy.html.

48. Quoted in Press, Washburn, "Digital Diplomas."

49. Carol Twigg, "Academic Productivity: The Case for Instructional Software," a report from the Broadmoor Roundtable, Colorado Springs, July 24–25, 1996. This paper is part of a series produced in connection with Educause's National Learning Infrastructure Initiative and is available at: http://www.educause.edu/ir/library/html/nli0002.html.

50. Arthur E. Levine, "The Future of Colleges: 9 Inevitable Changes," *Chronicle of Higher Education*, October 27, 2000, pp. B10–11.

51. Patrice M. Jones, Ron Grossman, "U. of C. Sets Controversial Course to Provide On-Line Business Classes," *Chicago Tribune*, May 13, 1999, p. 1; Patrick McGeehan, "UNext.com Signs Course Deals with Four More Universities," *Wall Street Journal*, June 23, 1999.

52. Quoted in Goldie Blumenstyk, "Temple U. Shuts Down For-Profit Distance-Education Company," *Chronicle of Higher Education*, July 20, 2001.

53. Quote comes from: Benjamin Lowe, "Fathoming Where the Money Goes," *Columbia Spectator*, February 7, 2001. See also: Scott Carlson, "After Losing Millions, Columbia U. Will Close Its Online-Learning Venture," *Chronicle of Higher Education*, January 17, 2003, and Chris Beam, "Year in Review: New Administration Brings Shifting Priorities," *Columbia Spectator*, May 19, 2003. The estimate of nearly $30 million comes from a faculty senate investigation finding that Fathom had lost Columbia $18.7 million as of 2001, and that Columbia was planning to spend another $10 million over the next two years to keep the site running as a "placeholder" for possible future operations; see: Ben Casselman, "Committee Reports on Fathom's Difficulties," *Columbia Spectator*, January 29, 2001.

54. See: David F. Noble, "Digital Diploma Mills. Part 4: Rehearsal for the Revolution," November 1999. The complete Digital Diploma Mills series is available at: http://smccd.net/accounts/onlineed/bios.htm. It was also published in David F. Noble, *Digital Diploma Mills: The Automation of Higher Education* (New York: Monthly Review Press, 2001).

55. Tiffany Waits, Laurie Lewis, et. al., *Distance Education at Degree-Granting Postsecondary Institutions: 2000–2001* (Washington, DC: U.S. Department of Education, National Center for Education Statistics, 2003), NCES 2003–017, pp. iii–iv, 24, available at: http://nces.ed.gov/pubs2003/2003017.pdf.

56. University of Maryland University College, Fiscal Year 2000–2003 Fact Sheets, *UMUC: Institutional Planning, Research and Accountability*, available at: http://www.umuc.edu/ip/fast00.html, /fast01.html, /fast02.html, /fast03.html.

57. Carol A. Twigg, "Expanding Access to Learning: The Role of Virtual Universities," Center for Academic Transformation, Rensselaer Polytechnic Institute, 2003, p. 29.

58. Carol A. Twigg, "New Models for Online Learning," Educause, September-October 2003, available at: www.educause.edu.

59. Carol A. Twigg, "Expanding Access," pp. 18, 26, 27, 29.

Chapter 9. The Path Forward

1. Martin Kenney, *Biotechnology: The University-Industrial Complex* (New Haven: Yale University Press, 1986), p. 32.

2. For a discussion of this ongoing problem, see: Russell Jacoby, *The Last Intellectuals* (New York: Noonday Press, Farrar, Straus & Giroux, 1987).

3. Donald Stein, personal interview, November 20, 2001.

4. Quoted in David C. Mowery, Bhaven N. Sampat, "Patenting and Licensing University Inventions: Lessons from the History of the Research Corporation," *Industrial and Corporate Change*, 10(2), 2001: 317–355, p. 321. Original source: Frederick Cottrell, "Patent Experience of the Research Corporation," *Transactions of the American Institute of Chemical Engineers*, 1932: 222–225.

5. David C. Mowery, Richard R. Nelson, et al., *Ivory Tower and Industrial Innovation: University-Industry Technology Transfer Before and After Bayh-Dole* (Stanford: Stanford Business Books, 2004), p. 42.

6. Richard R. Nelson, "The Market Economy, and the Scientific Commons," Laboratory of Economics and Management (LEM) Working Paper No. 2003/24, November 2003, available at: http://www.lem.sssup.it/WPLem/files/2003–24.pdf.

7. Arti K. Rai, Rebecca S. Eisenberg, "Bayh-Dole Reform and the Progress of Biomedicine," *American Scientist*, 91, January-February 2003; Arti K. Rai, "The Increasing Proprietary Nature of Publicly Funded Biomedical Research: Benefits and Threats," in Donald S. Stein, Ed., *Buying In or Selling Out? The Commercialization of the American Research University* (New Brunswick, NJ: Rutgers University Press, 2004), pp. 112–126, p. 124.

8. David Willman, "Stealth Merger: Drug Companies and Government Medical Research," *Los Angeles Times*, December 7, 2003 (see also four accompanying case studies); David Willman, "Lawmakers Assail NIH Conflict Rules; They Say the Agency's Efforts to Revise Its Policies on Drug-Firm Payments Fall Short," *Los Angeles Times*, May 13, 2004, p. 16.

9. Ted Agres, "Conflict Probe Expands to FDA," *The Scientist*, May 19, 2004.

10. Astrid James, Richard Horton, et al., "The Lancet's Policy on Conflicts of Interest," *The Lancet*, 363(9402), 2004: 2–3.

11. Rick Weiss, "House Panel Scolds NIH Chief, HHS," *Washington Post*, May 13, 2004, p. A27.

12. Regarding the ban, see: Jocelyn Kaiser, "NIH Proposes Temporary Ban on Paid Consulting," *Science*, 306, October 1, 2004: p. 27. Zerhouni's quote appeared in: Jocelyn Kaiser, "House Committee Slams NIH's Plan on Consulting," *Science*, 304, May 21, 2004: p. 1091.

13. Richard J. Bennof, "Federal Science and Engineering Obligations to Academic and Nonprofit Institutions Reached Record Highs in FY2002," Info Brief, National Science Foundation, June 2004, NSF 04–324, available at: www.nsf.gov/sbe/srs/infbrief/nsf04324/start.htm.

14. See: Denis O. Gray, Mark Lindblad, et. al., "Industry-University Research Centers: A Multivariate Analysis of Member Retention," *Journal of Technology Transfer*, 26(3), June 2001: 247–254.

15. Marcia Angell, *The Truth About the Drug Companies: How They Deceive Us and What to Do About It* (New York: Random House, 2004); Sheldon Krimsky, *Science in the*

Private Interest (Oxford, UK: Rowman & Littlefield, 2003), p. 229; Merrill Goozner, *The $800 Million Pill* (Berkeley, CA: University of California Press, 2004), p. 251. Under Goozner's plan, an independent federal agency would conduct trials of its own that compare existing medicines in order to develop best-practice guidelines for physicians.

16. Ken Getz, "Clinical Grants Market Decelerates," *CenterWatch*, 10(4), 2003.

17. Julie L. Nicklin, "Where Some Colleges See a Potential Donor, Others See a Target for a Lawsuit," *Chronicle for Higher Education*, July 17, 1998.

18. All of these Richard Hofstadter quotes are drawn from: Richard Hofstadter, "The Higher Learning in America," in Richard Hofstadter, C. DeWitt Hardy, *The Development and Scope of Higher Education in the United States* (New York: Columbia University Press, 1952).

Index

Abbott Laboratories, 115
"Academic capitalism," 69
Academic culture
 corporate-sponsored research
  and, 71
 openness within the sciences and, 73,
  194–196
Academic freedom
 American Association of University
  Professors (AAUP) and, 38–39, 204,
  207
 Bayh-Dole Act and, 69–70
 corporate intimidation/harassment
  and, 19–23, 83
 during McCarthy era, 43–44
 Edward Ross case and, 38
 German research model and, 32, 73,
  119
 industry funding of clinical drug trials
  and, 107, 103–110, 123–124
 medieval universities and, 28
 military funding and, 42–43, 72
 tenure and, 204–205

Academic governance structure, in
 American universities, 28–29
Academic-industrial complex, 140
Academic pork, lobbying for, ix,
 184–185
Academic research
 early history of patenting, 49–54
 funding for, 8
 growth in industry funding
  for, 139
 military funding and, 42–43
 ownership of, xi
Academic science
 competing research models and, 33
 true value of, 194–197
Academic tech-transfer agencies, ATTAs,
 proposal for independent licensing
 by, 229–231
Activase, 157
Adamany, David, 221
Adams, Henry Carter, 34
Adams, Michael F., 206
Adjunct faculty, 200, 201–203, 207

309

effects on faculty governance and
  academic freedom, 204–205
unions and, 210–212
Administrators
  commercialization and, 205–207, 209
  executive compensation, 205–206
Aerospace industry, university ties and,
  33
Affirmative action programs, 45
Africa, Yale and AIDS crisis in, 164–167
Agouron, 104
Agracetus, 147
Agricultural biotechnology, 163
Agriculture, genetic engineering and, 3,
  10–11
Akamai Technologies, Inc., 95, 96
Alfred University, industry funding at,
  139
Allen, George, 192
Allied Chemical, contract between U.C.
  Davis and, 95
Alzheimer's disease, 83
American Academy of Allergy, Asthma
  and Immunology, 129–130
American Association of University
  Professors, AAUP, 38–39, 204, 207
American College of Surgeons, 120
American Council on Education, 59
American Economics Association, 38
American Medical Association, AMA,
  119–120
American Thoracic Society, 77, 79
American universities
  academic governance structure in,
    28–29, 205
  historic relationship with American
    industry, 33–39
  Vietnam War protests and military-
    and-intelligence-related divestitures
    at, 45–46
Amersham Health, 191
Andreesen, Marc, 240
Andrews, Frederick, 61
Angell, Marcia, 81, 109, 237
Annals of Internal Medicine, 84
Annas, George, 128
Anticommons, tragedy of, 154–155
Antidepressants, suppression
  of negative research and,
  113–116, 238

Anti-intellectualism, utilitarianism and,
  26, 31
Antiwar movement, military funding
  debate and, 45–46
Apotex, 123, 124
Applied research, 14, 33, 194–195, 226
ARCH Development Corporation, 140
Archives of Internal Medicine, 110
Arendt, Hannah, 216
ARIAD Pharmaceuticals, Inc., 161
Aristotle, xiv
Arizona State University, ASU, 186–187
Armstrong, John, 193, 194
Arnold, Matthew, 31
Arnone, Michael, 182
Arrow, Kenneth, 62, 64
Arthritis
  corporate funding of drug trials and,
    110–111
  medications to treat, 67, 112
Association of American Medical
  Colleges, AAMC, 134, 135
Association of American Universities,
  AAU, 134, 135
Association of University Technology
  Managers, AUTM, 142–143,
    167–169, 191
  critiques of statistical analysis
    performed by, 143–146, 169–170
  Disney World, and annual meeting of,
    167–169
  patenting and licensing statistics issued
    by, 142–143
AstraZeneca, 82
AT&T, 33, 82
Atkinson, Richard, 111, 117
Atkinson, Richard C., 17, 57
Atomic bomb, 41
Atomic Energy Commission, 42, 63
Atrazine
  research on sexual development of
    frogs and, 20–23
  European ban on, 22
  Atrazine Endocrine Risk Assessment
    Panel, 21
Autoimmune Deficiency Syndrome,
  AIDS
  CCR5 receptor and, 148
  crisis in Africa—and at Yale, 164–167
  industry effort to suppress negative

research on vaccine for, 103–108
research, 83
Autonomy, university
   drug industry influence and loss of,
      122–124
   preserving, 228–229, 240
Avonex, 157
Avruch, Kevin, 214, 218
Axel, Richard, 157

Baker, Lynne Rudder, xiv
Balamuth, Fran, 166
Balanced Budget Act (1997), 128
Baptists, Brown University founded by,
   27
Barnes and Noble, 213
Bayh, Birch, 60, 66, 67
Bayh-Dole Act, 8–9, 17, 95, 98, 101,
   122, 146, 153, 156, 159, 190, 226
   academic culture and, 70
   critique of economic data used to
      support passage of, 64–65
   debate over economic legacy of,
      141–145
   history behind the passage of, 59–669
   industry criticism of, 190–192
   "march in" provision of, 67, 152,
      232–233
   precursor to, 65, 149
   proponents of, 142, 143
   proposals for amending, 225, 228,
      231–233
Baylor College of Medicine, p53 mouse
   controversy at, 152–153, 168, 233
Beard, Charles, 35
Beard, Mary, 35
Becker, Gary, 221
Beckman, John, 210
Bell Laboratories, 196
Bemis, Edward W., 38
Ben Franklin Partnership (Pennsylvania),
   175
Berdahl, Robert, 3, 8, 17, 23, 24
Berg, Paul, 240, 241
Berglund, Dan, 176, 179, 190
Berkeley Free Speech Movement, 1
Berring, Robert, 25
Bias, research
   government funding and, 83
   industry funding and, xx, 84, 110

Biogen, 56
BioSTAR (University of California), 19
Biotechnology, xiv, 19, 49, 58, 59, 80,
   121, 126, 141, 147, 172, 180, 188,
   241
   academic-industry alliances and the
      birth of, 56
   emergence of, 70, 176
   inflated expectations for, 188–189
   state funding for, 180
Blackburn, George, 116
Block, Ned, 199, 200
Blood, 133
"Blue-sky" research, xviii, 41, 196, 235
Blumberg, Peter, 166
Blumenstyk, Goldie, 22
Blumenthal, David, 74, 75, 86
Boards of trustees, history of, in
   American universities, 28–29, 35,
   39
Bodenheimer, Thomas, 110, 112
Bok, Derek, 137
Boots Pharmaceutical, 19, 20 (See also
   Knoll Pharmaceutical)
Bose, Amar Gopal, 143
Bose Corporation, 143
Bose, Vanu, 143
Boston College, 199
Boston Globe, 78, 114
Boston University, 76, 112, 185
   controversial investment in Seragen,
      141
Botstein, David, 93
Boyer, Herbert, 49, 52, 54, 55, 56, 58,
   66, 241
Boyle, James, 148
Bradley, Gwendolyn, 204
"Brain trusts," 31
Brand-name product development by
   universities, 141
Branscomb, Louis, 58
Bray, Karen, 212
Breast cancer gene, and restrictions on
   use, xi
Bremer, Howard, 66, 68
Brennan, Troyen, 111, 112
Brenner, Steve, 159
Brenner v. Manson, 148
Brentano, Robert, 13
Brewer, Dominic, 207, 208

Brigham Young University, 85
Brint, Steven, 216, 217
Brinton, Joyce, 168
Bristol-Myers Squibb, **BMS**, 5, 115,
    132, 156, 164, 165, 166, 191
Brookings Institution, 188, 189
Browdy and Neimark, 66
Brown, David, xv
Brown University, 97, 114, 210
    conflicts of interest in psychiatry
        department at, 114
    David Kern academic freedom case at,
        76–80
    founding of, 27
    Medical School at, 77, 78, 79, 80
"Bucks for Brains" initiative (Kentucky),
    180
Burger, Thomas, 191
Burger, Warren, 147
Busch, Lawrence, 14
Bush, George W., 82, 152
Bush, Jeb, 180
Bush, Vannevar, 40–42, 44, 51, 60, 83,
    185
Business-Higher Education Forum, 59
Business Week, xiv, 140, 215

Calgene, Inc., 95
California, "Enron model" of electricity
    deregulation in, xvii, 81
California Institute of Technology,
    (**Caltech**), 33, 36, 98
    Jet Propulsion Laboratory at, 43
California Institutes for Science and
    Innovation, **CISI**,(University of
    California), 17–18, 180
California State Senate, U.C. Berkeley—
    Novartis agreement hearing and,
    9–12
Campbell, Eric, 74, 86
Canadian Medical Association Journal,
    124
Cancer research, 5, 67, 74, 82, 84, 91,
    97, 141, 168
    conflicts of interest in, 131–133
    independent experts in, xvi
    patenting controversies related to, xi,
        156–157, 161
Canfield, James H., 31
Caplan, Arthur, 134

Carboplatin, 156
Cardiovascular disease, 83
Carnahan, Robert, 158
Carnegie, Andrew, 25
Carnegie Foundation for the
    Advancement of Teaching, 181,
    119, 203
Carnegie Mellon University, 176, 221
    Magnetic Technology Center at, 139
Carr, James A., 22
Carter, Jimmy, 64
Catch-up schools, research stature
    sought by, 170, 182–183, 184
    problems faced by, 187, 188, 190
CCR5 receptor, patent on, 148
Celebrex, 112, 169
Celera, 149
Cell phone research, 82
Centers for Disease Control, 79
Central Intelligence Agency, **CIA**
    university ties to, 42
    Vietnam War protests against, at
        Stanford, 45–46
Cerezyme, 157
Cerny, Joseph, 11
Chapela, Ignacio, 4, 14–16
Chapman, John Jay, 37
Chicago Tribune, xi
Chiles, Lawton, 158
Cho, Mildred, 81, 84
Chou, Joany, 96
Christian Scientists, 118
Chronicle of Higher Education, 5, 14,
    22, 85, 117, 182
Churness, Dana, 172, 173, 174
Cisco Systems, 173
Cisplatin, 156, 157
Citizenship, liberal education
    and, xxiii
Civil War, 30
Claremont Colleges, 183
Clinical drug research
    conflicts of interest and, 126–136
    corporate control over, 110–116
    data control and, 108, 112
    deficiencies in the oversight of,
        127–136
    human subjects and, 125–136
    litigation surrounding, 125–126,
        130–131

phases of drug testing in animals and humans, 127
proposal for oversight of, 237–239
Clinical trials
Cloning, 49, 55
Coalition on the Academic Workforce, 202
Cohen, Stanley, 49, 50, 52, 58, 66, 241
Cohen, Wesley, 145
Cold War, 43, 44, 72, 86
College of Natural Resources, CNR, (U.C. Berkeley)
Novartis agreement with, 3–4, 12, 16
College of Philadelphia, 27
College of William and Mary, 28
Colonial era (U.S.), colleges during, 27
Columbia University, 114, 186, 187, 203, 216, 230
Bristol-Myers agreement with, 5
cotransformation patent campaign at, 157–158, 186
Fathom, online-learning company formed by, 219, 221
founding of, 27
graduate student strike at, 210
Office of Clinical Trials at, 130
Office of Science and Technology Ventures at, 186
Vietnam War and opposition to defense industry ties with, 46
Colyvas, Jeannette, 150
Commager, Henry Steele, 26
Commercialism
Bayh-Dole Act and, 59–72
effect of, on knowledge commons, 54, 63, 145–149, 154, 159, 163, 227, 231
effect of, on teaching and humanities, 199–209
growing role of, in academic life, ix–xx
human clinical research and, 124–133
medical ethics and, 120
public interest secondary to profits, 155–163
public trust and, 118
students and effects of, 85–97, 158, 240
Communist Party, faculty purges and, 43–44

Community college systems, 45
Competition in higher education, and increase in, 182–185
Compton, Karl T., 36, 37, 151
Computer code, monopoly control over building blocks of, 148
Computer science field
commercial conflicts within, 95–96
intellectual property battles in, 159–160
Confidentiality agreements, 74, 85
occupational health investigations and, 76–80
Conflict of Interest Standing Committee, CISC,(UPenn), 131
Conflicts of interest in the academy, 225
biomedical research and regulation of, 99, 134–136
clinical drug trials and, 103–117
current federal rules pertaining to, 99–100, 234
debate over public disclosure of, 98–99, 101–102
distortion of mental health research and, 113–116
drug approval lobbying and, 116–117
failed federal attempts to regulate, 98–100, 134–136, 233–235
Harvard University debates on regulating, 93–94, 100
proposal for new federal regulation of, 233–237
Constant Gardener, The (Le Carré), 123
Consulting
fees, 233, 234, 235
proposal to regulate, 235
Contract research organizations, CROs, 129
Cooperative research-and-development agreements, CRADAs, 69
Coopers and Lybrand, 220
Cornell, Ezra, 30
Cornell University, 34, 210
Corporate-sponsored research, 3, 5, 9, 19, 55, 56, 71, 74, 81, 84, 136, 139
Corporate suppression of research, 19–23, 76–80, 83, 103–110, 112, 113–116, 122–124, 76–80
Correspondence schools, 221
Cottrell, Frederick, 51, 162, 228, 229

Council on Government Relations, 134
Crooks, Lawrence, 159
Crow, Michael, 150, 157, 185, 186, 187, 188, 219, 230

Dahlsten, Donald, 6, 7
Daily Californian, 3
Dangerfield, Anthony, 217
Dartmouth College, 119
Dasgupta, Partha, 194
Data control, clinical trials and, 108, 112
Data safety monitoring boards, DSMBs, 105, 106
Data Safety Quality Act of 2001, 23
Data withholding, and commercialism, 74–75
David, Edward E., 59
David, Paul, 194, 196
Davis, Gray, 17, 18, 180
Davis, Ralph, 66
Day, Robert, 132
DeAngelis, Catherine, 108
Debs, Eugene V., 38
Debt, student loan, xiii
Defense funding, of academic research, 42–43
Deferiprone, 123
DeForrest, Jack, 191
Department of Agriculture, 63
Department of Defense, DOD, 44, 63, 64
Department of Education, 203
Department of Health, Education, and Welfare, HEW, 65, 66, 67
Department of Health and Human Services, HHS, 99, 100, 127, 128, 130, 133, 234
Dewey, John, 37, 38, 204, 216
d4T (stavudine) patent, Yale's ownership of, 164–167
Diabetes drugs, 117
Diamond v. Chakrabarty, 147
Diamond v. Diehr, 147
Dickson, David, 58
Diclofenac, 112
Diet drugs, 111, 116, 117
Dietz, Francis, 78, 79
Dietz, Rick, 76, 78, 80
"Digital Diploma Mills" (Noble), 221

DiGregorio, Dante, 189
Dioxins, 82
Distance learning, ix, 218–223 (also see online education)
DNA sequences, patents on, 149
Doctors Without Borders, DWB, 164, 165
Doetschman, Tom, 154
Dolan, Jo Alene, 111
Dole, Bob, 60, 66, 67
Dong, Betty, 19, 20, 21, 23, 107
Dorfman, Nancy, 177
Dow Chemical, 33
Duke University, 139, 160
Duley, Jim, 191
Du Pont, 33, 71, 153

Eclectics, 118
Economist, The, 143
Ecorisk, Inc., 20, 21, 22
eCornell, 219
Edelman Medical Communications, 111–112
Edison, Thomas, 26
Edison Company, xviii
Educause, 219
Egg Company 2, (University of Southern California), 189
Ehrenberg, Ronald G., 169
Einhorn, David, 168
Einstein, Albert, 75
Eisenberg, Rebecca, 63, 64, 147, 154, 156, 161, 232, 233
Eli Lilly & Co., 82, 115, 122, 161
Elliot, Charles W., 29, 30, 31, 119
Ely, Richard T., 38
Embryonic research, exclusive licensing of, 51, 53, 61, 62, 63, 66, 98, 150, 151, 152
Emory University, 78, 208
  Charles B. Nemeroff conflict-of-interest case at, xvi
Emslie, Graham, 115
Endocrine disruptors, 21, 22
Endowment money, and start-up company investments, x–xi, 140–141
Engell, James, 217
Enron Corporation
  Harvard University and, xvii, 81

"Entrepreneurial university," 69
Entrepreneurship education, xix, 18, 89,
    138, 168, 178, 226,
    239–240
Environmental Health Perspectives, 22
Environmental Protection Agency, EPA,
    xvi, 21, 22, 23
*Environmental Toxicology and
    Chemistry*, 22
Epidemiology, 101
Epilepsy drugs, 116
Episcopalians, Columbia
    (as King's College) founded
    by, 27
Equity, 99, 105, 141
Etzkowitz, Henry, 58
Excerpta Medica, 111
Expressed sequence tags, ESTs, 149
Exxon Mobil, 82
    Global Climate and Energy Project
        (Stanford) and, 82–83
Exxon Research and Engineering
    Company, 59
Exxon Valdez oil spill, 82

Faculty
    arbitrary dismissals, due to political
        views of, 38–39
    entrepreneurial, 75, 87, 95–97
    McCarthyism and, 43–44
    part-time, 200, 203, 204, 206, 212
    university-industry ties and conflicts
        with, 14–17, 19–23, 103–108,
        76–80, 122–124, 131–133,
        159–160
Faich, Gerald, 116, 117
Fathom, (Columbia University), 219,
    221
Federal Bureau of Investigation,
    university ties to, 43
Federal Counsel on Science and
    Technology, FCST
    and statistics utilization rates of
        government-funded patents, 64
Federal funding for academic research
    decline in, 8
    strengthening rules for, 235
Federal government
    early relationship of the university to,
        34, 39–48

clinical research and oversight by,
    237–239
economic uncertainty and decline in
    higher education spending by, 57
post-World War II research financing
    by, 39
Sputnik I and the growth in higher
    education spending by, 44–45
Federal patent policy
    before Bayh-Dole, 61, 63
    overhaul of, 60–61, 63, 67–68, 69
    (See also Bayh-Dole Act)
Federal Reserve Bank of Minneapolis,
    175
Federal Technology Transfer Act, FTTA,
    passage of, 69
Feller, Irwin, xviii, 183, 184, 196
Fen-phen (diet drug), 111, 116, 117
    (See also Redux)
Ferguson, Niall, 200
Field, Hartry, 200
Financial aid, commercial pressures and,
    207–208
Financial disclosure rules, 101
Fineberg, Harvey, 82
Fischel, Daniel, 221
Flexner, Abraham, 29, 119–120, 221
Flock worker's lung, 79
Florida, Richard, 176, 178, 179, 197
Florida Gulf Coast University, FGCU,
    221, 223
Florida Progress Corporation, 158
Florida State University, FSU, 168, 169
Foerster, Norman, 32
Food and Drug Administration, FDA,
    20, 112, 115, 117, 126, 238
    drug approvals and, 129
    financial conflicts of interest at, 233
    human subject research and, 128
Forest Laboratories, 115
Fortune, 42
Fossil fuel companies, global warming
    debate and, 82
Franklin, Benjamin, 26
Fred Hutchinson Cancer Research
    Center, the "Hutch", (University of
    Washington), conflicts of interest in
    blood-cancer experiment performed
    at, 131–133
Freeling, Michael, 15

Frumkin, Donald, 78
Fulbright, J. William, 43, 46

Gardner, Phyllis, 93
Gates, Susan, 207
Gatorade, 169
Geiger, Roger L., 36, 43, 72
Gelbspan, Ross, 82
Gelsinger, Jesse, 125, 126, 130, 131
Gelsinger, Paul, 125, 126, 130
Genentech, 54, 55–56, 157, 161
General Accounting Office, GAO, 144
General Electric, 33, 37
Genetic disease testing patents, xi
Genetic engineering, 49, 53, 56
   clinical drug testing and, 125–127
   of corn, 15–16
   cotton patents and, 147
   of crops, 3, 10
   of mice, 152–154, 168, 233
Genetics Institute, Inc., 140
Genetic Systems, 56, 132
Genomic screening technologies, 87, 88
Genovo, Inc., 126, 134
GenPharm (See Taconic)
Genta Incorporated, 191
George Mason University, GMU, 176
   cuts to the humanities at, 212–214
George Washington University, Vietnam
   War protests and Army-related
   divestitures at, 46
Georgia Institute of Technology, Georgia
   Tech, 67, 139, 142, 143
German model of scientific research
   medical schools and, 32, 119
   tradition of openness and, 73
Geron Corporation, 151, 152
Getz, Wayne, 16
Ghosh, Sankar, 162
Ghostwriters, in university medicine, xv,
   111–112, 117
GI Bill, 44
Gilman, Daniel Coit, 30
Gilmore, James S., 212
GlaxoSmithKline, GSK, 113, 114, 115
Glaxo Wellcome, 161, 166. (See also
   GlaxoSmithKline)
Global warming, fossil fuel companies
   and public policy debate over, 82
Goldbloom, David, 122

Golden Rice, 163
Goldman, Charles, 207
Google, 141
Goozner, Merrill, 237
Gore, Al, 98
Government-University-Industry
   Research Roundtable, 193
Graduate students
   commercialization and effect on,
      85–97
   mentoring of, 85, 211
   as teachers, 200, 207
   unions and, 210–212
Graham, John D., 82
Gray, Denis O., 9
Gray, Paul, 34
Great Depression, 37
Greenspan, Alan, 214
Greenwich Village (New York City), 199
Greenwood, James, 233–234
Gregg, Judd, 157
Gregorian, Vartan, 79
Gruissem, Wilhelm, 6
Gutierrez, Andy, 7
Guttag, John, 95

Haas School of Business (U.C. Berkeley),
   5
Hale, George Ellery, 35
Hansen, John, 132
Harbridge House study, on utilization
   rates of government-funded patents,
   64, 65
Harley Davidson, 173
Harper, William Rainey, 30, 221
Harsche, Pat, 144
Hart, James Morgan, 32
Harvard Business School, xvii
Harvard Center for Risk Analysis,
   HCRA, 81
Harvard College, 28
   founding of, 27
Harvard Economic Service, 33–34
Harvard Electricity Policy Group,
   HEPG, xvii, 81
Harvard Magazine, xiv, 217
Harvard Medical School, 71, 81,
   87, 94
   Monsanto research agreement with,
      4–5

Harvard School of Public Health, 82, 101, 109, 111
  Center for Risk Analysis, HCRA, at, xix
Harvard University, 74–75, 99, 116, 117, 119, 161, 210
  Center for Ethics and Professions at, 101
  Clinical Research Institute at, 130
  conflicts-of-interest debate and, 93–94, 100
  debate over taking equity in faculty start-ups at, 140
  regional economic growth and, 177
  Russian Research Center at, 42
  venture-capital funds at, 140
HarvardWatch, xvii
Hayden, Tom, 10, 11, 12
Hayes, Tyrone B., 20, 21, 22, 23
Health care, rising cost of, 109, 121
Health care businesses, physicians' financial stakes in, 121
Health maintenance organizations, 121
Healy, David, 122, 227
Heath, David, 132
Heat Is On, The: The High Stakes Battle over Earth's Threatened Climate (Gelbspan), 82
Heller, Craig, 90
Heller, Michael A., 154
Hepatitis, 67
Herbicides, 20–23
Hewlett, William, 178
Hewlett Packard, 191, 192
Higher Learning in America, The (Veblen), 37
Hoechst, 71
  Massachusetts General Hospital and, 98
Hoey, John, 124
Hofstadter, Richard, 26, 28, 240, 241
Hogan, William, xvii
Hog farms, intimidation of researchers studying, 83
Hollinger, David A., 30, 217, 218
Homeopaths, 118
Honoraria, 234, 235
Honors Cooperative Program, 178
Hoover, Herbert, 35
Hopkins, Johns, 30

Horton, Richard, 112
Hospital for Sick Children, HSC, (Toronto), 123, 124
Hull, Jane, 172
Human genome, privatization of, 148–149
Human Genome Sciences, 148, 149
Humanities, 228
  commercial squeeze on, 212–218
  downsizing of, xviii, 211
  historical debates over place of, 32–33
Human subjects, commercialism and clinical research involving, 124–133
Humble Oil Company, 36
Hutchins, Robert M., 32
Hybritech, 56
Hypothyroidism, 20

IBM, 58, 139
Ibuprofen, 112
Immune Response Corporation, IRC, 103–108
Incubator programs, venture capital funds and, 189–190
Incyte, 149
Industry
  and historic relationship to the academy, 25–27, 33–39, 177–179
Industry leaders, on deleterious effects of commercialization of universities, 190–193
Industry-University Cooperative Research, (University of California), 19
Innovation
  Bayh-Dole Act and, 59–65, 231–233
  pipeline for, in jeopardy, 145–155
  role of universities in stimulation of, xviii, xx, 194–197
Insider trading, by university professors, 84
Institute for Bioengineering, Biotechnology, and Quantitative Biomedicine, QB3, 18, 180
Institute for Defense Analysis, Vietnam War protests against, at Columbia, 46
Institutional Patent Agreement program, IPA program, 65–66, 67

Institutional Patent Agreements, **IPAs**, 149, 231
Institutional review board, **IRB**, 128,132–133, 134, 136
Intellectual property, 148, 234
  legal battles over, within the university, 96, 158–162
  students, secrecy, and, 85–97
Intellectuals, views toward, in American history, 26, 31
Intelligence agencies, university ties to, 42–43
Internet, ix, 176
  origins of, x, 159, 160
Interstitial lung disease, **ILD**, 76, 77
Investigator objectivity, corporate sponsors and, 75–76
Iowa State University, USDA Agricultural Research Service lab at, 83
Irradiation technologies, 50, 51
Isner, Jeffrey, 126

Jackson Laboratories, "the Jax" (Maine), 153, 168
Jacoby, Russell, 31
Japan, competitive position of the U.S. relative to, x, 57
  Bayh-Dole Act and, 8, 60
Jefferson, Thomas, 26, 62
Job security, part-time academic workforce and, 204
Johns Hopkins University
  founding of, 32
  School of Medicine at, 119
  venture-capital funding at, 140
Johnson, Chris, 159
Johnson administration, college attendance during, 45
Jordan, David Starr, 38
Journal of the American Medical Association, **JAMA**, 20, 84, 85, 107, 108, 112, 115, 133

Kaashoek, M. Frans, 95, 96
Kahn, James, 103, 104, 105, 106, 107, 108, 109, 112
Kansas Corn Growers Association, 22
Kansas State Agricultural College, 38
Kapczynski, Amy, 164, 165

Kaplan, Henry, 133
Kazazian, Haig, xi
Keck Graduate Institute, 183
Keen, Karl, 24
Keller, Martin B., 114, 115
Kelly, J. Patrick, 5
Kendall, Ronald J., 21, 22, 23
Kennedy administration, college attendance during, 45
Kern, David, 76, 77, 78, 79, 80, 81, 227
Kerr, Clark, 1, 2, 3, 47
Kevles, Daniel J., 50
Kiang, Nelson, 85
Kimberley Clark, 173
King's College, 27, 119. (*See also* Columbia University)
Kirp, David L., 217
Kirschner, Ann, 219
Kmart, sponsored chairs at universities, 5
Knoll Pharmaceutical Co., 19, 20 (See also Boots Pharmaceutical)
Knowledge, for knowledge's sake, 32, 48, 240–241
Knowledge commons
  shrinkage of, 146–149
  threat to, 163
Knowledge-driven economy
  roots of, 58, 59
  requirements of, xiii, 155, 175, 196–197
Kodak, 139
Koffel, William, 95
Koren, Gideon, 123
Korn, David, 133, 134
Koski, E. Greg, 133
Kraft Foods, 82
Kramer, Peter, 191
Krimsky, Sheldon, 100, 108, 147, 237, 238
Kuhn, Charles, 77
Kuttner, Robert, xvii

La Follette, Bob, 31
Lagakos, Steven, 104, 105
Lam, Kit S., 92
Lancet, The, 111, 112, 233
Land-grant colleges, 29, 30, 134
Land grants, 34
Lang, Eugene, 212

Lange, Dale J., 84
LaPorte, Todd, 13
Latker, Norman, 65, 66, 67, 68, 69,
    149, 150
Lawrence Scientific School (Harvard),
    30
Lay, Ken, xv
Leahey, Michael, 130
LeBlanc, Paul, 183
Le Carré, John, 122
Lederberg, Joshua, 162
Legal fees and expenses, 158, 169
Lehigh University, 139
Leighton, F. Thomas, 96
Lerner, Joshua, 190
Leslie, Stuart W., 42, 179
Levine, Arthur, 220, 221
Lévi-Strauss, Claude, 216
Liaison programs, 139
Liberal arts education
    citizenship and, xix
    value of, 214–215
Licenses/Licensing (See also Material
    Transfer Agreements)
    Bayh-Dole Act and, 8, 59, 145
    commercialization and university
        receptivity to, 142
    exclusive, 53, 61, 62, 150–152, 192,
        231–233
    Federal Technology Transfer Act and,
        69
    nonexclusive, 53, 63, 67–68
    Stanford University and, 137–138
    third-party academic, 34, 162–163,
        228–231
    transgenic mice and, 153
Life sciences, data
    withholding/publication delays in,
        75
Life Sciences Greenhouses
    (Pennsylvania), 180
Link, Al, 177
Lister, Joseph, 119
Living organisms, patenting of, 147
Livingston, Jeffrey, 219
London School of Economics, 221
Long, Russell, 61, 65
Long Island University, 210
Los Alamos, Manhattan Project at, 41
Los Angeles Times, 233

Losey, John E., 15
Lou Gehrig's disease, 84
Lovejoy, Arthur O., 38, 204
Lowell, Abbott Lawrence, 31
Loyalty oaths, during McCarthy era, 44
Lycos, 176

Maclaurin, Richard C., 36
Madey, John, 160
Madey v. Duke University, 160
Magnetic resonance imaging, MRI, 159
Managed care, 121
    budget shortfalls and, 128
Manhattan Project, 41
Manning, JaRue, 95
Mansfield, Mike, 46
Manson, JoAnn, 116, 117
Market ideology, intrusion of, into
    academic life, x
Market-model university
    future of humanities threatened by,
        217
    rise of, 49–72
Markowitz, Marcia, 130
Marlboro College (Vermont), 183
Marsa, Linda, 41
Mars Incorporated, 24
Marsh, Donald J., 78, 79
Marshall, Garland, 96, 97
Martin, Paul, 132
Mash, Donald, 173
Massachusetts General Hospital, 71, 74,
    88
    Hoechst and, 98
Massachusetts Institute of Technology,
    MIT, xviii, 30, 33, 34, 51, 85, 139,
        153, 161, 173, 183
    Center for International Studies at, 42
    history of industry funding at, 35–37
    Lincoln Laboratory at, 43
    Media Laboratory at, 96
    Noyes-Walker controversy at, 35–37
    regional economic growth and, 177
    Research Laboratory of Electronics at,
        43
    Vietnam War and military research
        protests at, 45
Mass education systems, large
    enrollments and, 47
Massy, William, 70, 220

Material transfer agreements, MTAs, 146, 163

McCarthy, Joseph R., 43

McCarthyism, 2
faculty dismissals and, 43–44

McCulloch, James, 80

McTyre, Monica, 213

Medicaid, 121, 128

Medical colleges/schools
drug industry's penetration into, 108–110, 122–124
history behind, 118–121
proposal for federal oversight of clinical research at, 237–239

Medical-industrial complex, 121

Medical journals
conflict-of-interest disclosure policies at, 100
pseudoauthorship in, 111–112

Medical malpractice suits, 130, 131

Medical research
funding for, 42, 44, 128–129
industry control over, 108–117
post-World War II federal budget for, 121

Medical Society of Massachusetts, 116

Medicare, 121

Medicine
universities, the market, and, xviii, 108–110, 118–121

Medicine, Money, and Morals (Rodwin), 120

Medieval universities, self-governance in, 28

Melton, Douglas, 152

Memorial Hospital (Rhode Island), 76, 78, 80

Menand, Louis, 205

Mental health research, conflicts of interest and, 113–116

Mentoring, 32
commercialization and the effect on, 85, 87–97

Merck, 115, 149, 241

Merten, Alan G., 212, 213

Merton, Robert K., 73

Mesabi Range (Minnesota), 34

MetaMorphix, Inc., 140

Metzger, Walter, 33

Mexico, genetically modified corn and, 15–16

Michigan Life Sciences Corridor, 180

Michigan State University, MSU
cisplatin patent controversy at, 156–157
U.C. Berkeley-Novartis collaboration reviewed by team from, 13–17

Microfibres, Inc., 76, 77, 78, 79, 80

MICRO program (University of California), 19

Midwestern Association of Graduate Schools, 96

Milas, Alexander, 213

Military Authorization Act, 46

Military funding
of scientific research, 42–43
Vietnam War and opposition against, 45–46

"Military-industrial-academic complex," 43

Military-industrial complex, 45

Military R&D, at federal-contract laboratories, 43

Milken, Michael, 221

Miller, Merton, 221

Milstein, Alan, 130, 131

Minnesota Review, 215

Molecular biology, 6, 14, 56, 58, 108, 124

Monsanto, 71, 82
research agreement between Harvard Medical School and, 4–5

Mormons, 118

Morrill Act, 29

Moser, Richard, 207

Moses Maimonides, 119

Mosholder, Andrew, 114

Mowery, David, 154

"Multiversity," 47

Murrow, Edward R., 52

Muscular dystrophy, 67

Myriad Genetics, Inc., xi

Nanotechnology, 192

Nathanson, Neal, 134

National Academy of Sciences, NAS, 182, 196

National Association of State Universities, 134

National Bioethics Advisory Committee, 134
National Cancer Institute, 74
National Cancer Institute of Canada, 124
National Competitiveness Technology Transfer Act, 69
National Defense Education Act, NDEA, passage of, 44–45
National Defense Research Committee, 40
National Endowment for the Arts, NEA, establishment of, 45
National Endowment for the Humanities, NEH, establishment of, 45
National Governors Association, 182
National Institute for Drug Testing, NIDT, proposal to create, 238
National Institute of Mental Health, conflicts-of-interest inquiry, 114
National Institutes of Health, NIH, 14, 42, 45, 74, 99, 117, 121, 128, 144, 146, 151, 233
  adverse-event reporting and, 126
  expressed sequence tags and, 149
  financial conflicts of interest at, 233–234
  patents and, 67
National Labor Relations Board, NLRB, 210
National Research Council, 181
National Research Fund, 35
National Science Board, 184
National Science Foundation, NSF, xviii, 21, 45, 46, 57, 58, 99, 100, 180, 234
  creation of, 42
  Institutional Patent Agreement program at, 66
  Sputnik I and budget for, 44
Nature, 5, 15, 16, 22
Nature Neuroscience, xvi
Nelson, Gaylord, 65, 162
Nelson, Richard, 62, 64, 143, 145, 150, 154, 195, 232
Nelson, Robert M., 131
Nemeroff, Charles B., xvi
Netscape Communications, 240
Neurontin, 116

New Deal, 40
New England Journal of Medicine, NEJM, 81, 109, 110, 117, 121, 123, 133
New England's First Fruits, 27
New School University, 210, 212
  commercial ethos at, 216
Newsweek magazine, 60
New Wisconsin Idea, 171
New York Presbyterian Hospital, Office of Clinical Trials at, 130
New York Times, 49, 81, 129, 140, 152, 166, 211
New York University, NYU, the downsizing of teaching faculty at, 199–202, 204, 207, 210
NF-kB messenger protein, 161
Nixon, Richard M., 57, 59
Noble, David, 221
Nolan, Garry, 87, 88, 89, 90, 91, 92, 93, 94, 240
Nondisclosure agreements, NDAs, 95, 96
Nonexclusive licenses, 53, 63
North Carolina State University, venture-capital funding at, 140
Northwestern University, 35
Novartis, 115
  deal between U.C. Berkeley and, 3–7, 9–23, 25, 139, 236
Noyes, Arthur A., 35, 36
Nussbaum, Martha, xix
NYUOnline, 219, 221

Obesity, 116, 117
Occupational health investigations, corporate confidentiality and, 76–80
Office of Human Research Protections, OHRP, 128, 133
Office of Information and Regulatory Affairs, 82
Office of Management and Budget, OMB, Office of Information and Regulatory Affairs within, 82
Office of Naval Research, 42
Office of Scientific Research and Development, 40
Ohio State University, 139

Oil industry, influence on academic research, 82–83
Oil shock, 57
Olivieri, Nancy, 122–124, 227
Oncomouse, 153, 168
Online education, xiii, 218–223
Open scientific culture, industry interference with, 73–76
Open-source contracts, 159, 160
Optics, 58
Ornithine transcarbamylase (OTC) deficiency syndrome, 125
Owen-Smith, Jason, 59
Owning the Future (Shulman), 147

Pace University, 210
Packard, David, 178
Pajaro Dunes conference (1982), conflicts of interest problem and, 98
Palo Alto Research Center, 179
Part-time faculty, 200, 203, 206, 212
Pasteur's quadrant, 194
Pasteur's Quadrant (Stokes), 194
Patent-infringement suits, 160–162
Patents/Patenting, x, 142, 237
  academic history of, 50–54
  early views on, in academic medicine, 52
  Bayh-Dole Act and, 8, 9, 59–63, 64, 145
  double, 156–157
  on *ex vivo* human gene therapy, 148
  Federal Technology Transfer Act and, 69
  on genetically engineered cotton, 147
  on genetic diseases, xi
  of human genome, 148–149
  Institutional Patent Agreement program and, 65, 66
  of living organisms, 147
  on transgenic mice, 152–154
  upstream research, 154–155, 161
Patient consent forms, experimental drug trials and, 126, 134
Paxil, 113, 114, 238
Payan, Donald, 89, 92
Peace, Steve, 10, 11, 12
Peer-review systems, 110
  federal grant-making process and, 83, 184, 185

scholarly autonomy and, 39, 205
Penicillin, 41
Penn State University, **Penn State**, xiii, xiv, 139
Pentagon
  academic research funding and, 42
  antiwar movement and, 45–46
p53 mouse, 152–153, 168, 233
Pfizer Inc., 104, 115
Pharmaceutical drugs, escalating costs of, 109
Pharmaceutical industry
  cancer drug studies and, 84
  clinical research funding by, 128–130
  medical journals and, 111–112
  medical schools and, 108–109
  percentage of clinical drug trials paid for by, 237
Pharmacia Corporation, 112, 113
Pharmacology, xviii
Pharsight Corporation, 87
Phelps-Dodge Corporation, 39
Philip Morris, 82
Phillips, Robert A., 124
Plant and Microbial Biology Department, **PMB**, U.C. Berkeley-Novartis research agreement and, 3, 10, 12, 14, 15
Plant-molecular-genetics research, 71
Plant research, public-sector patenting and, 10, 11, 163
Polio vaccine, 52, 71, 104, 121
Popp, Richard, 87, 90, 93
Pork industry, silencing tactics and, 83
Positive Health Program (San Francisco), 104
Powell, Walter, 59
Pratt Institute, 210
Presbyterians, Princeton founded by, 27
President's Council of Advisors on Science and Technology, **PCAST**, 192
Prestige, pursuit of, 180–185
Prewitt, Kenneth, 216
Princeton University, 27, 34, 141
Pritchard, Richard, 124
Private sector, research dollars and, 8
Privatization
  agricultural research and, 10, 11
  Bayh-Dole Act and, 9, 69

of knowledge commons, 66, 146–149
of prisons, 81
spread of, into non-market spheres,
  xvii, 3, 5
*Proceedings of the National Academy of
  Science*, 21
Professoriate, downsizing of, 170,
  202–207
Professors' salaries, xiii, 200, 207, 209,
  217–218
Profits, 50, 53, 220, 227
  heart of academic life, and the
    intrusion of, 70, 140
  and putting public interest last,
    155–161, 162, 162
Progressive era, 31
Proprietary corporate culture, open
  scientific culture and, 74, 194–196
Providence Journal, 78, 80
Prozac, 113, 115, 122
Prusoff, William, 166
Pseudoauthorship, in medical journals,
  111–112
Psychiatry, pharmaceutical industry's
  influence and, 113–116, 122
Publication, 70, 73
  commercial restraints on, 19, 21, 22,
    36, 85–86
  delays of, 74, 75
  deleting information prior to, 75
Public domain for knowledge
  Bayh-Dole Act and, 63
  the shrinking of, 146–149
Public high school system, birth of, 30
Public interest, putting it last, 162–163
Public patrimony, preserving, 225–228
Public support, increased competition
  and, 184–185
Pulmonary hypertension, 116, 117
Purdue University, 61
Pure research model, 32, 33, 35, 227
Puritans, 27

Quaker Oats, 50
Queen's College, 27
Quist, David, 6, 15, 16

Radar, 41
Radiation Laboratory at MIT, 41
Rai, Arti, 147, 156, 232, 233

RAND, 62
rankings, college, 181–182, 199
Rausser, Gordon, 4, 6, 7, 8, 9, 10, 11,
  12, 19, 25, 26, 27, 29
Raytheon, 40
Reagan, Ronald, Bayh-Dole Act and, 69
Recombinant DNA technology, 49–50,
  52–55, 241
Redux, 111, 116, 117
Reformed Church, Rutgers (as Queen's
  College) founded by members of,
  27
Regan, Ward, 200, 201, 202, 210
Regeneration Technologies, 169
Reimers, Niels, 49, 50, 52, 53, 55, 66,
  68, 70
Relman, Arnold, 121–122
Remune, 103, 104, 106
Rennie, Drummond, 85
Rensselaer Polytechnic Institute, 30,
  189, 223
Research and Relevant Knowledge
  (Geiger), 42
Research assistants, RAs, 210
Research Corporation, 51, 156, 162,
  228, 229
Research Enticement Fund (Stanford),
  138
Research Laboratory of Physical
  Chemistry (MIT), 35
Research models, types of, 33, 194–196
Research tools
  proprietary restrictions on, 11, 74,
    152, 153, 154, 163
  National Institutes of Health reports
    on, 146, 153–154
Research Triangle Park, RTP, (North
  Carolina), 175, 177
Retin-A antiwrinkle cream, 116
Reynolds, Jesse, 6
Rezulin, 116, 117
Rice University, Ken Lay Center for the
  Study of Markets in Transition at,
  xv
Rich, Stuart, 117
Rickover, Hyman, 61, 64
Rigel Pharmaceuticals, Inc., 87, 88, 89,
  90, 91, 92, 94, 240
Right-to-know laws, 77
Rine, Jasper, 16

Rise of the Creative Class, The (Florida), 179
Rochon, Paula, 110
Rockefeller, John D., 30
Rockefeller Foundation, 163
Rocket propulsion, 41
Rodin, Judith, 211
Rodwin, Marc A., 120
Roentgen, Wilhelm, 119
Roizman, Bernard, 96
Rolnick, Arthur, 175
Roosevelt, Franklin, Vannevar Bush and, 39, 40, 41
Rosenberg, Barnett, 156
Rosenberg, Nathan, 145
Rosenberg, Steven A., 74
Rosenfield, Andrew, 221
Ross, Edward, 38
Rothenberg, Michael, 87, 88, 89, 90, 91, 92
Rothman, Kenneth, 101
Route 128 region (Boston), 173, 175, 176, 177, 178
Royal Society (Britain), 154
Royalties, 94, 140, 142, 148, 151, 153, 156, 157, 159, 161, 165, 167, 191
Rush Medical College, 117
Rutgers University, founding of, 27

Sabbaticals in industry proposal, 239
Sage, Henry W., 34
Salaries, 235
  for professors, 200, 207, 209, 217–218
  for university presidents, 205–206
Salk, Jonas, 52, 71, 103
Sampat, Bhaven, 67, 143, 155
Sandelin, Jon, 138, 142
Sandoz, 4
San Francisco Bay Guardian, 17
San Francisco General Hospital, 104
Savio, Mario, 1, 2
Saxenian, Annalee, 178
Schaefer, Lynne, 168
Schiffer, Stephen, 200
Scholarly independence, drug companies and, 109
School rankings, 181–182, 199
Science, 13, 65, 134, 153, 154, 161, 163
Science: The Endless Frontier, 41

Science and the Private Interest (Krimsky), 147
Science funding, post-World War II, 39–44
Scient, 173
Scientific research, German model and, 119
Scientist, The, 159
SCIRun, 159
Scott, Christopher, 18
Seattle Times, 132, 133
"Second academic revolution," 69
Secrecy in science, 62, 74, 75, 85, 86, 124
Securities and Exchange Commission, SEC, 84, 166
Seely-Brown, John, 179
Selectide, 92
Selective serotonin reuptake inhibitors, SSRIs, suicide and, 113–116, 122
Semiconductors, 58–59
Senate Finance Committee, 61
Seragen, 141
Servos, John, 37
Severson, James A., 155, 156
Sexton, John, 204
Shakespeare, Einstein, and the Bottom Line (Kirp), 217
Shalala, Donna, 127, 134, 135
Shane, Scott, 189
Shank, Peter, 77
Sheffield Scientific School (Yale), 30
Shleifer, Andrei, 200
Shulman, Seth, 147, 148
Silber, John R., 141, 185
Silicon Valley, 173, 175, 176, 177–178
Singer, Jerome, 159
Site management organizations, SMOs, 128
Smullin, Louis, 43
Social sciences
  commercial squeeze on, 212–218
  downsizing of, xiv
Social Transformation of American Medicine, The (Starr), 118
Society of University Patent Administrators, 66, 144
Socrates, xix
Soderstrom, Jon, 164
Sohio, 71

Sondius-XG, 141
Spear, Robert, 13
Specter, Arlen, 151
Spitzer, Eliot, 113
Sputnik I, federal government's funding
of higher education and, 44
St. Louis University Medical School, 97
Stanford, Jane, 38
Stanford, Leland, 38
Stanford Industrial Park, 178
Stanford Research Institute, 178
Stanford Research Park, 189
Stanford University, 33, 35, 49, 71, 87,
93, 94, 97, 154, 173, 183, 221
Applied Electronics Laboratory at, 43
Center for Biomedical Ethics at, 81
Cohen-Boyer inventions and, 49–56
commercial strains on mentoring at,
87–94
Edward Ross case at, 38
equity stake in Google and, 141
Global Climate and Energy Project at,
82
Office of Technology Licensing (OTL)
at, 137–138
regional economic growth and,
177–179
Vietnam War and opposition to
intelligence agency connections
with, 45–46
Starbucks, x
Starr, Paul, 118, 120
Start-up companies, 80, 87, 89, 94, 95,
96, 97, 121, 178, 188, 189, 192
faculty investments in, xv–xvi, 56,
100, 108–109, 126, 131
Genovo, Inc. (UPenn), 126, 131
investment of endowment money in,
x–xi, 140–141
Rigel Pharmaceuticals, Inc. (Stanford
University), 90, 94
Saragen (Boston University), 141
State funding, decline in, 8, 18–19
State Sciences and Technology Institute,
SSTI, 176, 179
State universities, local industry and, 34
Steele, Glenn D., Jr., 140
Steenbock, Henry, 50
Stein, Donald, 208, 209, 226
Stem cell research, 151–152, 153, 233

Stiglitz, Joseph, 154
Stock holdings, 56, 94, 106, 234
Stokes, Donald, 194
Strategically Targeted Academic
Research Centers, STAR, (New
York), 180
Student evaluations, part-time faculty
and, 203–204
Student Labor Union Group, SLUG,
(New School University), 212
Student loan debt, xiii
Students, commercialization and effect
on, 85–97, 158, 240, 199–209
Students for a Quality Education, SQE,
(George Mason University), 212,
213
Students for Responsible Research, SRR,
(U.C. Berkeley), 3, 5–6
Suicide, and antidepressant drugs,
113–116, 122
Sullivan, Louis W., 99
Sulston, John, 154
Swanson, Robert, 54, 55, 56
Syngenta, 3, 14, 20, 21, 22, 23 (See also
Novartis)
Synthroid (levothyroxine), 19, 20

Taborsky, Petr, 158, 240
Taco Bell, 213
Taconic, 153
Tax breaks, public subsidies and, xx, 8,
29, 46, 69, 166–167
Taxol, 168
Teaching, commercial squeeze on,
xii–xiii, 170, 199–210
Teaching assistants, TAs, xiii, 210
Technology initiatives, regional
economic development and,
171–190
Technology Plan, (MIT), 36
Technology transfer, 137–138, 142,
143–144, 145, 149
Institutional Patent Agreement (IPA)
program and, 65
nonexclusive licenses and, 53, 63,
67–68
Technology transfer offices, 66, 70, 137,
149, 156, 166, 230
operational costs for, 169–170
Temple University, 219

Tenure, xvi, 87, 203, 206, 210, 228
  academic freedom and, 39, 204–205
Terman, Frederick, 177, 178
Texas A&M, 183
Texas Tech University, 21, 22, 23, 183
Thalessemia, 123
Third-party licensing, 51, 156, 162–163,
  228–231 (See also Research
  Corporation)
Thomas, Charles, 81
Thomas, E. Donnall, 132
Thomas Edison program (Ohio), 175
Thompson, Dennis F., 101
Thompson, Tommy, 171, 172
Thomson, James, 151
Thursby, Jerry, 142, 156
Thursby, Marie, 142
Thyroid medications, 19, 20
Time magazine, 60, 203
"Title policy," 63
Tobacco industry, influence on research,
  xvi, 82, 84
Toronto Star, 124
Trade secrets
  confidentiality agreements and, 74, 76,
  77, 158
Transgenic mice, 152–154, 168, 233
Trial data, corporate control over, 108
Trust, academic medicine and, 118
Tufts University, 100, 108, 126, 210
Tuition and fees, increases in, xii–xiv,
  xx, 199, 202–203, 205
Tuition assistance, 45, 208
Twigg, Carol, 220, 223
Tyson, Laura D'Andrea, 5

UNext.com, 221
Unions, adjuncts, graduate students and,
  210–212
United Auto Workers, 210
United States, intellectual heroes of, 26
Universities
  during the McCarthy era, 43–44
  federal government and, 34, 39–48
  market model of, 49–72
  medicine and the market, a history of,
  118–121
University and Small Business Patent
  Procedures Act, 59, 67 (See also
  Bayh-Dole Act)

University Business, 183
University-industry cooperation, history
  behind, 57–72
University-Industry Cooperative
  Research Projects Program, (at the
  National Science Foundation), 57
University-industry research centers,
  UIRCs, 139
University-led commercial initiatives,
  track record of, 189–190
University of Akron, 34
University of Arizona, 39, 182, 183
University of California at Berkeley,
  U.C. Berkeley, 1, 2, 97, 162
  Ignacio Chapela tenure case at, 14–17
  Lawrence Livermore Laboratory at, 43
  Novartis deal with, 3–7, 9–23, 25,
  139, 236
  open source contract dispute at,
  159–160
  Tyrone Hayes case at, 20–23
University of California at Davis, U.C.
  Davis
  Allied Chemical and Calgene contracts
  with, 95
  Ray Valentine controversy at, 95, 98
University of California at Los Angeles,
  UCLA, 117
University of California at San
  Francisco, UCSF, 18, 49, 55
  Betty Dong case at, 19–20, 21, 23,
  107
  James Kahn case at, 103–108, 109
University of California Student
  Association, 10
University of Chicago, 32, 34, 38, 43
  ARCH Development Corporation,
  140
  Joany Chou case at, 96
  Michael Milken/UNext case at, 221
University of Cincinnati, 154
University of Erfurt (Germany), 23
University of Florida, 81, 168, 169, 215
  Charles Thomas case at, 81
  lucrative inventions at, 168–169
University of Houston, 183
University of Illinois, 71, 239
University of Iowa, 32
University of Kentucky, 34, 180, 183
University of Louisville, 141, 180

University of Maryland University College, 221
University of Massachusetts, xiv
University of Michigan, 63, 121, 166
University of Minnesota, 161
  Mines Experiment Station run by, 34
University of Mississippi, 187
University of Nebraska, 31
University of New Mexico, 159
University of North Carolina (Chapel Hill), 34, 83
University of Oklahoma, 130
University of Pennsylvania, UPENN, xi, 94, 116, 119, 210, 211
  Gelsinger case at, 125–126, 130, 131
  Office of Clinical Trials at, 130
  Wharton School at, 33
University of Pennsylvania Law Review, 166
University of Pittsburgh, 141
University of Rochester, 169
University of South Florida, USF, (Tampa), Petr Taborsky case at, 158, 240
University of Texas at Austin, xvi, 183
University of Texas Medical Branch (Galveston), Karen Wagner case at, 115
University of Texas Southwestern Medical Center, Graham Emslie case at, 115
University of Toronto
  David Healy case at, 122–123
  Nancy Olivieri case at, 123–124
University of Tulsa, 139
University of Utah
  breast cancer gene controversy at, xi
  College of Pharmacy at, 139
  open source contract dispute at, 159
University of Virginia, xiv, 26
University of Washington, 130
  Fred Hutchinson Cancer Research Center at, 131–133
  experimental research and conflicts of interest at, 131–133
University of Wisconsin, UW Madison, 31, 174
  Biostar program at, 172, 180
  McCarthyist era and, 43
  Richard Atkinson, and the

ghostwriting controversy at, 111, 117
University of Wisconsin system, UW, 38, 50, 151, 171, 233
University presidents
  salaries of, 205–206
  selection of, 205
University rankings, 181–182, 199
"Upstream research," proprietary restrictions on, 154–155, 161
U.S. Air Force, 42
U.S. Army, 42, 46
U.S. Congress, 81, 98, 99
  Bayh-Dole Act passed by, 147, 175
  Bayh-Dole hearings in, 61, 69–70
  Federal Technology Transfer Act passed by, 69
  Hearings on the Harvard Center for Risk Analysis in, 82
  National Defense Education Act passed by, 44–45
U.S. Constitution, 62
U.S. Navy, 42
U.S. News and World Report, 181–182, 199
U.S. Patent Office, 148, 158, 231
U.S. Supreme Court, 147, 148, 160
Uses of the University, The (Kerr), 2
Utah System of Higher Education, 219
Utilitarian movement, in American higher education, 26, 29–31, 91, 104, 227
  modern day advocates of, 26, 171, 195, 240, 227
Utilitarian research model, 33

Vaccines (whooping cough, tetanus, diphtheria, measles, and rubella), 121
Vacuum Oil Company, 36
Valentine, Ray, 95, 98
Vanderbilt, Cornelius, 30
Vanu, Inc., 143
Varmus, Harold, 153
Veblen, Thorsetn, 37
Venture capital spending by universities, xi, 18, 70, 121, 140, 170, 176, 180, 189–190
Veysey, Lawrence, 31, 34
Vietnam War, 2, 54, 57

protests against university-military/intelligence ties during, 45–46

Virex, 97

Virtual Temple (Temple University), 219

"Visiting Important Professors Program," at Wyeth-Ayerst, 116

Vocationalism, 29–32

Wagner, Karen, 115

Walker, William, 36

Wall Street Journal, 20, 81, 95, 96, 143, 166

Walsh, Jonathan, 145

W. Alton Jones, 21

Ware, Donald R., 158

Warner-Lambert, 117

Washington Post, xv, 56, 60, 112

Washington University, 71, 96

Wayland, Francis, 29, 30

Wayne State University, 5

Weapons development, at federal-contract laboratories, 43

Weapons manufacturers, Vietnam War and opposition against, 45–46

Webster, Andrew, 58

Weiss, Ted, 99

Weissman, Robert, 66, 68

Westinghouse, 33

West Point, 30

Wharton School (Univesity of Pennsylvania), 33

Wheeler, Benjamin I., 30

White, Andrew D., 29, 30, 32

Will, Thomas Elmer, 38

Williams, Jeffrey, 215, 216

Williams, R. Stanley, 192

Wilson, Duff, 132

Wilson, James, 126, 134

Wilson, Woodrow, 31

Wing, Rod, 182, 183

Wing, Steven, 83

Wisconsin Alumni Research Foundation, **WARF**, 50, 51

stem cell case at, 151–152, 153, 233

Wisconsin Economic Summit, 172

Wisconsin Idea, 31, 171

Wissenschaft, 32

Wold, William, 97

Wolfe, M. Michael, 112

World AIDS Conference, 164

World Congress on Information Technology, 213

World Intellectual Property Organization, 154

World War I, 40

World War II, 46, 72, 121, 185

effect of, on funding of higher education, 39, 40

federal patent policy after, 63

World Wildlife Fund, 21

Wyden, Ron, 192

Wyeth-Ayerst, 111, 115, 116, 117

Xalatan, 150

Xerox Corporation, 179

X-rays, 119

Yale Daily News, 165

Yale University, 34, 210

AIDS drug controversy at, 164–167

Yamaha, 141

Zahn, James, 83

Zapol, David, 87, 88, 89, 90, 91, 93

Zapol, Nikki, 88

Zapol, Warren, 87, 94

Zemsky, Robert, 220

Zerhouni, Elias, 234

Zerit, 164, 166

Ziagen, 166

Zimpher, Nancy, 173

Zoloft, 113, 115